D0477652

WITHDRAWN

BEST FOR BRITAIN?

BEST FOR BRITAIN?
The Politics and Legacy of Gordon Brown

SIMON LEE

ONEWORLD

OXFORD

A Oneworld Book

Published by Oneworld Publications 2007
Copyright © Simon Lee 2007

ISBN 978–1–85168–537–0

Typeset by Jayvee, Trivandrum, India
Cover design by eDigital Design
Printed and bound in Great Britain
by Biddles Ltd, King's Lynn

Oneworld Publications
185 Banbury Road
Oxford OX2 7AR
England
www.oneworld-publications.com

Learn more about Oneworld. Join our mailing list to
find out about our latest titles and special offers at:

www.oneworld-publications.com

This book is printed on paper made
from fully managed and sustained
forest sources.

FSC

TT-COC-002303

© 1996 Forest Stewardship Council A.C.

For my father, Norman Arthur Lee,
with love and thanks

Contents

PART II: Gordon Brown's Domestic Policy Agenda

PART III: Gordon Brown's Foreign Policy Agenda

Preface

As I wrote this book, British politics entered a vital phase. The transition from Tony Blair to Gordon Brown was set within the context of a series of important anniversaries with major contemporary resonances. The three-hundredth anniversary of the 1707 Act of Union, which joined the kingdoms and parliaments of England and Scotland into the United Kingdom and Parliament of Great Britain, passed with scarcely a hint of official celebration. Which other state would have allowed its tercentenary to pass without pomp and circumstance? After ten years of New Labour, the fact that Tony Blair chose not to mark the final months of his premiership with a major birthday celebration is a measure both of the ambiguity of his political legacy and the constitutional uncertainty surrounding the future of the British Union. However, Blair's successor is a Scotsman who represents a Scottish constituency but wishes to make important policy choices for the English (not least because devolution has constrained his discretion to intervene elsewhere). In such circumstances, a celebration might have appeared an indulgence too far.

With delicious timing, the elections for the Scottish Parliament and the English local and mayoral elections were held just two days after the tenth anniversary of New Labour's accession to power and on the twenty-eighth anniversary of Margaret Thatcher's 1979 General Election victory. For those who believe that the New Labour modernisation project has been little more than a consolidation and extension of many of the core tenets of Thatcherism, the elections served as a timely referendum on and political obituary for the Blair decade.

Blair's personal political legacy to Gordon Brown is a country ill at ease with itself. The United Kingdom's continuing commitment to the Bush Administration's 'coalition of the willing' in Iraq and Afghanistan and its domestic repercussions – the 7/7 London bombings and a series of high-profile trials and police operations against alleged terrorists – have contributed to a palpable sense of domestic insecurity. And the two-hundredth anniversary of the passage of the 1807 Act to abolish the slave trade in the British Empire, and the ensuing debate about reparations, has coincided with a series of teenage murders that has highlighted difficult, and unresolved, questions about community cohesion and integration.

Neither is Blair's foreign policy legacy particularly rosy. The celebrations of the fiftieth anniversary of the signing of the Treaty of Rome served only as a reminder of Blair's failure to place the United Kingdom at the heart of Europe. The commemorations of the twenty-fifth anniversary of the Falklands War and the completion of a successful military operation in the South Atlantic stood in stark contrast to the faltering campaigns in Iraq and Afghanistan. Blair and Robin Cook's shared ambition to establish an ethical dimension to British foreign policy is long-forgotten.

Beset by weakening political authority, Tony Blair had to rely on the votes of Conservative MPs to secure a parliamentary majority for the renewal of the United Kingdom's 'independent' nuclear deterrent, in the face of the rebellion of eighty-eight Labour backbenchers. This, the largest parliamentary rebellion since the March 2003 vote on the invasion of Iraq, allied to the revelation of negotiations about the possible stationing of US anti-ballistic missile defence systems in Britain, highlighted the major internal divisions within the Labour Party about the future direction of British foreign policy.

Moreover, the capture and detention of fifteen British military personnel by Iranian forces, set against the backdrop of the unanimous decision of the United Nations Security Council to pursue further sanctions against Iran for its refusal to suspend its nuclear enrichment programme, emphasised how Blair's political legacy will be associated with the United Kingdom's stance on Weapons of Mass Destruction. Despite Blair's ten years in office, the debate on the extent to which British foreign policy goals should be aligned either with those of the United States or the European Union remains unresolved.

Given this rich political and historical context, my purpose in writing this book is simple: to identify and explain the political ideas and policy choices of Tony Blair's successor, Gordon Brown. This entails asking important questions about political legacies, electoral arithmetic and national identity.

First, the political gift bequeathed to Britain by Tony Blair on his resignation was not his sole creation. It is a legacy shared with many; above all with his principal political nemesis: Gordon Brown. Brown is unique among the major figures of modern British politics. No other candidate for the leadership of their political party or the office of Prime Minister of the United Kingdom inherited such a major political and economic legacy. Understanding its nature and how voters (both within the Labour Party and beyond) will respond to it is the key to Brown's future as party leader and Prime Minister. This book explores that political legacy and sets out Brown's principal domestic and foreign policy choices.

None of his predecessors as Chancellor of the Exchequer enjoyed such unprecedented power over the conduct of domestic economic and social policy as did Brown during his decade at the Treasury. No previous Chancellor exercised such power that at times they appeared to challenge or defy the Prime Minister's authority. Neither has any previous candidate for the leadership of their party and state entered the contest with the political advantage of a record of ten years' economic growth and financial stability. Paradoxically, despite his ubiquity as Chancellor of the Exchequer, many members of his political party – and most voters – remain in the dark about what Gordon Brown's leadership will mean both for the Labour Party's ideology and policy and for the future of the United Kingdom. This book sheds light on those questions, by illuminating the key features of Brown's 'British Way', his political agenda for the future of the United Kingdom.

My second inspiration arises from simple electoral arithmetic. At the time of writing (and before the 'Brown Bounce' which accompanied the opening weeks of Brown's premiership) the Labour Party, for the first time in fifteen years, was experiencing opinion poll results which, if they were a general election, would condemn it to defeat. By the end of December 2006 – the end of David Cameron's first year as party leader – the Conservative Party was consistently enjoying a greater than ten percentage point lead over the Labour Party. Moreover, when voters were asked if they would be more likely to vote for a Brown-led Labour Party, the margin of the Conservatives' poll lead widened. Between May 1997 and May 2005 the Labour Party lost 3.9 million voters and saw its share of the popular vote decline from 44.3 per cent to 35.2 per cent. Only 21.6 per cent of the electorate voted for New Labour in May 2005. Nearly twice as many (38.6 per cent) did not even bother to vote. Only the inequities of the first-past-the-post electoral system allowed the Labour Party to translate so few votes into 355 (fifty-five per cent) of the seats at Westminster.

For the parliamentary Labour Party, and in particular for the forty-four Labour MPs with wafer-thin majorities of fewer than 3,000 votes, the choice of Gordon Brown as Tony Blair's successor was vital. It was equally important for the Labour Party as a whole. When New Labour was first elected, in May 1997, John Prescott promised to double the party's membership. In the subsequent decade, membership more than halved, from 417,000 to 198,026 (as of 31 December 2005). The financial consequences of this collapse in popular membership have been catastrophic. During 2005, the Labour Party's income was £35.3 million; its expenditure £49.8 million (plus an additional actuarial loss of £1.17 million arising from the party's pension scheme). With net liabilities (including the pension fund liabilities) of £27.25 million at the end of December 2005, the Labour Party is technically insolvent and its capacity to attract new funding has been severely compromised by the 'cash-for-honours' scandal. The choice of Gordon Brown as leader is vital to the future of the Labour Party as an election-fighting and vote-winning machine.

My third inspiration was the question of the future of England. Four deficits at the heart of the New Labour project affect the governing of England and its people. First, New Labour's constitutional reforms have led to a democratic deficit in participation, accountability and legitimacy for most English people. The people of the other constituent nations of the United Kingdom have seen their opportunities for democratic citizenship extended by the creation of elected institutions at Holyrood, Cardiff and Stormont. With the exception of the citizens of Greater London, who vote for their assembly in City Hall, the English people have been denied similar democratic empowerment.

Second, since July 1998, the citizenship postcode lottery has been compounded by a second parallel policy deficit, created by the Treasury's centralised prescription for policy design and resource allocation in England, carried out through the biennial Spending Reviews and their accompanying Public Service Agreements. The overwhelming majority of the English have been denied the opportunity for the constitutional checks and balances on Treasury power that devolution has afforded to the people of Scotland, Wales and Northern Ireland. Understanding if and how Gordon Brown intends to redress these constitutional and policy problems is central to an evaluation of the 'British Way' and whether, at the expense of democratic citizenship and accountability for England, it will be best for the British state.

There is a third and parallel resource deficit in England. In 2006–2007, the total planned identifiable public expenditure on services in Brown's native Scotland was £8,265 per person, 21.1 per cent higher than the £7,121 per person in England. England's identifiable public expenditure was ninety-seven per cent of the United Kingdom average, while Scotland's was 117 per cent.[1] The pre-Thatcher 'Barnett Formula' for allocating territorial expenditure was supposed to narrow such differences but, despite having, as Chancellor, been as pro-active in fiscal policy as any of his predecessors, a central component of Brown's economic legacy is his failure to redress this territorial imbalance. In the pre-devolution political era, when people were encouraged to think of public services in terms of citizenship rights, rather of the narrower, self-interested, terms of individual consumption, such inequities might not have mattered. For a Scotsman representing a Scottish constituency yet intent on imposing his reform agenda upon England, such statistics are potentially political dynamite.

Finally, there is an identity gap, created by New Labour's reluctance to recognise England as anything more than a source of sporting or cultural identity. From the early days of 'Cool Britannia' to more recent proposals for citizenship education that affect England alone, New Labour's reforms embraced a careful conflation of England with Britain and Englishness with Britishness. Cool Britannia meant 'Frozen England'. Even though around 95 per cent of the United Kingdom's migrant population and identifiable ethnic minorities live in England's towns and cities, the possibility of reflecting and embracing that multi-ethnic and multi-cultural reality in a collective, inclusive, English civic and democratic identity has been studiously avoided. As I will show, this has been particularly evident both in Gordon Brown's speeches (especially those made to English audiences) and in the draft legislative programme and constitutional reform agenda announced during the early weeks of the Brown Government.[2]

How Gordon Brown squares these circles will, largely, determine his prospects for securing an historic fourth consecutive General Election victory for his party. His plan is to identify a 'British Way' of politics; a successor to Tony Blair's 'Third Way'. Brown's New Unionism seeks nothing less than a new British Enlightenment, a restoration of British identity and an accompanying negation of the identity of England as a political community and rival to the United Kingdom. Britain, and Britishness, will be the focal point of citizenship.

The problem confronting the 'British Way' is that popular support for the Labour Party has eroded in England. At the 2005 General Election, although the Labour Party won 286 (fifty-five per cent) of English seats, it polled 65,000 fewer votes and saw its share of the vote fall by six per cent when compared with the 2001 General Election. No fewer than thirty-seven of the forty-seven seats that Labour lost in 2005 were lost in England. Should the Labour Party lose a further twenty-nine English MPs at the next General Election, it would no longer enjoy the democratic mandate of a majority of English seats. In these circumstances, a future Labour government would have to rely on the support of MPs from Scotland, Wales and Northern Ireland to pass legislation affecting England. The constitutional volatility of such a scenario for the future of the United Kingdom would be compounded if the Labour Party were forced into coalition with a Liberal Democrat Party led by Sir Menzies Campbell, another Scot representing a Scottish constituency. In such circumstances, if the Conservative Party held 265 or more English seats and therefore a majority of English constituencies, it could claim the sole political legitimacy to speak for England.

Three vital political challenges confront Gordon Brown. First, he must simultaneously carve out a distinctive domestic and foreign policy agenda while addressing the question of New Labour's political legacy. He must distance himself from the unpopular elements of Tony Blair's administration, so that they quickly become associated solely with Blair. The 'British Way' is his means to that end. Second, he must reverse the electoral and financial fortunes of the Labour Party and inspire a new generation of activists and donors to provide the foot-soldiers and funding to deliver a fourth consecutive General Election victory. Like John Major succeeding Margaret Thatcher, Brown must persuade a highly-sceptical electorate that his administration will deliver the first term of a new and progressive political project for Britain, rather than a fourth term of tired New Labour. Finally, he must persuade English, and above all floating voters in the key marginal constituencies of Middle England, that they should not repeat the pattern of May 1979 by deserting the Labour Party in favour of an untried and untested Conservative Party.

I hope this book will enable the reader to decide for themselves whether Gordon Brown will be able to find effective responses to these three challenges. I offer my own judgement in the conclusion. However, it would not have been possible for me to write it (or any of the preceding chapters), without the support of the Department of Politics and International Studies at Hull University. Whatever insight I am able to offer into Brown's thinking and policies is largely the result of my having spent the past decade teaching undergraduates about the politics of New Labour. This has given me the chance to study in detail the speeches and policy documents that have emanated from Gordon Brown, The Treasury and from Brown's key economic adviser and closest political confidant, Ed Balls.

For this opportunity, I must thank our Head of Department, Professor Lord Norton of Louth. I also wish to express my gratitude to my other colleagues for their respective encouragement for and interest in this project. In particular, I wish to thank my friends Justin Morris, Richard Woodward, Colin Tyler and Claire Hairsine, for their constant good humour, which has been invaluable to me when I was in danger of losing mine. I am equally grateful to Sir Alex Ferguson, the players of Manchester United and my fellow occupants of Block 204 of the Stretford End, who have offered me such an exciting escape from the world of politics and academia, at least until the Glazer family takeover at Old Trafford. I also owe a considerable personal debt both to Mike Harpley at Oneworld for commissioning this book in the first place and to Ann Grand for her meticulous preparation of the manuscript. Finally, my greatest inspiration remains the love and support I have enjoyed from my sister Chris Clarke, my brother-in-law Roy Clarke, my niece Joanna and my nephew Adam and above all, my father, to whom this book is dedicated.

Introduction

ELECTORAL ASSET OR LIABILITY?

When his political and economic legacy is compared with the track record of his principal rivals both for the leadership of the Labour Party and the office of Prime Minister, Gordon Brown's claim to best for Britain should be unassailable. As his eleventh and final Budget report reminded the British people: 'Over the past ten years, the Government's macroeconomic framework has delivered more stability in terms of GDP growth and inflation rates than in any decade since the war'.[1] Indeed, the United Kingdom's current economic expansion 'is not only without precedent in the post-war history of the UK but is also the longest on post-war record for any G7 economy and the longest expansion of any OECD country'.[2] As the longest expansion 'since records began in the year seventeen hundred and one', the 'Brown Boom' stands in stark contrast to David Cameron's notoriety as economic adviser to Norman Lamont at the time of 'Black Wednesday'.[3] Ironically, Black Wednesday (16 September 1992), which saw the United Kingdom's departure from the Exchange Rate Mechanism, actually ushered in fifty-nine consecutive quarters of economic prosperity. Brown's central role in helping to secure an unprecedented three consecutive Labour Party General Election victories shines in comparison to Cameron's dismal failure as chief policy co-ordinator for the Conservative Party in the 2005 General Election campaign.

Despite Brown's rich political and economic legacy (until the trend was reversed in the early weeks of his premiership), opinion polls at first displayed a worrying trend for Gordon Brown and the Labour Party: voters only grudgingly acknowledged Brown's economic skills. In a YouGov poll, conducted at the 2007 Budget, just forty per cent of respondents identified Brown as an asset for the Labour Party; this figure exceeded those who regarded him as a liability by only two per cent. Forty-four per cent acknowledged that he was doing a good job as Chancellor but thirty-six per cent stated that he was not. Only ten per cent rated his performance over the past ten years as 'excellent', compared to twenty-seven per cent who thought it 'good'. No fewer than nineteen per cent thought Brown's record 'poor', with twenty-nine per cent rating his performance as merely 'fair'. Forty-six per cent thought the Budget unfair; comfortably exceeding those (thirty-four per cent) who thought it fair. Moreover, only twenty-one per cent thought the Budget would leave them a little or a lot better off, compared to forty-five per cent who thought it would leave them a little or a lot worse off. Despite a two-penny cut in the basic rate of income tax, seventy-five per cent of those questioned thought a future Labour government would raise taxes. Most worryingly for Brown, more people (thirty-five per cent) preferred Tony Blair as Prime Minister to him (twenty-five per cent). Most worryingly for the Labour Party, thirty-nine per cent indicated their intention to vote Conservative, compared to only thirty-one per cent support for Labour.[4] This reflected a broader trend; five other polls conducted between 19 January and 8 March 2007 recorded an average 38.5 per cent vote for the Conservative Party and only 31.6 per cent for Labour.[5]

These polls appeared to confirm a long-term trend in British public opinion: Gordon Brown's political stock with the general public had been waning for some time. At the 2005 Budget, fifty-two per cent thought Gordon Brown, as Chancellor, was doing a better job than Tony Blair, as Prime Minister (seventeen per cent). In 2006, thirty-seven per cent thought Brown was doing the better job, compared to an endorsement of Blair by twenty-two per cent. However, in March 2007, only thirty per cent thought Brown was better, compared to twenty-four per cent for Blair.[6] When Brown first became Chancellor, his net approval rating was +thirty-two per cent and the public's Economic Optimism Index (EOI) registered a healthy +nineteen per cent. Brown's approval rating had been negative only twice (in September and November 2000) but in December 2006, despite having delivered sustained prosperity, it stood at zero (forty-six per cent were satisfied and an equal percentage dissatisfied).[7] In January 2007, the EOI registered −thirty-nine per cent, not only the second worst figure during Brown's tenure but also one of the worst since records began at the time of the International Monetary Fund crisis in April 1976.[8] During 2006, the best recorded figure for the EOI was −twenty-three per cent, in January and October.

Even before he succeeded Tony Blair, the public appeared to be losing faith in the prudence of the 'Iron Chancellor'. A February 2007 YouGov poll revealed that more people (twenty-nine per cent) thought David Cameron would make a better Prime Minister than Gordon Brown (twenty-four per cent). More people (thirty per cent) also thought the Conservatives would run Britain's economy well, compared to twenty-seven per cent for the Labour Party.[9] In November 2005, as David Cameron prepared to assume the leadership of his party, a Populus opinion poll revealed that more people (thirty-seven per cent) would prefer to vote for a Brown-led Labour Party than a Cameron-led Conservative Party (thirty-five per cent). However, once Cameron had assumed the leadership the following month, he immediately established a six per cent lead over Brown (forty-one per cent to thirty-five per cent); a lead that he maintained until the May 2007 elections. That lead was never less than four per cent and by March 2007 was a record thirteen per cent (forty-two per cent to twenty-nine per cent).[10] With similar polls recording an eleven per cent lead for a Cameron-led Conservative Party over a Brown-led Labour Party, Labour backbenchers became increasingly nervous about their prospects of retaining their seats, let alone recording a fourth consecutive General Election victory.[11] A survey of sixty-two MPs from among Labour's 100 most marginal constituencies found that only thirty-four were Brown supporters. Of the remainder, ten wanted a challenger to Brown to come forward and fourteen, though without enthusiasm, regarded his leadership as inevitable.[12] In the months before he became Prime Minister, it was clear that neither prospective voters nor the parliamentary Labour Party were at all certain that Gordon Brown would be best for Britain.

A 'PSYCHOLOGICALLY FLAWED' POLITICIAN?

Like Margaret Thatcher, Gordon Brown is a politician who tends to divide people and opinion. As the odds of his following Tony Blair as Labour Party leader shortened every passing week, questions were raised about his suitability to succeed him as Prime Minister of the United Kingdom of Great

Britain and Northern Ireland. Former colleagues very publicly questioned his credentials. Charles Clarke, a former Cabinet colleague, accused Brown of being a control freak, who 'thinks he has to control everything' and was 'totally, totally uncollegiate'.[13] Lord Turnbull, the former Permanent Secretary to the Treasury, endorsed this judgement, claiming that Brown had not allowed Cabinet colleagues 'any serious discussion about priorities. His view is that it is just not worth it and "they will get what I decide"'. Turnbull further suggested that 'you cannot help admire the sheer Stalinist ruthlessness of it all'.[14] Clarke and Turnbull identified possibly serious character flaws in the Prime Minister-in-waiting, variously accusing him of being a perfectionist, not a risk-taker, lacking political courage, suffering delusions of Blair having to anoint him as his chosen successor and, in Turnbull's words, of having 'a Macavity quality. He is not there when there is dirty work to be done'.[15]

This was not the first time that Gordon Brown attracted personal and political opprobrium. For example, 'someone who has an extremely good claim to know the mind of the Prime Minister' once told the *Observer* journalist Andrew Rawnsley: 'You know Gordon, he feels so vulnerable and so insecure. He has these psychological flaws'.[16] It was widely assumed that these non-attributable remarks came from Alistair Campbell, then the Prime Minister's Chief Press Secretary. Such was the sensitivity between the Blair and Brown camps concerning the Prime Minister and Chancellor's working relationship and such was the enduring furore surrounding such poisonous character assassination that when Lance Price, a former Downing Street spin doctor, suggested that the source of the remarks had been the Prime Minister and not Campbell, Tony Blair chose to confirm, at Prime Minister's Question Time, that he had never used those words.[17]

More certain, and of greater moment for the unity of the Labour Party, is that Brown has divided his Cabinet colleagues. His colleagues in Blair's last Cabinet openly endorsed his candidature, not least because of the lack of a credible alternative successor. They concentrated instead on declaring their participation in the deputy leadership contest. In stark contrast, former, Blairite, Cabinet colleagues rallied to oppose Brown's succession. Brown was pictured leaving Downing Street grinning, following a discussion over the precise timing of Blair's resignation. After a week of open warfare between their camps, Charles Clarke accused Brown of 'absolutely stupid' behaviour. Clarke further asserted that Brown lacked confidence, was nervous and therefore must 'prove his fitness' to succeed.[18] Subsequently, Clarke and fellow Blairite Alan Milburn launched the *2020 Vision* website. Ostensibly, its purpose was 'to set out the new ideas that can give New Labour renewed momentum'.[19] However, among others, the website had been endorsed by both Frank Field, MP and Peter Mandelson, who had demanded there be a challenger to Brown, so the suspicion remained that a concerted attempt was being made to persuade David Miliband to stand. Miliband declined, and publicly backed, albeit belatedly, Brown's candidature.

Much of the debate emanated from the uncertainty surrounding Brown's political ideas and policies. Would his programme for government be any different from that fashioned during the past decade of New Labour? From the Labour Party's perspective, would Brown have a sufficiently bold political vision to revive a government had lost momentum and direction during its third term? Would his domestic and foreign policy agenda have enough energy to reverse the trend in the opinion polls before the next General Election?

Gordon Brown's personal and political biographies have been extensively and expertly documented but less attention has been paid to his political philosophy and policy agenda.[20] And although his relationship with Tony Blair has been picked over with the finest-toothed of political combs, less insight has been offered into what a Brown premiership means for the United Kingdom.[21] This book fills those gaps, offering the reader a detailed analysis of Gordon Brown's political and economic inheritance and a careful evaluation of his major speeches and policy announcements, especially those made since the 2005 General Election and Tony Blair's decision not to serve a full third term as Prime Minister.

Part One explores the evolution of Gordon Brown's political philosophy in a political odyssey that has witnessed his transformation from a withering critic of capitalism to the most powerful advocate of the interests of the City of London's financial markets. This odyssey is divided into four phases: the first two, explored in Chapter One, go from Brown's formative years at university to his first decade as an MP at Westminster. This period saw his advocacy of British industrial modernisation through supply-side socialism and parliamentary socialism, a vision rooted firmly in the values and traditions of the Labour Party.[22]

Following Labour's third consecutive General Election defeat, Brown entered a third phase, in which he began to distance himself from the

Labour Party's history and ideas. A new vision of a 'British Way' of politics and a British model of political economy emerged, based on the monetary stability and fiscal prudence of supply-side liberalism and the nationalisation of policy design and resource allocation in England.

Following New Labour's 1997 General Election landslide victory, operational independence for the Bank of England and, in March 1999, Brown's redefinition of the role of the Treasury and Blair's decision not to stand aside in favour of his Chancellor, Brown's political philosophy slowly began to evolve towards its fourth, continuing, phase. Chapter Two demonstrates how this phase has been characterised by a Messianic conversion to the liberalism of Adam Smith (who, like Brown, was born in Kirkcaldy). Brown has set out the parameters of a New British Enlightenment, based on a sympathetic liberalism that articulates a moral defence of the virtues of the market, entrepreneurship and competition. He has also returned to the American liberalism of the 1930s New Deal and 1960s Great Society programmes, first taught to him by his father. Like Margaret Thatcher and Tony Blair, Gordon Brown has based his future modernisation programme for Britain on an ideology of liberalism, implemented through statecraft that entails the further rolling forward of the frontiers of centralised state control over England and its people.

Part Two is devoted to a detailed explanation and analysis of Gordon Brown's domestic policy agenda. Chapter Three explores the 'British model' of political economy. This model was devised by Gordon Brown, in partnership with his economic adviser Ed Balls, during a decade at the Treasury. While the 'British model' has delivered an unprecedented period of sustained monetary stability and economic growth, in Chapter Three, I will demonstrate how the 'Brown Boom' has failed to remedy the long-term supply-side weaknesses of the British economy and has been built on rising taxation and growing public and private imprudence. Most importantly, the 'British model' has seen Balls and Brown abandon the Labour Party's historic commitment to the state-led industrial modernisation of the United Kingdom's manufacturing industries. An alternative economic model has emerged, based on support for the City of London's liberalised financial markets, the domestic property market and investment in the United Kingdom's defence, aerospace and pharmaceutical industries. Although it has helped to deliver three consecutive General Election victories, the model has left a legacy of greater inequality in the distribution of income and wealth.

Chapter Four sets out Brown's agenda for the public services. Once, the Labour Party nationalised industries and failing sectors of the economy; this chapter explains how, under Brown's stewardship, the Treasury implemented a top-down technocratic statecraft of 'constrained discretion', which allowed it to limit the freedom of institutions in the public sector to spend taxpayers' money. This enabled it to nationalise policy design for, and the allocation of resources to, public spending bodies in England. Through the Treasury's biennial spending reviews and the framework of the Public Service Agreements, Brown has been able to engineer a top-down, centralised, strategy for public service reforms. Because it has bypassed or eliminated many of the previous checks and balances on executive power, including those exercised by the Prime Minister, the Cabinet, Parliament, local government and individual citizens, constrained discretion has delivered both a seemingly-permanent reform revolution and a significant increase in funding for public services, notably health and education. However, there is growing evidence that the political legacy of an approach based on partnerships with the private sector and a consumer-led approach to public service delivery is a burgeoning disillusionment with the resulting 'postcode lottery' in the availability of services. The trend in public opinion polls demonstrates a widespread perception that increased resources have not been matched by corresponding increases in the quality of public services.

Chapter Five addresses important questions of national identity and citizenship, by exploring Gordon Brown's vision of the 'British Way' of politics. A successor to Tony Blair's 'Third Way', the New Unionism of the 'British Way' seeks an answer to the 'Kirkcaldy and Cowdenbeath Question', the successor to the pre-devolution 'West Lothian Question'. These questions ask why Scots, representing Scottish constituencies, should be able to decide policy matters that affect England alone. Devolution has ensured that the effects of those policy choices will not be experienced by Scottish voters but it has denied English voters the equivalent opportunity to hold their politicians directly to account. This chapter highlights how Brown's British Way is based on examples of Englishness and English history, conflated (or misconstrued) as examples of Britishness and British history. It also demonstrates Brown's increasingly desperate attempts to defend and revive the British Union against the dual threat of the Scottish National Party and resurgent English nationalism.

Part Three sets out Gordon Brown's foreign policy agenda. Chapter Six outlines his New Atlanticism and his quest for a global New Deal on poverty. Although many have expected Brown to distance the Labour Government from the 'war on terror' in Iraq and Afghanistan, the chapter demonstrates that Brown is as much – if not more – of an advocate of the 'special relationship' with the United States as Tony Blair or Margaret Thatcher. In outlining his proposals for an International Finance Facility and supporting the recommendations of the Commission for Africa, the 'Make Poverty History' campaign and the Stern Review of the economic costs of climate change, Brown's foreign policy agenda has deepened rather than challenged the tenets of the neo-liberal 'Washington Consensus' that has dominated the theory and practice of global governance for the past quarter century.

In Chapter Seven, Brown's passionate Atlanticism is contrasted with the open Euroscepticism of his pro-European realism. The roots of Brown's opposition to sterling's participation in European Monetary Union can be traced to his defence of the British Model of Political Economy, his broader advocacy of an Anglo-American model of capitalism and a 'Global Europe' vision for Europe that largely accords with Margaret Thatcher's speech to the College of Europe, in Bruges. The March 2000 Lisbon Summit of the European Union was pivotal in legitimising the Treasury's attempts to move towards a more liberal and deregulated market economy. The chapter further highlights how Brown's vision for the future of the EU – 'Global Europe' – embraces both a vehement opposition to any movement towards an ever-closer political union and a desire for supra-national convergence towards his British model.

The Conclusion summarises the economic legacy of Brown's decade at the Treasury and explores the nature of his political inheritance from Tony Blair. The period before the next General Election will be a battle of ideas between Brown and David Cameron to decide who is the most effective occupant of the common ground in British politics and the truest advocate of twenty-first century liberalism. I will explore the preparations for the Brown Government, as laid out in the conduct of the second Comprehensive Spending Review and how particular attention will be paid to the challenges and opportunities arising from demographic and socio-economic change, globalisation, technological change, global uncertainty over security and environmental sustainability. A key point of departure from Blair's foreign policy is Brown's determination to engage in a battle for hearts and minds as a means of defeating international terrorism.

Brown has promised a new kind and a new style of politics. The book concludes by evaluating whether he will be 'best for England' and whether he can be 'best for Britain'. My conclusion is that the early months of the Brown Government have demonstrated his determination to advance ideas, policies and a legislative programme for England that will champion Britain, the United Kingdom and Britishness, through the negation of democratic citizenship in England and the national identity of England as a distinct political community.

PART I

Gordon Brown's Political Philosophy

Chapter 1

From Supply-Side Socialism to Supply-Side Liberalism

WINNING THE BATTLE OF IDEAS

During his life, Gordon Brown has undertaken a lengthy personal ideological journey. Part One is dedicated to mapping that journey. Brown's elevation to the role of Labour Party leader and Prime Minister of the United Kingdom of Great Britain and Northern Ireland has come almost forty years since he went up to Edinburgh University as the university's youngest-ever undergraduate and twenty years after Neil Kinnock appointed him to his Shadow Cabinet.

During long political careers, it is not especially surprising if a politician's ideas evolve . However, what is truly remarkable (and will be surprising to the uninitiated) in Brown's political philosophy is the extent to which he has abandoned the ideas of the mainstream Scottish Labour Party and its socialist heritage. Brown has instead embraced the liberalism and moral political economy of Adam Smith and the Scottish Enlightenment, whose moral sense, and sentiments, have moved him to closer to the values he first learned from his parents.

I begin by identifying the importance of his parents' values as the personal inspiration for Brown's political career, followed by an exploration of the first phase of Brown's political philosophy, to emphasise its origins in the mainstream Labour Party tradition of parliamentary socialism. I shall then consider the key aspect of the second phase, a commitment to supply-side socialism and the Labour Party's ambition to implement a techno-cratic, state-led industrial modernisation programme as its alternative to Thatcherism. Following the Labour Party's fourth consecutive General Election defeat in April 1992 and Tony Blair's election as Labour Party leader in July 1994, Brown's political philosophy entered a third phase of supply-side liberalism. Following the Labour Party's election victory in May 1997, Brown's philosophy entered its fourth and current phase, during which he has abandoned the socialist tradition within the party. As an alternative, Brown has embraced the moral sentiments of Adam Smith. These third and fourth phases are analysed in Chapter Two.

WINNING THE BATTLE OF IDEAS: SETTING THE AGENDA FOR MODERNISATION

Winning the battle of ideas has been particularly important to recent British Prime Ministers. They have identified this battle as one of two prerequisites for the implementation of their respective modernisation agendas. (The other was the learning of vital lessons from the perceived failures of previous governments and designing policies to avoid their repetition.) For Margaret Thatcher, being able to implement the policies she deemed best for Britain depended on 'winning not just power but the battle of ideas'.[1] Her closest ideological ally, Sir Keith Joseph, argued that by the mid-1970s the Conservative Party, like British politics in general, had become 'stranded on the middle ground' that had arisen from 'the left-wing ratchet' of Keynesian social democracy.[2] The Tories had therefore been 'inhibited from fighting a vigorous battle of ideas', when they should have been frankly analysing 'the developments of the whole post-war settlement, as it grinds into a dead end'.[3] When the first Thatcher Government was elected, in May 1979, Sir Keith Joseph proclaimed to the House of Commons:

> The new government bring with them a different analysis and a different set of policies. The analysis takes into account the lessons that we have learnt from the past during periods of Conservative Governments and, certainly, Labour Governments. A fresh set of policies will arise out of that analysis.[4]

Tony Blair followed a similar path. In his 1994 Labour Party leadership election statement, *Change and National Renewal*, Blair stated that the Labour Party 'must do more than just defeat the Conservatives on grounds of competence, integrity and fitness to govern. We must change the tide of ideas'.[5] As leader, in April 1995 Blair told the special Labour Party conference on the new party constitution that Britain needed 'new energy, ideas and vision – a government free of dogma, not hidebound by ideology but driven by ideas'.[6] New Labour would learn the lessons of Labour's landslide election victory in 1945: 'the need for a clear sense of national purpose [and] the need to win the battle of ideas'.[7] Its task would be 'nothing less than national renewal', necessitating 'economic renewal, social renewal and political renewal'.[8] The 1997 Labour Party General Election manifesto asserted that its aim was 'to put behind us the bitter political struggles of left and right that have torn our country apart for too many decades'. New Labour would be the 'party of ideas and ideals but not of outdated ideology. What counts is what works. The objectives are radical. The means will be modern'.[9]

Once he became Prime Minister, Tony Blair followed the precedent set by Margaret Thatcher; definitive statements of the ideology underpinning his modernisation programme were not published until well after he had entered 10 Downing Street. (The 1979 Conservative Party manifesto made no mention of privatisation, the signature policy of Thatcherism[10] and 'Thatcherism' itself was not coined until after she had become Prime Minister and even then was a product of her opponents.[11]) Neither Blair nor his closest academic ally, Anthony Giddens, published definitive statements of the 'Third Way' renewal of politics until the year after his election.[12] Bill Clinton had used the term 'Third Way' before but not until six years into his presidency.[13] Like Thatcher, Blair attempted only to give retrospective ideological coherence to his government's modernisation programme.

Gordon Brown is different. Not since Margaret Thatcher has British politics witnessed a Prime Minister whose speeches are so frequently and so richly punctuated with quotations. Thatcher's speeches of the late 1970s were littered with references to the work of philosophers and economists, with a relatively narrow focus on conservative thinkers and the liberal political economy of Adam Smith, Friedrich Hayek and Milton Friedman.[14] In comparison, two features stand out in Brown's speeches. The first is the sheer eclecticism of the sources from which his politics come. In a collection of fourteen selected speeches, the 'further reading' (based on the sources cited), listed 122 authors, ranging from major Enlightenment philosophers (Adam Smith, David Hume, Francis Hutcheson and Adam Ferguson), senior religious figures (Pope John Paul II, the Archbishop of Canterbury and the Chief Rabbi), major literary figures (notably John Milton, François Voltaire, James Joyce and George Orwell), American Presidents (Abraham Lincoln, Robert Kennedy and George W. Bush) to an international rock musician (Bono Vox) and an Eskimo poet. The second is the conspicuous absence of references to major Labour Party politicians or political thinkers. Only fifteen sources in the edited collection had a direct link with the Labour Party and were outnumbered more than two-to-one by references to liberal and conservative philosophers or politicians.[15] This, in itself, is an important indication of the evolution of Brown's political philosophy.

Long before he had the opportunity to contest and win the Labour Party leadership or contest a General Election as Prime Minister, Brown drew up a detailed blueprint of his modernisation agenda. He was determined to win the battle of ideas by specifying his philosophy beforehand rather than retrospectively. In so doing, he not only demonstrated how far his political thinking had moved from its radical socialist origins but also how much it had returned to the values and lessons his parents taught him during his childhood.

Brown has said that he sees winning the battle of ideas not only as key to domestic modernisation but also to Britain's foreign policy goals. He has argued that the Cold War was disputed and won not only with military and intelligence weaponry but also through 'a cultural Cold War – a Cold War of ideas and values', fought 'not just through governments but through foundations, trusts, civil society and civic organisations'.[16] That cultural Cold War must now be renewed: Brown identified as crucial to defeating international terrorism the isolation of 'murderous extremists' through the mobilisation of 'the essential decency and moderation of all our communities ... to win the battle of ideas and minds'.[17] The existence of the Internet means that this battle must now be fought in the interests of the moderate majority at the global level.[18]

RESOLVING THE PROGRESSIVE DILEMMA

Gordon Brown is intent on fighting the battle of ideas and wants to launch a new phase of British national renewal. The thesis underpinning his 'British

Way' is that 'as the tasks of government change, the way we govern must change, not just new policies but new politics too. A new politics founded on responsibilities as well as rights'.[19] Given that Brown worked closely with Tony Blair from their election to Westminster in the June 1983 General Election, it is important to establish whether, and to what extent, the tenets of Brown's political philosophy are different from Blair's. Of particular concern to Labour Party members and voters is the question of whether Brown will return the Labour Party to any of the traditional core values that New Labour is held to have abandoned. It is also important to establish whether Brown's philosophy will be capable of resolving the progressive dilemma between liberalism and social democracy which has blighted the Left's electoral prospects in British politics since the end of the First World War.

When Tony Blair was first elected, he appeared genuinely committed to a fundamental ideological realignment of British politics.[20] This realignment would have seen first, the Labour Party and the Liberal Democrats working increasingly closely and second, a referendum on the voting system, in an attempt to resolve the 'progressive dilemma' of British politics. This dilemma, as depicted by David Marquand, had prevented the Labour Party from constructing a successful progressive coalition on the Left of British politics similar to that which had been led by the Liberal Party before 1914. The electoral consequence from 1918 was the distribution of the majority of votes on the Left at successive General Elections but a predominance of Conservative governments.[21]

Throughout the twentieth century, the largest share and, in most cases, the majority of voters at British General Elections tended to cast their votes for social democratic parties of the Centre-Left. However, because those votes were divided between the Labour Party, the Liberal Party and various other parties of the Left (notably the Social Democratic Party during the early 1980s) and because of the vagaries of the first-past-the-post electoral system, the Conservative Party was able to hold power for sixty-eight of the century's years, more than twice as long as its social democratic opponents. Blair's Third Way promised to resolve the progressive dilemma, by drawing 'vitality from uniting the two great streams of left-of-centre thought – democratic socialism and liberalism – whose divorce this century did so much to weaken progressive politics across the West'.[22]

This ambition was given concrete form by the participation of Liberal Democrats in a Cabinet committee and the appointment in December 1997

of the Liberal Democrat peer and leading social democratic thinker, Lord
Jenkins, as head of an independent commission into the future of the voting
system.[23] The General Election manifesto had stated 'We are committed to
a referendum on the voting system for the House of Commons'.[24] However,
by the time the Jenkins Commission had reported, in October 1998, the
realpolitik of New Labour's 179-seat majority at Westminster (delivered by
the existing first-past-the-post voting system) had won the day. The quest
for ideological realignment was quickly abandoned and the commitment to
introduce a more proportionate and fairer voting system left to wither on
the vine.[25]

Within a few months of the election of the first Blair Government,
prominent social democratic commentators exhibited their disillusionment with the Third Way. They argued that Blair lacked a public philosophy
and the Third Way marked the death of Labour re-distributionism and signified the establishment of a neo-liberal consensus in British politics.[26]
Bryan Gould, a prominent member of Neil Kinnock's Shadow Cabinet,
argued that 'New Labour is not Labour renewed. It is Labour rejected,
Labour renounced. New Labour is a negative. New Labour is and is meant
to be, Not Labour'.[27] For his part (having left the Labour Party to join the
Social Democratic Party but returned following Blair's election as leader),
the former Labour MP, David Marquand, contended that Tony Blair's
defining characteristic – and 'what makes New Labour new' – was the
acceptance of 'the foundational assumption of the Thatcher counter-revo-
lution in political economy', namely 'free choice in the marketplace [and]
the entrepreneurial ideal of the early nineteenth century'.[28]

Blair failed to resolve the progressive dilemma in British politics: the
question naturally arises as to whether Gordon Brown can do any better. He
has frequently reminded the Labour Party that:

> ... when we make a compelling case and trust the progressive instincts
> of the British people we can build a shared sense of national purpose,
> we can build a progressive consensus that inspires the country, a con-
> sensus that prosperity and justice for all can advance together.[29]

However, when Brown's political rhetoric and statecraft as Chancellor of
the Exchequer are taken into account, in terms of the location of Brown's
political philosophy in relation to the history of ideas in progressive politics
in general and the Labour Party's traditions in particular, they appear to

point in opposing directions. On the one hand (as I shall set out in greater detail in Chapter Four), Brown's actions as Chancellor place him firmly in the Fabian tradition of technocratic modernisers, who have no qualms about basing their politics on, in the words of W. H. Greenleaf, 'wise and authoritative direction from above'.[30] In their quest for national efficiency (and mirroring Brown's quest for a shared sense of national purpose), since the era of Sidney and Beatrice Webb, Fabian modernisers have placed their faith in socialism becoming, as Sidney Webb said, 'more and more the business of elaborately trained experts'.[31] From his decision to give responsibility for setting interest rates to the unelected Monetary Policy Committee (consisting of economists and financial experts) to his increasing proclivity for commissioning studies on important matters of public policy from individual technical experts beyond the scrutiny of democratic institutions, Brown has governed in the Fabian technocratic tradition.[32]

On the other hand, Gordon Brown's political rhetoric, at least during the two earliest phases of the evolution of his political philosophy, places him sturdily in the tradition of English ethical socialism and the thinking of, among others, R. H. Tawney, George Orwell and T. H. Marshall. In *English Ethical Socialism*, Dennis and Halsey define this tradition by its positive commitment to fraternity, liberty and equality, harnessed to 'a sense of the enormous contribution that a society's past makes to its present morality and institutions and that its present choices and failures to choose will be profound in their consequences'.[33] Above all, ethical socialism embraces 'a shared belief in the power of moral character to perfect a person and ennoble a nation' and, in short, advances 'a theory of personality and society which places moral motivation as the mainspring of individual conduct and social organisation'.[34] In this tradition, R. H. Tawney argued, during the inter-war period, that Britain's problems were attributable to the absence of the spiritual and ethical foundation necessary for economic and social affairs.[35] Tawney's socialism was 'above all personal, moral and religious'.[36]

These characteristics shaped Gordon Brown's socialism in the formative years of his political development. During his childhood, the Brown family's politics were, like Tawney's, personal, moral and religious. As Brown told the 2006 Labour Party conference, his father was a minister of the Presbyterian Church of Scotland but 'his motivation was not theological zeal but compassion' and he was 'more of a social Christian than a fundamentalist'.[37] What he particularly learned from his father was the importance of public service as a person's duty to others and the importance of community and of civic associations as the basis of community. As a consequence, Brown's religion 'is built on a far greater sense of people's importance and potential'.[38]

The specific values taught by his parents were 'duty, responsibility and respect for others', allied to a belief in 'honesty and hard work and that the things that matter had to be worked for'. Every individual had the opportunity to leave their mark on the world, for good or ill, and therefore everyone had a duty to use whatever talents they possessed 'to help people least able to help themselves'. However, while some people possessed a talent, their ability would remain 'lost and forever unfilled' unless they had supportive people to champion them. Consequently, Brown joined the Labour Party 'out of faith – faith in people, that they should have the opportunity to realise their potential'. For this reason, 'at all times the Labour Party must stand for more than a programme: we must have a soul'.[39]

Moral sense and the ethical dimension of politics have been central to Brown's philosophy all his adult life. His parents 'were more than an influence, they were – and still are – my inspiration. The reason I am in politics'. They taught him that 'each of us should live by a moral compass' and by 'a simple faith with a fundamental optimism'.[40] Like the English ethical socialists, Brown believes in the power of character, inspired by fundamental moral sentiments, to perfect a person and ennoble a nation and defines the 'British Way' in terms of the moral character and particular qualities of the British people.[41] Brown has used speeches on Britishness to argue that a society's past contributes to its present morality and institutions and that the choices it makes – and any failures to choose – will have profound consequences.[42] In 2006, Brown reminded the Labour Party conference of his belief that the values of opportunity and responsibility 'are even more relevant to the future of our country as we face profound change [from] the momentous challenges of terrorism and security, global economic competition ... the threat to our planet from climate change'.[43] However, the moral sense and moral sentiments of the Scottish Enlightenment thinkers, which will shape the policies of the Brown Government are far removed from the tradition of ideas that shaped Brown's political philosophy during its earliest phase.

PHASE ONE: BROWN'S ETHICAL AND PARLIAMENTARY SOCIALISM

The importance of politics as a moral duty was evident from the beginning of Gordon Brown's political career: and he was politicised at a very early age. As he recounted to his biographer, the journalist Paul Routledge: 'I grew up and became politically aware in the early Sixties when the Tory government was failing and the idea of change – even for a twelve-year-old – was an important thing'.[44] In November 1972, when standing (successfully) for the post of Rector of Edinburgh University at the age of 21, Brown's manifesto stated 'I am an idealist, a radical and a reformer ... Society's problems today are not technical but social and moral. I believe the university must play a leading role in setting social and moral standards in a civilised society'.[45] Similarly, when Brown attended a vital meeting of the Scottish Labour Party executive in November 1981, he identified the importance of drawing up a party manifesto that would 'start a moral crusade backed by the vast majority of party members'.[46]

The importance of ideas in the development of Brown's moral crusade was vividly illustrated towards the end of his tenure as Rector when Brown helped assemble and edit a collection of essays, *The Red Paper on Scotland*. This collection demonstrates the extent to which, during the 1970s, his politics were firmly in the mainstream of the Scottish Labour Party. It was published against the backdrop of the peak of the Wilson Government's travails with the consequences of Britain's relative economic decline, the genesis of Thatcherism as a critique of post-war social democratic modernisation and the resurgence of Scottish nationalism following the discovery of North Sea Oil. The *Red Papers* series was intended as the Left's ideological counterweight of *The Black Papers on Education*, an important symbol of the emergence of the New Right in British politics.[47]

In his introduction to *The Red Papers*, entitled 'The Socialist Challenge', Brown developed the thesis that a combination of the Royal Commission on the Constitution (the Kilbrandon Report), the issue of North Sea Oil and Britain's wider economic crisis had fostered 'a barren, myopic, almost suffering consensus which has tended to ignore Scotland's real problems – our unstable economy and unacceptable level of unemployment, chronic inequalities of wealth and power and inadequate social services'. The key question confronting Scotland was 'who shall exercise power and control the lives of our people?' and what sort of social structure could 'guarantee to people the maximum control and self management over the decisions which affect their lives, allowing the planned co-ordination of the use and distribution of resources, in a co-operative community of equals?'[48] Brown's answer was that Scotland's social conditions and political predicament demanded 'a new commitment to socialist ideals', including 'a new social vision for Scotland'[49] that was humane, democratic and revolutionary.

At this time, Brown's politics were couched in impeccably socialist terms and expressed in a commitment to community democracy, a planned economy and the empowerment of workers. His political economy identified capitalism as the cause of Scotland's economic and social problems, rejecting the alternative explanations of national suppression and London mismanagement, although, he claimed, 'we have had our share of both'. First, Brown asserted, the root cause of Scotland's problems was 'the uneven and uncontrolled development of capitalism and the failure of successive governments to challenge and transform it'. Second, Brown claimed, capitalism had for centuries 'sacrificed social aspirations to private ambitions' and thereby stultified the 'real resources of Scotland', which lay in 'the collective energies and potential of our people' rather than North Sea Oil or the 'ingenuity of native entrepreneurs' which was to be championed by Margaret Thatcher and Sir Keith Joseph.[50]

Brown identified 'the long standing paradox of Scottish politics ... the surging forward of working-class industrial and political pressure (and in particular the loyal support given to Labour) and its containment through the accumulative failures of successive Labour Governments'. In the 1920s, socialism had been 'a qualitative concept, an urgently-felt moral imperative, about social control' but that heritage had been lost. The rise of modern Scottish nationalism should be understood as 'less an assertion of Scotland's permanence as a nation than a response to Scotland's uneven development'.[51] Intriguingly, he did not dismiss the nationalist cause out of hand. On the contrary, he merely suggested that, because of the urgency of Scotland's problems, Scottish socialists could not support 'a strategy for independence which postpones the question of meeting urgent social and economic needs until the day after independence'.[52] By implication, a Scottish nationalism which accorded priority to those social and economic needs would be worthy of support. At the same time, Brown argued that Scottish socialists could not give 'unconditional support to maintaining the integrity of the United Kingdom – and all that entails – without any guarantee of radical social change'. This was because the question was 'not one of structures nor of territorial influence but of democracy', of how working people in Scotland could increase their control over 'the decisions which shape their lives and the wealth they alone produce'.[53]

To redress the 'gross inequality' he identified in Scotland, Brown advocated 'policies for mobilising social and economic as well as educational resources in an overall strategy for ending inequality'. What would be required was nothing less than 'a massive and irreversible shift of power to working people, a framework of free universal welfare services controlled by the people who use them'[54]. Moreover, socialism would have to be won 'at the point of production – the production of needs, ideas and particularly of goods and services'. Existing economic strategies had failed to generate 'a new economic base for sustained economic growth', not least because of the clear industrial divide between 'the giants of finance and industry on an international scale (including British multinationals, second only to the Americans) and the small firms on the national market'.[55]

As a socialist alternative, Brown argued for a planned economy to cure 'a vicious circle of low productivity, bad labour relations, low investment and poor entrepreneurship'. He rejected 'the familiar tried formulas of wider incentives, tax reliefs, assured labour markets, growth areas and native entrepreneurs' because such 'public intervention will only be as effective as the efficiency of the private sector permits'.[56] In short, the private control of industry had become 'a hindrance to the further unfolding of the social forces of production'. Whether through investment in state-owned industries or through the application of intermediate technology, what was needed was 'the erosion of the power of the market – and of the multinationals who now manipulate the market – to determine the social priorities that are the forging ground for socialist progress'.[57]

To empower the workers, Brown rejected as inadequate proposals for worker shareholdings, favouring the co-ordination of workers' activity in different industries and unions. This could be achieved through the revival of the Institute of Workers' Control, which had been proposed at the time of the occupation of Upper Clyde Shipbuilders during the Heath Government. In relation to the wider question of the relationship between socialism and nationalism, Brown argued that Scottish identity had been forged on the anvil of successful British capitalism. Responding to the

Scottish National Party's (SNP) agenda, Brown asserted that they had, mistakenly, presumed 'the familiar priorities of wealth and power over people' and assumed 'the subservience of Scottish workers to private international controls'.[58] In short, the SNP had merely brought the professional and commercial classes back into politics.

For Brown, in the mid-1970s, the way forward for the Labour movement in Scotland lay in the creation of 'a socialist society, a coherent strategy with rhythm and modality to each reform to cancel the logic of capitalism', achieved through 'social reorganisation – a phased extension of public control under workers' self-management and the prioritising of social needs set by the communities themselves'.[59] Claiming that devolution had become 'all things to all people', including 'the insertion of a sixth tier of government which threatens to make us the most over-governed country in Europe',[60] Brown concluded his socialist challenge by focusing on the opportunity presented by events 'to force the pace towards socialism in Britain as a whole'. This could be accomplished by convincing people of the need for social control, as had been understood by 'Scotland's socialist pioneers, Hardie, Smillie, Maxton, Maclean, Gallacher, Wheatley and others'.[61]

Gordon Brown's list of Scotland's socialist pioneers was significant, demonstrating his commitment to a gradual, parliamentary socialism, rather than to a more radical form of political organisation. The most significant of these Scottish pioneers to Brown's political philosophy was James Maxton, Independent Labour Party MP for the Glaswegian constituency of Bridgeton from the 1922 General Election until his death in July 1946. Maxton's philosophical influence was reflected in the prominence of his work in Brown's PhD thesis.[62] For example, during the late 1920s, Maxton had campaigned for the Independent Labour Party's manifesto, Socialism in Our Time, which had called for 'a new approach to politics' and contended that 'on the issues of Socialism and the abolition of poverty there is no room for compromise'.[63]

James Maxton also developed the notion of 'the third alternative ... neither a long period of misery under capitalism, nor a great economic and social collapse'. He claimed the third alternative 'aims at securing political power by the ordinary political machine, aims at developing industrial power by strengthening of the trades unions and at increasing economic power by strengthening the co-operative movement'.[64] (Maxton's development of this concept may explain why Brown never felt comfortable with and refused to use the term 'Third Way' when Chancellor of the Exchequer.)

Shortly before Maxton's death, as Brown recorded in his biography, Winston Churchill described him as 'The greatest gentleman in the House of Commons'. After he died, the *Daily Mail* asserted that he had given Westminster 'a moral authority'.[65] Brown has sought to impart this quality of moral authority to his politics and, following in the footsteps of James Maxton, to his parliamentary career.

PHASE TWO: SUPPLY-SIDE SOCIALISM

Having unsuccessfully contested the Edinburgh South constituency in the May 1979 General Election (which he lost by only 2460 votes, reducing the Conservative majority by nearly one thousand votes), Brown was elected to Westminster in the June 1983 General Election as MP for the Fife constituency of Dunfermline East. Brown was elected with 18515 votes (no less than 51.5 per cent of the votes cast) and a majority of 11301.

Brown made his maiden speech on 27 July 1983, choosing a debate on social security.[66] The choice of his personal, political and historical reference point is deeply instructive: the 1942 Beveridge Report, written by a card-carrying member of the Liberal Party, with not a reference to any ideas of the Labour Party. (Twenty-four years later, he was to choose the 1944 White Paper on Employment and the goal of full employment identified by John Maynard Keynes, another Liberal Party member, as his reference point when setting out the Blair Government's economic policy objectives.) In this maiden speech, he sought to defend the welfare state as a correction to the wrongs wrought by Victorian values, citing Winston Churchill, not Ramsay McDonald, Clement Attlee, Harold Wilson, James Callaghan or any other previous Labour Party leader. He began his speech by highlighting the impact of de-industrialisation on the people of Dunfermline East and the assault on social justice inflicted by 'mass unemployment and its inevitable consequence, mass poverty'. Using normally unpublished statistics from the Government's Manpower Services Commission, Brown identified 'a new arithmetic of depression and despair' that had arisen from the Thatcher Government's desire to cut welfare benefits for the unemployed.[67]

In Scotland, welfare dependency had increased. In 1979, 405,000 were on supplementary benefit; by July 1983, 750,000 received means-tested benefits. Paradoxically, even with benefits as low as £26 per week, the government argued that they were a disincentive to employment, although a study from the influential think-tank, the Institute for Fiscal Studies, indicated that only one claimant in 40 was receiving more income than they would have received from employment. Brown asserted that to seek to cut unemployment benefit was not a necessary act of economic policy, as Nigel Lawson implied, but 'an act of vindictiveness to the poorest in our community'. Brown's conclusion was that the Government was 'proposing and enshrining a new definition of the national minimum, a new poverty line and a new safety net'.[68] This would not only contradict the tenets of the 1942 Beveridge Report but also be 'devoid of all logic, bereft of all morality and vindictive even beyond monetarism'.[69]

Gordon Brown thus began his parliamentary career by demonstrating his commitment to social justice. He underlined that commitment by co-editing (with Robin Cook) a study of poverty and deprivation in Scotland. Brown's introduction highlighted the new poverty in Scotland, where more than one million people existed on or below the Government's official poverty line. He attributed Scotland's high level of deep-seated poverty to the industrial and occupational structure of the Scottish economy and, in particular, the highly uneven and uncontrolled character of Scotland's economic development.[70] Brown claimed the welfare state was now endangered by 'a new Tory social ideology which is doing to the legacy of Beveridge what "monetarist" dogma has done to the heritage of Keynes'. He noted that the New Right's proposals for the welfare state would mean market forces would determine the shape and price of social services. This meant the Friedman–Hayek analysis underpinning this agenda was 'as much at odds with the facts of life in a complex society and the climate of social values as is Mrs Thatcher's incantation of Victorian bliss'.[71]

As an alternative, Brown advocated the Left should re-assess its social strategy to address changing circumstances, if not the ideological challenge posed by the Thatcherite New Right. The Left should argue the case for equality and identify badly-needed new principles for social security. In this, he drew on the thinking of R. H. Tawney and identified five initiatives that would 'narrow the space between valley and peak ... by radically reforming the existing tax, social security and welfare systems'. The initiatives were: an end to mass unemployment, a legal minimum wage, a more generous definition of the minimum 'safety net', raising the levels of public expenditure on the areas and groups most in need and the redistribution of income and wealth, by re-establishing the principles that 'those who cannot afford to pay tax should not have to pay it' and 'taxation should rise progressively with income'.[72]

Brown extended these ideas beyond Westminster, using the very public platform of the Labour Party's annual conference. He castigated the second Thatcher Government for an approach to the welfare state that was about 'the redistribution of poverty among the poor when it should be about the redistribution of wealth from rich to poor'. He was equally contemptuous of those who had left the Labour Party in 1981, claiming that 'the Social Democrats cannot fight the new Right because they *are* the new Right'. He also asserted that there was more talent 'stagnating at the Labour Exchange than speculating on the Stock Exchange'.[73] Given Brown's later role at the Treasury as the champion of the interests of the City of London, the length of his ideological odyssey from his early parliamentary socialist roots becomes apparent.

From his first election to Westminster until the Labour Party's fourth consecutive General Election defeat (in April 1992), Gordon Brown's political philosophy remained firmly within the traditions, aims and values of the Labour Party and indeed, those of the broader labour movement. He was a consistent and skilled advocate of state-led industrial modernisation. His analysis of the United Kingdom's relative decline was clear and consistent with that of the party leader, Neil Kinnock. In his manifesto for state-led industrial modernisation of 'machines and methods', Kinnock defined democratic socialism as 'the politics of production' and identified essential measures to plan investment in and expansion of the manufacturing industry.[74] This was the period of development of Brown and the Labour Party's supply-side socialism.

To differentiate it from the Thatcher Government's medium-term financial strategy, the Labour Party promised a medium-term industrial strategy and 'a science-based, high-tech future'[75] in which the Party's commitment to supply-side socialism would reflect the fact that 'The Conservatives are the party for the City. We are the party for industry'.[76] Demonstrating a growing commitment to macro-economic stability and fiscal prudence, the Labour Party would pursue 'a policy of sustained and balanced growth' but would be prepared to follow the French and Germans in harnessing 'private resources for publicly-led investment'.[77] Above all, the Party would be committed to the modernisation of Britain, providing the stable conditions and the strategic policies to help industry succeed. For the economy, modernisation would mean 'a modern industrial policy, based on partnership between government and industry, where government encourages long-term investment in skills and technologies'.[78] To finance and deliver its industrial modernisation programme and to correct the short-termism and failure of the City of London's financial markets to invest sufficiently in manufacturing industry, the Labour Party committed itself to a National Investment Bank, a National Recovery Programme, an Investment Decade for Britain and the establishment of a British Technology Enterprise and English Regional Development Agencies.[79]

In 1989, Brown published *Where There is Greed*, a withering critique of Thatcherism that reflected his commitment to supply-side socialism. In it, he accused Margaret Thatcher of betraying Britain's future by failing to make the public investments necessary for industrial modernisation. For him, the 1980s had been 'a decade not of achievement but of missed opportunity', during which the free market had failed, creating 'under-funded and over-extended' public services and 'an industrial desert'.[80] This failure had arisen because of Thatcher's doctrinaire prejudice and short-term vision, in which her blind conviction that the British decline could be attributed to the over-reaching state had obstructed the 'greater role for organised and supportive interventions by the state [in] education and training, in innovation and in technology support and in enhanced long-term investment'. Unaided, the market would fail to 'educate and train our workforce, plan and fulfil national research goals or restore or even compensate for our battered infrastructure'.[81]

Brown's alternative was to re-cast the state as catalyst and co-ordinator and introduce a new supply-side socialism, whose principal themes would be 'investment in skills and science, with teamwork, collective effort and the involvement of the workforce'.[82] This would deliver 'the necessary remedial action: supply-side measures to stimulate investment in the regions, in education and research and to ensure proper balance in the economy'.[83] Based on a classically technocratic and rational approach to national self-interest, Brown's series of co-ordinated supply-side interventions would attend to the under-investment in Britain's infrastructure, not least her 'overcrowded, underfinanced, under-planned, under-maintained and sometimes dangerous transport system'.[84]

This was Kinnock's 'politics of production' writ large. Brown's state-led modernisation agenda firmly attached him to the Labour Party tradition of Harold Wilson's white heat of technology, with its Ministry of Technology and the Callaghan Government's National Enterprise Board. More broadly, he had set out a classic developmental state model, whose focus on the development of national productive powers through public investment was solidly in the tradition of the nineteenth-century German political economist, Friedrich List.[85] In his great work, *The National System of Political Economy*, List set out, for industrialising economies seeking to catch up with their more advanced competitors, the definitive alternative to Adam Smith's liberal economics.[86] Rather than following Smith's example of believing that 'politics and political power cannot be taken into consideration in political economy', List argued that political power should be used to increase both internal prosperity and foreign commerce by nurturing the nation's productive powers.[87] Brown's supply-side socialism set out an agenda to harness political power for the purpose of state-led industrial modernisation.

Supply-side socialism underpinned the Labour Party's 1992 General Election campaign and manifesto. Only three months before the election, the Labour Party launched *Made in Britain*, a statement of the economic and industrial policy priorities of a potential Labour government.[88] At its launch, John Smith, the Shadow Chancellor, emphasised two important facets of Labour's strategy: first, that it would clearly divide Labour and the Tories on industrial policy and second, that Labour's industrial policies would be prudent, costing no more than around £1.1 billion, because 'the first responsibility of government is to create a stable economic framework so that business can plan and invest for the future'.[89] Despite the Labour Party's very public commitment to macro-economic stability and fiscal prudence and the fact that the backdrop of the General Election was the worst domestic recession since the 1930s, supply-side socialism still sent the Labour Party to its fourth consecutive General Election defeat. It won only 271 seats (albeit a net gain of forty-two seats over the 1987 General Election) and took a 34.4 per cent share of the vote (up by only 3.6 per cent from Labour's poor performance in 1987).

In his role as Shadow Chief Secretary to the Treasury, Gordon Brown had attempted either to remove costly proposals from the Labour Party's

Policy Review documents or to preface spending commitments with the qualification that they would be implemented only when economic circumstances allowed.[90] However, even such prudential supply-side socialism was insufficient to persuade enough of the electorate to vote for Labour, especially in the more affluent marginal constituencies of the English Midlands and Home Counties. John Major's Conservative Party piled up a record total of 14.09 million votes, against the Labour Party's 11.56 million. Despite the domestic recession, a month before the election, a MORI opinion poll revealed the Conservative Party to have an eleven per cent lead over Labour on the question of economic competence. Forty-seven per cent of respondents thought John Major best equipped to manage the economy, compared to only 31 per cent support for Neil Kinnock.

Supply-side socialism had failed politically. If the Labour Party were ever to govern Britain again, a major review was needed: one that would not only be confined to policy and strategy but would also embrace the ideas and political philosophy of the Labour Party.

PHASE THREE: FROM SUPPLY-SIDE SOCIALISM TO SUPPLY-SIDE LIBERALISM

The need for fundamental change and a wholesale reinvention of the Left was well-understood by the group of politicians who, after John Smith's death, became the principal architects of New Labour's modernisation under Tony Blair. In his leadership election statement, Blair asserted that the Labour Party: 'must do more than just defeat the Conservatives on grounds of competence, integrity and fitness to govern. We must change the tide of ideas'.[91]

Gordon Brown had understood this need long before. Following the Labour Party's General Election defeat, he was one of a number of Shadow Cabinet members who studied the Democratic Party's campaign strategy and platform for the November 1992 American Presidential election. Brown learnt three, very specific, lessons from Labour's defeats and Clinton's victory. The first was that, for the Labour Party, 'the most important thing is that we lay down the principles that guide our future policy': winning the battle of ideas, rather than detailing policy, must become the party's over-riding priority.[92] Brown felt Clinton had won because he had:

... found an echo throughout America for his central idea that government had responsibilities to the whole community to deal with the huge problems of unemployment, the weaknesses of the American manufacturing sector and training in skills and, of course, for the argument that there were entrenched economic interests, privileged elites in American society, that were denying people opportunity.[93]

Brown's focus was still on supply-side issues but his second great lesson from Clinton's victory opened an alternative ideological framework for his modernisation agenda. This lesson concerned the central importance of globalisation in economic policy. Brown contended that 'we're living in an increasingly global economy. There's global sourcing of companies, a global capital market, 24-hour speculative activity'. Allied to the other great challenge, that of how the microelectronics revolution was affecting industry and services and completely changing the working of the economy, the third lesson the Labour Party would have to learn was that 'increasingly, the most important thing about national economic strength is the level of skill in the economy. Government has a responsibility to ensure that training, education and investment are maintained at a satisfactory level'.[94]

This was a supply-side socialist politician, who at a Party conference less than a decade before had lambasted financial speculators and supported Kinnock's politics of production as an alternative to the Conservatives' politics of the City. Brown now proposed a wholesale redefinition of the political economy of the Labour Party and its long-standing assumptions about the respective roles of the state and market. Globalisation, and the need to maintain Britain's international competitiveness, provided Gordon Brown with ideological grounds on which he could justify major changes in the Labour Party's economic and social policy priorities.

From this point, Brown's political philosophy would increasingly embrace a neo-liberal perspective on globalisation, with its advocacy of market liberalisation and deregulation and its unshakeable faith in entrepreneurial initiative as the prime agency of innovation and social change (exercised through competition and risk-taking in open markets). As I shall show in Chapter Three, in economic policy terms, this transition in Brown's thinking was given additional momentum and consolidated by two events: first, the Treasury and Bank of England's political and economic humiliation on 'Black Wednesday', when sterling's humiliating departure from the European Exchange Rate Mechanism followed the defeat of the

Government's monetary policy by financial speculators and second, Brown's appointment of Ed Balls as his personal economic adviser. Balls's liberal political economy, and particularly his critique of some of the central assumptions of macro-economic policy, helped propel Brown away from supply-side socialism and towards supply-side liberalism.

THE POLITICS OF POTENTIAL

Brown's political economics might have been in flux but he still sought to define a new politics that would sustain his conviction that 'prosperity requires a just society. Individuals must be given the opportunity to realise their potential to the full'.[95] Brown followed Neil Kinnock's, and the Labour Party Policy Review's, vision of socialism for the 1990s, based on a rejection of the failed 'old ideologies – command economy at one extreme, crude free market economics at the other', in favour of the individual's freedom to develop their potential.[96]

In this vein, Brown wrote a Fabian pamphlet: *Fair is efficient: a socialist agenda for fairness*, in which he sought to put the case for a new economics that would demonstrate how 'attacking poverty and a lack of opportunity at their source is the route both to a fairer society and a more prosperous economy'.[97] To achieve this, progressive taxation, the welfare state and good public services would have to be at the heart of the Labour Party's fairness agenda. The philosophical basis underpinning the new economics was that socialism's objective:

... had always been that every individual should have the opportunity to realise his or her potential to the full, to enable people to bridge the gap between what they are now and what they have it in themselves to become.[98]

Moreover, the Labour Party's vision of fairness had 'always meant more than an aspiration to provide opportunities for all. It also embodies an analysis of society which shows how we can achieve this'.[99]

Brown contended that socialism's unique contribution had been to understand that:

... the strength of society – the community working together – is essential not only to tackle the entrenched interests and accumulations of power that hold ordinary people back but also positively to intervene to promote the realisation of potential. In other words, the power of all of us is essential to promote the potential of each of us.[100]

Even though Brown's political economy was now pointing firmly in the direction of supply-side liberalism, he continued to set out his political agenda within the English ethical socialist tradition. He recalled that R. H. Tawney had acknowledged 'the importance of both spreading individual opportunities to all and of the community in making personal freedom meaningful'.[101] Tawney's *Equality* stated that a society would only be free:

> ... in so far and only in so far, as within the limits set by nature, knowledge and resources, its institutions are such as to enable all its members to grow to their full stature, to do their duty as they see it.[102]

Brown also reminded his readers of Aneurin Bevan's mantra that 'democratic socialism is a child of modern society'.[103] Therefore, Brown's new economic egalitarianism would be concerned with modernisation and would ensure the availability of the helping hand of government at critical moments in people's lives.[104]

At this time of reflection for the Labour Party, Brown contributed significantly to a collection of essays, *Reinventing the Left*, edited by the future Blair loyalist, David Miliband. The theme of the collection was the identification of a politics of autonomy, to provide the basis for a radical new identity for the Left, countering the anti-politics of the New Right's neo-liberalism. For Miliband, the four underlying themes of this reinvention of the Left were the extension of personal autonomy in an increasingly interdependent world, an integration of public action and market decisions to secure social interests, a politics defined by relations of power beyond the labour process as well as within it and the need to surmount traditional modes of political organisation both within and beyond the nation state.[105]

Brown's contribution to the reinvention of the Left was to elaborate upon his concept of the politics of potential. Brown advocated a new popular socialism, based on four foundations of a new redistribution of power, through an enabling state, a new constitutional settlement embracing devolved power wherever possible, the reconstruction of the idea of community as a prerequisite for re-inventing government and a new economic egalitarianism.[106] These tenets were derived from three ethical principles identified by the writers of the 1918 Labour Party constitution but which

Brown held to be as true as ever: first, that 'individual potential is far greater than can be realised in a wholly capitalist society', second, that 'individuals are not just self-centred' and third, that 'not only individuals thrive best in a community and that the potential of the individual is enhanced by membership of a community but also that a strong community is essential for the advancement of individual potential'.[107]

Brown contended that in the nineteenth century, controlling the means to life had meant controlling the means of production, distribution and exchange but this ignored the environmental impact of production and consumption. Now, in the interests of enhancing individual freedom, controlling the means to life meant 'controlling the environment of which the economy is a part and that requires collective action'.[108] Subsequently, under New Labour, for Brown it was to mean controlling the process of resource generation and allocation through centralised and prescriptive control of the domestic policy process in England. Treasury power was to be exercised in a manner that denied the notion of a politics of autonomy. Furthermore, in his attempted redefinition of the notion of community, Brown argued that people are interdependent and both emerge from society and are part of it. However, rather than being spontaneous, community, 'the idea that people see themselves as mutually dependent [must] be constructed and not just assumed'.[109]

Brown contended that 'in recognition of our interdependence people must accept their responsibilities as individuals and as citizens and community action should never be a substitute for the assumption of personal responsibility'. This broader notion of community should be separated from the narrower notion of the centralised state, to protect individual rights and to enable the community to explore how its affairs might be organised 'in a decentralised way, more sensitively and flexibly'. Brown argued that 'hierarchical and centralised bureaucracies designed in the 1940s and 1950s simply do not do the job in a rapidly changing, information-rich, knowledge-intensive society'.[110] In practice, Brown and Balls's development of the British model of political economy, based on the principle of 'constrained discretion', has witnessed a new form of centralisation of political power, in which communities' autonomy has been restricted to administering central policies under the guise of 'new localism' (see Chapter Four).

The potentially dangerous implications for accountability in Brown's agenda were immediately identified by one of his fellow essayists in

Reinventing the Left. Anne Phillips did not dissent from Brown's multiplication of the possible avenues along which citizens might participate in decisions but she did query whether such a process could be based upon 'a community that does not – and may never – exist' and whether Brown's lack of precision in his definition of community might extend into 'a lack of precision over democratic accountability and control'. This, in turn, could scupper any radical transfer of power from the centre to communities.[111] Phillips' comments were prescient. This is precisely what happened in England following the election of the Blair Government: unprecedented personal autonomy was extended to the individual as consumer but the political autonomy of the individual as citizen was severely constrained. Because England has been by-passed by the process of political devolution implemented in the other constituent nations of the United Kingdom, enhanced democratic accountability has been denied to its communities. As an alternative to a genuine politics of autonomy, in the reform of their public services these communities have instead been offered 'earned autonomy' by the Prime Ministers and 'constrained discretion' by the Chancellor of the Exchequer (see Chapter Four).

THE TRIUMPH OF THE TECHNOCRATIC OVER THE ETHICAL

In defining a new politics of potential, Gordon Brown revisited the theme of the importance of developing the potential of people, first learnt from his parents. He also began to revisit ethical socialism and the moral dimension of his political philosophy. This process continued when, after the Labour leader, John Smith's, sudden death, Brown co-edited the volume of tributes to his life and work with the journalist James Naughtie. In his essay on Smith's socialism, Brown highlighted three features also readily identifiable in his own thinking: first, the importance of there being a purpose in politics; second, the importance of recognising the relationship between economic prosperity and social justice and third, and most significantly, the importance of the relationship between Christianity and socialism. Brown underscored how Smith had depicted R. H. Tawney as an uncompromising ethical socialist and himself drawn attention to the importance of 'applying our moral principles in a way which results in practical benefits to our fellow citizens'.[112]

This theme was developed further in Brown's introduction to an anthology of socialism he co-authored with the Labour MP, Tony Wright. In it, Brown provided the clearest statement yet of his concept of socialism. Having identified the values of equality, community and democracy, Brown and Wright asserted that:

> Perhaps the most distinctive feature of British socialism historically has been its insistence on the moral basis of politics. A century ago this kind of ethical socialism may have looked like an aberration in terms of general socialist doctrines but it has been triumphantly vindicated.

In short, socialism had always been 'a matter of moral choice [and] more of an ethic of society than an economic doctrine'.[113] Brown and Wright contended that while 'there should be no doubt that socialism is primarily an ethical doctrine', at the same time its moralism 'should be severely practical'. British socialism had always combined the ethical with the practical by sustaining 'a dual focus on efficiency and equality'.[114]

This meant that an unregulated economy would be 'incapable of delivering either a decent economy or a decent society' and therefore 'capitalism had to be socialised in the public interest'.[115] In its preoccupation with public ownership, Wright and Brown contended that British socialism had provided 'a classic inversion of ends and means, historically understandable but morally and intellectually deficient'. However, following the Labour Party's modernisation of its archaic 1918 constitution, it was now understood that the public interest need not necessarily conflict with the continued existence of markets. On the contrary, rather than seeking to abolish markets, the key task for the state would now be 'to set standards in a way that ensures that markets work in the public interest'.[116]

While the public interest would remain constant, the role of the state would be redefined in a dynamic way, such that government would become 'partner, catalyst, enabler, financier or simply regulator, rather than owner, employer or manager only; just as government may be local and international as well as national'. The modern state would engage in active partnerships in pursuit of public interest objectives, for 'public and private, state and market, capital and labour, national and international: these are the components of a modern partnership economy'.[117] Rather than a choice between capitalism and socialism as forms of ownership, the contemporary choice would be between 'responsibility and irresponsibility, social market and unsocial market, a stakeholder economy and footloose capitalism'.[118] Furthermore, the socialist version of community should be 'an argument about power and its control, enabling people to participate in the decision processes that affect their lives'. The notion of social responsibility arising from the stakeholder economy would go 'far beyond traditional notions of devolution and de-centralisation [and] an encouragement to participation and involvement [to] redistribute power from State to individual'.[119]

Brown and Wright's choice of 'stakeholder economy', with its implications for a radical redistribution of political and economic power, was significant. On 7 January 1996, Tony Blair had made a major speech in Singapore, which focussed on the concepts of trust and the stakeholder economy. Blair had defined trust as 'the recognition of a mutual purpose for which we work together and in which we all benefit' and the stakeholder economy as one 'in which opportunity is available to all, advancement is through merit and from which no group or class is set apart or excluded'. For Blair, trust and stakeholding not only provided the economic justification of social cohesion but also the key to achieving competitiveness in an increasingly competitive global economy.[120]

For the Labour Party, the implications of pursuing such an agenda would have been profound. It would have meant not only a commitment to tackle long-term and structural unemployment but also a wholesale reform of the welfare state. For Will Hutton, writing in the *Observer*, the speech had 'lapses into a language of platitudinous generality'. Despite this, it was hailed as having initiated 'a political exchange of fundamental importance'[121] within and between Britain's two major political parties and to signify a genuine departure in British politics, which might inspire 'a reformist political programme in five chief areas: the workplace, the welfare state, the firm and the City, the constitution and economic policy more generally'.[122]

In the event, the radicalism of stakeholding and its major ramifications for Labour Party policy were sufficient for it to disappear from both Brown and Blair's thinking. During the six months between the Singapore speech's and the publication of the Labour Party's major policy statement, *New Labour, new life for Britain*, the concept of stakeholding was hollowed out.[123] Its radical constitutional, financial and corporate governance reforms, which would have upset both British businesses and the City of London, were either diluted or removed.[124]

The Labour Party focussed instead on learning the three key lessons of the Attlee Government's General Election victory of 1945: first, 'the need for a clear sense of national purpose'; second, the need to win the battle of ideas' and, third, 'the need to mobilise all people of progressive mind around a party always outward-looking, seeking new supporters and members'.[125] These themes, and the language used to describe them, were redolent of the previous two decades of Brown's political philosophy but the actual words were spoken by Tony Blair. The Labour Party now focussed relentlessly on 'nothing less than national renewal', which would require 'economic renewal, social renewal and political renewal'.[126] From this time, until the 1997 General Election, Tony Blair made the definitive statements of New Labour's political philosophy, because he, not Brown, had succeeded John Smith as the Labour Party's leader.

Tony Blair located his political philosophy firmly within the ethical socialist tradition, describing it as 'the only one that has stood the test of time'.[127] He acknowledged his personal debt to the Scottish moral philosopher, John MacMurray, and his view that life had 'a moral purpose that encompassed the notion of duty'.[128] For Blair, socialism was:

> ... never about nationalisation or the power of the state; not just about economics or politics even. It is a moral purpose to life; a set of values; a belief in society, in co-operation, in achieving together what we are unable to achieve alone.[129]

Paradoxically, while Blair's philosophical focus was on ethical socialism, Gordon Brown's role, as Shadow Chancellor of the Exchequer, was the overseeing of the Labour Party's policy agenda for domestic economic and social modernisation. His desire to micro-manage and centrally prescribe policy development and resource allocation increasingly placed him within the top-down, technocratic Fabian tradition of Labour modernisers. More importantly, as Brown focussed increasingly on globalisation, macro-economic stability, fiscal prudence and the long-standing supply-side weaknesses of the British economy, the philosophical basis for his political economy became more attuned to supply-side liberalism than supply-side socialism.

Brown's movement towards supply-side liberalism was accelerated by the events that followed John Smith's death. On 31st May 1994, Brown had dinner with Tony Blair at *Granita*, a restaurant in Islington. During the meal, Brown agreed to lay aside his own ambitions to lead the Labour Party, in favour of Blair's candidature. The price extracted by Brown was to secure an unprecedented control over the design and delivery of domestic economic and social policy. In the aftermath of the dinner, a draft memorandum (later leaked to *The Guardian*) was drawn up, purportedly by Peter Mandelson. Originally, the memorandum read:

> In his Wales and Luton speeches, Gordon has spelled out the fairness agenda – social justice, employment opportunities and skills – which he believes should be the centerpiece of Labour's programme and Tony is in full agreement with this and that the party's economic and social policies should be further developed on this basis.[130]

On the leaked copy of the memorandum, Gordon Brown had crossed out 'is in full agreement with' and instead written 'has guaranteed this will be pursued'.[131] By so altering the wording, Brown skilfully ensured that he, rather than Blair, the potential future Prime Minister and First Lord of the Treasury, would be the prime mover of New Labour's domestic modernisation agenda.

CONCLUSION

The Labour Party's economic and social policy agenda for the 1997 General Election was shaped by Gordon Brown's growing fixation on globalisation and its implications for Britain's domestic policy choices. The political rhetoric of the Party's key policy documents and 1997 General Election manifesto remained technocratic and pragmatic. The promise was of a partnership between government, shareholders, managers and workers, who would put behind them 'the old battles: public versus private, state versus market'.[132] New Labour was 'a party of ideas and ideals but not of outdated ideology ... what counts is what works'.[133] In practice, Brown was proposing to tackle Britain's long-standing supply-side weaknesses by harnessing the energy of the market, dynamic entrepreneurs and successful companies. Competition would be used as 'a spur to innovation, investment and improved productivity – the vital organs of a dynamic economy'.[134] Consumers would be provided with better information, to enable them to exercise greater individual choice. Ironically, the last time such faith had been shown in the dynamic properties of open markets, competition and individual enterprise was in January 1988. Then, at the height of Thatcherism, the Department of Trade and Industry published, *DTI – The Department for Enterprise*, the definitive statement from Whitehall of the Thatcher Government's determination to 'champion all the people who make it happen, rather than just individual sectors, industries or companies'.[135]

The supply-side liberalism of Gordon Brown's nascent 'British model' of political economy was now to gamble that it could deliver modernisation by harnessing and manipulating the actions and investment of private market agents, such as corporations, entrepreneurs and consumers, in the same way that supply-side socialism had previously orchestrated nationalised industries, trades unions and public corporations.

Chapter 2

The New British Enlightenment

INTRODUCTION

During the decade that Gordon Brown served as Chancellor of the Exchequer, his political philosophy evolved significantly. The purpose of this chapter is to chart and explore that philosophical journey, which has left an important political legacy, both for the United Kingdom and for Brown personally, as Prime Minister.

The evolution of Brown's thinking is best understood by dividing its development during his decade at the Treasury into two periods. In the first, from May 1997 until April 1999, Brown laid down and refined the tenets of his supply-side liberalism. With the notable exception of one lecture, in November 1997, in which he set out the principles of his 'British Way' of politics,[1] Brown focussed relentlessly on the development of the British model of political economy (which I shall explore at greater length in Chapter Three). Key economic policy reforms were implemented, notably granting to the Bank of England's Monetary Policy Committee its operational independence over the setting of interest rates, the announcement of the decision that the pound would not be joining the Euro for the lifetime of the Parliament and the completion of the year-long Comprehensive Spending Review and new fiscal policy framework.

During this consolidation of supply-side liberalism, Brown concentrated on showing how fiscal prudence, macro-economic stability and supply-side liberalism would provide the British economy with a policy

environment in which to meet the challenges of globalisation. The culmi-
nation of this particular phase was the delivery of two speeches in the spring
of 1999. In the second, Brown announced to the Institute for Fiscal Studies
that the Treasury's new mission would be no less than the modernisation of
the British economy. Fifty years of 'sterile and self-defeating conflicts
between state and market, managements and workforce, public and private
sectors' would be brought to a decisive end by the pursuit of 'a new national
purpose based on an end to short-termism and an understanding of the
need to take a long-term view of government, industry and the financial
community.'[2] Brown's renewed engagement in the battle of ideas was not to
be limited to economic modernisation. On the contrary, as his first speech,
given five weeks before to the Smith Institute had indicated, Brown's quest
for a new national purpose would take him beyond the parameters of economic modernisation, to the much broader themes of national identity,
constitutional reform and key aspects of global governance.[3]

The development of this fourth phase in Brown's political philosophy
was made possible because he, unlike his Labour predecessors as
Chancellor, was not preoccupied with devaluation or balance-of-payments
crises. Moreover, the combination of the decisions to give operational independence to the Bank of England's Monetary Policy Committee and to conduct fiscal policy through a series of biennial Spending Reviews driven by
the Treasury gave Brown the licence to roam across government departments and explore policy issues previously beyond the remit of the
Chancellor. Exploiting this freedom, Brown embarked on a series of lectures and keynote speeches in which he sought to set out his vision of 'the
new Britain and a new and inclusive vision of Britishness for the twentieth
century'. Brown envisaged a re-discovery of British values, during a transition 'from an over-centralised and uniform state – the old Britain of subjects – to a pluralist and decentralised democracy – the new Britain of
citizens'.[4] This vision would encompass 'a new understanding to the rights
and responsibilities of the citizen and to the reach and role of government',
involving 'a credible and radical view of citizenship as responsible citizenship and a new view of the state as an enabling state'.[5]

In the event, and following from the earlier phases of ethical socialism,
parliamentary and supply-side socialism and supply-side liberalism, this
phase of Brown's political philosophy has seen him embrace a sympathetic
liberalism and moral political economy. These ideas have underpinned the

development of his 'British Way', in domestic policy and his vision for 'Global Europe' and an Atlanticist New Global Deal for poverty and development, in foreign policy. There are a number of remarkable aspects of this phase. As Prime Minister, Brown's 'British Way' is the fourth post-war modernisation programme to be based on liberalism; in developing this sympathetic liberalism, Brown has largely abandoned the socialist tradition of ideas within the Labour Party's history of thought in favour of the philosophy of the Scottish Enlightenment in general and the moral sentiments of Adam Smith in particular; he has returned to the personal, moral and religious philosophical origins of his childhood by drawing extensively on the insights of the Chief Rabbi, Jonathan Sacks and the increasing influence of Enlightenment thinking has drawn him into ideological territory long occupied by the British and Conservative New Right.

In articulating the tenets of his new British Enlightenment, this former, passionate, socialist critic of capitalism has aligned his moral compass to some of the most vigorous defenders of free-market capitalism. This threatens to leave British politics stranded on the ideological common ground first identified by Sir Keith Joseph more than thirty years ago.

THE LIBERAL CENTURY

Seldon and Ball called their 1994 collection of essays *The Conservative Century*. The Conservative Party was electorally dominant in the twentieth century, holding office for more than twice as long as its political opponents were in government.[6] However, in ideological terms, the century would more accurately be described as 'The Liberal Century'. In its first half, the Asquith Government succeeded in laying the foundations for the welfare state and the redistributive taxation system needed to finance it. It legislated for two of the most vital constitutional changes in the United Kingdom's modern political history (the 1911 Parliament Act and the 1914 Government of Ireland Act) and placed the trades unions within a stable legal framework for the first time.[7]

During the latter half of the century, two card-carrying members of the Liberal Party inspired the social democratic 'First Way' of post-war reconstruction. For a generation of politicians – both from Left and Right – John Maynard Keynes specified a macro-economic blueprint for winning both the Second World War and the peace after it.[8] He did so by identifying the ideological and policy conditions for full employment.[9] Sir William Beveridge performed a similar task in relation to the welfare state.[10]

From the mid-1970s, 'The Liberal Century' entered a new phase. Margaret Thatcher and Sir Keith Joseph sought to modernise Britain, by harnessing conservatism and the Conservative Party to the market liberalism of Adam Smith, Milton Friedman and Friedrich Hayek.[11] Thatcher frequently referred to the importance of the moral philosophy of Adam Smith in her redefinition of conservatism and Sir Keith Joseph summarised his new philosophy for government for his senior civil servants at the Department of Industry, adding a reading list which included Adam Smith's *Theory of Moral Sentiments* and *The Wealth of Nations*.[12] When Nigel Lawson defined 'New Conservatism' in August 1980, he noted how new Conservatives had turned to new sages, such as Friedrich Hayek and Milton Friedman, precisely because these thinkers had reinterpreted 'the traditional political and economic wisdom of Hume, Burke and Adam Smith in terms of the conditions of today'.[13] Thus, the 'Second Way' of Thatcherite modernisation owed a significant philosophical debt to liberalism.

Tony Blair's 'Third Way', with its mantra that 'government should not try to run business. The days of picking winners are over' and its retention of the philosophy that 'the role of government in a modern economy is limited but critical', largely left untouched the liberalism of the political economy of its predecessors.[14] Indeed, in the extension of the role of consumer choice and private finance to the organisation and funding of public services, the 'Third Way' rolled forward the frontiers of market-led modernisation.

This raises the key question of whether the Labour Government led by Gordon Brown will embark on a 'Fourth (British) Way' modernisation project, also underpinned by liberalism. The answer is resoundingly in the affirmative, demonstrated by the fourth and latest phase in the development of Gordon Brown's political philosophy. A careful analysis of Brown's speeches and policy statements reveals that he has drawn on the liberal political philosophy of the Scottish Enlightenment, the American liberalism of the 'New Deal' and 'Great Society' Democrat programmes and an eclectic mix of liberal philosophers, whose ranks include Alexis de Tocqueville, John Stuart Mill, T. H. Green, J. A. Hobson, J. M. Keynes, William Beveridge, Jonathan Sacks, Michael Sandel and Michael Walzer.

GORDON BROWN'S MORAL SENSE: 'THE BEST HEAD AND THE BEST HEART'

The key figures who emerged from the heart of the fourth phase of the development of Gordon Brown's political philosophy might seem surprising, given Brown's political and philosophical provenance as a Labour Party politician and ethical socialist. They make more sense when we recall Brown's admission that his parents gave him a world view that was personal, moral and religious. Like Margaret Thatcher and Tony Blair before him, his modernisation programme is for the restoration of British national purpose. Like Thatcher, Brown's project is firmly rooted in the moral sense and moral sentiments of the Scottish Enlightenment, and in particular the moral philosophy and political economy of Adam Smith. For Thatcher, and her closest ideological ally, Sir Keith Joseph, the harnessing of conservatism to liberalism was a genuine Messianic conversion. Brown has simply returned to the philosophy of Adam Smith, a fellow Langtonian, a citizen of the 'Lang Toun' [long town] of Kirkcaldy, where Brown spent his childhood years.

Giving the Pope Paul VI memorial lecture in 2004, Brown advanced three propositions for the reintroduction of moral sense into British politics and political economy: first, 'that our dependence on each other should awaken our conscience to the needs not just of neighbours but of strangers'; second, 'more than that, our moral sense should impel us to act out of duty and not just self interest'; and third, 'that the claims of justice are not at odds with the liberties of each individual but a modern expression of them that ensures the dignity of all – and there is such a feeling as a moral universe'.[15] Brown noted how the great Enlightenment philosophers saw that 'liberty was not at odds with justice or duty but liberty and duty advanced together'. Citing Martin Luther King, Brown spoke of 'an inescapable network of mutuality, together woven into a single garment of destiny'. Brown's belief was that:

> ... even if we are strangers in many ways, dispersed by geography, diverse because of race, differentiated by wealth and income, divided by partisan beliefs and ideology, even as we are different, diverse and often divided, we are not and we cannot be moral strangers for there is a shared moral sense common to us all: call it as Lincoln did – the better angels of our nature; call it as Winstanley did – the light in man; call

it as Adam Smith did – the moral sentiment; call it benevolence, as the Victorians did; virtue, the claim of justice, doing one's duty. Or call it as Pope Paul VI did – 'The good of each and all'.[16]

Where Thatcherism focused on Smith's invisible hand of the pursuit of individual self-interest, as the key to the restoration of an entrepreneur-driven enterprise culture and the creation of a property-owning, share-owning popular capitalism, Brown focused on *The Theory of Moral Sentiments* and Smith's helping hand that matched the invisible hand of his wealth of nations. Brown sought to emphasise Smith's selflessness, in contrast to Thatcherism's self-interested individualism.[17] Brown noted how as he died, Adam Smith:

> ... was writing a new chapter for his *Theory of Moral Sentiments* entitled 'On the corruption of our Moral Sentiments' which is occasioned by 'the disposition to admire the rich and great and to despise or neglect persons of poor and mean condition'.[18]

The importance that Brown attaches to the philosophy of Adam Smith provides insight into his frequent use of the term 'prudence'. What began as a simple concern with being careful in how he spent taxpayers' money has developed into a complex concern with prudence as the expression of moral duty towards others.

In the opening sentence of the first paragraph of Part One of *The Theory of Moral Sentiments*, Adam Smith places sympathy at the heart of his exploration of moral sentiments: 'How selfish so ever man may be supposed, there are evidently some principles in his nature, which interest him, though he derives nothing from it except the pleasure of seeing it'.[19] In the political economy of Gordon Brown, from his specification of the Blair Government's central economic objectives, the moral sentiment and virtue of prudence played a more salient role.[20]

For Smith, there were at least two proper objects of prudence. The lesser of these was 'the care of the health, of the fortune or the rank and reputation of the individual, the objects on which his comfort and happiness in this life are supposed principally to depend'. The superior level of prudence embraced 'wise and judicious conduct, when directed to greater and nobler purposes than the care of the health, the fortune, the rank and reputation of the individual'.[21] While Smith regarded security as 'the first and the principal object of prudence', he regarded the superior prudence of the great general, statesman or legislator, as supposing 'the utmost perfection of all the intellectual and of all the moral virtues'.[22] Prudence is 'the best head joined to the best heart' and, when combined with other virtues, constituted the noblest, for Smith. By the same token, imprudence, combined with other vices, constituted the 'vilest of all characters'.[23]

SYMPATHETIC LIBERALISM: CLAIMING ADAM SMITH FOR THE LEFT

Gordon Brown understood that he could not claim to be a truly prudential politician, in possession of 'the best head joined to the best heart', unless he could reclaim Adam Smith's work from the New Right. On 25 April 2002, Brown chaired an 'Enlightenment Series' lecture at Edinburgh University. The theme was 'Can both the Left and Right claim Adam Smith?', so Brown invited the audience to consider whether Adam Smith would have felt more at home in the left-of-centre Smith Institute (named after the late John Smith MP) or the right-of-centre Adam Smith Institute. That question has been broached in *Radical and Egalitarian: An Interpretation for the Twenty-First Century*, written by a fellow Scot, Professor Iain McLean of Oxford University, in which he sought to set out the case for Adam Smith to be reclaimed by the Left as a radical and egalitarian.

Developing his thesis, McLean argued that the importance of Adam Smith's Scottishness has been understated and that his radical egalitarianism was rooted in the Scotland that he grew up in.[24] By the same token, that could also be said of Gordon Brown. McLean has identified a 'subterranean' theme of his book as 'once a Presbyterian, always a Presbyterian, even if you reject the doctrines of the Church of Scotland'. Adam Smith's tastes for frugality and egalitarianism are 'uncannily similar' to those of Gordon Brown, for 'both the eminent sons of Kirkcaldy are puritanical about ostentation in clothes or tastes. "Prudence" is the favourite word of both'.[25]

The most importance convergence between Adam Smith and Gordon Brown lies not in the realm of their respective characters but in their philosophy and political economy. For any politician, their understanding of market failure (that is, where markets fail to deliver either an efficient allocation or sufficient and affordable supply of vital public goods) will determine where and when they resort to government intervention. McLean has noted how Brown and Smith concur that 'the central question of political economy is where the boundary between the market and the state should lie, in the face of partial market failure'.[26] Indeed, he contends that 'what we might call a social-democratic reading is truest of all to the historical Adam Smith'.[27] This is superior to the New Right's libertarian conservative interpretation because that 'does not acknowledge the depth of Smith's analysis of market failure, nor of his case for redistributive taxation'.[28] For example, Smith's first maxim of taxation anticipated progressive taxation by stating: 'The subjects of every state ought to contribute towards the support of the government, as nearly as possible, in proportion to their respective abilities'.[29] The source of Smith's profound egalitarianism is his focus on the human moral sentiment of sympathy: it is 'our capacity for sympathetic insight into others that allows us to take up the role of impartial spectator towards ourselves'.[30] By reflecting on our own behaviour and how that must appear to other people, we have the capacity not only to liberate ourselves from our own faults but also to identify the condition of others and to offer them a helping hand.

At the root of Smith and Brown's philosophy is their sympathetic liberalism and belief in humans' possession of an innate moral sense. McLean's thesis is that this common philosophical platform has led them to share six main arguments. First, both oppose rent-seeking by vested interests. For Brown, this means that producer interests should not be treated as being synonymous with the public interest. Second, both reject selfishness as the sole motive of human life, reflected in Brown's exploration of the moral limits of markets. Third, both Smith and Brown understand market failure and fourth, have identified the role that the state has to play in correcting it but, fifth, recognise that the state does not have to provide public goods itself. Sixth, Brown shares Smith's four maxims of taxation, announcing that he had them at his side when preparing his 2002 Budget.[31]

The increasing influence of Adam Smith's ideas on Brown's political philosophy and the simultaneously diminishing importance of the Labour Party's tradition of ideas in general and ethical socialism in particular was demonstrated in October 2006 when Brown gave the Donald Dewar Memorial Lecture (a tribute to the former First Minister of Scotland and principal architect of Scottish devolution). Brown used this opportunity not only to chart Dewar's 'rich and complex political legacy' but also to set out his vision for politics and government in the twenty-first century. The common denominator was the central importance of the philosophy of the Scottish Enlightenment. Having made a solitary (and brief) reference to the importance of equality and the work of R. H. Tawney in Dewar's politics, Brown explored at length how the idea of liberty, understood as individual empowerment rather than a narrow selfish individualism, had come alive in the Scottish Enlightenment. Indeed, it had been at Glasgow University, where Dewar had studied, that Adam Smith had delivered the lectures which 'first laid the foundations of a modern moral philosophy and political economy'.[32]

Having located both Dewar's and his own politics firmly within the ideological tradition of the Scottish Enlightenment, Brown now set out his vision for politics in the twenty-first century. His thesis was that:

> If the challenges of the last half of the last century focused on economic instability and prosperity, unemployment and underinvestment in our public services, the major challenges ahead are now also terrorism and security, global economic competition and climate change and meeting the rising aspirations of individuals and the yearning for stronger communities.[33]

These challenges could be met through a partnership which gave equal place 'to the active, responsible citizen, the empowered community and [an] enabling, empowering government working together'. However, this would only be accomplished with the rediscovery of 'our rich culture of rights and responsibilities', by remembering that the state was the servant and not the master of the people and by forging a partnership between 'individual civic society and the institutions of government'. This would be possible for the British people, because their passion for liberty had not degenerated into self-interested individualism; what Jonathan Sacks terms 'a British libertarianism'.[34] On the contrary, that possibility had been denied precisely because of the influence of Adam Smith and the Enlightenment writers. Smith, in *The Wealth of Nations*, stated 'All for ourselves and nothing for other people, seems, in every age of the world, to have been the vile maxim of the masters of mankind'[35] and in *The Theory of Moral Sentiments* (for Brown, Smith's most important book), he showed how 'the helping hand of individuals supporting other individuals' complimented the invisible hand of *The Wealth of Nations*.[36]

In consecutive years, Brown invited both Alan Greenspan, Chairman of the United States' Federal Reserve and Mervyn King, Governor of the Bank of England, to deliver the Adam Smith Memorial Lecture in Kirkcaldy,

Smith's birthplace and Brown's home town. Ironically, Greenspan used his lecture to emphasise the legacy of Smith's 'invisible hand' and its importance for 'the relative economic stability we experience daily' rather than Brown's 'helping hand' interpretation of Smith's moral sentiments.[37]

King closed his lecture by announcing that Adam Smith was to be the new face on the Bank of England's £20 note; Smith's portrait duly appeared on the new issue of 13 March 2007.[38] This action – and its timing – was deeply symbolic. Not only was Adam Smith the first Scotsman to appear on a Bank of England note but he appeared just one week before Brown was to deliver his eleventh (and probably final) Budget statement. Even greater political symbolism lay in the fact that Smith's image replaced Edward Elgar's. Not only is Elgar widely regarded as the quintessential English composer but also his *Pomp and Circumstance March No 1* is the setting for the words of *Land of Hope and Glory*, the theme often used at sporting events, such as the Commonwealth Games, as an unofficial English national anthem. Elgar's replacement came in the year of the 150th anniversary of his birth, which prompted an Early Day Motion for his reinstatement in the House of Commons. However, Brown stood firm: two Unionist sons of Kirkcaldy triumphed over an icon of English national identity.

THE RE-MORALISATION OF BRITAIN

Adam Smith's work has become increasingly influential on Gordon Brown's agenda for both domestic economic and social reform and his approach to tackling global poverty. However, a second vital philosophical datum point for the calibration of his moral compass is the work of the Chief Rabbi, Jonathan Sacks. References to Sacks's *The Politics of Hope* and, more recently, *The Dignity of Difference* have littered Brown's speeches and Sacks's thesis of the moral dimension of politics and the market economy resonates, with increasing power, with Brown's sense of moral duty.[39] Sacks argues that the dominant concepts of a free society, the liberal and the libertarian, have shared the ideal of 'an arena in which the state guarantees the freedom of the individual to realise his or her own choices'. It has been assumed both that 'morality has no part to play in politics beyond fair procedures and the transparency and accountability of governments' and that therefore 'morality itself is a purely individual concern'.[40]

For Sacks, it is evident that social order has failed and has instead delivered social disorder. The alternative is to restore a liberal order and a civil society which rest on covenantal moral relationships arising from families, friends and citizens rather than governments. Salvation lies in a re-moralisation of society through a 'politics of hope' that will develop 'a public language of shared values rather than private claims' to enable people to identify the goods which we hold in common.[41]

This is precisely the public language of shared values in which Brown has attempted to articulate his 'British Way' (see Chapter Five). The world of self-interested individualism, in which morality is privatised and relationships defined in terms of contracts and vested interests, must be rejected and replaced with a stronger recognition by society of the importance of covenantal obligations, in which the moral component is exercised through loyalty and fidelity to one's family, friends and community and the voluntary associations which constitute the basis of civil society.[42]

In *The Dignity of Difference*, Sacks addressed a question at the heart of Brown's politics: globalisation. Sacks's thesis is that the politics and economics of globalisation possess 'an inescapably moral dimension', because both create problems and both raise issues that cannot be resolved by either one alone.[43] Sacks's proposal for the resolution of such matters is a covenant of hope based on recognition of 'the dignity of difference'.[44] The free market is acknowledged as 'the best means we have yet discovered for alleviating poverty and creating a human environment of independence, dignity and creativity'. However, Sacks held that the market 'has done more than open up extremes of poverty and wealth. It has subverted other institutions – families, communities, the bonds that link members of a society to a common fate'.[45]

In conditions of 'maximal uncertainty' and reflecting Brown's increasing emphasis on the importance of moral sense and moral sentiments, Sacks asserted that human behaviour should be guided by six simple moral principles: control, contribution, creativity, co-operation, compassion and conservation. These six are the prelude to a seventh: the 'new global covenant of human solidarity',[46] which would serve as an overdue corrective to the demoralisation of society during the past half century, which has signalled 'both a loss of moral meanings and a loss of hope'.[47]

The way forward in political economy, for example, is to make the moral case for the market economy, recognising that 'mankind was not created to serve markets. Markets were made to serve mankind'.[48] By exploring the moral dimensions of the market in a global age, it will be possible for us to identify 'the values that should guide us if we are to create a more humane world'. For Sacks, 'the ethical imperative is ubiquitous and non-negotiable. Beyond every "is" lies the claim of "ought" '.[49] This is precisely what Brown is attempting domestically in his 'British Way' for politics and internationally in his 'global New Deal' promises. By drawing on the insights of Enlightenment thinkers, Brown is seeking to expose the moral dimensions of contemporary markets and the moral sentiments that can help to create a more humane world.

Sacks's moral political economy has likewise drawn on the work of Enlightenment thinkers such as David Hume and Adam Smith. In *The Dignity of Difference*, Sacks cited Smith's famous observations in *The Wealth of Nations* about the invisible hand to highlight the fact that 'markets work on the basis of self-interest rather than altruism'.[50] Nevertheless, for Sacks 'The very act of market exchange is the supreme embodiment of the idea of the dignity of difference' because, as long as everyone has something to contribute, the division of labour and Ricardo's *Law of Comparative Advantage* will ensure that 'everyone gains through the contribution of others'. (David Ricardo was another Enlightenment thinker. His theory of comparative advantage argued that 'by specialising in producing and trading those goods for which they have greater cost advantage, nations and their populations maximise their access to wealth and welfare'.[51])

In short, the market offers 'the paradigm of the win-win scenario and the non-zero-sumness of human relationship', which in turn has 'not merely economic but moral and spiritual consequence'.[52] The best hope for avoiding conflict and war is to engage in market exchange because 'Unlike the battlefield, the market is an arena in which both sides can win'.[53]

Jonathan Sacks has provided Gordon Brown with an important moral justification for the market and his advocacy of trade liberalisation and deregulation as the key to human development (see Chapter Six). Rather than basing his political economy on questions of efficiency of allocations and individual self-interest, Sacks's work seeks to base future human exchange on the basis of a covenant and not a contract. Unlike a contract, a covenant is 'not limited to specific conditions and circumstances'; it is 'open-ended and long-lasting [and] not based on the idea of two individuals, otherwise unconnected, pursing personal advantage. It is about the

"We" that gives identity to the "I" '.[54] Gordon Brown's 'war against poverty', Global New Deal and International Finance Facility are simply Sacks's proposal of a global covenant transposed onto the global international stage.[55] For Brown: 'What is morally wrong cannot be economically right' and so we must move 'from economics to morality, from enlightened self interest that emphasises our dependence on the other to the true justice that summons us to our duty'.[56]

CIVIC SOCIETY AND THE MORAL LIMITS OF MARKETS

For Gordon Brown, the key to giving further effect to the moral sentiments of Adam Smith's 'helping hand' and Jonathan Sacks' 'politics of hope' is the restoration of civic society. Giving the Hugo Young Memorial Lecture in 2005, Brown noted how 'it was Britain and British ideas that led the way into the modern world by focusing on benevolence, improvement, the civic society and the moral sense as necessary for social progress'.[57] Brown wants to restore these qualities to British society but they can only be realised through families, voluntary associations, churches, faith groups and public service. Brown claimed that: 'we, the British people, have consistently regarded a strong civic society as fundamental to our sense of ourselves – that moral space, a public realm in which duty constrains the pursuit of self-interest'.[58]

Brown's childhood in Kirkcaldy taught him the value of the 'network of civic society'. Speaking at the National Council for Voluntary Organisations' (NCVO) conference in 2000, he described how a town with strong community and voluntary organisations at its heart could make people 'feel they belonged and, in turn, could contribute, as part of an intricate network of trust, recognition and obligation'.[59] The free and co-operative association in civic society which Brown wishes to promote is based on the Scottish Enlightenment philosophers' concept of moral sense, that is, 'a set of moral sentiments of dispositions that all human being possess in common': human sociability as 'a shared feeling of mutual sympathy'. The British way 'is not to exalt self-interested individualism but throughout the centuries to foster a uniquely rich and continuously-evolving relationship between individual community and state, a strong vibrant civil society where there is opportunity for all'.[60]

In another lecture in 2000, the Arnold Goodman Lecture, Brown argued that responsible citizenship meant 'respect for order, family and responsibility with agreement to pursue the values of civic society and a shared sense of social purpose'.[61] To the NCVO, he stated that the most important aspect of civic society is that it is not a contract, that is, 'a deal based on self-interest and sustained through the external force of law' but rather a covenant; 'an agreement that is morally based and internally sustained, through shared values, common purposes and mutual obligations'.[62] From this, in Brown's perspective, two key consequences follow:

> ... the new covenant – and the society it leads to – will be one in which we extend opportunity and demand responsibility in return [and] the outcome will be an active civic engagement, not a passive civic obedience, restoring the principles of voluntary and community action to a central social place.

Brown wants people to give 'active social expression to our shared moral impulses to sympathy, fairness, self-control and duty', to exercise the personal responsibility which he claims was ignored by 'the social engineering of the old left'.[63]

The problem with Brown's vision of civic society is that it sits very uneasily with the emphasis on competition and the pursuit of risk, profit and innovation in liberalised markets that are at the heart of the British model of political economy (see Chapter Three) – a model that has encouraged active and contractual individual entrepreneurship and consumerism. Civic society is also difficult to reconcile with (and to a significant degree contradicts) the Treasury's nationalisation of policy design and resource allocation in England (see Chapter Four), which has actively discouraged covenantal citizenship. On the one hand, Brown has sought to promote the virtues of voluntary action because of its four great practical strengths: its local character, its greater flexibility to innovate, its individual, personal approach and its capacity to strengthen citizenship. Because contemporary social problems would not lend themselves to 'a standardised, uniform, one-size-fits-all solution or to an impersonal approach', Brown claimed that the state has had to devolve power to 'those organisations that have the deepest local knowledge and the broadest capacity for innovation and the greatest experience in the one-to-one approach'.[64] On the other hand, the devolution of political power has by-passed England, where eighty-five per cent of the United Kingdom's citizens live.

The political legacy of Brown's decade at the Treasury was a postcode lottery for citizenship and civic society. For his fellow Scots, the re-establishment of the Scottish Parliament enabled Scotland's rich tapestry of voluntary associations to interact with a new forum holding devolved and autonomous political power with which civic society and the extension of active democratic citizenship worked in partnership.

His legacy to England was very different. He stated, in July 2000, that he believed a new relationship was taking shape between the individual, communities and government: 'Call it a giving age, active citizenship, call it community – it is Britain becoming Britain again'.[65] In 2005, to the *Volunteering* conference, Brown again outlined his vision of Britain as a civic society: 'Call it community, call it civic patriotism, call it the giving age or call it the new active citizenship, call it the great British society – it is Britain being Britain'.[66] However, Brown failed to explain why, in the other constituent nations of the United Kingdom, 'new active citizenship' meant the devolution of political power to democratically-elected institutions but in England, the political framework for voluntary action and civic society must be of passive citizenship, administrative devolution to unelected and locally unaccountable bodies and micro-management in accordance with the priorities of the biennial Spending Reviews and Public Service Agreements.

In Brown's political philosophy, one of the key functions of civic society is to impose limits on markets, referring to Michael Sandel's identification (in the Tanner Lecture series *What Money Can't Buy*) of the 'moral limits of markets' as 'the dimensions of life that lie beyond consent, in the moral and civic goods that markets do not honour and money cannot buy'.[67] Sandel identified what money cannot buy by distinguishing two reasons why market valuation and exchange should not be extended to certain areas of life. First, 'when people buy and sell things under conditions of severe inequality' market exchanges are not necessarily voluntary. Coercion might arise when, for example, someone living in poverty has to sell a kidney to feed their family. Second, if certain moral or civic goods are bought and sold for money, the resulting market exchange and valuation has a degrading effect on those goods and practices. Sandel illustrated this moral limit to the market using the example of prostitution which, while it may not be illegal, is inevitably morally degrading for the prostitute. Furthermore, the excessive role for markets in important aspects of public life will have a corrupting impact on citizenship as defined by the republican tradition, whose particular concept of citizenship argues that 'to be free is to share in self-rule, i.e. citizens' freedom depends on their capacity to participate in shaping the forces that govern their collective destiny'. However, to exercise that freedom, citizens must first 'possess or come to acquire certain qualities of character or civic virtues'.[68]

This aspect of Sandel's thesis on the moral limits of markets is particularly interesting for Brown's concept of citizenship. Sandel noted that citizenship may be defined in liberal terms, which emphasise 'toleration and respects for the rights of others' or in republican terms, in which it aims:

> ... to cultivate a fuller range of virtues, including a moral bond with the community whose fate is at stake, a sense of obligation for one's fellow citizens, a willingness to sacrifice individual interests for the sake of the common good and the ability to deliberate well about common purposes and ends.[69]

For Brown, who regards politics as a moral duty, the republican concept of citizenship is much closer to his own, even though the core elements of his 'British Way' and the values and virtues of the national character he has identified include the virtues of tolerance and respect for the rights of others.

From Sandel's perspective, the problem with Brown's political legacy is that, through market-driven reforms of public services, it has extended the role of markets into certain aspects of public life yet has simultaneously diminished English citizens' self-rule by denying them the political devolution that would enable them democratically to participate in shaping the forces that govern their collective destiny. In 1999, at the Smith Institute, Brown spoke of a transition from 'an over-centralised and uniform state – the old Britain of subjects – to a pluralist and decentralised democracy – the new Britain of citizens'.[70] However, that commitment has long been abandoned.

In defining the limits to markets, Brown cited *Spheres of Justice*, the work of the political philosopher Michael Walzer, in which Walzer developed the notion of 'blocked exchanges' to denote those aspects of life which money cannot buy and where market exchanges cannot represent value, for example, the sale of human beings as slaves, freedom of speech and political and civil rights.[71] Brown also noted how in his book *Equality and Efficiency*, the economist Arthur Okun saw that 'the market needs a place and the market needs to be kept in place'.[72] Okun's thesis for policy-makers was that government needs the market-place as both a support, to provide the tax revenue to finance public services and as a counterweight, to check and balance the centralised power of the state. At the same time, the market needs government to make and enforce property rights and the rule of law and to provide the human and physical infrastructure.[73]

Okun's emphasis on the role of markets as check and balance highlights a further, salient, aspect of Brown's emphasis on civic society. In all his major speeches on this topic, Brown has drawn almost exclusively on comparisons with and examples from the United States. He has cited John Dilulio, who served in the first term of George W. Bush's administration as Director of the White House's Faith-Based and Community Initiatives, President Kennedy, in his instigation of the Peace Corps, President Clinton's AmeriCorps, President George W. Bush's Freedom Corps,[74] the 'superb' www.mentoring.org website and corporate giving through 'Business Strengthening America'.[75] Brown has quoted Robert Kennedy and mentioned his own late father's belief in Martin Luther King's words that 'everybody could be great because everyone can serve'.[76] For Brown's philosophy, the apposite point about the United States is that there, individuals and civic associations operate within the democratic framework of a written constitution, in which centralised political power is heavily checked and balanced. Democratic citizenship therefore operates, as it does in Scotland, in parallel with civic society. Brown's legacy to England is to have operated at the Treasury for a decade without similar constitutional checks and balances on his political power.

BROWN'S COMMON GROUND WITH THE NEW RIGHT

As Gordon Brown's personal political philosophy has become increasingly distant from the history of ideas of the Labour Party and ever more dependent on liberal political thinkers, so he has moved ever closer to the ideological foundations of the New Right. In particular, he has moved on to philosophical ground shared not only with Margaret Thatcher and Keith

Joseph but also with the contemporary neo-conservatives whose ideas have informed the policies of George W. Bush's administration. A conspicuous feature of Brown's speeches in recent years is his increasing use of quotations from prominent American conservative commentators, philosophers and historians.

When Brown gave the first Donald Dewar Memorial Lecture in 2006, he cited the prominent conservative commentator, David Brooks, writing in an article for the *New York Times*:

> If the big contest of the twentieth century was between planned and free market economies, the big questions of the next century will be understanding how cultures change and can be changed, how social and cultural capital can be nurtured and developed, how destructive cultural conflict can be turned to healthy cultural competition.[77]

Citing a commentator from the Right in a lecture dedicated to an eminent colleague and friend from the Left was in itself extraordinary and the choice of Brooks particularly interesting. Brooks had been on the liberal Left of American politics until 5 April 1983, when he participated in a televised debate with Milton Friedman, doyen of the New Right. As Brooks later recalled, this encounter was his road to Damascus moment in his conversion to the political ideology of the Right because 'The show was essentially me making a point and he making a two-sentence rebuttal which totally devastated my point and then me sitting there with my mouth hanging open, trying to think what to say'.[78] Brown's intellectual conversion may not have been as sudden as Brooks' but he too appears to have undertaken an equally significant philosophical odyssey.

In his quest to reintroduce morality into the British political conversation, Brown has cited the work of the American conservative philosopher, James Q. Wilson. For Brown's political philosophy, Wilson's *The Moral Sense* provides an important further and direct connection to the Scottish Enlightenment through its exploration of the sources of moral sentiments: 'human nature, family experience, gender and culture'.[79] Wilson also furnished a comprehensive analysis of the four aspects of the moral sense: 'sympathy, fairness, self-control and duty'.[80] Brown wants to bring these four qualities to British politics, both through his own example and by virtue of the policies he wishes to implement. For example, he entitled his speech to the 2005 Labour Party annual conference 'Politics as a moral duty'.

In this particular speech, Brown acknowledged his personal moral compass, set by what his parents had brought him up to believe. His lodestone was not only 'to do my best and to work hard but to treat everyone equally, to respect others, to tell the truth, to take responsibility' but also to understand that 'for every opportunity there was an obligation, for every demand a duty, for every chance given a contribution to be made'. Having identified the importance to his politics of a moral sense, Brown identified the Labour Party's moral cause: 'that every child has the best start in life, that no one is left behind ... a vision that defines us as a community and as a country inspires a new sense of mission'.[81] Moral sentiments could thus be linked directly to the continuing project of national renewal and with Brown's redefinition of Britishness.

James Q. Wilson portrayed his thinking as 'a continuation of work begun by certain eighteenth-century English and Scottish thinkers, notably Joseph Butler, Francis Hutcheson, David Hume and Adam Smith'.[82] The particular importance that Brown attached to this work was demonstrated when he spoke at the 2006 Cheltenham Literature Festival. Asked whether he had found wisdom or inspiration in any contemporary novel, Brown responded that the sole contemporary influence on his work had been Wilson's *Moral Sense*, because of its emphasis on the importance of shared communal bonds and values to modern life.[83] In the Pope Paul VI Memorial Lecture in 2004, Brown had asserted that Wilson had 'so brilliantly' described the moral sense as 'a small candle flame flickering and spluttering in the strong winds of passion and power, greed and ideology'.[84]

Given his desire to fashion a New British Enlightenment, it is perhaps not surprising that Brown should admire a political philosopher who has argued that 'we all live in a world shaped by the ambiguous legacy of the Enlightenment'.[85] However, what will surprise socialists and social democrats in general, and Labour Party politicians in particular, is that Brown aligns his personal moral compass by reference to the ideas of a man so intimately connected with the American Right. These links are reflected not only in Wilson's position as Ronald Reagan Professor of Public Policy at Pepperdine University, California but also his role as the Chairman of Academic Advisors to the free-market American Enterprise Institute. Awarding Wilson the Presidential Medal of Freedom in July 2003, George W. Bush described him as 'the most influential political scientist in America since the White House was home to Professor Woodrow Wilson'.[86]

Wilson's purpose in *The Moral Sense* was 'to help people recover the confidence with which they once spoke about virtue and morality'.[87] This means engaging in an age-old war, 'a cultural war, a war about values': a war in which Brown wishes to engage as the basis of his 'hearts and minds' security and foreign policies against international terrorism (see Chapter Eight). For Wilson, moral sense means 'an intuitive or directly felt belief about how one ought to act when one is free to act voluntarily (that is, not under duress)',[88] defining 'ought' as 'an obligation binding on all people similarly situated'.[89] In choosing 'sympathy, fairness, self-control and duty' as his four examples of moral sense, Wilson wished to challenge what he portrayed as the 'fatally flawed assumption of many Enlightenment thinkers, namely, that autonomous individuals can freely choose or will, their moral life'.[90]

As an alternative, Wilson sought to identify those aspects of moral life that are universal and refined in the crucible of parent-child and extended relationships among families and peers. This led him to the conclusion that moral sense entails 'a network of commitments that we have and that we share with others' and which includes loyalties to 'our towns and teams, our nations and people [which] transcend the costs and benefits of daily transactions'.[91] This vision accorded closely with Brown's personal experience of community and civic associations while growing up in Kirkcaldy. Wilson's thesis was that, in many of the ideologies of the nineteenth and twentieth centuries, the idea of commitment had been replaced by the idea of choice. However, Wilson concluded that the freedom people want 'is not unconstrained choice; it is rather the opportunity to express themselves, enrich themselves and govern themselves in a world that has already been organised and defined by a set of intuitively understood commitments'.

Wilson dismissed the idea of 'autonomous individuals choosing everything – their beliefs and values, their history and traditions, their social forms and family structures' as vainglorious.[92] Wilson found solace from individual autonomy over values and morality in the insights of the Enlightenment thinkers' notion of sympathy as an 'innate sensitivity to the feelings of others' and the idea that 'The natural sociability of mankind gives rise to sentiments of sympathy, fairness and reciprocity in every culture that we can imagine'.[93] Each person's 'moral sense, however weak or imperfect, helps explain social order because that sense grows out of, and reflects, the fact that we are social beings, dependent on one another'.[94] Brown has placed precisely these qualities at the heart of his definition of the values and character of Britishness (see Chapter Five).

Brown focussed on Wilson's concept of character, which Wilson defined as the 'distinctive combination of personal qualities by which someone is known (that is, a personality) and moral strength or integrity'.[95] Brown's is the Aristotelian vision of becoming virtuous by the practice of virtue, by practice rather than precept, an habitual morality. In this regard, Brown also cites the work of another American academic, Joseph Campbell, who focussed on the importance of heroes and myths for the contemporary world. In *The Power of Myth*, using the example of Martin Luther King, Campbell defined a hero as 'someone who has given their life to something bigger than themselves'.[96] For Campbell, the importance of myths is that they help put the mind in touch with the rapture of being alive, providing 'clues to the spiritual potentialities of the human life'.[97] They also offer 'life models' but these have to be 'appropriate to the time in which you are living'.[98]

For Campbell, the contemporary world has unfortunately become demythologised but nevertheless it needs 'myths that will identify the individual not with his local group but with the planet'. Campbell's model is the thirteen colonies that, through the Declaration of Independence, decided to act together in the national interest against their British colonial rulers.[99] Campbell claimed that when the United States belatedly entered the First World War, it cancelled that Declaration and 're-joined the British conquest of the planet'.[100] For Campbell, myths serve four functions: mystical, cosmological, sociological and pedagogical. While the mystical and cosmological might not be important to the politics of Gordon Brown, the sociological and pedagogical clearly are. The sociological function of myths is 'supporting and validating a certain social order' while their pedagogical function is to teach people 'how to live a human lifetime under any circumstances'.[101]

In his political philosophy, Brown is attempting to create the myth of Britishness (see Chapter Five), to support and validate the social order of modern British society. He has sought to turn Enlightenment thinkers, notably Adam Smith, into heroes and draw on Smith's moral sentiments to teach the British people how to live their lives under different circumstances. Recently, in his book *Courage: Eight Portraits*, Brown identified exemplars and icons whose personal belief and moral purpose enabled 'these people of courage' to be 'driven and sustained by higher ideas'.[102] What is particularly interesting about Brown's selection is that none of the people of courage emanated from the Labour Party or the wider Labour movement. Indeed, the only politicians included in the group are Martin Luther King, Robert Kennedy, Nelson Mandela and Aung San Suu Kyi.

David Brooks and James Q. Wilson are not the only prominent American conservative philosophers who have been praised in Brown's speeches. He has also paid fulsome tribute to Gertrude Himmelfarb and her book, *The Roads to Modernity*.[103] Brown identified with Himmelfarb's analysis because she, like him, sought to reclaim the philosophy of the Enlightenment and restore it to the British, who helped create it. An intriguing aspect of Brown's praise for Himmelfarb is that much of her academic work has drawn attention to the nineteenth-century British morality that helped inspire Margaret Thatcher's belief in Victorian values.[104] Himmelfarb is also a significant figure, ideologically, by marriage: her husband is Irving Kristol, one of the principal architects of American neo-conservatism.[105]

In *Roads to Modernity*, Himmelfarb sought to identify the three 'alternative approaches to modernity, alternative habits of mind and heart, of consciousness and sensibility' pursued by Britain, the United States and France.[106] These differences could be attributed to a variety of factors, notably:

> ... the very different political characters of the countries and the relationship of classes within these political systems; the nature and authority of the churches and their role in the state; economies at various levels of industrialism and subject to different kinds and degrees of government regulation; and all the other historical and social circumstances that were unique to each country and helped to shape its temper and character.[107]

Himmelfarb asserted that the British approach was based on moral philosophers who were sociologists, being 'concerned with man in relation to society, they looked to the social virtues for the basis of a healthy and humane society'. In contrast, the American approach was based on an attempt to furnish 'a new "science of politics" ' that would establish the new republic on a sound foundation of liberty. The French chose an alternative third approach, making 'reason the governing principle of society as well as mind, to "rationalise", as it were, the world'.[108] Himmelfarb depicted the British approach as a non-revolutionary, reformist 'sociology of virtue', characterised by a social ethic and moral sense, compared to the American 'politics of liberty' and the French 'ideology of reason'.

Himmelfarb noted how many of the Scottish moral philosophers of the Enlightenment chose to identify themselves as 'North Britons' rather than as Scots. David Hume, for example, changed the spelling of his name from the Scottish 'Home' to the Anglicised 'Hume'.[109] Other important Enlightenment thinkers were English, notably John Locke, Isaac Newton and the Earl of Shaftesbury.[110] Therefore, it would be more appropriate to describe them all as thinkers of the British rather than the Scottish Enlightenment. This aspect of Himmelfarb's thesis is the most pertinent to the development of Gordon Brown's 'British Way', since he too has sought to emphasise his British, rather than his Scottish, identity. Furthermore, Himmelfarb claimed that the distinctive feature of the political economy of the British Enlightenment was its basis in moral philosophy. Adam Smith advocated capitalism for the sake of economic, civil and religious freedom rather than for the sake of monetary gain and 'by far the most important effect of commerce: its civilising, moderating and pacifying effect on peoples and societies'.[111] This too accords with Brown's interpretation of Smith's work and his moral defence of capitalism and the virtues of the City of London.

Himmelfarb concluded that Adam Smith's moral vision of political economy currently characterises the United States.[112] This is a further source of its appeal to Gordon Brown; by basing his political philosophy on the moral sense and sentiments of Adam Smith, he is now able to justify his advocacy of trade liberalisation, his 'New Atlantic' foreign policy and his past work at the International Monetary Fund (conducted in partnership with the United States Treasury), in terms of a shared philosophical platform (see Chapter Six).

Intriguingly, in her Epilogue, Himmelfarb also noted that Margaret Thatcher, who revived the notion of Victorian values, could have gone back further, to Adam Smith and the moral philosophers, to discover the moral sense that was 'the genesis of those values and that gave then an undeniably social character'.[113] Thatcher and Sir Keith Joseph in fact did this, drawing extensively on both *The Wealth of Nations* and *The Theory of Moral Sentiments*. This serves to illustrate the philosophical and political bedfellows Gordon Brown has risked having to share with in aligning his moral compass so firmly to the philosophers who inspired the New Right. His key challenge as Prime Minister is to win the battle of ideas in British politics, by persuading people that Adam Smith's true legacy is the 'helping hand' of government, rather than the pursuit of selfish individualism more redolent of David Cameron's liberal conservatism (see Chapter Eight).

CONCLUSION

When Gordon Brown began his political career his moral compass was firmly aligned to ethical socialism and the development of a withering critique of capitalism based on a moral sense passed on by his parents. Brown is now an equally adamant advocate of the market economy and, in particular, the liberty and opportunity open markets offer for the fulfilment of individual potential. Brown's political philosophy has evolved from supply-side socialism via supply-side liberalism to its current sympathetic liberalism. The constant element throughout this political and philosophical odyssey has been Brown's moral sense and commitment to politics as a moral duty. However, rather than looking to R. H. Tawney and the English ethical socialist tradition for his political ethics, Brown has turned to the moral sentiments of Adam Smith and the thinkers of the Scottish Enlightenment.

Like his predecessors Margaret Thatcher and Tony Blair, Gordon Brown has attached great importance to winning the battle of ideas in British politics as the prerequisite for the successful implementation of his modernisation agenda. Also like his predecessors, liberalism will provide the primary ideological underpinning to his politics, maintaining a long-standing tradition in British politics. The liberalism of John Maynard Keynes and William Beveridge provided the platform on which the full employment and welfare state of the post-war First Way settlement was built. When the efficacy of that settlement was challenged in 1976 by the Callaghan Government and then largely dismantled by the 'Second Way' of Thatcherism, liberalism was once more harnessed to traditional Conservative values. When Tony Blair's 'Third Way' succeeded the eighteen years of Conservative rule, it placed its faith in the capacity of liberalism, entrepreneurial initiative and market competition to reform the United Kingdom's ailing public services.

Brown's New British Enlightenment has launched a fourth 'British Way' of modernisation, which draws on the liberalism of the moral sentiments of Adam Smith.

These moral sentiments are the political legacy of the three phases of Gordon Brown's philosophical odyssey. In Parts Two and Three, I shall explore their impact on Brown's domestic and foreign policy choices.

PART II

Gordon Brown's Domestic Policy Agenda

Chapter 3

The British Model of Political Economy

INTRODUCTION

Economic policy is the most important dimension of Gordon Brown's political legacy: his credibility as successor to Tony Blair was based on his record as the prudent 'Iron' Chancellor of the Exchequer for the whole Blair Government decade. The essence of Brown's appeal, both to the Labour Party and to the electorate as a whole, is of a political heavyweight, who has succeeded in delivering a decade of stability, prudence and prosperity.

This legacy can be contrasted with that of Brown's Labour predecessors, whose failure allowed the Labour Party to be cast as the party of devaluation. Brown, in his 'British Model' of political economy, took important lessons from the failures of the past and delivered an unprecedented decade of growth. More importantly, in the run-up to the next General Election, and with his record set against Brown's economic legacy, David Cameron can be cast as a political lightweight. Cameron has no experience of serving as a Cabinet minister but does have the dubious record of being a special adviser to Chancellor Norman Lamont at the time of 'Black Wednesday'.

Black Wednesday (16 September 1992) was the day sterling left the European Exchange Rate Mechanism (ERM), as the City of London's financial speculators, led by George Soros, routed Lamont (then Chancellor), the Treasury and the Major Government's 'unassailable' economic policy. It was a national political humiliation, from which the Conservative Party never regained its previous reputation for economic competence.[1]

Ironically, that humiliation marked the onset of the longest period of sustained economic growth in the United Kingdom's modern history.

During his decade as Chancellor, Gordon Brown constructed an institutional and policy model that he and Ed Balls described as the 'British Model'.[2] This model received much praise, especially from abroad. Highlighting its openness and flexibility, the Executive Board of the International Monetary Fund (IMF) welcomed 'the UK economy's remarkable performance that has lasted for more than a decade', while IMF staff reported that 'during 1996–2005, the growth of real GDP [Gross Domestic Product] per capita was higher and less volatile than in any other G7 country'.[3] By July 2007, the UK economy had grown for fifty-nine consecutive quarters, including forty quarters under Brown's stewardship. The Treasury has noted that this expansion 'is not only without precedent in the post-war history of the UK but is also the longest on post-war record for any G7 economy and the longest expansion of any OECD country' and it would take 'at least nine years before the UK's current expansion could be eclipsed by another G7 country'.[4] By redefining (three times) the Treasury's official definition of the United Kingdom's economic cycle, so that the previous cycle was both held to have begun in 1997–1998 and to have ended in early 2007, Brown ensured that his time at the Treasury delivered a decade of growth. This encouraged Brown to boast that Britain was experiencing its longest period of sustained growth since the start of the Industrial Revolution and 'since records began in the year seventeen hundred and one'.[5]

In this chapter, I shall outline the principles of Gordon Brown and Ed Balls's British model of political economy and evaluate the extent to which the 'Brown Boom' delivered prudence and a sustainable prosperity. When, in May 1999, Brown redefined the role of the Treasury as nothing less than the modernisation of the British economy, he claimed that this broke 'decisively with the short-termist, secretive and unstable record of macroeconomic policy-making of the past two decades by setting a credible framework' for monetary and fiscal policy.[6] It is undoubtedly true that Brown's economic legacy, in terms of stability, is better than that of any of his modern peacetime predecessors as Chancellor. However, I shall also demonstrate that Brown's legacy is equally one of consistent private and increasing public imprudence.

None of the longstanding supply-side weaknesses of the United Kingdom economy, such as under-investment in education, training, transport and communications infrastructure, have been redressed during the 'Brown Boom'. The 'British model' resolved the previous tensions between the interests of industrial modernisation and manufacturing on the one hand and those of the City of London on the other. This resolution was accomplished by simply abandoning the Labour Party's historic and Brown's former commitment to wholesale industrial modernisation through supply-side socialism and casting macro-economic policy decisively in the interests of the City. However, it has not insulated the United Kingdom's economy from instability. On the contrary, as the IMF has noted, by encouraging the United Kingdom economy to become even more closely linked to global financial markets, the 'British model' has increased the vulnerability of the United Kingdom economy to global risks and contagion.[7] Moreover, rather than rejecting the core tenets of Thatcherism, Brown, with all the zeal of a convert, has embraced and celebrated entrepreneurship and the merits of economic development through risk-taking, market liberalisation and deregulation. The passionate socialist critic of the market has been transformed into the Labour Party's most vocal champion of capitalism.

THE ROLE OF THE TREASURY

The Treasury lies at the heart of the British model of political economy and has frequently been at the centre of the narrative of British decline. It has been held to have subordinated long-term investment in the United Kingdom's industrial success to the short-term political expediency of 'stop-go' or 'boom-bust' economics, with artificially inflated periods of economic growth timed to coincide with General Election campaigns. The Treasury has been accused of possessing 'a contempt for production', of being part of a 'core institutional nexus' (with the Bank of England and the City of London) at the heart of British society which has been held to have frustrated consecutive state-led modernisation programmes.[8] Under previous Labour Governments, the Treasury oversaw sterling's departure from the Gold Standard in 1931 and damaging sterling crises and devaluations in July–August 1947, September 1949 and November 1967. The ultimate humiliation occurred in September 1976 when a Labour Chancellor of the Exchequer applied to the IMF for $3.9 billion (then the largest credit ever extended by the IMF) to finance the UK's balance of payments crisis and the repayment of short-term credit.

Although the Treasury has retained its historic role as the guardian of the public finances and the guarantor of monetary stability, the 'British model' of political economy defined a new mission for the Treasury: the modernisation of the British economy. In Brown's definition, the Treasury was to be 'not just a Ministry of Finance but also a Ministry working with other departments to deliver long-term economic and social renewal'.[9] In practice, working with other departments has meant the Treasury exercising an unprecedented degree of control over the design of policy and the allocation of resources through the Treasury-led biennial Spending Reviews, ten-yearly Comprehensive Spending Reviews and the Public Service Agreements. However, because of devolution to elected institutions in other parts of the United Kingdom, the 'British model's' political power has only been exercised in England, where no such constitutional checks and balances operate on Treasury power (other than in London).

The economic policies of the Macdonald, Attlee, Wilson and Callaghan Labour Governments were undermined by the constraints on domestic modernisation programmes generated by the global commercial interests of the City of London. Attempts to create modernising agencies to rival the Treasury, notably the Department of Economic Affairs and Ministry of Technology in the 1960s and the National Enterprise Board in the 1970s, led to conflict regarding the Treasury's domination over economic policy. This reached its zenith in the failed social revolution of the National Plan, when the Wilson Government attempted to fashion 'a state of competitive existence' between the Treasury and the newly-created Department of Economic Affairs (DEA), led by George Brown, but actually only delivered an economic strategy based on 'two diametrically opposed policies'. As early as 1971, George Brown suggested that 'Some Government, some day, will re-create a department on the lines of the DEA and limit the out-dated authority of the Treasury'.[10]

Gordon Brown deliberately did not follow George Brown's 1960s model. Rather than limiting the authority of the Treasury by creating an alternative focal point for economic modernisation, he made modernisation the remit of the Treasury. Its power was strengthened and deepened. By establishing the Treasury as the pilot agency of the state of British development, the 'British model' surmounted the creative tension that once existed between rival economic departments in Whitehall. And by ceding responsibility for monetary policy to the Bank of England's Monetary Policy Committee (MPC), the Treasury was given the space and opportunity to intervene, in a way unprecedented in peacetime, in economic and social policy (see Chapter Four). The creation of the MPC made possible the new developmental role for the Treasury. The domestic modernisation programmes of previous Labour Governments had been undermined by inflation and devaluation. Freed of these constraints, the elite of the bureaucracy at the Treasury identified and selected the sectors of the United Kingdom economy to be developed: the City of London's financial and commercial services, the property market, defence and aerospace manufacturing and science-based industries (notably pharmaceuticals and biotechnology).

In these sectors, the 'British model' sought to develop market-improving methods of state intervention and administrative guidance and to supervise competition in accordance with the principles of Brown and Balls's doctrine of 'constrained discretion'. As the price that had to be paid for maintaining economic stability, this doctrine limited the freedom of public spending bodies in England to determine their own policy choices and to allocate their resources as they saw fit. The 'British model' imposed centrally-determined policy choices and decisions about resource allocations on hospitals, schools and local authorities in England.

Because of the Blair Governments' large parliamentary majorities after May 1997 and their proclivity for policy to be designed in Whitehall by unelected committees of technical experts (most notably the Monetary Policy Committee), the Treasury has operated in a political system that has given it 'sufficient scope to take initiative and operate effectively' as the lead agency of British modernisation.[11] The Treasury has operated as a pilot, using a mix of powers to steer policy design and resource allocation in England, by-passing (with the exception of Greater London) the process of creating elected, devolved institutions that now operate in the other constituent territories of the United Kingdom and constrain the Treasury's power there.

DEVISING THE 'BRITISH MODEL': THE ROLE OF ED BALLS

It is important to understand Brown's economic legacy as a 'British model' of political economy, rather than the narrower notion of a 'British model' of economic policy. The model embraced a particular understanding of the appropriate relationship between and respective roles for the state and market. The 'British model' is based on the fatal conceit of being able 'not only to support but positively enhance markets'. Brown's closest economic advisers have contended that 'markets are a powerful means of advancing the public interest'.[12] Markets can be made to work better by manipulating the behaviour of the private market to act for the general public good, in the manner that previous Labour governments sought to orchestrate nation-alised industries, trades unions and the other components of the architecture of the public domain. Like his predecessors as Prime Minister, Margaret Thatcher and Tony Blair, Brown cast his model in terms of a free economy accompanied by a strong state, prepared to defend the commercial interests of corporations, both at home and abroad.[13]

The British model was driven by the Treasury and devised by Brown in partnership with Ed Balls (appointed Secretary of State for Children, Schools and Families in June 2007 and formerly Economic Secretary to the Treasury). As Brown's Economic Adviser from 1994 to 1999 and Chief Economic Adviser to the Treasury from 1999 to 2004, Balls was not only Brown's closest confidant but also a major influence on Brown's thinking about economic policy. No other individual was as influential in shaping the political economy of both Gordon Brown and New Labour during the decade of the Blair Governments. It was Balls who provided Brown with an analysis of the failure of macro-economic policy under both Labour and Conservative Governments and during the era of both the post-war social democratic 'First' and Thatcherite 'Second Ways' of British modernisation. This analysis shaped the agenda for economic policy that later was to be termed (by Balls) the 'British model' of stability and prudence. The model provided Brown with an alternative economic policy to United Kingdom participation in the Euro and placed fiscal prudence at the heart of domestic economic policy.

Gordon Brown and Ed Balls first met in October 1992, at Brown's instigation.[14] Within two months, Balls had published a pamphlet, through the Fabian Society, in which he identified the agenda for national economic policy which was to shape much of Brown's subsequent economic strategy for the next decade. Balls' thesis was that Britain had suffered 'a misguided and ultimately unsustainable bout of economic self-destruction' for the second time in little more than a decade. Leaving the ERM on Black

Wednesday had torn off its 'fig leaf' and exposed 'the vacuum of ideas and institutions at the heart of British economic policy-making'.[15] Balls filled that ideological and institutional vacuum by firmly rejecting the 'European brand of monetarism' that had been implemented by the ERM. He wanted Labour to offer 'a break from the past' and in particular the 'dangerous and unworkable' economic implications of the Maastricht Treaty, specifically the 'economically and politically misconceived project' of monetary union, in its envisaged form and under the declared timetable. The central lesson from the ERM debacle was that 'Britain's European monetary commitments must be complementary to, not an excuse for the absence of, a credible national economic policy'.[16] The British model would furnish the requisite credibility.

For Balls, if the United Kingdom economy were simply to go for growth, by slashing interest rates and loosening fiscal policy, this, in the absence of institutional reform, would be 'a recipe for disaster'. Not only had individuals and institutions been discredited by the events of recent years but 'the entire theory and practice of UK economic management'.[17] An alternative economic strategy was needed, pursuing macro-economic stability, set within a European framework but drawing on a range of other important policies to stimulate 'balanced, industry-orientated growth and full employment'.

Delivering this model needed two prerequisites: first, 'a transparent, accountable and predictable monetary policy', that would permit sterling to re-enter the ERM without the need for the Government to pledge not to devalue the pound and second, 'a medium-term industrial strategy', that emphasised both the direct responsibilities of government, (that is, fiscal policy, public infrastructure and education) and its indirect role in fostering profits, investment and higher living standards for all.[18]

The first element of Balls' alternative economic strategy required 'active macro-economic management', that is, lower interest rates and higher public investment as a remedy for recession and rebuilding confidence not the 'Old-style Keynesianism' of short-term government borrowing and tax cuts which 'pursued for too long, simply leads to high and rising inflation, unwieldy fiscal deficits and finally damaging recessions'. To avoid boom-bust cycles and achieve low and stable inflation, economic growth and full employment, administration of monetary policy would have to be taken away from the Treasury because 'no one had mastered the art of boom-bust

economics better than the Treasury'. Balls considered that the power of the
Treasury remained absolute and that 'This degree of centralised and unaccountable executive and bureaucratic power over economic policy [was]
inefficient and out of date'.[19] This was quite a statement from a man who
later, as the Chancellor's Chief Economic Adviser, wielded unprecedented,
unaccountable, centralised and bureaucratic power until his election to
Parliament at the 2005 General Election.

Balls's remedy for macro-economic instability was 'a carefully reconsti-
tuted and statutorily-controlled central bank, empowered to pursue low
and stable inflation'. The Bank would have a number of characteristics.
First, the Bank's decision-making council, appointed by government,
should include representatives from industry and the unions as well as the
City of London. Second, the Bank should answer directly to Westminster;
its Governor giving regular testimony to House of Commons committees.
Third, although autonomous, it would administer a monetary policy
approved by the House of Commons, which would have the power 'to over-
ride a decision by the Bank in extreme circumstances'. However, the Bank
should not be responsible for supervising the City of London's financial
markets. This arrangement would deliver 'a transparent, accountable and
predictable monetary policy', providing, most importantly, credibility and
meaning for the subsequent 'British Way' and 'British model' of political
economy, that 'a Labour chancellor would be free to concentrate on the
many other aspects of policy'.[20]

LEARNING THE LESSONS OF THE PAST

A central feature of the 'British model' is that claims to have learnt vital
lessons from the mistakes made by previous British governments. The central conceit of the model is that, unlike its predecessors, it has managed to
identify a successful formula for reconciling domestic economic, social and
political modernisation with the constraints of global financial markets and
the need to maintain the United Kingdom's international competitiveness.
Globalisation has been used as a political weapon to justify important
changes in domestic and social policies and to discipline popular expectations of what the role of the state should be. The cost of significant areas of
public welfare (notably pensions) have increasingly been transferred from

the state, the corporation and the general taxpayer to the individual. Like Thatcherism before it, Brown's model identified the unfettered capitalism of the City of London, the liberalised markets for property and financial services and the consumer demand driven by those sectors as the key agents of economic modernisation. When Brown first entered Parliament, the Labour Party had based its electoral strategy on becoming the 'Party of Production' in contrast to the Conservative 'Party of the City': Brown's legacy is to have based his 'British model' on the City and the services sector rather than manufacturing industry and predominantly consumer rather than producer interests.

The 'British model' learnt one important lesson learnt from past British economic mismanagement: politicians and policy-makers paid insufficient attention to economics when making key decisions. This was true of Churchill's disastrous return in April 1925 to the pre-1914 'gold standard' of global fixed exchange rates backed by gold reserves, in which the pound sterling was set at its pre-1914 level of $4.86. This decision eventually led, in 1931, to the Labour Party being labelled the 'Party of Devaluation'. It was also true of the Attlee Government's decision, in 1946, to re-enter sterling into a fixed exchange rate system with the dollar set at the pound's pre-war rate of $4.03. The Wilson Government was equally culpable in its 1964 decision to reject devaluation, only to be forced into it in November 1967, resulting in deflation, rising unemployment, fiscal retrenchment and the resignation of James Callaghan from the Chancellorship. From Balls' perspective, too little economics also led to the Major Government's decision to withdraw an over-valued pound from the ERM on 'Black Wednesday', having ushered in the longest recession since 1945.[21]

Giving the Ken Dixon Lecture, at the University of York in 2004, Balls declared the 'British model' to be 'post-monetarist', because of monetarism's mistaken foundation on the discretionary fine-tuning of the macro-economy, based in turn 'on an assumed long-term trade-off between unemployment and inflation'.[22] In Brown and Balls's opinion, Milton Friedman proved as long ago as 1968 that an expansionary monetary policy and fiscal policy could not deliver, let alone sustain, full employment.[23] The monetarist model had 'collapsed intellectually and empirically'; its failure, both in continental Europe and domestically in the pre-1993 ERM, was because of its 'inflexibility in prioritising low money supply growth as the route to low inflation and growth', just when the liberalisation of capital markets and innovation in financial products was undermining the seemingly stable relationship between the growth of the money supply and inflation. A means had to be found to deal with the problem of 'time inconsistency', that is, the temptation to make a dash for short-term growth at the expense of long-term stability.[24] The British model claimed to have resolved that matter and made 'a decisive step forward to a credible model of macro-economic policy-making in Britain' through Bank of England independence and the introduction of a Code for Fiscal Stability.[25]

EMPOWERING THE TREASURY THROUGH 'CONSTRAINED DISCRETION'

In 1997, in his first major announcement as Chancellor of the Exchequer, Gordon Brown identified the central economic objectives of the Blair Government to be 'high and stable levels of growth and employment', which would be achieved by rebuilding 'British economic strength with a modern industrial base, high levels of investment and a culture of entrepreneurship'.[26] These objectives were couched in terms of a reaffirmation of a commitment made in the May 1944 White Paper *Employment Policy*: the acceptance 'as one of their primary aims and responsibilities the mainte-nance of a high and stable level of employment after the war'.[27] Brown con-tended that a new paradigm of monetary and fiscal policy was needed to achieve these goals.[28] The policy needed to escape from 'the short-termism of the past' and the economic instability that had characterised the British economy for most of the twentieth century, basing its break-out on 'the solid rock of prudent and consistent economic management, not the shift-ing sands of boom and bust'.[29] Long term commitments to monetary stabil-ity, fiscal stability, higher levels of investment in people and businesses, far-reaching modernisation of the welfare state, free trade and 'constructive engagement' with Europe were needed.[30]

From the outset, Brown and Balls based their 'British model' on the principle of 'constrained discretion'; the key to policy-making 'in a modern open economy'.[31] 'Constrained discretion' meant limiting the freedom of agents and institutions, especially those spending taxpayers' money, so that they could not undertake any actions that would undermine or challenge the priorities of the Treasury's economic policy agenda. The Treasury's vital insight was that:

> ... the discretion necessary for effective economic policy – short-term flexibility to meet credible long-term goals – is possible only within an institutional framework that commands market credibility and public trust with the government constrained to deliver clearly defined long-term policy objectives and with maximum openness and transparency.[32]

For Balls, the ERM failure demonstrated that the stability and low inflation required to realise and sustain high and stable levels of growth and employment would not be achieved by adhering to destabilising 'fixed and intermediate policy rules'.[33] As an alternative, constrained discretion would limit the capacity to destabilise macro-economic policy and performance by requiring policy-makers to deliver long-term objectives through institutional arrangements. In return for this commitment, policy-makers would benefit from 'the maximum operational flexibility that is consistent with achieving that goal [of stability]'.[34] Constrained discretion would be credible through aligning policy-makers' incentives with long-term objectives: flexibility, through the devolution of operational responsibility for decision-making to front-line agents and transparency, through both the provision of clear, precise and publicly-stated objectives and the regular reporting of agents' performance against their objectives.

Constrained discretion placed particular importance on the principle of credibility in policy-making: 'the elusive elixir of modern macro-economics'.[35] The then chief Economist (and later Governor of the Bank of England), Mervyn King, noted how credibility was 'a question of whether announced intentions are believable'. This was a matter of trust but markets were naturally suspicious, given the propensity of politicians to manipulate economic policy for short-term advantage. For King, credibility was:

> ... not an all or nothing matter. Policy is neither credible nor incredible but rather a continuous variable. Therefore, because the current behaviour of economic agents would depend on their expectations about the future actions of monetary authorities, the key to credibility for the British model would be the maxim: 'Say what you do and do what you say'.[36]

The vital lesson Balls learnt from the ERM debacle was that because the globalisation of international capital markets was 'the most significant change in the world economy', it was evident that 'the power of "the markets" is always and everywhere' and would 'immediately punish any government which strays from the macro-economic straight and narrow'.[37]

From Brown and Balls' perspective, basing their British model on the principle of constrained discretion had two huge political advantages. First, it legitimised constraints on the freedom of policy-makers and other actors, including those in receipt of public expenditure, as dictated by their commitment to institutional arrangements and policy objectives prescribed by the Treasury. Second, it simultaneously legitimised a division of labour whereby Brown, Balls and other elite Treasury officials were able to design policy and determine resource allocation at the centre, while those in charge of delivering public goods and services were responsible for administering policy priorities as dictated by the demands of constrained discretion. Policy design was effectively nationalised, through the Treasury's biennial Spending Reviews and attendant Public Service Agreements and thereby became increasingly divorced from administration in the delivery of public services, with major implications for policy, performance and, above all, democratic accountability in England (see Chapter Four).

Despite Brown's assertion that 'old command and control systems of management are not the way forward',[38] constrained discretion had engineered a top-down, technocratic, highly-centralised and Treasury-driven approach to domestic economic and social modernisation that would become one of the definitive features of policy-making under New Labour.

THE 'BRITISH MODEL' OF MONETARY POLICY

The principle of constrained discretion was applied first to monetary policy. This too was an area where the British model learnt lessons from past experience. During the 1970s, the final decade of the post-war social democratic 'First Way' of British modernisation, annual inflation averaged thirteen per cent, peaking at nearly twenty-seven per cent in August 1975, during Dennis Healey's tenure as Chancellor of the Exchequer . During the 1980s, the era of the Thatcherite 'Second Way', annual inflation averaged seven per cent (compared with three per cent in Germany and five per cent in the United States), peaking in the early 1990s at more than nine per cent. This meant that between 1980 and 1997 the United Kingdom's economy suffered the second highest annual average inflation rate among the Group of Seven (G7) industrialised economies, with only France and Italy suffering greater variability.[39]

The 'British model' derived four key lessons from this experience. First, Britain had suffered from poor institutional arrangements: correct monetary policy should be a stabilising force for the economy. Second, monetary policy had been based on a fundamental misunderstanding about the relationship between inflation and unemployment: unemployment could be cut by stimulating demand, albeit with the trade-off of higher inflation. In practice, any reductions in unemployment had been temporary and inflation had accelerated. Third, because monetary policy decisions had been taken by politicians, this fostered the suspicion that decisions were based on short-term political expediency rather than the long-term interests of the economy. Fourth, because monetary policy decisions had been taken in secret, there had been a lack of transparency, with little or no explanation for the conduct of policy.[40] To rectify these parallel deficits in effectiveness and transparency, one of Gordon Brown's first major policy announcements, in May 1997, was the aforementioned transfer of responsibility for meeting the Government's monetary policy objectives to a newly established Monetary Policy Committee (MPC) of the Bank of England. The Committee would be responsible for honouring the Labour Party's manifesto commitment to match the Major Government's inflation target of 2.5 per cent or less.[41]

Constrained discretion would be achieved through three policies: first, sound long-term objectives, through a symmetrical inflation target (requiring the MPC to respond when the inflation rate was too low, as well as too high). Such symmetry would avoid any deflationary bias and would not target both inflation and the short-term exchange rate.

Second, a commitment to credible institutional arrangements, through a division of labour in economic policy: the Government would set the broader economic strategy and objectives for monetary policy and the MPC would take the monthly decisions on how to meet the Government's inflation targets. Since the MPC would be composed of the Governor and four executives of the Bank, plus four members appointed by the Chancellor and with a non-voting Treasury official in attendance, its operational independence would be very heavily constrained. Not only (given the Chancellor's influence over the appointment of Governor) would the

Treasury effectively appoint a majority of the MPC but the presence of the non-voting Treasury official would ensure that the Chancellor was fully briefed by someone not distracted by the responsibility of voting. Co-ordination of monetary and fiscal policy and the capacity to respond to sudden events would be achieved through an 'Open Letter' system. Where inflation was one per cent higher or lower than the Government's target, an open letter would be sent by the Governor of the Bank of England to the Chancellor accounting for the divergence and explaining what remedial action would be taken.[42]

Third, monetary policy would have maximum transparency, through the publication of both the minutes of the monthly meetings and of the votes of the members of the MPC.[43] However, the publication of individual voting patterns would inevitably lead to certain MPC members being cast as 'doves' or 'hawks' depending on their preparedness to adjust interest rates to meet the Government's inflation target.

On 10 December 2003, Gordon Brown confirmed that the new inflation target for the MPC would no longer be based on the Retail Price Index (RPIX). Instead, the MPC would be required to set monetary policy to achieve a target of two per cent inflation, measured by the annual increase in the Consumer Price Index (CPI). If inflation were to deviate by more than one per cent from this target, the MPC would be required to send an open letter of explanation to the Chancellor.[44]

This change apart, Brown's legacy to monetary policy is to have maintained macro-economic stability. The Treasury has claimed during the decade from 1997–2007, 'the UK has enjoyed more stability in terms of GDP growth and inflation than in any decade since the war'. This is reflected in the fact that:

> ... inflation, on the RPI measure, has remained within a range of ¾ to 4¾ per cent over the past ten years, compared with a range of 1 to 11 per cent in the 1990s, 2½ to 22 per cent in the 1980s and 5 to 27 per cent in the 1970s.

The Treasury has also pointed to 'the longest period of sustained low inflation for the past 30 years' and (Japan excepted) lower average inflation in the United Kingdom for the past decade than any other G7 economy.[45]

However, in abandoning the RPI (X) measure of inflation, in favour of the CPI-based system, the 'British model' excluded the cost of mortgage interest payments from its calculations. This meant the official calculation of inflation excluded the major item of expenditure for the majority of households in the United Kingdom. These payments were a principal source of inflation during the housing boom of the 1980s and 1990s, when the rise in average house prices far outstripped the rise in the general cost of living. This meant that June 2007, when Gordon Brown succeeded Tony Blair as Prime Minister, according to the Office for National Statistics (ONS), while CPI annual inflation had fallen from 2.5 per cent in May 2007 to 2.4 per cent in June, RPI (X) inflation had risen from 4.3 per cent in May to 4.4 per cent in June, reflecting the 0.25 per cent rise in mortgage interest rates during May. Even if mortgage interest payments were excluded from the calculation of RPI (X) annual inflation, at 3.3 per cent in June 2007, this was still 0.9 per cent higher than the Brown Government's own calculation.[46] In effect, the Government claimed political credit for a measure of inflation that bore little relation to the true price increases affecting individuals and households in the real economy. The ONS also said that the 'British model' gave 'the MPC the flexibility to respond decisively to unexpected economic events over recent years'.[47] It also meant that during his tenure as Chancellor of the Exchequer, Gordon Brown enjoyed unprecedented power over the conduct of domestic policy.

Brown's decision to set up the MPC has had two important effects: first, unlike his post-war Labour predecessors (Sir Stafford Cripps, James Callaghan, Roy Jenkins and Denis Healey) whose respective periods at the Treasury witnessed the sacrificing of modernisation programmes on the altar of sterling crises, devaluation, public spending cuts and trades union unrest, Brown was not preoccupied with the macro-economy and the immediate responsibility for administering monetary policy. Second, having been freed of the responsibility for setting interest rates, Brown had the time and policy space to intervene in many areas of domestic policy not previously thought to be within the Treasury's compass. This nationalisation of policy design and resource allocation had been implemented through the new fiscal policy framework, the second element of the 'British model' of political economy.

THE 'BRITISH MODEL' OF FISCAL POLICY

Gordon Brown's fiscal policy inheritance when he entered the Treasury in May 1997 was the failure to control public spending during the 'First' and

'Second Ways' of British modernisation. For example, during the Wilson Governments, public spending increased from 38.1 per cent of GDP in 1964–1965 to a post-war record of 49.5 per cent of GDP in 1975–1976. Furthermore, despite the Thatcher and Major Government's rhetorical ambition to roll back the frontiers of the state, from 1978–1979 and 1996–1997 the average annual real growth in public spending had been 1.9 per cent, driven upwards by, for example, a 3.1 per cent average annual increase in health spending.[48] There had been a rise in net government debt from 31 per cent of GDP in 1988–1989 to 44 per cent of GDP in 1996–1997[49] and the tax burden, as a share of GDP, had risen slightly from 34.25 per cent to 36.25 percent.

However, although the UK's tax burden in 1997 was greater than that of either the United States or Japan, Britain remained 'a strikingly low-tax country', especially when compared with its European competitors.[50] In the run-up to the 1997 General Election, Brown's predecessor as Chancellor, Kenneth Clarke, pledged to impose on public spending an austerity policy without precedent in post-war history; limiting the planned average annual real percentage growth in public spending to just 0.4 per cent in 1996–97 and 1999–2000. This would have had severe implications for vital areas of public service, notably the health service, where spending between 1997–98 and 1999–2000 was planned to increase by an annual average of only 0.6 per cent.[51]

From this experience, the 'British model' derived two key lessons for fiscal policy. First, it should take a prudent approach, adjusting for the economic cycle and building in a margin for uncertainty. Second, policy should be open and transparent, to be achieved by setting stable fiscal rules and clearly explaining fiscal policy decisions.[52]

Speaking at the Lord Mayor's Dinner (to the City of London) in 1997, Brown declared that the first principle of constrained discretion, sound long-term objectives, would be imparted to fiscal policy by two fiscal rules. First, the so-called 'golden rule'; over the economic cycle the Government would borrow only 'to finance public investment and not to fund public consumption' and second, the 'sustainable investment rule'; the United Kingdom's net debt as proportion of GDP would be kept 'at a prudent and sensible level' over the economic cycle.[53] The 'golden rule' was later defended as 'a clear rule based on widely accepted and internationally agreed accounting principles'. It was conceded that a better measure of inter-generational equity (how the burden of taxation would be divided between current and future generations of taxpayers) would have been a 'balance sheet' approach to borrowing and spending; monitoring indicators such as net worth. However, according to Ed Balls, this approach would not have been feasible at the time because of many technical and methodological issues.[54]

The 'British model' had chosen to follow a rule which committed it, unlike its predecessors, not to borrow money to finance current expenditure (for example to spend on welfare benefits) but only to borrow for capital investment in new infrastructure and building projects. This potentially gave a dangerous hostage to fortune because, as the experience of the Major Government during the early 1990s had demonstrated, the onset of a deep recession might lead to significantly lower levels of revenue and demand significantly higher levels of spending to pay for unemployment benefit and the maintenance of effective demand in the national economy. The strength of the recovery from recession might not be sufficient to absorb the increases in taxes needed to generate compensatory budgetary surpluses to counteract the earlier borrowing. Furthermore, in the run-up to a General Election, voters might not be attracted by the merits of fiscal discipline when public services urgently needed money. The principal political advantage of the 'golden rule' was left to the Treasury to define the precise duration of the 'economic cycle'. Consequently, it might be possible for New Labour to extend or abbreviate the cycle to create the most favourable scenario for meeting the 'golden rule'.

In relation to the sustainable investment rule, Brown and Balls chose to commit the Blair Government to maintaining debt below forty per cent of GDP in each year of the economic cycle. There was no particular reason to select this specific. They could equally well have chosen thirty eight per cent or forty-two per cent. The Maastricht convergence criteria for participation in the EMU (Economic and Monetary Union) had set a level of net debt at sixty per cent of GDP, so when New Labour took power the United Kingdom already enjoyed one of the lowest figures for net debt among industrialised economies. That low debt level was a tribute to two decades of privatisation and massive under-investment in the public services and the national infrastructure (as anyone who regularly travelled by train or used the NHS during the early 1990s could have testified). Consequently, it might have been argued that, in the face of such long-term neglect, the

'British model' should have been less conservative in its plans for increased public sector capital investment.

Gordon Brown also planned to increase the role of the Private Finance Initiative (PFI) and Public–Private Partnerships (PPPs) in total capital investment. Paradoxically, on the capital markets the Government could borrow to finance investment at a lower interest rate than the private sector. Adhering to the sustainable investment rule threatened both to brake the capacity to modernise the crumbling national infrastructure and unnecessarily to inflate the cost of modernisation, by a superfluous reliance on private sector investment which, as railway privatisation had already demonstrated, might never materialise. Furthermore, the Blair Government inherited a situation in which the Major Government's post-ERM controls of public spending and buoyant tax revenue from consecutive years of economic growth made both fiscal rules eminently achievable, even before the Blair Government committed itself to the Major Government's planned austerity policy on public spending for 1997–1998 and 1998–1999.

The efficacy of the rules-based approach may have been exaggerated by both Balls and Brown. As the Institute for Fiscal Studies (IFS) suggested, 'Both are reasonable rules of thumb but neither has particularly firm analytical or statistical foundations as defined operationally ... the direct economic importance of strictly obeying the rules as defined has been overstated'.[55] The problem with such rules was that they led Gordon Brown

> ... to stake his credibility on predictions or premises that rely on an unrealistic degree of forecasting accuracy [placing] a rhetorical weight on strictly meeting his definition of the rules that neither their theoretical nor statistical foundations can reasonably be expected to bear.[56]

For example, the Treasury predicted in the 2005 Pre-Budget Report that the golden rule would be met by a cumulative surplus of only £12.8 billion over the twelve-year economic cycle which would conclude in 2008–2009. However, as the IFS demonstrated, the Treasury's average absolute error in forecasting just one year ahead in public sector net borrowing averaged twelve billion pounds (at 2005–2006 prices) during 1977–1978 to 2004–2005.[57] Moreover, since one of the principal motivations of the golden rule was to achieve inter-generational fairness in the distribution of the costs and benefits of taxation and expenditure, there was no obvious rationale for achieving a budget surplus, as opposed to a budget balance, since a surplus would appear unduly to penalise the current generation of taxpayers. Nor was it clear why fiscal policy should not embrace a similar degree of transparency and delegation as monetary policy through the transfer of responsibility for providing official tax revenue forecasts to an independent agency.[58]

In applying the second principle of constrained discretion to fiscal policy (commitment to credible institutional arrangements), Brown and Balls considered whether to duplicate the role of the MPC in monetary policy and create an independent fiscal committee to adjudicate on questions of taxation and expenditure. However, according to Ed Balls, this option was ruled out because 'the wider political complexity of fiscal policy making – the different impacts that the different levers have on a range of different objectives of which stabilisation is only one – would have implied a politically unsustainable break with UK parliamentary tradition'.[59] However, this argument could also have been made about passing operational control over interest rates to the MPC, since monetary policy could be said to have an impact on a range of objectives other than price stability, notably the international competitiveness of manufacturing industry and the United Kingdom's balance of payments position.

To address the third principle of constrained discretion (credibility through maximum transparency), the 'British model' introduced the 'Code for Fiscal Stability'. The Code specified how the five principles of the Government's fiscal policy (transparency, stability, responsibility, fairness (including between generations) and efficiency) would relate to its formulation and implementation. The Code would require fiscal policy to adhere to clearly stated objectives and rules, have its underlying key assumptions independently audited and its issues regularly and openly reported. Although the Chancellor of the Exchequer would continue to make the key decisions in fiscal policy, in 2004, Ed Balls explained the Treasury would also publish full five-year forecasts for the public finances, twice-yearly statements of the economic and other underlying assumptions informing public finance projections, the government's estimates of the output gap and cyclically adjusted fiscal aggregates so that progress against the fiscal rules could be assessed across the economic cycle and an end of year fiscal report and long-term public finance report, which would furnish a detailed analysis of the long-term projections for public finances over the next fifty years.[60]

The final element of the rules-based British model of fiscal policy was the year-long Comprehensive Spending Review (CSR), incorporating no fewer than thirty zero-based reviews, not only of departmental spending plans but also their objectives and policies. The CSR was to be followed by three Biennial Spending Reviews, before a second CSR. This innovation in fiscal policy particularly signified the manner in which Gordon Brown took an iron grip on the conduct of domestic economic and social policy, a grasp not seen in earlier peacetime Chancellorships (see Chapter Four). Monetary policy had been insulated from manipulation for short-term political gain but fiscal policy was more politicised. The ability of the rules-based approach to deliver prudence and credibility would largely depend on the precise definition of the economic cycle over which the fiscal rules had to be met.

The credibility of the British model has been undermined by Gordon Brown's politically-inspired redefinition of the economic cycle on three occasions. In July 2005, it appeared that Brown would not meet his first golden rule (not to borrow to finance current government spending over the economic cycle). He used an appearance before a Select Committee (of the House of Commons) to announce, without warning, that the Treasury had calculated that the economic cycle had started in 1997–1998, not in 1999–2000 as had previously been claimed.[61] Had Brown gone by the earlier definition of the economic cycle, he would have broken his golden rule by £5.5 billion, because of the £15.1 billion deficit on the current budget recorded in 2005–2006. Brown announced a second unanticipated redefinition of the economic cycle in December 2005, extending the economic cycle by three years, coming to an end in 2008–2009.[62] Once more, the redefinition appeared to be little more than a political convenience to ensure that Brown met his golden rule. Brown completed a hat-trick of unannounced redefinitions of the economic cycle a year later, when in his 2006 Pre-Budget Report statement he announced that the end of the economic cycle (which the 2006 Budget had confirmed at 2008–2009), would be early 2007.[63] This neatly defined the economic cycle as coinciding precisely with the beginning and (anticipated) end of Brown's Chancellorship and thereby enabled him to claim that his economic legacy to Britain was unbroken economic growth.

Brown's politically-driven redefinitions of the economic cycle meant that the golden rule of fiscal policy was met (according to the IFS) with a margin of around £11.6 billion (0.1 per cent of GDP).[64] As the Treasury noted: 'the introduction of strict fiscal rules and clear objectives for fiscal policy have put the public finances on a more sound and sustainable footing than in previous economic cycles' and that a surplus of 0.1 per cent of GDP for the current cycle was 'in contrast to the last cycle's average deficit of 2.0 per cent of GDP and the 1977–78 to 1986–87 cycle's average deficit of 1.8 per cent of GDP'.[65] This performance appears less creditable, if we remember that, in his 2001 Budget statement, Brown confidently forecast that the budget would be in surplus to the tune of £118 billion over the economic cycle. By the time of his (pre-election) 2005 Budget, the forecast surplus had decreased, to only five billion pounds. The IFS estimated that around one quarter of this fiscal deterioration was the result of policy decisions to increasing spending but the remainder reflected unexpected weakness in tax revenues.[66]

The problem with the British model of fiscal policy is that it has delivered only short-lived fiscal prudence. Brown's initial austerity policy reduced public spending to 37.7 per cent of GDP in 1999–2000, its lowest level since 1960–61. Having been in deficit by only £1.4 billion (0.2 per cent of GDP) during his first year in office, the budget produced surpluses from 1998–99 until 2000–01(artificially buoyed by the £22.5 billion raised from the auction of mobile phone licences). Brown's fiscal prudence delayed substantial new investment in the public services, especially health and education, until after the publication of the 2000 Spending Review. However, it did enable him to reduce public sector net debt, as a share of national income, from 43.6 per cent of GDP in May 1997 to 31.3 per cent by the 2001 General Election. By contrast, during the Blair Government's second term, Brown's increasing fiscal imprudence led to public sector net debt rising by 3.7 per cent to 35.0 per cent of GDP by the 2005 General Election. Further deterioration has seen net debt rise to £515.9 billion or 37.5 per cent of GDP by the end of June 2007.[67]

In 2007, the IFS judged Brown's fiscal legacy to Alistair Darling, his successor as Chancellor, to be four-fold. First, he increased public spending from 40.8 per cent of GDP in 1997–1998 to 42.0 per cent in 2007–2008, about £25.0 billion in cash terms. Second, during the same period he increased receipts by about 2.8 per cent of GDP, about £39.6 billion. Third, he reduced net borrowing by around 1.1 per cent of GDP, about £14.6 billion. Fourth, he reduced net public debt by 5.4 per cent of GDP, around £74.4 billion.[68]

This golden legacy may rapidly dissipate. His third redefinition of the economic cycle, abbreviating the current economic cycle by two years, enabled Brown to engineer a small surplus on the cycle, at the expense of starting the next economic cycle with two years which are likely to see current budget deficits.[69] This means Alistair Darling is likely to have much greater difficulty in meeting the golden rule, unless it is redefined or he follows Brown's precedent and politically manipulates the economic cycle, further undermining the credibility of the British model of fiscal policy.

THE TRIUMPH OF THE CITY

One of the most distinctive features of the British model of political economy was its abandonment of the Labour Party's long-standing commitment to state-led industrial modernisation. The British model increasingly chose instead to champion the interests of the City of London. Brown claimed that a 'new industrial policy' had replaced 'the old centralisation of national champions, picking winners or offering special subsidies to loss makers, with a level playing field for all'.[70] In practice, Brown's industrial policy was to continue the practice of picking winners. Indeed, he picked precisely the same winners as the Thatcher and Major Governments before him: the City of London and the financial services sector; the property market, defence manufacturing, civil aerospace; and pharmaceuticals. Each of these was supported by major policy initiatives, institutional innovation or large-scale subsidies. At the same time, the British model attempted to bridge the long-standing productivity gap between the United Kingdom economy and its major competitors through a series of interventions, driven by Brown's supply-side liberalism.

The abandonment of manufacturing was the only element of Ed Balls's December 1992, post-ERM analysis that was not incorporated into the British model. The second element of his alternative economic strategy was the adoption of a medium-term industrial strategy', as a counterweight to the Conservatives' previous medium-term financial strategy. Balls claimed that sustainable growth and full employment would not be achieved without a manufacturing and export-led recovery, brought about by a macroeconomic platform and supported by the micro-economic management of laws, regulations and taxes to foster dynamism and enterprise to ensure that 'individual actions serve the public interest'.[71] Balls thus framed one of the definitive characteristics and potential flaws of the future British model; the belief that state intervention could manipulate private market agents such as entrepreneurs and corporations (as if they were public sector agencies) to change their pattern of behaviour from short-term under-investors to long-term investors.

In his analysis, Balls took the inspiration for his 'non-monetarist alternative' from Australia, asserting that 'the Australian experience [of the 1980s] should be a model for what must happen in the UK'.[72] In the 1980s, the Australian Labour Party won five consecutive General Election victories (in 1983, 1984, 1987, 1990 and 1993) first under Bob Hawke and then, from December 1991, under Paul Keating's leadership; it did not lose office until 2 March 1996. The Labour Administration negotiated a Prices and Incomes Accord through a series of corporatist arrangements: the National Economic Summit Conference, the Tax Summit, the Economic Planning Advisory Council and the Australian Labor Advisory Council. Balls contended that the Australian example recognised 'the need to put profits and investment before higher real wages and built a public consensus around the need to do so'.[73]

For Balls, economy-wide wage restraint was a prerequisite for the success of a medium-term industrial strategy. To implement this in the United Kingdom, four steps would be necessary. First, a consensus, embracing public and private employers and the unions and endorsed by both the Confederation of British Industry and the Trades Union Congress, to deliver 'the kind of wage inflation that is needed to boost profits, investment and jobs'.[74] Second, the creation of a Council of Economic Advisors to provide independent advice to industry, the unions and the electorate about sustainable rates of pay inflation and the damage that would arise from high settlements. Third, an independent Central Bank to pay – and announce that it was paying – specific attention to the rate of inflation in average earnings when setting monetary policy. Irresponsible pay settlements would be rewarded with higher interest rates. Fourth, a return to the ERM (but only when German interest rates had fallen), to provide an external discipline on pay.[75]

In terms of the viability of this alternative strategy for state-led industrial modernisation, Balls conceded that the United Kingdom's history of statutory incomes policies was far from encouraging and that the problem of short-termism might well run too deep.[76] The desire to cast off, once and for all, the image of being the party of devaluation had not yet been accompanied by a similar desire to distance the Labour Party from the demise of the Social Contract in the 1979 'Winter of Discontent'. However, by the time Gordon Brown became Chancellor, the idea of a medium-term industrial strategy had been abandoned. There would not be a return to the corporatism of beer and sandwiches at Number 10. The British model would reduce expectations and discipline wage inflation in the public sector through an initial freeze on wages, dictated by the austerity policy of public spending during the Blair Government's first two years in office. Wage discipline would be imposed on the private sector through the threat of higher interest rates, playing on workers' increasing indebtedness and exposure to large-scale mortgage borrowing.

Gordon Brown and Ed Balls picked the City of London as the key winner to be backed. For the British model the City has provided the most tangible evidence of the benefits to innovation and entrepreneurship brought about by meeting the challenges of globalisation with a policy approach based on competition, liberalisation and deregulation of markets. In June 2006, at the Lord Mayor's Dinner, Brown proclaimed:

> The message London's success sends out to the whole British economy is that we will succeed if like London we think globally. Move forward if we are not closed but open to competition and to new ideas. Progress if we invest in and nurture the skills of the future, advance with light touch regulation, a competitive tax environment and flexibility. Grow even stronger if this is founded on a strong domestic market built on the foundation of stability.[77]

Brown (and Balls) admitted that financial and business services accounted for only twelve per cent of the national economy and 1.1 million jobs across Britain but London was celebrated as, paradoxically, the home of twenty per cent of cross-border lending, thirty per cent of world foreign exchange turnover, forty per cent of the over-the-counter derivatives market and seventy per cent of the global secondary bond market.[78] The major beneficiaries of the British model were the leading United Kingdom banks, whose 2006 net earnings totalled more than forty billion pounds.[79] Previous Labour Chancellors regarded the City as the class enemy, likely to undermine the prospects of domestic modernisation by serving as the catalyst for balance-of-payments' and devaluation crises but Brown paid homage to this global centre of casino capitalism. He asserted that 'we can demonstrate that, just as in the nineteenth century industrialisation was made for Britain, in the twenty-first century globalisation is made for Britain'.[80]

Also speaking in the City of London in 2006, Balls paid fulsome tribute to the liberalisation and deregulation of the City of London by the Thatcher Government's 'Big Bang' of late 1986. He also pointed to how much of the Treasury's work during Brown's early years as Chancellor was devoted to the creation of a new, independent and unified regulator, the Financial Services Authority, to redress the City's critical competitive weakness: a 'fragmented, overlapping, burdensome, self-regulatory system'. Although civil manufacturing (with the notable exception of aerospace and pharmaceuticals) was left to compete without significant state intervention, Balls argued that 'we cannot take London's status for granted'.[81]

Consequently, Brown established the Chancellor's High Level Group of leading City financiers to work in partnership and 'ensure the continued global success and competitiveness of UK financial services'.[82] The first meeting of the Group was attended by Lord Aldington, Chairman of Deutsche Bank; ironically, the previous Lord Aldington, a year before the 'Big Bang' celebrated by Balls, had chaired a House of Lords' Committee that had warned the Thatcher Government that there was the possibility of 'a major social and economic crisis in our nation's affairs in the foreseeable future', if national attitudes and policy in Britain towards trade and manufacturing did not change radically.[83] The 'British model' chose to ignore such warnings and abandoned the modernisation of civil manufacturing for the Labour Party to become the 'party of the City'.

THE SUPPLY-SIDE FAILURE

The 'British model' has not altogether neglected manufacturing, for the Blair Government continued the long-standing tradition of large-scale state financial assistance to the aerospace industry. Despite British Aerospace (BAe) and Rolls-Royce being highly profitable trans-national corporations, under Brown the Treasury sanctioned £980 million of repayable launch investment for the Airbus A380 'super-jumbo' aircraft. Despite this subsidy, the Treasury refused to intervene in BAe's later sale of its twenty per cent stake in the Airbus consortium, a commercial decision that has threatened the long-term future of civil aircraft manufacturing in Britain. BAe chose to concentrate on the defence sector which, during Brown's tenure, remained the manufacturing sector receiving the largest public investment. In December 2005, the Blair Government published its Defence Industrial Strategy, setting out its vision for the United Kingdom's future defence requirements and the industrial capacity that would be needed to procure the equipment needed. Other than in the realms of the City of London and the warfare state, it would be unthinkable for the 'British model' to sanction such large-scale state intervention.

The extent of the failure of the model to redress any of the long-standing supply-side weaknesses of the United Kingdom economy was demonstrated by the fact that Ed Balls contended that, for the Brown Government, 'raising skills levels is the central economic challenge of the next decade'.[84] This begged the question of what the Treasury had been doing to address these issues from 1997 to 2007. According to the IFS, business investment in the United Kingdom had been a paradox in recent years: on the one hand, corporate profitability and company balance sheets appeared 'unusually healthy' on the other, investment expenditure appeared anaemic, despite the cost of capital being low and pre-tax real rates of return on corporate capital (both net and gross of depreciation and relative to net or gross capital employed) being 'close to 40-year highs'.[85] During 2006, business investment fell by 4.7 per cent and had only grown by a paltry 3.25 per cent in 2005.[86] Leading analysts described this performance as 'disappointing'.[87] Investors continued to prefer to exploit the freedom offered by the City of London's liberalised markets to invest overseas or trade speculatively.

The 'British model' also failed to bridge the productivity gap between the United Kingdom and its leading competitors. In 2005, ONS figures showed that productivity per worker in the United Kingdom remained nine per cent below the G7 average and twenty-five per cent behind the United States. This marked a considerable improvement on 1997, when the United Kingdom had been fifteen per cent behind the G7 average and twenty-eight per cent behind the United States.[88] The productivity gap had been narrowed but not bridged. At the outset of his tenure as Chancellor, Brown promised that the Blair Government would 'identify the barriers to growth and productivity' and then 'relentlessly work to remove them'.[89] A year later, Brown laid down a challenge to 'the country's business leaders and to every shareholder, every employee, every citizen of the country' to work together 'to bridge the productivity gap'. Invoking 'a sense of national economic purpose, to agree a new long term direction for Britain', Brown portrayed the role of government as ensuring lasting stability, the role of industry as investment for the long term and the role of the financial community as a refusal 'to resort to the short-termism and stop-go attitudes which have bedevilled us since the war'.[90]

Neither finance nor industry rallied to Brown's patriotic cause: the necessary investment was not forthcoming. Brown's decision, in his inaugural July 1997 Budget, to abolish the tax credits paid to pension funds and companies, as a disincentive to the payment of dividends rather than the reinvestment of profits, returned to haunt him a decade later. An attempt to counter short-termism, at a time of pension fund surpluses and holidays, was retrospectively portrayed as a hidden, 'stealth tax' which may have caused a shortfall of up to seventy-five billion pounds in existing assets.[91]

The most damning evidence that 'British model' had not redressed supply-side weaknesses came from its failure to reverse the trend of United Kingdom current account deficits (which cover all transactions in goods, services, income and current transfers); indeed, it strengthened and deepened those deficits. The United Kingdom had experienced current account deficits every year since 1984 and a trade deficit every year since 1982 (and in all but six years since 1900). ONS figures show that in 2006, the United Kingdom recorded a deficit of £47.8 billion (–3.7 per cent of GDP), an increase from the 2005 deficit of £29.2 billion (–2.4 per cent of GDP). The deficit on trade in goods was £83.6 billion. This deficit was in no sense balanced by a £29.2 billion surplus on the United Kingdom's trade in services. Thus, the overall deficit on trade in goods and services was £54.4 billion (–4.3 per cent of GDP), compared to £44.5 billion in 2005 (–3.6 per cent of GDP).[92]

This is the price that the national accounts have had to pay for the British model's neglect of domestic manufacturing industry, which remains the most internationally-tradable sector of the global economy. Despite its undoubted success, the City of London's earnings are nowhere near sufficient to compensate for the lost employment, output and income from the loss of more than one million manufacturing jobs during Brown's Chancellorship. Manufacturing may account now for less than twenty per cent of GDP but, as the United Kingdom's trade figures will attest, it is still the principal source of export revenue for Brown's successor.

THE RISK OF VOLATILITY AND CONTAGION: THE MYTH OF LOCKED-IN STABILITY

One of Gordon Brown's most frequent boasts has been that the 'British model' has 'locked-in' stability. In practice, the model cannot lock in stability, because the openness of the City of London's financial markets means that the door is set ajar for volatility and contagion. In recent years, the United Kingdom has had to borrow from abroad to finance its continuing current account deficit, with the consequence that inward investment (United Kingdom liabilities) now exceeds outward investment (United Kingdom assets). Since 1995, the level of the United Kingdom's external assets and liabilities has more than trebled. At the end of 2006, total net assets stood at £5279 billion but total net liabilities had risen to £5544.2 billion. This meant that during the year, the United Kingdom's net liabilities had risen, by £124.8 billion, from £140.4 billion at the end of 2005. This signified a deterioration from liabilities equivalent to – 11.4 per cent of GDP at the end of 2005 to – 20.6 per cent of GDP at the end of 2006[93] and that 'net UK overseas liabilities as a percentage of GDP were at their highest for 30 years'.[94]

Between 1966 and 1994, under Labour and Conservative Governments, assets had tended to exceed liabilities, reaching a record £86.4 billion in 1986. However, from 1995 and throughout Brown's tenure as Chancellor, ONS statistics show the UK recorded a net liability.[95] Furthermore, in 2005, for the first time since 1990 direct investment in the United Kingdom was greater than direct investment abroad.[96] That trend continued during 2006, with direct investment abroad of £43.2 billion far exceeded by direct investment in the United Kingdom of £75.8 billion.[97] Such imbalances risked loss of confidence by and willingness among foreign investors to continue to fund the United Kingdom's deficits, with potentially destabilising consequences for the future value of sterling, especially since sterling operated outside the collective stability of the Eurozone.

The significance of the United Kingdom's current account deficit has been doubted, on the grounds that United Kingdom residents' assets are weighted towards equity-type investments, which have higher average returns than debt-type assets. Moreover, if the stocks of assets and liabilities are adjusted to their market value, United Kingdom assets continue to exceed liabilities. However, even this optimistic analysis has its doubters; Stephen Nickell, in his paper *The UK Current Account Deficit and All That*, concluded that the current position is only 'probably sustainable' and that there risks arise from 'a continuing and rapid increase in the trade deficit' that could undermine the United Kingdom's favourable adjusted net asset position. These include a 'significant fall in the long-term returns on equity relative to returns on debt'; a movement by foreign residents towards equity-type investments through major purchases of United Kingdom companies; and 'a large and permanent real appreciation of sterling' that would 'significantly reduce UK assets relative to UK liabilities'.[98]

This appears a dangerously complacent conclusion, given the rapid deterioration in the United Kingdom's trade and current account balances, the sheer scale of its assets and liabilities (around four times GDP)and the fact that the determination of whether the United Kingdom's international investment account moves further into deficit is in the hands of private corporations and investors (both British and foreign) and outside the Treasury's direct control. As the recent deterioration in the United Kingdom's international investment demonstrates, the 'British model' could not lock in stability any more than could the economic policies of previous United Kingdom governments, because of the freedom enjoyed by agents in liberalised financial markets to invest and disinvest for profit wherever they please, without checking with Gordon Brown's moral compass or sense of national economic purpose.

A LEGACY OF PRIVATE IMPRUDENCE, DEBT AND INEQUALITY

During Gordon Brown's time as Chancellor, economic growth was overwhelmingly consumer-led and borrowing-driven. It was not investment-led. People took advantage of the opportunities offered by liberalised and deregulated financial and property markets to borrow record amounts of money, which they set against the rising value of their assets – notably their houses and shares. This capacity to borrow was assisted by the innovations with which liberalised financial markets found new ways to finance debt. Where once home-buyers would have been limited to borrowing up to three times their current salary, it was now possible for them to borrow up to six times.

Neither did Brown's sense of moral purpose extend to prudence and thrift in the use of credit cards. Admittedly, during 2006, total spending in the United Kingdom on credit cards fell by two per cent, from £122 billion to £120 billion. However, that decline (the first fall for more than forty years), was more than offset by a fifteen per cent increase in spending on debit cards, which rose to £195 billion. Figures from the Association of

Payment Clearing Systems (APACS) showed that in December 2006, spending on plastic cards reached a record high of thirty-one billion pounds, including £19.6 billion from 472 million transactions conducted on debit cards, up 15.3 per cent from the previous year.[99] Total United Kingdom personal debt stood at £1,291 billion by the end of December 2006, an annual increase of 10.6 per cent (around £114 billion). Of this total, £1,078 billion was secured against property, an annual increase of 11.5 per cent. The remaining £213 billion was consumer credit lending to individuals (an annual increase of 6.2 per cent), of which £54.9 billion was owed on credit cards. This meant that the average United Kingdom household's debt was £53,326 including mortgages or £8,791 excluding mortgages. These debts cost an average of £3,400 a year to service. Indeed, the average United Kingdom adult now owed £27,445 (including mortgages), including £4,524 of debt held on credit cards, motor and retail finance deals, overdrafts or unsecured personal loans.[100]

An increasing number of people cannot manage their debts. During the financial year 2005–2006, the Citizens Advice Bureau (CAB) received 1.4 million requests for advice on debt problems, an annual increase of eleven per cent. During January 2007 alone, the number of cases of debt problems rose to 83,000, an annual increase of fifteen per cent. The CAB has estimated that it would take its clients an average of seventy-seven years to pay back their average debt of £13,000, because that amount is nearly 17.5 times their average monthly income.[101] The 'British model' did little to curb the United Kingdom's addiction to credit and borrowing. On the contrary, it fed the habit, because it was the motive force behind the 'Brown Boom' decade of economic growth. In February 2007, Credit Action stated that the United Kingdom's personal debt has been increasing by one million pounds every 3.85 minutes.[102]

The problem for Gordon Brown in his Prime Ministership is that such high levels of debt may have consequences for the United Kingdom's economic performance in the next economic cycle. Brown did not attempt to dampen the growth of debt by setting a tax on consumer credit. In the 1980s, under the then Chancellor, Nigel Lawson, the Treasury did contemplate the introduction of a one per cent tax on outstanding consumer credit (including mortgages). Lawson concluded that the consumer- and property-led boom of the late 1980s was 'to a considerable extent a once-and-for-all occurrence: the change from a financially regulated to a financially deregulated economy'.[103] He was wrong: under Lawson's successors, notably Brown, the United Kingdom has become locked into a permanent condition of financial risk, volatility and debt-financed consumption.

In the housing market, there is little sign of an end to the 'Brown Boom'. In January 2007, the Halifax House Price Index showed that the annual rate of house price inflation was 9.9 per cent, with the average house costing £186, 954 – an increase of 605 per cent since January 1983.[104] During 2006, such was the inflation in the housing market that the typical house increased in value by forty-five pounds per day, compared to a daily increase of £12.50 during 2005. However, during 2006, the number of first-time buyers was estimated to have fallen by seven per cent to 315,000, a decline of 37.4 per cent on their 1997 level (503,000) and the lowest total since 1980. This reflected an eleven per cent rise in the price of the average United Kingdom first-time house purchase, to £151,565, an increase of ninety-five per cent since 2001. House price inflation has meant a ninety-one per cent increase in the average mortgage, to £123,435 in 2006, For the first-time buyer in London, the average purchase price has risen to £250,819, requiring an average deposit of £53,136.

Such rampant house price inflation appears unsustainable. The gap between the average income of the first-time buyer and that of people in their twenties has widened significantly during Brown's stewardship of the economy. In 1997, when the Blair Government first took power, the average first-time buyer's income was £16,053, only 1.1 per cent greater than the average full-time earnings of people between the ages of twenty-two and twenty-nine years (£15,839). However, by 2001, the gap in incomes had widened to more than twenty per cent and by 2006 to more than thirty-five per cent. Average houses are now unaffordable for first-time buyers in ninety-three per cent of towns in the United Kingdom, compared to only thirty-seven per cent in 2001.[105] Housing has become so expensive that thirty-three per cent of mortgages taken out during November 2006 were 'interest only' (compared to twelve per cent during June 2006) and of these twenty-six per cent did not incorporate a repayment plan for the capital borrowed.[106] Fewer and fewer young people are now able to enter the housing market and in much of the United Kingdom entrance is beyond the range of many people, including key workers in the public services. The housing market has become an engine of increasing inequality in income and wealth, with inflation in asset values far outstripping the effects of limited redistribution arising from the tax credit reforms implemented by Brown.

Gordon Brown sought to infuse his 'British model' of political economy with the same moral purpose that he brought to public life; the commitment to duty and the service of others. However, the evidence of executive pay and remuneration to workers in the City of London suggests that their reward has been of a very different – pecuniary – form and of an order of magnitude far removed from the income of the average citizen. A survey of 1340 FTSE 100 directors found that directors' pay for the financial year 2005 rose by twenty-eight per cent, from £590 million to £753 million. Of this, no less than £678 million was paid to just 540 full-time executives (an average of £1.24 million).This compared with an increase in average earnings of 3.7 per cent and an inflation rate of 2.5 per cent. While the average pay of Tesco's 368,000 workers fell from £12,713 to £11,594, the pay of Tesco's Chief Executive rose to £5.4 million; 466 times the average remuneration of a Tesco employee.[107] There was little evidence to suggest that the explosion in executive pay in 2005, to seventy-six times that of the average worker (compared with a ratio of 10:1 in 1980), has been either performance-related or the product of labour market risk. On the contrary, research from the Work Foundation suggested that there was scant justification for paying FTSE 100 directors many times the Prime Minister's £186,000 a year salary. For Iles, in *The Risk Myth*, this 'winner-take-all' and excessive level of remuneration constituted both 'a form of market failure', because it threatened the long-term competitiveness of these companies and a major social cost, because 'inequality matters. High levels of inequality in wider society act as a brake on social mobility and high levels of inequality within organisations act as a brake on performance'.[108]

CONCLUSION

The 'British model' of political economy delivered forty consecutive quarters of economic growth during Gordon Brown's Chancellorship. This was a much better-sustained performance than those of any of his predecessors, Labour or Conservative. In acknowledging that undoubted success, we must also recognise that the 'British model' largely failed in its attempt to rally the private sector to a shared sense of national economic purpose. At the start of his tenure, Brown promised not to pursue 'a policy of "Whitehall knows best" ' but to be 'a supporter and friend of all that is best in British entrepreneurial culture'.[109] In the event, he discovered that, left to themselves to enjoy the freedom of liberalised markets, British entrepreneurs may choose the culture of short-termism and domestic under-investment that prompted Whitehall intervention in the past.

The effect of the 'British model' of political economy was to reinforce competitive advantage. Its winners were the City of London, investors in the housing market and the Treasury (which enjoyed unprecedented power over the design of policy and the allocation of resources in England). Its losers were manufacturing industry and first-time buyers on the property market. Brown's economic legacy was to reinforce rather than reverse the trend towards greater inequality in income and wealth established during the Thatcher and Major Governments. Furthermore, implementing the 'British model' was a quintessential top-down, technocratic exercise. Despite its claims to have accorded priority to economics over politics, it was a highly-politicised agenda, driven by a committee of two: Gordon Brown and his former Chief Economic Adviser and closest political confidant, Ed Balls. Vital decisions concerning macro- and micro-economic policy were entrusted to a series of unelected committees and experts appointed or approved by Brown, much of whose work was beyond the democratic scrutiny of the British people.

Despite a decade of hyperactivity in the publication of Treasury reports, there is little evidence that any of the principal long-term supply-side constraints on the performance of the United Kingdom economy have been alleviated. The long tail of under-performing companies and individuals first highlighted by the Commission on Public Policy and British Business immediately before the election of the Blair Government has remained.[110] The fact that Brown's tenth and final Pre-Budget Report identified the challenge for the next decade as the creation of 'a new British framework for investment and innovation, a British strategy to make the next stage of globalisation work for the British people' was itself testament to the extent of the failure of the British model to redress significantly the long-term supply-side weaknesses of the United Kingdom economy.[111]

Initially, Gordon Brown was prudent for a purpose. During the Blair Government's first term, he demonstrated his commitment to macro-economic stability and fiscal prudence to the City of London's investors while showing both his Cabinet colleagues and the trades unions in the public sector that there would be no sudden windfall from the election of a Labour Government. Latterly, during the Blair Government's second and third terms, Brown was increasingly imprudent, for the purpose of investing in the public services. However, as I shall show in Chapter Four, the speed with which public spending has increased the resources available to public services, combined with the combination of a centrally-driven, permanent revolution of market-based reforms, meant that the 'British model's' growing fiscal imprudence yielded a disappointing dividend and legacy in terms of performance and productivity for England's public services.

Chapter 4

Reforming the Public Services: The Nationalisation of Policy Design and Resource Allocation

INTRODUCTION

In its 1997 General Election manifesto, the Labour Party made some bold commitments to public services. It promised that 'education will be our number one priority and we will increase the share of national income spent on education as we decrease it on the bills of economic and social failure'.[1] In fact, the National Health Service (NHS) was the Blair Government's number one priority. New Labour wanted 'to save and modernise the NHS'.[2] It promised to do this by ending the Conservatives' internal market in health care and by increasing spending on the NHS in real terms every year. This was to be accomplished (while still adhering to the Conservatives' very low planned public spending allocations for the first two years in office), by reallocating spending 'from economic failure to investment'.[3] To bring about the necessary changes in the NHS, there was to be 'continuity as well as change or the system cannot cope. There must be pilots to ensure that change works. And there must be flexibility, not rigid prescription, if innovation is to flourish'. The fundamental purpose of reform would be 'to restore the NHS as a public service working co-operatively for patients, not a commercial business driven by competition'.[4]

New Labour has delivered on its spending commitments. Up to 2007–2008, education spending, in real terms, increased annually by an average of 4.6 per cent. This compares with a paltry 1.5 per cent average annual real terms' increase from 1979 to 1997. Health spending under New Labour increased by an average annual rate of 6.1 per cent, compared with a 3.1 per cent annual increase during the Thatcher and Major Governments.[5] The planned total public expenditure for the Department of Health for 2007–2008 is £104.1 billion, an 8.1 per cent increase in real terms, following 7.8 per cent and 5.1 per cent real terms increases in the previous two years.[6]

Although money has clearly been provided for the modernisation of the public services, paradoxically, opinion polls have repeatedly demonstrated a consistent level of general public dissatisfaction with the returns from that investment, in terms of the quality of service experienced. For example, in May 2007, a MORI opinion poll identified that more people (fifty-one per cent) disagreed than agreed (thirty-eight per cent) that in the long term the government's policies would improve the state of Britain's public services.[7] And despite the investment, morale among workers in the public sector remained much lower than in the private and not-for-profit sectors. No fewer than thirty-nine per cent of managers in the public sector believed morale to be low in their organisation, compared to only sixteen per cent of private sector managers and six per cent of not-for-profit managers.[8]

Even before he became Prime Minister, Gordon Brown was warned by Dr Jonathan Fielden, Chairman of the British Medical Association's Central Consultants and Specialists' Committee, that morale in the NHS was 'at an all time low' and that 'political meddling has brought it to its knees'. His allegation was that the NHS in England had seen: 'incoherent policy dividing and fragmenting. No long term strategy for sustained improvement ... The real barriers to progress are government policies – we all bear the scars on our backs from these – patients, the public and notably the profession'. Having promised to abolish the internal market in the NHS, he accused the Blair Government of leaving a legacy that had gone from 'the Bazaar to the

Bizarre: a messianic belief in the market, redirecting billions of pounds into poor-value-for-money schemes'. As incoming Prime Minister, Fielden exhorted Brown to 'Go on Gordon go for it; get your legacy in days where Tony has failed in a decade!', by valuing and giving back leadership to the medical professions and by freeing the NHS from 'political meddling'.[9]

During his tenure at the Treasury, Gordon Brown certainly engaged in extensive 'political meddling' in the public services, especially in England, where the absence of devolution had resulted in the absence of institutional and democratic checks and balances on the exercise of micro-management through centralised prescription. Brown further entrenched his control over domestic policy by sitting on eighteen of the thirty-two principal ministerial committees of the Cabinet, including all those concerned with reform of the public services. Brown, rather than Blair, chaired the Cabinet committee on Public Services and Public Expenditure, whose terms of reference were 'to review public expenditure allocations and to make recommendations – including on Public Service Agreements – to Cabinet, and to review progress in delivering the Government's programme of investment and reform to renew the public services'.[10] To understand Brown's policies for and legacies to the public services, in this chapter I will show that, where once the Labour Party nationalised industries and failing sectors of the economy, under Gordon Brown's stewardship the Treasury implemented a technocratic statecraft of constrained discretion. This enabled it to nationalise policy design and the allocation of resources for public spending bodies in England.

Through the Treasury's biennial spending reviews and the framework of the Public Service Agreements, Brown engineered a top-down framework of centralised prescription over public services reform. Because it bypassed or eliminated many of the previous checks and balances on executive power (including those exercised by the Prime Minister, his Cabinet colleagues, Westminster, local government and individual citizens), constrained discretion delivered both a seemingly permanent revolution of reforms and a significant increase in funding for public services, notably health and education. Thus, it was possible for modernisation to alienate both public sector workers and their representatives at a time of record investment. There was also increasing evidence that the political legacy of an approach based on partnerships with the private sector and a consumer-led approach to public service delivery was a growing disillusionment with the resulting postcode lottery in the availability of services. The perception was widespread that increased resources had not been matched by corresponding increases in the quality of services.

BROWN'S CONSTRAINED DISCRETION VERSUS BLAIR'S EARNED AUTONOMY

The reform of public services in England caused the most bitter of the battles over domestic policy between Gordon Brown and Tony Blair. This battle was the most visible legacy of the *Granita* accord, when Brown stood aside from the contest to succeed John Smith as Labour Party leader in return for a central role in domestic policy formulation. The battle also produced two rival but essentially similar models for modernisation, advanced by the Treasury and the Prime Minister. Tony Blair set out his model of 'earned autonomy', which was enshrined, for example, in the July 2000 publication *The NHS Plan*. This plan (made for England alone, a fact not once acknowledged in it) promised that investment and reform would be implemented through 'a new system of earned autonomy' that would 'devolve power from the centre to the local health service as modernisation takes hold'.[11] The Treasury advanced its alternative model of 'constrained discretion'. This demanded commitment, through institutional arrangements and procedural rules, to clear and sound long-term policy objectives, in return for 'the maximum operational flexibility that is consistent with achieving that goal'.[12] In other words, the freedom of schools, hospitals, local government and other providers of public services was to be limited, in return for accepting the Treasury's national standards as the political price to be paid for receiving the money for modernisation.

Both modernisation models followed the same centralised prescription for and nationalisation of policy design, standards and resource allocation for public services in England (not feasible elsewhere in Britain, because of devolution). Blair's model of 'earned autonomy for schools, hospitals, local government and other public services' had enabled 'locally-elected representatives to adopt approaches to public services reflecting their own national priorities and concerns' – but only in Scotland, Wales and Northern Ireland.[13] In England, Blair held that 'devolved delivery can only operate with national standards and accountability'. Public services' reform must be based on a clear demarcation between central government's prescription for an 'overall vision' – that is, policy design and specification of 'national standards' (again for England alone, a fact not once acknowledged) – and the delivery of that vision by subordinate layers of administration 'by devolution and delegation to the front line'.[14]

Brown's Treasury model of modernisation claimed that the 'command and control systems of public service management employed in the past had serious drawbacks; in particular they lacked devolution, transparency and accountability'. Constrained discretion purported to be 'bottom-up not top-down, with national government enabling powerful regional and local institutions to work by providing the necessary flexibility and resources'.[15] However, the fact that the Treasury specified that it, rather than England's regions and localities, would provide the necessary 'flexibility and resources' was ample testament to the degree which Brown too had nationalised policy-making and resource allocation in England. The crucial difference between Blair and Brown's intended nationalisations was that New Labour's commitment to Spending Reviews and their accompanying Public Service Agreements gave Brown the means by which to institutionalise his framework for domestic economic and social policy and to ensure the subordination of Blair's.

One way in which the rivalry between Blair and Brown affected the reform of the public services was encapsulated in the row over health service funding in January 2000. During a television interview with David Frost, and against the backdrop of Lord Robert Winston's (a leading fertility expert) accusations that his Government had failed to deliver NHS reform and funding, Blair committed himself to raising health spending to the European Union average over five years. He stated 'If we run the economy properly, I am entirely confident we will get those five per cent real term rises'.[16] Not only did Blair's statement break an agreement with Brown that additional funding would be dependent on future economic growth and reform but it also committed the government to a target that was 'huge, imprecise and moving'. Andrew Rawnsley, in *Servants of the People*, reported that Brown was purportedly incandescently angry that Blair had pre-empted his Budget statement.[17]

To reassert his control over this vital aspect of the public services' agenda, in March 2001 Brown commissioned a review of the long-term trends affecting the NHS.[18] Blair responded, in August, by commissioning his own review of health strategy.[19] However, the triumph of Brown over Blair was signalled in April 2002 when the spending profile identified by the (Brown-commissioned) Wanless Report as necessary for the United Kingdom to catch up and sustain best practice in healthcare became the basis for government policy. The July 2002 Spending Review announced a growth in the United Kingdom's health spending of 7.3 per cent in real terms per annum until 2008, matching the Wanless Report's blueprint for annual average real increases of between 7.1 and 7.3 per cent during this period.[20]

THE PERMANENT REVOLUTION OF CONSTRAINED DISCRETION

The permanent revolution of modernisation and reform of the public services in England reflected the influence of the hypothesis of the reinvention of government, first put forward in the early 1990s. This reinvention sought to transform the public sector, creating 'entrepreneurial government', which, according to Osborne and Gabeler in *Reinventing government*, would 'constantly use their resources in new ways to heighten both their efficiency and their effectiveness'.[21] Among the characteristics of entrepreneurial government Osborne and Gabeler described were:

... the promotion of competition between service providers, the empowerment of citizens by 'pushing control out of the bureaucracy, into the community', the measurement of the performance of public agencies by 'focusing not on inputs but on *outcomes*', the redefinition of clients for services as 'customers', who would be offered 'choices – between schools, between training programs, between housing', a preference for market mechanisms over bureaucratic mechanisms and a focus 'not simply on providing public services but on *catalyzing* all sectors – public, private and voluntary – into action to solve their community's problems'.[22]

Rejecting the 'Reaganite' mantra that government was not the solution but the problem, the hypothesis of entrepreneurial government asserted that 'the central failure of government today is one of *means*, not *ends*'.[23] The focus was not on the quantity of government: Osborne and Gabeler's hypothesis was that 'we have *the wrong kind of government*' and that consequently what was needed was better government or 'to be more precise, we need better *governance*' (which they defined as the process by which society collectively solves its problems and meets its needs).[24] This needed managerial systems that separated 'policy decisions (steering) from service delivery (rowing)'.[25] The steering role would require government to 'set policy, deliver funds to operational bodies (public and private) and evaluate performance [but] seldom play an operational role themselves'.[26] However, while entrepreneurial government would allow service delivery to be contracted out to the private sector or the third sector of civic society groups and voluntary, not-for-profit associations, steering (policy design, resource allocation and governance) could not. Policy design must remain the province of government, so that decisions could be taken collectively, markets regulated, a sense of equity and altruism be maintained and unprofitable public and social services be sustained, so as not to overburden the third sector.[27]

The hypothesis of entrepreneurial government is an accurate depiction of the Treasury's approach to the governance of public services during Brown's Chancellorship. The separation of policy design and resource allocation and service delivery was institutionalised, through the control mechanisms of the two Comprehensive Spending Reviews, the intervening biennial Spending Reviews and their attendant Public Service Agreements. Under previous Labour Prime Ministers, from Attlee to Callaghan, the relationship between the Treasury and government departments was characterised by negotiation through policy networks within Whitehall. Public services were delivered through hierarchical or vertically-integrated agencies. The Treasury had been able to exercise only discretionary authority over policy and resources, because its power was 'constrained by the exercise of countervailing power by each autonomous spending department' (Thain and Wright: *The Treasury and Whitehall*).[28] Under the Thatcher and Major Governments, negotiated discretion in expenditure planning and public service delivery had been abandoned only temporarily. Privatisation led to a departure from the principles of hierarchical or vertically-integrated public service provision towards provision based on contractual relationships. The boundaries between the public and private sectors had become blurred.

During Gordon Brown's tenure as Chancellor, the previous constitutional and practical checks and balances on Treasury power were largely removed. This was a paradigm shift, from negotiated discretion to centralised prescription for the control of policy and the allocation of resources for the public services. Competition was introduced between service providers in the public services in England. Public Service Agreements, performance indicators and output measures institutionalised an emphasis on the measurement of performance and a focus on outcomes, not inputs. The clients of public services were redefined as customers. There was an almost messianic faith in markets and the capacity of the private sector to innovate and to enhance efficiency and productivity in the use of resources.[29]

THE SPENDING REVIEWS AND PUBLIC SERVICE AGREEMENTS

The principal instruments through which the Treasury nationalised the design of policy and allocation of resources for the public services were the Comprehensive Spending Reviews (1998 and 2007), the intervening biennial Spending Reviews (2000, 2002 and 2004) and their accompanying Public Service Agreements (PSAs). Although these instruments gave the Treasury a greater degree of centralised control over the budgetary and policy-making processes, they did not necessarily ensure that resources flowed consistently to the public services or indeed that the resources allocated for modernisation were spent effectively or in an equitable manner.

The first year-long Comprehensive Spending Review (CSR), which covered 1999–2000 to 2001–2002, established the Treasury's central prescription for policy and resources. It incorporated thirty-six zero-based reviews by the Treasury not only of individual departmental spending plans but also their objectives and policies. Effectively, the Treasury was reviewing the rationale of policy and even long-held assumptions about policy were open to challenge. One sixth of these reviews were conducted cross-departmentally, to ensure integration and co-ordination. However, because expenditure was planned to grow by only 2.25 per cent on average in real terms over the CSR's life, this meant a period of austerity for the public services.[30] Public spending under the Major Government had grown more quickly, at an annual real terms' average of 2.4 per cent. Indeed, at the end of the Blair Government's first term, total public spending was 2.6 per cent of national income lower than when New Labour had taken office. In 1999–2000, at 37.4 per cent of GDP, public spending was at its lowest level since 1960–1961.[31] Health spending had also declined as a share of national income, from 5.5 per cent of GDP in 1996–1997 to 5.4 per cent in 1999–2000 and education spending likewise, from 4.7 per cent of GDP to 4.4 per cent.[32]

No change in the available resources for the public services occurred until the year before the 2001 General Election. The July 2000 Spending Review announced that current public spending would increase by an annual average of 2.5 per cent. However, spending on health would increase by 6.1 per cent in real terms from 2000–2001 to 2003–2004, while education spending would increase by 5.4 per cent.[33] The July 2002 Spending Review planned to accelerate spending on these key services: in the five years to 2008, education spending in England would grow by six per cent a year in real terms and health spending in the United Kingdom by an average of 7.3 per cent.[34] The momentum was maintained by the July 2004 Spending Review, which planned expenditure growth for education in England of 4.4 per cent between 2004–2005 and 2007–2008. By 2007–2008, NHS spending was planned to increase to ninety-two billion pounds, compared to only thirty-three billion in 1996–1997.[35]

Whether this significant acceleration in investment in the public services delivered an improvement in the quantity and quality of services depended on the Government's ability to translate investment into enhanced efficiency. Through the Spending Reviews, the Treasury identified three 'building blocks' of its approach to raising the productivity of the public services: first, a focus on outcomes as the central aim of policy, as opposed to the solitary focus on inputs; second, constrained discretion for local service providers, 'increasing their operational freedoms and flexibilities, subject to appropriate minimum standards and regular performance monitoring'; third, improved governance of public services, through 'reforming institutions to reflect the importance of clear objectives, appropriate incentives and good performance information in the achievement of higher productivity'.[36] There was also a greater emphasis, notably in the preparation of the second CSR, on the catalytic role of the private and third sectors, to complement the role of the public sector.

The essential contradiction in the Treasury's approach to the reform of the public services in England was that constrained discretion could in practice operate only by decreasing the freedom and flexibility of local communities and public spending bodies to make autonomous choices about the design (as opposed to the administration and delivery) of policy.

Constrained discretion meant limited freedom. Furthermore, the Treasury's 'appropriate minimum standards' facilitated the nationalisation of policy design and resource allocation in England. The Treasury's 'regular performance monitoring' fed an audit culture, in which a fixation on meeting performance targets and indicators all too often led to a neglect of the broader picture of effective delivery of public service.

PSAs were introduced in the July 1998 report of the first CSR. As part of the 'money for modernisation' agenda, PSAs incorporated 'new objectives and measurable efficiency targets', monitored by a Cabinet Committee chaired by the Chancellor of the Exchequer.[37] From the very outset of the Blair Government's reform of the public services, Gordon Brown had thus engineered an institutional structure and approach to policy-making that allowed him to micro-manage policy design and resource allocation. When the July 2000 Spending Review was published, it announced the strengthening and deepening of performance measurement, through the introduction of Service Delivery Agreements (SDAs) and Technical Notes. SDAs explained how the government aimed to deliver its targets in the PSAs and how it itself would modernise and reform to give better value for money. The Technical Notes underpinned departmental PSAs and would specify the precise performance criteria against which PSA targets would be measured.[38] The Treasury thus possessed an extensive framework for monitoring progress in the reform and modernisation of public services.

The degree to which the creation of the biennial Spending Reviews, PSAs, SDAs and Technical Notes enhanced the Treasury's power not only over the public services but also over 'the strategic direction of the Government', soon became apparent to the rest of Whitehall and to Westminster. The Treasury Select Committee accused the Treasury of exerting 'too much influence over policy areas which are properly the business of other departments and that is not necessarily in the best interests of the Treasury or the Government as a whole'.[39] It was not thought desirable for the Treasury to set both 'the framework within which departments should operate, using the Spending Review and PSA process and to act as the sole assessor of whether or not departments are achieving their objectives'.[40] It recommended that the Treasury's power to monitor PSAs should be curtailed, by reducing the dominance of Treasury ministers on the Public Services and Public Expenditure Cabinet Committee (a recommendation the Treasury never accepted). However, it also conceded that Parliament lacked the resources to hold the Treasury to account, because 'the Treasury's role in allocating public expenditure, determining, monitoring and adapting PSAs and influencing policies which have economic effects is opaque, hidden behind a curtain of Whitehall secrecy'.[41]

This open acknowledgement that Westminster lacked the resources to hold it fully to account meant that a major constitutional check on the centralised prescription-writing of the Treasury's constrained discretion had been removed. However, it soon became apparent that the objective of micro-managing reform of the public services through performance targets had been too ambitious. The number of targets was almost halved between the July 1998 and July 2002 Spending Reviews. This trend continued in March 2004, when the Treasury published the results of its Devolved Decision Making Review.[42] This specified fewer nationally-set targets and a greater emphasis on locally-determined outcomes. This change was tantamount to an admission that the Treasury's command-and-control approach had been inflexible and denied local management the autonomy needed to develop effective local performance management. This trend continued in the 2007 CSR, when the number of PSAs was further reduced to 'less than a third of the number of PSAs' in the 2004 Spending Review.[43] In a similar vein, in October 2006, introducing the White Paper on local government, Ruth Kelly, then Secretary of State for Communities and Local Government, announced a 'new settlement between central government, local government and citizens', which promised a 'radical reduction in national targets and the introduction of a lighter touch inspection system'. In practice, this still meant around 200 performance indicators for local government in England (compared to the previous 'between 600 and 1,200 indicators'[44]). It showed how centralised and nationalised policy design, resource allocation and performance monitoring had become in England under constrained discretion, when the retention of such a large measure of centralised prescription could be presented as a radical act of devolution.

HELPING MARKETS WORK BETTER: GORDON BROWN ON PUBLIC SERVICES

In *Microeconomic Reform in Britain*, Ed Balls and his co-editors held that a central assumption underpinning the policy of constrained discretion was that 'markets are a powerful means of advancing the public interest'. The essential conceit of constrained discretion was that the Treasury had the capacity 'not only to support but positively enhance markets'.[45] Such intervention was held to be necessary because 'markets can fail to deliver socially optimal outcomes requiring intervention to make markets work in the public interest'.[46] In healthcare, the role of state was vital because of:

> The existence of multiple market failures ... [and] ... price signals don't always work; the consumer is not sovereign; there is potential abuse of monopoly power; it is hard to write and enforce contracts; it is difficult to let a hospital go bust; and we risk supplier-induced demands.[47]

The provision of healthcare by the market would 'lead to neither the most efficient nor the most equitable outcome, jeopardising the delivery of opportunity and security for all'.[48]

For Gordon Brown, there was a key test of whether the appropriate balance had been established between the market and the state in the delivery of public services:

> whether the public interest – that is, opportunity and security for all – and the equity, efficiency and diversity necessary to achieve it, are best advanced by more or less reliance on markets or through substituting a degree of public control or ownership for the market; and whether, even when there is public sector provision, there can be contestability.[49]

Brown identified the failure of the Labour Governments of the 1960s and 1970s 'to take on vested interests' and criticised post-war politicians on both sides of the political spectrum for wrongly seeing the centralised state as 'the main, and sometimes the sole, expression of community'.[50] Brown's thesis was that the relationship between the state and the market must be renegotiated, because of the way in which globalisation and technology had challenged traditional assumptions. There must be an agreement 'on where markets should have an enhanced role and where market failure has to be addressed'. The public interest must not be confused with public ownership or producer interests. Nor must the Labour Party 'adhere to failed means lest we fail to achieve enduring ends'.[51]

This was when Brown invoked his thesis of the importance of civic society and the moral limits of markets (see Chapter Two). On the one hand, by identifying that there were certain 'moral and civic goods that markets do not honour and money cannot buy', Brown sought to clarify the limits of market provision.[52] On the other, by arguing that market failure should be redressed 'not by abolishing markets but by strengthening markets and enabling them to work better', Brown also sought to show the role markets could play in the delivery of public services. Rather than replace market failure with state failure, Brown asserted that the application of the same public interest test to each could deliver 'equity, efficiency and diversity by reforming and modernising the public realm for the decades ahead, in particular through devolution, transparency and accountability'.[53]

Brown claimed that markets could be enabled to work better by the provision of 'fair and accurate information' to the consumer, fair competition among suppliers, low barriers to entry, producers who are 'not monopolists with the power to dictate prices' and mobility, through the freedom of capital, labour and consumers to go elsewhere. Competition must be embraced, rather than greeted with suspicion, because without it 'vested interests accumulate' and an entrepreneurial culture celebrated as a source of market dynamism and innovation. Where the market had delivered 'insufficient investment and a damaging short-termism', the state must intervene 'to enable markets to work better and for the long term'.[54] For example, by publicly funding health care, the state could surmount the absence of consumer sovereignty. It could overcome the 'chronically imperfect and asymmetric information', the failure of private insurance to 'cover all of the people all of the time' and the fact that essential medical and surgical specialities had, by their very nature, to be delivered locally and therefore, by definition, were 'akin to natural monopolies'.[55]

The problem with Brown's 'pro-market principles' was that while they may have been readily applicable to the liberalised and deregulated markets of the City of London and the privatised utilities, they were less easily applicable to the public services. Brown pointed out how increased investment had been matched by policies such as 'devolution with multi-year budgets for primary care and hospital trusts'; 'more payment by results'; and 'NHS foundation hospitals with greater management flexibility'. He emphasised the importance of the Private Finance Initiative (PFI) as an approach 'quite distinct from privatisation', which had seen the private sector 'rightly helping in public service delivery'.[56] The Treasury's rationale for PFI was that it enabled the public sector 'to take advantage of private sector management skills incentivised by having private finance at risk'. It also claimed it would only use PFI 'where it is appropriate and where it expects it to deliver value for money', based on 'an assessment of the lifetime costs of both providing and maintaining the underlying asset and of the running costs of delivering the required level of service'.[57]

The Treasury maintained that the PFI had been used only where it could deliver efficiency, equity and accountability and offer value for money but 'not at the expense of the terms and conditions of the staff'.[58] The problem was that a large body of evidence challenged these assertions, and the PFI, both in theory and practice. First, the PFI was seen to have undermined the public service ethos, because it fostered privatisation and turned public services into commodities that had become detached from their role of serving the public, rather than private interests.[59] Second, the PFI was driven by the Treasury's desire to keep borrowing off the public sector balance sheet, rather than to improve public services. Third, PFI projects were known to be more costly than conventionally funded public sector projects, because the private sector had to borrow at higher interest rates than government. PFI contracts also had very high start-up costs, because of the number of lawyers and consultants employed by both public and private agencies,[60] and the private sector demanded high returns from PFI projects, which further inflated their cost to the taxpayer and were not in the public interest.[61] Fourth, there was significant evidence that workforces employed by private contractors experienced worse pay and conditions than those enjoyed by public sector workers.[62] Finally, there was little evidence of the genuine transfer of risk from the public to the private sector to justify the premium cost of PFI contracts. Pollock and Price, in *Public risk for private gain?* noted that risk transfer was 'largely unevaluated for central government PFIs'and therefore there was little empirical basis for the claimed benefits.[63]

A detailed analysis (by Pollock and others) of Treasury evidence for cost and time over-run concluded that the PFI was 'A Policy Built on Sand'.[64] The Treasury claimed that eighty-eight per cent of PFI schemes had been delivered on time, whereas seventy per cent of non-PFI projects were delivered late and seventy-three per cent over budget. Treasury guidance required the estimated costs of non-PFI projects to be inflated by as much as twenty-four per cent 'to take into account the risks of cost and time over-runs'.[65] However, an evaluation of five reports on the PFI, including the Treasury report, *PFI: meeting the investment challenge*,[66] concluded that 'there is no evidence to support the Treasury's chief justification for the policy, namely, that PFI generates value for money savings by improving the efficiency of construction procurement. Government policy guidance on optimism bias is flawed and misleading'.[67]

Parliamentary scrutiny of PFI debt refinancing revealed that the Government had received only £93 million as its dividend from voluntary sharing arrangements with private PFI contractors, compared with the expected £175–200 million. By contrast, the refinancing of four early PFI projects enabled private investors to raise their rate of return from between 15.5 and 23.0 per cent (before refinancing) to between 56.0 and 71.3 per cent (after refinancing).[68] This was hardly a shining legacy for Brown's approach to public service reform.

Despite the evidence of the limits of market-based reforms of the public services, Brown further asserted that 'even when a market is inappropriate, old, centralised, command and control systems of management are not the way forward'. His alternative, for the NHS and other public services, was 'a decentralised means of delivery compatible with equity and efficiency'.[69] Brown endorsed the balance between national standards and local autonomy of Tony Blair's 'earned autonomy' model for public services, claiming that:

> ... national targets work best when they are matched by a framework of devolution, accountability and participation – empowering public ser-vices to make a difference ... Local autonomy without national stan-dards may lead to increased inequalities between people and regions and the return of the postcode lotteries.[70]

Brown pointed out there had been 'more devolution to English regions in the last few years than in the preceding one hundred years', emphasising the freedom given to Regional Development Agencies (RDAs) to consider local needs in budgets affecting public services in the fields of economic develop-ment and planning.[71]

Like Blair, Brown never explained why constrained discretion and cen-trally prescribed targets must only apply to public services in England. Likewise, outlining 'the modern model for the British NHS', Brown never once acknowledged that, in practice, this market-based model only related to England.[72] The result was a postcode lottery of citizenship rights and funding for public services.

It could not be said that the postcode lotteries had returned because, under the pre-Thatcher Barnett Formula (which the reforms of Brown's

'British model' by-passed (see Chapter Three)), these lotteries in the funding of public services between and within the nations of the United
Kingdom never went away. For example, Treasury statistics showed that in
2006–2007, identifiable expenditure on services per head in England was
£7,121, less than ninety-seven per cent of the United Kingdom average. By
contrast, in Scotland, identifiable expenditure was 117 per cent. In England,
per capita spending on health was ninety-eight per cent of the United
Kingdom average and for education and training ninety-seven per cent; in
Scotland, the equivalent was 112 per cent and 117 per cent.[73]

With identifiable spending also significantly higher in Wales and
Northern Ireland, such inequalities in funding enabled the Scottish
Parliament and the National Assembly for Wales to offer free public services
for which English people were charged. For example, from 1 April 2007,
patients in Wales were entitled to free prescriptions; people in England were
charged at least £6.85. Welsh breast cancer patients at an English hospital in
Shrewsbury received the drug Herceptin for free, while English patients had
to pay £47,000 for the equivalent drug.[74] The extent to which cancer patients
from deprived communities in England were disadvantaged by the NHS
Cancer Plan was duly highlighted by parliamentary scrutiny.[75]

A further anomaly of Brown's legacy to the public services in England
was that he never explained why English devolution had to mean merely
administrative decentralisation to unelected and appointed agencies (not
least the RDAs and their northern consortium, the Northern Way), within
tightly prescribed national standards, when devolution of policy and
resources was sanctioned for the Scottish Parliament and National Assembly
for Wales.[76] It was claimed that the pre-1997 model of public service delivery
lacked 'devolution, transparency and accountability', which had suppressed
local initiative, constrained innovation, undermined employees' morale,
ignored local needs and circumstances and potentially led 'to the delivery of
one-size-fits-all, poor quality services to diverse communities'.[77] Brown
claimed that during his tenure, the Treasury's alternative model had seen
'decentralised public service delivery to ensure greater freedom and flexibility to local providers'.[78] However, rather than granting the freedoms enjoyed
by Scottish and Welsh communities to decide autonomously how to allocate
resources and design policies, the Treasury retained tight control of that
process in England, through a top-down nationalisation of resource allocation, policy design and performance measurement.

THE LEGACY OF CONSTRAINED DISCRETION

At the Labour Party conference of September 2005, referring to the 7 July 2005 bombings of the London transport system, Gordon Brown referred to the emergency services as 'the quiet heroes of our country', examples of 'public service at its best, not just a career but a calling, the ethic of duty, care, compassion and service'.[79] Brown further asserted that the Labour Party had 'not talked enough about their ethical foundations, of what, at root, gives purpose to our politics and builds trust in public service'.

Brown's moral compass showed him that 'in return for what we received we had a duty to put something back, one moral community of fairness to all, responsibilities from all'.[80] Brown identified the legacy to the public services from a decade of reform and investment as the expansion in the number of people that recruited to improve them; 92,000 more teaching assistants, 36,000 extra teachers and 85,000 additional nurses, compared with 1997.[81] However, there was growing evidence of public disillusionment with, and an imminent political backlash against, the dividend from the investment in and reform of the public services.

As Brown prepared his campaign for the Labour Party leadership, in March 2007, an ICM poll of voting intent found that no fewer than seventy-one per cent of voters questioned thought, in overall terms, that the extra money the government had spent on public services such as health and education during the past decade had been spent badly; only twenty-five per cent thought it had been spent well.[82] The lack of public confidence in the Blair Government's ability to reform the public services was reflected in the March 2007 Ipsos Mori quarterly Delivery Index, which found that fifty-seven per cent of respondents did not agree that its policies would improve the state of Britain's public services, compared to only twenty-nine per cent who did. No fewer than forty-nine per cent of respondents expected the NHS to get worse, far exceeding the nineteen per cent who expected it to get better. In May 2005, just before the General Election, thirty-seven per cent had expected the NHS to improve and only twenty-eight per cent to worsen. Most worryingly, among Labour supporters, an equal number (thirty-three per cent) expected the NHS to improve as did to worsen. This constituted a significant reversal from November 2006, when thirty-five per cent had expected an improvement and only twenty-seven per cent a deterioration.[83]

An Ipsos MORI opinion survey conducted to mark the tenth anniversary of the Blair Government also found that public belief in the government's policies to improve the state of the public services had declined since the 2005 General Election: the number of people agreeing that services would be improved (forty-three per cent) was only narrowly exceeded by the number disagreeing (forty-five per cent). By March 2007, the number agreeing had declined to twenty-nine per cent, compared to fifty-seven per cent who thought public services would not be improved. No fewer than forty-nine per cent of respondents thought the NHS would get worse over the next few years, compared with nineteen per cent who thought it would get better. At the time of the 2005 General Election, thirty-seven per cent had thought things would get worse, compared to twenty-eight per cent who thought the NHS would get better. Sixteen per cent thought the NHS would get much worse and only three per cent that it would get much better. In education, the picture was more encouraging. In March 2007, thirty-three per cent of respondents thought that the quality of education would improve over the next few years and only twenty-four per cent that it would get worse, maintaining a positive trend of public opinion sustained over the past four years.[84]

An ICM poll on political trust, conducted at the end of May 2007, recorded that more respondents (forty-one per cent) trusted David Cameron to improve the quality of education in schools, compared to forty per cent support for Gordon Brown. The same poll found Cameron leading Brown by forty-two per cent to thirty-seven per cent in relation to public trust over improvement of the NHS. However, the results revealed that the further south the poll was conducted, the larger became Cameron's lead over Brown – widening in the South to four per cent (forty-three versus thirty-nine per cent) on schools and five per cent (forty-one versus thirty-seven per cent) on the NHS. In the key battleground of the English Midlands, Cameron's lead was much more pronounced; five per cent on schools (forty-two versus thirty-seven per cent) and twelve per cent on the NHS (forty-five versus thirty-three per cent). However, in relation to competence, Brown enjoyed a massive twenty-five per cent advantage (fifty-four versus twenty-nine per cent), a twenty per cent lead in terms of being a strong leader (fifty-three versus thirty-three per cent) and a crushing seventy-eight per cent lead in experience (eighty-five versus seven per cent). Despite these advantages, Brown's overall lead in terms of making a better Prime Minister was only two per cent (forty-five versus forty-three per cent).[85] It is clear that winning the battle of ideas and policies on the reform of public services will be one of the key contests in the run-up to the next General Election.

PERSONALISED PUBLIC SERVICES: THE AGENDA FOR THE BROWN GOVERNMENT

There will be no slackening in the pace of the reform of public services in England under the Brown Government. On the contrary, Gordon Brown has indicated that the momentum of the reform process will, if anything, increase. Barely a week after he became Prime Minister, Brown announced a 'once-in-a-generation' review of the NHS. The new Health Secretary, Alan Johnson, promised that there would be 'no further centrally dictated, top-down restructuring to primary care trusts and strategic health authorities for the foreseeable future' (although Johnson did not rule out further top-down restructuring after that); instead, the review would ensure that 'a properly resourced NHS is clinically led, patient-centred and locally accountable'.[86] For his part, welcoming the review, Gordon Brown stated, 'No institution touches the lives of the British people like the NHS. It is part of what makes Britain the place it is'.[87]

Johnson and Brown's statements encapsulated several distinct features of public services reform under the Brown Government. First, nowhere in Johnson's statement (nor in the Department of Health press release which accompanied it) was there any mention that the NHS review would apply only to England. Not for the first time, a quintessentially English policy was presented as being British; a frequent occurrence during the early weeks of the Brown Government. (Ed Balls, Secretary of State for Children, Schools and Families, also portrayed his agenda as if it would apply to schools and children throughout the United Kingdom; the civil servant who edited the accompanying press release had to add a note at the bottom of the page ' *This press notice relates to "England"*'.[88])

Second, the NHS review was to be led by Professor Ara Darzi, a leading surgeon, who would become a Health Minister by his appointment to the House of Lords. Once more, whereas devolution in the other constituent nations of the United Kingdom extended the democratic control of citizens over policy design and resource allocation in the reform of public services, in England, the process would be driven by an unelected technocrat, who the citizens of England would be unable to hold to account at the ballot box. Third, despite Johnson's denial of a top-down restructuring, which would be locally accountable, the NHS review in England would be centrally conducted by Whitehall. The nationalisation of policy design and resource allocation would continue.

Brown's conviction is that 'by combining continuing modernisation of our public services with continuing investment, we can better harness the ethos of public services to meet the needs of the people we serve'.[89] He has identified a series of challenges, domestic and external, which confront the public services. Externally, issues arise from globalisation: security, economic and environmental challenges. Domestically, Brown has identified:

> ... the challenge of ever-rising individual aspirations, people's desire for an individual, often personalised tailor-made service that is customised to meet their needs and their requirements, allied to a new range of public needs and the continual quest for value for money.[90]

This challenge will be met by cutting administration budgets by five per cent in real terms and re-allocating the one billion pounds saved into front-line services. These changes will be augmented by selling thirty-six billion pounds of surplus assets and saving an additional two billion pounds a year by setting unchanged or reduced figures for the 2007 Spending Review settlements for government departments including the Cabinet Office, Treasury, the Department of Constitutional Affairs and the administration of the Department for Work and Pensions.[91]

For Brown, the next stage of reform entails 'personalised services tailored to people's needs'. In practice, his Government has committed itself to:

> ... exciting and innovative new areas of policy, greater choice, greater competition, greater contestability, there will be greater accountability, there will be new approaches to the responsibilities as well to the rights of citizens, there will be a coming together with the third sector and social enterprise so that we can do more.[92]

We should note that while Brown developed these ideas within a discourse about Britain and Britishness, devolution means that this agenda will apply only to England, unless the devolved institutions of the other constituent parts of the United Kingdom decide to follow his lead. Brown has promised 'reforms that create greater citizen empowerment and accountability so that people have more control over the services that serve them'.[93] His problem is that the legacy of the principles and practice of constrained discretion is that the nationalisation of policy design and resource allocation in

England is still based on the denial of precisely that empowerment and accountability, at the community level.

Brown has described a model of 'the double devolution of power from Whitehall to the Town Hall and then from the Town Hall to citizens and communities'.[94] But this model only devolves the power to take decisions over the administration of public services within the constrained discretion (or limited freedom) of the nationalised framework of the Spending Reviews and Public Service Agreements. The greater choice and competition that will come from personalising and individualising public service delivery will empower people as consumers, rather than as citizens.

This personalisation and the double devolution of administrative power has been planned within the context of the 2007 Second CSR. Although this will allocate resources only for 2008–2009 until the end of 2010–2011, it will set the framework for public services reform (at least in England) for the next decade. In quantitative terms, the major financial challenge to Gordon Brown as Prime Minister will remain the deceleration of the overall increase in public spending. Until 2010–2011, spending is planned to increase by an average of only 1.9 per cent per year in real terms, a slower rate of increase than under the previous two Spending Reviews; a pattern which will be repeated in the planned spending for individual programmes. For example, the Department for Education and Skills will increase average education spending in England by 2.5 per cent a year in real terms (5.3 per cent in nominal terms) during the period of the CSR.[95] This is a significantly lower level of planned spending compared to the average 5.6 per cent per year real increases during the 2000 Spending Review, the 6.0 per cent annual real growth during the 2002 Spending Review and the 4.4 per cent annual real terms increase during the 2004 Spending Review.[96]

The fat years are over for the public services, at least for the foreseeable future. Reforms will have to be implemented in a context of tighter budgets. One of the key doubts surrounding the 2007 CSR is whether it can deliver the anticipated 2.5 per cent annual efficiency savings needed to fund the reallocation of resources into front-line services. When Brown reported the findings of the July 2004 Spending Review, they were accompanied by the publication of the Gershon Review of public sector efficiency. This identified potentially twenty billion pounds of efficiencies in public spending by 2007–2008.[97] However, by the end of September 2006, departments and local authorities had reported annual efficiency gains totalling only £13.3 billion.[98]

Considerable scepticism has surrounded whether these amount to actual tangible savings that can result in the reallocation of resources to front-line services. A report from the Work Foundation pointed out a potential contradiction in the Treasury's agenda for the public services.[99] On the one hand, the Gershon Review's efficiency programme would result in significant cuts in staffing in public services. On the other, if the Brown Government continued to emphasise the importance of choice and the personalisation of services, there would need to be enough spare capacity in those services to make the exercise of individual choice feasible.

This was painfully demonstrated by the inability of English NHS Trusts to reduce possible infections by isolating new patients, because of the lack of hospital beds. In 2006–2007, no fewer than fifty-five (fourteen per cent) of English NHS Trusts stated that they could not keep their patients, staff and visitors safe by ensuring the risk of hospital-acquired infection was reduced, compared to only 7.2 per cent of Trusts in the previous year.[100] The imperatives of greater choice and greater efficiency contradicted one another. Moreover, there remain significant, but as yet unaddressed, practical obstacles to meeting the objective of efficiency, not least because of weaknesses in recruitment and the threat of 'significant industrial relations problems in the future'.[101]

In his March 2007 Budget statement, Brown announced that for public sector workers covered by the independent Pay Review Body, the overall headline awards in 2007–2008 would average 1.9 per cent, their lowest level for a decade.[102] Public service trades unions were particularly angered by the fact that while the Pay Review Body's recommendation of 2.5 per cent for NHS workers was accepted by the government, Brown chose to stage the pay award in England and Wales (an extra 1.5 per cent from 1 April 2007 and an additional one per cent from 1 November 2007) to keep the award within his two per cent target for public sector pay increases. Members of UNISON, the largest public sector union, unanimously voted to reject the offer. The unions' anger at the staging of the award was exacerbated when it was announced that the NHS in England had recorded a net surplus of £510 million in 2006–2007, compared to a deficit of £547 million during the previous year.[103]

Although trades unions such as UNISON actively supported Gordon Brown's candidature for Labour Party leader, they have demonstrated that they do not share his vision for the reform of the public services. One union-sponsored study asserted that 'the discussion around public service reform has been distorted by a distracting emphasis on market mechanisms and private sector involvement'. However, while 'in theory, such reforms have been thought to offer a route to consumer choice, competitive discipline and managerial innovation', in practice the reforms had 'foundered on the fact that such solutions are not readily applicable to the practical realities of public services'. In particular, such reforms left a legacy of fragmented services, disrupted collaborative relationships, poorer working conditions, higher costs and monopoly profits, 'short-term cost-cutting and distortion of priorities' and the compromising of 'the principles of social equity and public accountability that should underpin all public service reform'.[104] The trades unions maintained that a distinction must be drawn between public services and the private provision of consumer goods and the government must acknowledge the different expectations of each. UNISON has continued to maintain that 'markets will at best only ever be marginal and at worst could be a serious obstruction to the real challenges of public service improvement'.[105]

Venting his frustration at the slow pace of change in the reform of the public services, Tony Blair famously stated, 'I bear the scars on my back after two years in government' and frequently thereafter referred to 'the forces of conservatism' that were threatening modernisation.[106] When he singled out the need to 'take on the forces of conservatism in education' and urged teachers to end the 'culture of excuses', he received a furious reaction from the representatives of professional groups and trades unions representing public sector workers.[107] Gordon Brown's insistence on maintaining – and possibly accelerating – the pace of reform in the public services means that as Prime Minister he can expect similar scars from the 'forces of conservatism'.

BALANCING PERSONAL ASPIRATIONS AND PUBLIC EXPECTATIONS WITH RESOURCES

One of the biggest challenges confronting Gordon Brown as Prime Minister is how to meet the greatly increased public expectations generated by a decade of investment in the public services and the Blair Government's consumer-led approach to reforming service delivery. Despite the fresh momentum that the 2007 CSR brought to the process of public services' reform, the Brown Government did not start with anything resembling a clean sheet but had to work within the restrictions of the legacy of a decade of constrained discretion.

Following Tony Blair, and the Third Way's example of the knowledge-based economy, Brown identified education as the future basis of economic success and what was going to make Britain great in the modern world. His problem is that, because education policy is devolved to the Scottish Parliament and (to a lesser extent) the National Assembly for Wales, his power to intervene can only affect England's schools. Once more, the fact that he represents a Scottish constituency will be used against him by polit-ical opponents, both at Westminster and in the media. Brown used a suc-cession of Budgets during New Labour's second and third terms to by-pass local authorities and allocate funding directly to head teachers. For exam-ple, Brown's 2006 Budget speech announced new direct payments to schools (worth £270 million in 2006–2007 and £440 million in 2007–2008), which meant that total per-pupil spending in the state sector increased by an annual average of 5.3 per cent between 1996–1997 and 2007–2008.[108] In a television interview in January 2007, Brown said that education is:

> ... the priority, it will have pride of place and indeed it's my passion ... We used to talk about education, education, education [but now] If anything it's excellence, excellence, excellence, for the next few years. Excellence for all.

Brown also said he believed that Britain (in effect, England) 'can move to a world-class education system over the next few years'; one that concentrates on individual tuition.[109] Furthermore, Brown stated that 'our education system should keep people in part-time or full-time education until at least eighteen'.[110]

Brown's ambition for schools in the United Kingdom is, once again, likely to be disrupted by devolution. The school leaving age in Scotland and Wales can be raised only with the consent of their Parliament and National Assembly. At best, the Scottish Parliament may anticipate possible reform in England by introducing such a measure at an earlier date, thereby embarrassing the Prime Minister. At worst, the devolved institutions might adopt an alternative policy, to assert their genuine political auton-omy and resist any attempt to orchestrate policy from Westminster and

Whitehall, in pursuit of a 'British Way' of United Kingdom-wide public services' reform.

Brown also indicated that, through the introduction of more Foundation Schools and Academies, he will continue the unpopular trend towards greater diversity of education provision in England and the dilution or dismantling of the comprehensive system. Brown believes in greater variety and diversity of education institutions because 'It puts pressure on the other schools to do better'. He has further identified 'more choice also within the school, within the classroom itself, as being the next stage'[111] Brown claimed that the Blair government had reached only the foothills of educational progress and he looked forward to 'exciting new innovative areas, whether it be greater choice, greater competition, greater contestability and greater local accountability'.[112]

In effectively reiterating Tony Blair's famous mantra 'education, education, education' and embracing the Blairite faith in consumer choice and market competition as the key agents for modernisation in England's public services, Gordon Brown confronted an immediate fiscal challenge to the affordability of his ambition of educational excellence for all. In his 2006 Budget speech, noting the £3,000 disparity between spending per pupil in state schools (£5,000) and in private schools (£8,000), Brown declared, 'our long term aim should be to ensure for one hundred per cent of our children the educational support now available to just ten per cent'. To deliver, by 2011, the same level of capital investment per state pupil enjoyed by private school pupils in 2006, Brown announced 'a total of thirty-four billion pounds new investment over five years'.[113] However, the misleading nature of this statement and the disparity between Brown's aspirations for educational attainment and spending and the cost of translating that aspiration into an actual policy commitment was highlighted in research prepared by the Institute for Fiscal Studies (IFS) for the House of Commons' Education Select Committee.

The IFS noted that Brown's statement led to tabloid newspaper headlines such as '£34 Billion Schools Bonanza'.[114] However, that figure could only be arrived at by adding together the entire planned capital spending for the period between 2006–2007 and 2010–2011. The implication of Brown's speech had been that there would be 'a significant increase in the rate of growth of new school capital spending in the public sector'. This was not the case. In truth, school capital spending in 2010–2011 would be only £0.9 billion higher in real terms than in 2007–2008, a very different figure from Brown's thirty-four billion pounds.[115] By presenting a cumulative total as if it were an annual increase, Brown had repeated the same trick that he had played eight years earlier when announcing the July 1998 CSR.[116] More damningly, the IFS calculated that to raise per capita education spending on the United Kingdom's projected 7.2 million state pupils in 2010–2011, to the level enjoyed by private school pupils, would cost an extra seventeen billion pounds a year in real terms. If, under a Brown Government, state school spending were to increase at the Treasury's projected 2.25 per cent underlying the real annual rate of growth of the economy, it would take until 2024 to close the gap between the public and private sectors.[117] A pupil aged eleven when Brown first announced his aspiration would be twenty-nine years old by then.

Challenged on the apparent lack of progress on educational attainment during a decade of New Labour government, Brown disputed that the educational glass was half empty rather than half full. Having claimed that the number of pupils achieving the benchmark of five 'good' GCSE A* – C grades had improved from forty-five per cent to sixty per cent, he was reminded that when two of those five had to be in mathematics and English, the percentage fell to forty-five per cent. Brown retorted that that still meant 'a big improvement' in overall terms and that he didn't think 'any parent looking at the schools today will doubt there's been improvement'.[118] The problem for Brown, with all New Labour's public service reforms, is whether the electorate thinks there has been enough improvement, given the additional taxpayers' money invested in education and health. As the aforementioned trends in opinion polls suggest, the legacy of a decade of constrained discretion is not necessarily promising.

CONCLUSION

After a decade of constant reform and significant investment in the public services, Gordon Brown was able to point to a major legacy. For example, by 2007–2008 (compared with 1997–1998), health spending in the United Kingdom would be eighty-five per cent higher in real terms. Where a quarter of a million patients were waiting for more than six months for an operation when New Labour took power in May 1997, a decade later almost no one had to wait that long.[119] Despite this investment, as the trend in the public opinion polls has suggested, there remains widespread public dissatisfaction at the dividends of a decade of reform.

This is understandable, given the regularity with which the media has been presented with reports questioning the efficiency and equity of the allocation of public resources. Public confidence is unlikely to be enhanced when a parliamentary select committee identifies that, despite record investment and succession of massively expensive administrative reorganisations, the Department of Health still lacks the present-year information needed to manage NHS finances 'in the most effective manner'. Within the wider NHS, 'there is a lack of financial management expertise ... a need to strengthen communication between those responsible for the finances and for the delivery of local health services'.[120] Such weaknesses in financial management and accounting led to a £560 million shortfall in 2005–2006 of the resources needed for the 'Agenda for Change' pay initiative. This resulted in an overall deficit for the NHS in England, at a time of record real terms investment.

This is not a proud legacy of a decade of the Treasury's model of constrained discretion. The nationalisation of policy design and resource allocation in England meant that public services in general, and the NHS in England in particular, had become ever more centralised. Patricia Hewitt, the former Secretary of State for Health acknowledged that with its net budget for England planned at 90.7 billion for 2007–2008:

> If the NHS were a country, it would be the 33rd biggest economy in the world, larger than new European Union transition economies like Romania and Bulgaria ... The NHS is four times the size of the Cuban economy and more centralised.[121]

While it may have suited the Treasury, little in organisational theory or empirical evidence suggested that maintaining such a centralised structure could necessarily plan policy, allocate resources or deliver services in the most effective manner. There was also the additional legacy of the huge deficit in, and cost to, democratic citizenship rights which constrained discretion bequeathed to the people of England. There has been taxation but insufficient representation of the views of citizens in their communities. As one parliamentary select committee concluded, 'with the powers already conferred on unaccountable regional bodies there is a democratic deficit and with the existing devolution of powers and resource allocation to Scotland, Wales and Greater London', devolution in England must be addressed'.[122]

Despite a decade of frenetic reform, it is evident that the pace of renewal of the public services in England is not going to slacken under the Brown Government. On the contrary, he has indicated that the intensity of reform will, if anything, increase under his leadership. Brown wholeheartedly endorsed the Blair Government's Policy Review of the public services; therefore, in future, citizens will experience public services that are 'increasingly personalised to meet their needs'. The vision that Brown has embraced is of government creation of 'self-improving institutions of public service, independent of centralised state control, drawing on the best of public, private and third sector provision ... a new concept of modern public services: one built around the user of the service'.[123] This choice-based vision is rooted in the belief that 'the UK is also now a consumer society', in which consumers are 'highly educated and sophisticated'.[124]

It is also a vision for England's public services founded on the empowerment of individuals through deliberative forums and participation in third-party organisations, rather than through the extension of citizenship rights via directly elected, devolved institutions, as in the other constituent nations of the United Kingdom.[125] The Treasury hopes that a greater reliance on voluntary organisations, families and individual responsibility for the provision of social welfare will reduce the future burden on the hard-pressed taxpayer. The need to limit the tax burden on corporations and entrepreneurs, to maintain their international competitiveness in global markets, is being used as a powerful rhetorical device to reduce expectations of the role of the state in service provision. The role of the voluntary sector is being championed as a source of individual and community empowerment, an effective partnership between the state, society and the individual and a means of enhancing the moral virtues of duty and service to others.[126]

The danger for the future of the public services is that this model has overly focussed on the individual as consumer and is too far removed from the public domain of citizenship, equity and public service. The Brown Government has trusted individual consumer choice, the entrepreneurship of private corporations and the social entrepreneurship of voluntary organisations as the prime agents of reform and modernisation in the public services. This risks perpetuating the hollowing out of democratic citizenship and public trust in England. Citizens will only trust the public domain if they believe that public services are governed by an ethic of equity and service.[127] If people believe that the provision of health care and education is governed by an ethic of competition and profiteering no different from services provided in private markets, even more Labour Party members and voters may desert a political party whose history is bound up so closely with the provision of public goods and services by public agencies.

The good news for Gordon Brown was that there was early evidence of a (at least short-term) 'leadership bounce' in public opinion on the reform of public services, before he became Prime Minister. This trend continued during the early weeks of his government. The Ipsos MORI May 2007 Government Delivery Index reported that the number of people agreeing that the government's policies would improve the state of Britain's public services had risen to thirty-eight per cent, while the number disagreeing had fallen to fifty-one per cent. This meant that the figure for net optimism had improved to –fourteen per cent, compared to –thirty per cent in March 2007. Specifically, the net optimism figure for the NHS had improved to –fourteen per cent (twenty-four per cent versus thirty-eight per cent). However, there was be no room for complacency; the net optimism figure for the quality of education had fallen from nine per cent to seven per cent.[128]

The public's priorities remained the same during the early weeks of the Brown Government as they were during the decade of the Blair Government. In May 2007, a YouGov poll found that cutting NHS bureaucracy was the highest-ranked objective for the Brown Government, with eighty-seven per cent of people advocating it. Eighty-eight per cent of respondents thought it desirable that a Brown Government should focus on policy and delivery, not celebrity, seventy-six per cent that pharmacists should be able to carry out routine procedures such as blood-pressure tests, seventy-two per cent that general practitioners should be required to extend the opening hours of their surgeries and seventy per cent that arrangements should be made for school pupils who struggle with mathematics to have one-to-one tuition.[129]

The greatest challenge confronting the Brown Government remains its capacity to meet the public's high expectations of what public services can deliver for them as individuals. The greatest political legacy of a decade of reforms in England's public services – reforms that enhanced the role of the individual as consumer within internal markets and through competition among providers but weakened the ethic of public service – is that people now expect a lot more. They have paid more tax. They want more for it. If the Brown Government does not deliver, the next General Election could be lost on the key battlegrounds of health and education.

Chapter 5

The British Way of Identity and Citizenship

INTRODUCTION

During the Blair Government's second term, one of the most conspicuous features of Gordon Brown's speeches was his gradual switch from a preoccupation with macro-economic stability and fiscal prudence to a fixation with Britain and Britishness. Recent speeches to the annual Labour Party Conference were replete with references to Britain, Great Britain or Britishness (fifty-nine in 2003, fifty-one in 2004, fifty-four in 2005 and forty-two in 2006). Whether at home, attending the 'Great Britons' Awards or delivering the British Council Annual Lecture or abroad, during visits to Africa, Brown missed no opportunity to associate himself with Britain and Britishness. To restore a shared sense of national patriotic purpose, which he believes Britain and the British to have lost, in various speeches he has proposed a series of measures, including the establishment of a British youth national community service, a British Day, the reclaiming of the Union flag 'as a flag for Britain, not the British National Party' to be honoured and not ignored, a National Veterans' Day, the introduction of a biometric British National card, and English language and British history lessons for immigrants.[1]

In this chapter, I shall explore the definition and rationale of the British Way and consider its fundamental flaws. The 'British Way' is Brown's attempt to refine the political asymmetries of citizenship, identity and power that arise from the unique nature of the British Union and have been deepened by the Blair Government's constitutional reforms in general and its devolution agenda in particular. It is also Gordon Brown's means of maintaining the unprecedented Treasury control over policy design and resource allocation in England that was entrenched during Brown's tenure as Chancellor of the Exchequer and will be maintained during his time as Prime Minister.

The British Way is fundamentally flawed: not only did the Blair Government fail to deliver (in England) its tenets but it is also sustained by historical illustrations and literary references that are almost exclusively about England and Englishness, conflated or misconstrued to become examples of Britishness and British history. Brown has attempted to confine expressions of English identity to the realm of sport but his attempts to ingratiate himself with English football supporters have led to ridicule.

The legacy of the British Way is to have denied the citizens of England the liberty for all, responsibility from all and fairness to all that Brown has identified as the defining characteristics of Britishness. The historical and literary examples Brown has used to substantiate it actually point towards the possibility of an alternative 'English Way', based on an inclusive civic identity and a devolved and more plural approach to politics, policy design and resource allocation.

THE BRITISH WAY: LIBERTY FOR ALL, RESPONSIBILITY FROM ALL, FAIRNESS TO ALL

From the beginning of the Blair Government in May 1997, the New Labour project was characterised by significant similarities and differences in the politics and political economies of Gordon Brown and Tony Blair. One notable difference was the manner in which Brown deliberately shunned the concept of the 'Third Way'. He used the term only once, in an early speech on Britain's role in Europe where 'the third way of economic reform' was contrasted with New Labour's rejection of 'both the federal way and the regulatory way ahead'.[2]

In ideological and rhetorical terms, as I tried to show in Chapters Two and Three, the quintessential characteristic of the British Way is the liberalism of the political philosophy and economy which underpins it. The British Way does not reflect the history and ideas of the Labour Party and its socialist and social democratic traditions; Brown has drawn much more heavily on liberalism, citing the work of John Locke, Adam Smith, Alexis de Tocqueville, John Stuart Mill, T. H. Green and J. A. Hobson. On one notable occasion, when the British Way did actually draw on the work of a prominent socialist, Brown wrongly attributed the quotation 'a poverty of aspirations' to Aneurin Bevan; as Alan Johnson noted, it was in fact said by Ernest Bevin.[3]

As I showed in Chapter Two, Brown has used Himmelfarb's analysis of the paths to modernity in Britain, the United States and France to highlight the superiority of the British reformist 'sociology of virtue', rooted in Enlightenment liberal moral philosophy and characterised by a social ethic and moral sense, over its American 'politics of liberty' and French 'ideology of reason' rivals. Himmelfarb argued that Adam Smith's moral vision of political economy is characteristic of the contemporary United States and has supported George W. Bush's Administration's vision of compassionate conservatism.[4] Brown has endorsed the work of the one of the most prominent American conservative philosophers, James Q. Wilson, precisely because he draws on the Enlightenment notions of moral sentiments and moral sense.[5]

Another salient feature of Brown's British Way, visible during his tenure as Shadow Chancellor and Chancellor of the Exchequer, was his very distinct statecraft. The desire to micro-manage and centrally prescribe policy design and resource allocation in England placed Brown firmly in the technocratic tradition of managerial modernisers. The British Way does not contemplate or sanction the 'marked bias towards individual autonomy' characteristic of Dennis and Halsey's description of English ethical socialism as 'a theory of personality and society which places moral motivation as the mainspring of individual conduct and social organisation'.[6] While maintaining the link between moral motivation and human conduct, only rarely has the British Way drawn on the work of R. H. Tawney or other Labour Party thinkers.[7] Nor have Brown's examples of best practice in public policy or civil society been drawn from the European social democratic tradition. On the contrary, his notion of 'moral sense' comes from liberalism and the thinking of Adam Smith and Adam Ferguson, while the British Way's examples of best practice in civil society have been predominantly North American.

The thesis of the British Way was developed first in Brown's November 1997 Spectator/Allied Dunbar Lecture. Rejecting both the idea of the declining relevance of national identity and the alternative political project of supranational federalism, Brown sought to define British identity in terms of a distinct national character and three 'qualities of a people, of the collective experience they have shared over time'. First, the British Way was manifest in a commitment to liberty through the protection of the individual against the arbitrary power of the state. This was achieved not by the pursuit of crude individualism but by the exercise of mutual responsibility and duty, initially through civil society associations and latterly through the welfare state and NHS. Second, the British Way was adaptable, including the willingness 'to embrace, not fear, constitutional reform ... to break up centralised institutions that are too remote and insensitive and so devolve power'. Third, the British Way was to pursue an outward-looking and internationalist patriotism.[8]

Brown did not develop this theme further until April 1999, when, in a speech at the Smith Institute, he claimed that 'throughout the centuries' the British Way had been 'to foster a uniquely rich and continuously evolving relationship between individual community and state, a strong vibrant civil society where there is opportunity for all'. Casting aside the narrower neo-liberal and Thatcherite concept of Britishness as individualism, the shared British values to be rediscovered were 'creative enterprise and hard work, of outward-looking tolerance and fairness' and also 'public service and a practical outward-looking internationalism'. Brown conceded that these values were 'not necessarily unique' to Britain but none the less, their combination could give rise to 'a special and unifying identity'. Through the rediscovery of these values, Britain could move 'from an over-centralised and uniform state – the old Britain of subjects – to a pluralist and decentralised democracy – the new Britain of citizens'.[9]

However, the definitive statement on the British Way was not articulated until July 2004, when Brown gave the British Council Annual Lecture. In his speech, he sought to weave what he depicted as three muscular and robust 'core values of Britishness' with three distinct national qualities. These six values and qualities: 'being creative, adaptable and outward looking, our belief in liberty, duty and fair play' had, he declared, combined to fashion both 'a distinctive Britishness' and a unique British political settlement, balancing the rights and responsibilities of individuals, communities and the state.[10]

Brown further asserted that these values and qualities should be mobilised both to organise Britain's institutions and to generate a specific political agenda. First, the 'British desire for liberty' and its attendant 'strong sense of civic duty and fair play', which had engendered the British Way of encouraging and enhancing the status of voluntary and community organisations, should now be used to 'refashion the settlement between individual, community and government'. Second, to complement and augment the British Way's restoration and enhancement of local initiative and mutual responsibility in civic affairs, the local institutions of government should be strengthened 'to empower people in their own neighbourhoods'. Third, the British Way's strong sense of duty, fair play and commitment to public service should be harnessed to make citizenship serious.

For Brown, this meant a national debate about the responsibilities and rights of citizenship, embracing 'new literature, new institutes, new seminars, new cross-party debate' and the reclaiming of the Union flag from the British National Party to become 'a flag for all Britain – symbolising inclusion, tolerance and unity'. Britishness would embrace a commitment to 'liberty for all and responsibility from all but fairness to all'.[11]

A MATTER OF POLITICAL ASYMMETRY

One of the principal motives for Brown's increasingly frequent promulgation of his British Way is simple electoral arithmetic. In the seventeen United Kingdom General Elections held since 1945, the Labour Party has won a majority of seats in England on only five occasions (1945, 1966, 1997, 2001 and 2005). Its average of 241 seats and 40.8 per cent of the vote in England compares with the Conservative Party's average of 262 seats and 43.3 per cent of the vote. In the 1997 and 2001 General Elections, the Labour Party won almost twice as many seats in England as the Conservative Party. However, at the 2005 General Election, in winning 286 seats (thirty-seven fewer than in 2001), the Labour Party polled 65,000 fewer votes than the Conservatives. Should it lose a further twenty-one seats at the next General Election, to have a majority on any legislation affecting England the Labour Party would have to rely on its (currently sixty-eight) MPs from Scottish and Welsh constituencies or the votes of other political parties. Such a scenario would appear unsustainable.

While this might have been tolerated in pre-devolution times, Brown appears to comprehend only too readily that this is unlikely to be the case post-devolution. Having campaigned at the 2001 and 2005 General Elections with the policy of 'English votes for English Laws', the Conservative Party has increasingly questioned the legitimacy of the Brown-led Labour Party's right to govern England while holding only a minority of English seats.[12] In February 2006, in a speech entitled 'Modernisation with a purpose' (aping Brown's frequent references to 'prudence with a purpose'), David Cameron announced the creation of a Democracy Task Force, chaired by the former leadership candidate Kenneth Clarke MP.[13] The Task Force addressed a number of key constitutional questions, including the case for equality arising from 'the West Lothian Question (or more accurately) the English question'.[14] Brown has seized every available opportunity to deflect demands for English devolution by trying to convince the English that their political identity must be British and that they should not demand the equivalent political and citizenship rights to their compatriots within the British Union. His task has been made more difficult by a series of hostile opinion polls. For example, an ICM opinion poll in May 2006 showed that fifty-five per cent of those questioned in England (and fifty-two per cent in the United Kingdom) opposed the idea of an MP for a Scottish constituency becoming Prime Minister.[15]

Public disquiet had been fuelled by the thousands of job losses and budget deficits in the NHS in England, a pattern conspicuous by its absence elsewhere in the United Kingdom. The Government would have lost important votes on policies for England (notably health and social care in July and November 2003 and higher education in January and March 2004) had voting been restricted to English MPs. The ban on smoking in public places in England was affected by the votes of 93 MPs from other parts of the United Kingdom. Above all, Tony Blair's final Cabinet contained the anomaly of John Reid, Home Secretary (and former Health Secretary), with responsibility for prisons, police and the criminal justice system in England but not in his native Scotland and Douglas Alexander, Transport Secretary, responsible for England's railways, roads and airports but not those in his Paisley and Renfrewshire constituency.

These imbalances in accountability highlight the peculiar political asymmetries of the United Kingdom. England accounts for almost eighty-four per cent of the UK's population and almost eighty-six per cent of its income. If England were an independent state, its population of 50.1 million and GDP of £861 billion (figures from 2004) would make it both one of the largest member states of the European Union and a prospective member state of the G7/G8. Yet paradoxically, within the British Union, England has not enjoyed an identity as a distinct political community. As an adjunct of the British state (and as the Encyclopædia Britannica states), 'Constitutionally, England does not exist'.[16] This lack of identity ferments the long-standing discontent over the iniquities of the Barnett Formula, the pre-Thatcherite mechanism for the territorial allocation of public spending between the constituent nations of the United Kingdom, which was left unchanged by the legion of reforms unleashed by Brown's British model of fiscal policy. A further source of discontent is that, on a strictly pro rata basis, England's population should be represented by 549 rather than 529 Westminster constituencies. These asymmetries made for a potent undercurrent of English discontentment under the three-hundredth anniversary (in 2006) of the Union of the English and Scottish Parliaments.

The implications of these asymmetries were acknowledged in 1973, when the report of the Royal Commission on the Constitution concluded that such political asymmetries could not be redressed by a United Kingdom federation, with a federal Parliament and a Parliament in each of the constituent countries, because of domination by 'the overwhelming political importance and wealth of England'. Nor could the constitutional imbalances embraced by the United Kingdom be corrected by artificially dividing England into a number of federal provinces of equal status; 'this would be unacceptable to the people of England'.[17] The accompanying Memorandum of Dissent pointed out that to grant significant additional political rights to Scotland and Wales, while denying them to the people of England, would result in an inequality of political rights that would not be 'right or acceptable'.[18]

THE NEGATION OF CITIZENSHIP IN ENGLAND

The British Way has fashioned a uniquely British political settlement. It has balanced rights and responsibilities such that citizens and communities in England are denied the opportunity of an autonomous democratic voice and accountability which the devolved institutions have provided elsewhere in the United Kingdom. Interviewed in the *Guardian* in February 2006, Brown promised 'more power for individuals and for neighbourhoods' but used his May 1997 policy choice of 'making the Bank of England independent' as a specific example of the executive both giving up power and building trust in the public realm. Brown claimed that Britain was ready 'to shape a new constitutional settlement' based on 'a new compact between the local and the national and between the executive and the legislature'. This in turn would be based on 'the primacy of the Commons and the enhanced accountability of the second chamber'.[19]

This constitutional settlement merits closer scrutiny. The Bank of England is not independent. The Monetary Policy Committee (of nine appointed, not elected members), exercises a degree of administrative autonomy over the setting of interest rates but only within the monetary policy framework and inflation target laid down by the Treasury and the Chancellor of the Exchequer. What Brown presented as devolution of political power was, in practice, a delegation of administrative responsibility that provided Brown with an institutional alibi for unpopular economic policies. Brown claimed that the 'British idea of liberty' had found new strength through 'the empowerment of each individual' and through responsibility being exercised through 'new forms of active civic engagement'.[20] However, there could never be a new compact between the national and the local in England until the central executive devolved political power (as opposed to merely administrative responsibility) to directly elected local governments, democratically accountable to local citizens and with no centrally pre-scribed performance indicators and output targets.

Speaking in 2001, Brown's solution to his English conundrum was 'a Britain of regions and nations', which divides (and thereby conquers) England's political identity as a discrete nation.[21] In his vision, the nations are Scotland, Wales and Britain; the regions are England's. England does not – and must not – exist as an autonomous distinct political community. In an address to the 2005 Sustainable Communities Summit in Manchester, Brown asserted that regional policy was entering a third phase, in which 'the top-down centralised systems of regional and urban policy – the *dirigiste* systems of the mid-twentieth century' would be set aside, in favour of local indigenous capacity'. Brown promised that 'the Treasury and central government generally will continue to devolve power away from the centre'.[22] However, to illustrate this 'true devolution of power', Brown cited the examples of the Regional Development Agencies, the Northern Way, the pilot Local Area Agreements, Sure Start, the New Deal for Communities and the Safer Communities Initiative. The common denominator of these

English (not British nor United Kingdom) initiatives was that they had all been designed by central government and operated within the constrained discretion demanded by the Treasury. Brown's periodically-stated commitment to the reinvigoration of elected local government and to increase openness and transparency by 'reforming undemocratic institutions'[23] (specifically the House of Lords) would leave his power as Prime Minister and that of the Treasury in England unchecked. Local government would continue to function within the national framework of Spending Reviews and Public Service Agreements. The House of Lords would remain a subordinate revising chamber. The British Way envisaged that the identity of England as a nation would be limited to the cultural and sporting.

THE KIRKCALDY AND COWDENBEATH QUESTION

Tam Dalyell MP first posed the 'West Lothian Question' in pre-devolution 1977; the question is a modern incarnation of Gladstone's travails over Irish 'Home Rule'. Dalyell described the 'absurd situation' of MPs representing Scottish constituencies being able to vote on areas of policy affecting England, when MPs representing English constituencies would not be able to exercise similar political rights in the Scottish Parliament.[24]

The political asymmetries and postcode lottery in democratic accountability and citizenship fostered by the Blair Governments' constitutional reforms created the post-devolution 'Kirkcaldy and Cowdenbeath Question', to which the British Way was to become Brown's answer. Why should Brown or any member of the Westminster Parliament representing a Scottish (or Welsh or Northern Irish) constituency, be able to exercise unchecked and unbalanced power (including voting rights) over the allocation of resources and the design of policies affecting the people of England, when those same policies do not directly affect their own constituents, their schools and hospitals and when the English electorate cannot directly vote them into or out of office?

The British Way is ultimately about the exercise of political power and the desire to maintain the unprecedented power that Brown's illiberal statecraft of 'constrained discretion' exercises over the design of policy and resource allocation in England, when devolution to the Scottish Parliament and Welsh Assembly denies him such power elsewhere. As Chapter Four illustrated, policy design in England was effectively nationalised through the Comprehensive Spending Reviews and the Biennial Spending Reviews and their accompanying Public Service Agreements. This was allied with New Labour's failure to remove caps on the finances of English local government and to reverse the centralisation (so steadfastly opposed by Old Labour in Opposition) enacted by the Thatcher and Major Governments. Any extension of English citizenship, political rights and genuine democratic autonomy would challenge the power of the Treasury and the right of Prime Minister Brown, as an MP for a Scots constituency, to govern England.

Brown has made the same political calculation as did Blair. Genuine political autonomy over policy and resources might be permissible in the heartlands of Scotland and Wales, where Labour is guaranteed its lion's share of seats but nothing more than administrative devolution can be countenanced in the more volatile marginal constituencies of southern England. Tony Blair's desire to maintain and deepen central control was defined in terms of the application of the concept of 'earned autonomy' to reform of public services. Devolution empowered 'locally-elected representatives to adopt approaches to public services reflecting their own national priorities and concerns' but in England alone Blair prescribed that 'devolved delivery can only operate with national standards and accountability'. By complying with this overall vision of centralised prescription over policy design and resource allocation, England's schools, hospitals, local government and other public services had 'earned autonomy' to administer 'by devolution and delegation to the front line'.[25]

For Brown, Treasury power was exercised through the application of the principle of 'constrained discretion' to the 'British Model' of fiscal policy. Through the biennial Spending Reviews and their accompanying Public Service Agreements, the Treasury was sanctioned only heavily-constrained administrative discretion (as opposed to genuine political autonomy) to public spending bodies in England, in accordance with the Treasury-determined spending totals, policy choices and performance indicators.[26] The price of fiscal discipline for England, purportedly to help maintain confidence among the City of London's investors, was to remove the autonomy and trust characteristic of the genuinely pluralistic and associative democracy envisaged by ethical socialists. For England, 'constrained discretion' was technocrat-speak for 'limited freedom' and the negation of English citizenship.

The constitutional imbalances in accountability and legitimacy raised by devolution in general, and the Cowdenbeath and Kirkcaldy Question in particular, were vividly illustrated by the fate of the project to establish a British youth national community service, modelled on the United States' AmeriCorps. On 17 May 2004, Gordon Brown and the then Home Secretary David Blunkett announced the creation of a commission chaired by the then Chief Executive of Scottish Power, Ian Russell (an interesting choice to lead a commission whose work was intended to help strengthen British identity, given that in March 2002 Russell had led thousands of bagpipers in a St Andrew's Day parade through the streets of New York). The Russell Commission was asked to draw up plans for a national community service scheme for young people. Brown had intended the 'national' element of the Commission's work to mean 'British'. However, the Commission's work was pre-empted by the Scottish Executive's launch, a week earlier on 11 May, of 'Project Scotland', a national youth volunteering programme for sixteen to twenty-five year old Scots.

Launching the 'ScotsCorps' programme, Jack McConnell, Scotland's First Minister, stated that Project Scotland was intended to enable Scotland 'to move from a culture of dependence to a culture of responsibility' and to help young Scots to show their national pride and display 'the kind of Scotland that our country will become'.[27] There was no mention of any desire to promote a civic British identity to complement a new Scottish identity. Ironically, one of the founding corporate partners of Project Scotland was Scottish Power and one of the project's principal supporters was none other than Ian Russell. He justified his company's sponsorship as 'the chance to help young Scots attain their fullest potential and the opportunity to invest in people now in order to improve our nation's future competitiveness'.[28]

One Scot (Brown) had commissioned another Scot (Russell), in charge of a Scottish company (Scottish Power), to produce a report on a United Kingdom volunteering project that would celebrate the values of a civic British identity, only for it to be pre-empted by another Scot (McConnell) and the Scottish Executive's own project on Scottish volunteering which celebrated instead the values of a civic Scottish (but not British) identity.

The peripheral nature of the influence of the Russell Commission's work on volunteering in Scotland and Wales was demonstrated by the fact that of the Commission's thirty-six public consultations, only one was held in Scotland and one in Wales.[29] When the Russell Commission published its report, *A National Framework for Youth Action and Engagement*, it did not acknowledge that the 'national' in its title now meant 'English', not 'British', because the devolved administrations in Scotland and Wales had chosen to pursue autonomous initiatives. The Commission conceded that its framework 'could be applied throughout the UK but the final decisions regarding implementation will rest with each administration'.[30] While the implementation of the Commission's work in England was to be funded by £45 million of public money matched with £55 million of private sponsorship, the devolved institutions were allocated £19.5 million for implementation. This – significantly more generous – allocation of public money was provided even though the devolved institutions had decided to set aside the Commission's work in favour of their own programmes, notably Project Scotland. Since the publication of the Russell Commission's report, a new charity – '*V*' – has been created to fund volunteering among 16–25 year olds. However, it is confined to developing close partnerships with voluntary organisations in England.

Thanks to devolution, the legacy of Gordon Brown's ambitions to promote civic British identity through a culture of volunteering is the highlighting of the manner in which devolution has constrained his power to intervene on questions of citizenship in England.

THE FLAWS OF THE BRITISH WAY

There are many further flaws in the British Way. Brown has asserted that it embraces adaptability, the willingness to embrace rather than fear constitutional change and the devolution of power, to break up remote, centralised institutions. In April 1999, Brown claimed that the whole of Britain would benefit from 'the birth of new centres of power and initiative'; that this new Britain would embrace a 'commitment to participatory democracy' and that it would be built on 'a new set of constitutional arrangements and a unifying and inclusive idea of citizenship'.[31] However, the greatest political asymmetry in and anomaly of devolution is that it has (so far) circumvented the vast majority of the electorate in England (and by extension, the United Kingdom). Only the electorate of Greater London has its own Mayor and Assembly, which leaves 86.4 per cent of England's electorate (72.3 per cent of the United Kingdom electorate) still beyond the pale of devolution. Even if the electorate of the North East of England is taken into account (an electorate which overwhelmingly rejected a Regional Assembly with few meaningful powers in a referendum in November 2004), devolution has still by-passed 81.2 per cent of England's voters and 68.0 per cent of the United Kingdom's electorate.

The British Way identifies the NHS as quintessentially British, where 'national is unquestionably "British" '.[32] This ignores the fact that, with the onset of devolution elsewhere, only in England does the internal market continue to operate. (Similarly, in relation to education, only in England have schools continued compulsory Standard Assessment Tests.) This is a significant divide in the reform of public services; for the NHS in England, 'national' now unquestionably means 'English', not 'British', unless the Government needs 'British' votes from Scots, Welsh and Northern Irish MPs to pass unpopular English reforms.

Further flaws and contradictions in the British Way arise in relation to the pursuit of an outward-looking and internationalist patriotism, which was criticised both at home and abroad. In the majority of his speeches about Britain and Britishness, Brown has tended to avoid the question of the legacy of the British Empire. However, in a speech at the British Museum, many of whose most important artefacts attest colonial plunder, Brown asserted that 'we should be proud ... of the empire'.[33] During a visit to Tanzania in January 2005, Brown told a BBC *Newsnight* film crew, 'the days of Britain having to apologise for our history are over ... we should celebrate much of our past rather than apologise for it and we should talk, rightly so, about British values'.[34] Brown specifically linked imperialism with enduring British values of enterprise and internationalism by claiming that the Empire gave Britain a greater global reach than any other country. Drawing on his belief in a moral sense of duty, Brown also asserted that missionaries had been driven to Africa by their particular sense of duty.[35]

The hostile reaction to Brown's defence of the British Empire was led by Thabo Mbeki, President of South Africa. Mbeki described Brown's comments as 'a real surprise and a matter for serious concern' and noted that the United Kingdom had never apologised to those whom it had colonised. Mbeki endorsed an alternative depiction of the British Empire: 'genocide, vast ethnic cleansing, slavery, rigorously enforced racial hierarchy and merciless exploitation'. As an alternative to Brown's vision, Mbeki preferred 'to celebrate those who campaigned for colonial freedom rather than the racist despotism they fought against'.[36] Brown's favourable disposition towards the Empire might be understandable in terms of the high profile of Scots in the Empire's construction but it is somewhat contradicted by his tendency regularly to cite the work of the English radical liberal theorist, J. A. Hobson, one of the greatest critics of imperialism.[37]

THE CONFLATION OF ENGLAND WITH BRITAIN

The most intriguing element of and greatest flaw in Brown's British Way is the extent to which it can only be sustained by drawing on examples of English history or writings specifically about England and the English and reinventing them as if they were about Britain and the British. For example, identifying the British affirmation of freedom and liberty and commitment to fairness for all, Brown cited the signing of the Magna Carta at Runnymede in 1215. He also quoted 'from early opposition to the first poll tax in 1381 to the second', 'the civil war debates – where Rainborough asserted that "the poorest he that is in England hath a life to live as the greatest he" ' and the Bill of Rights in 1689.[38] These are all examples of English history, predating the Act of Union and the creation of the United Kingdom.

While its historical significance and political, social and religious implications have been widely debated, the salient feature of the Peasants' Revolt of 1381 against the third poll tax (following those of 1377 and 1379) is that it was quintessentially English. It was a revolt led by Englishmen (notably Wat Tyler) against the English Exchequer's attempts to meet the costs of England's war with France and arose in the English counties of Essex, Kent, Norfolk, Suffolk and Hertfordshire and did not spread any further north than York, Beverley and Scarborough. Similarly, the Putney Debates of 1647 were conducted by the General Council of the New Model Army at the end of the first English Civil War. They were debates conducted among Englishmen about what actually constituted the English nation and had nothing to do with Britain or Britishness. The debates brought forward 'utterly irreconcilable notions of English particularity, what amounted to two different claim-rights to the kingdom, two different notions of what it was to be English'. Colonel Thomas Rainborough was a member of a very small Republican faction in the Commons who spoke up for the aspirations of ordinary English soldiers. He claimed that law limiting the franchise was 'the most tyrannical law under heaven'; pondering 'what we have fought for ... if it was not to free the population from "the old law of England ... that enslaves the people of England" '.[39]

The British Way is even more dependent on reinventing literary Englands as if they were about Britain and Britishness. Identifying liberty as the primary British value, Brown claimed that Voltaire said that Britain had given to the world the idea of liberty.[40] What Voltaire actually wrote in his *Letters concerning the English nation* was that 'the civil wars of *Rome* ended in slavery and those of the *English* in liberty. The *English* are the only people on earth who have been able to prescribe limits to the power of Kings by resisting them'. Moreover, Voltaire noted that the English were 'not only jealous of their own Liberty but even of that of other nations'[41]. Voltaire identified an essentially English tradition that had nothing to do with Britain or Britishness. In his July 2004 British Council lecture, Brown also cited Montesquieu's statement that 'ours was "the freest country in the world" '.[42] 'Ours' was not Britain. Montesquieu wrote, about England and its constitution, 'England is the freest country in the world'.[43] Cronk, in his 1994 'Introduction' to Voltaire's *Letters*, describes their true importance as that they constitute 'the earliest expression of Enlightenment thinking' and describe 'the rise of empiricism from Bacon to Locke as an English phenomenon in opposition to the French tradition of rationalism'.[44] Likewise Montesquieu, because of his focus on the effectiveness of the balance of power and checks and balances in its constitution and the importance of its commerce to its general spirit, has been described by Pangle, in *Montesquieu's Philosophy of Liberalism* as 'the most influential foreign champion that England ever had'.[45]

Brown further suggested that Edmund Burke's 'little platoons' reflected 'both a British desire for liberty and a strong sense of civic duty and fair play'. However, when Burke stated that 'to love the little platoon we belong to in society, is the first principle (the germ as it were) of public affections', he was comparing revolutionary France specifically with England, and his native Ireland, rather than Britain.[46] In asserting that the superiority in the wealth of England, compared with pre-revolutionary France, could be attributed to the English form of government, Burke specified 'I speak of England, not of the whole British dominion'. When the nation contemplated the French revolutionary model of government, Burke was also adamant that the nation 'must feel as Englishmen and feeling, we must provide as Englishmen'.[47] Burke sought to advance a conservative nationalism, based on 'the whole representative majesty of the whole English nation', to counter a flourishing radical Enlightenment version of English nationalism. Despite his Irishness, Burke sought not only to become 'an *embodiment* of the English national character' (Furniss, in *Cementing the Nation*) but also to redefine that national character, based on a reinvention of the English constitution.[48] That reinvention embodied an explicit rejection of the 1689 Bill of Rights, which Brown had identified as an exemplar of the British 'golden thread of liberty'. Far from Burke's work amounting to an endorsement of the Act of Union between Britain and Ireland, if the predictions about the dangers of the future in Burke's *Reflections on the Revolution in France* are taken seriously, the Act of Union can be seen as 'a disruptive and even revolutionary moment' and 'a precarious political gesture'.[49]

   Constructing the British Way, Brown misquoted or misrepresented as exemplars of British qualities and values, literature about England and Englishness provided by Thomas Gray, William Wordsworth, William Hazlitt, Lord Henry Grattan, Alexis de Tocqueville, George Orwell and Winston Churchill. To illustrate both the triumph of human spirit and the tragic waste of human potential in British history, Brown elected to cite Thomas Gray's *Elegy in a Country Churchyard* and its reference to 'Some mute inglorious Milton'.[50] To celebrate Britishness, Brown had chosen an English elegy, by an English poet, written in an English rustic setting. Referring to another English poet, William Wordsworth's 'flood of British freedom', Brown did not indicate that the quote came from a poem entitled *England, 1802.* In this particular poem, Wordsworth declared, 'Milton! Thou shouldst be living at this hour: England hath need of thee' and duly summoned up a string of English authors, including Shakespeare.[51] Brown also cited the English political essayist William Hazlitt: 'we have and can have "no privilege or advantage over other nations but liberty" '.[52] Hazlitt's exact words were not 'we' (Britons) but 'an Englishman has no distinguishing virtue but honesty: he has and can have no privilege or advantage over other nations but liberty. If he is not free, he is the worst of slaves, for he is nothing else'.[53]

   Another prominent example of misquotation and misrepresentation in the cause of the construction of New Unionism came when Brown noted that the nineteenth-century Irish statesman Lord Grattan said, 'we can get a Parliament from anywhere ... we can only get liberty from England'.[54] A member of the Irish Parliament (and who served as a member of the British Parliament for fifteen years until his death in June 1820), Henry Grattan actually said, 'you can get a king anywhere, but England is the only country with whom you can participate in a free Constitution'.[55] This statement formed part of Grattan's famous 'Declaration' speech to the Irish Parliament of the 16 April 1872.[56] It was not a tribute to British liberty was but an impassioned demand for Irish freedom and legislative independence from Great Britain. The following month, the Lord Lieutenant, the Duke of Portland, proclaimed that the British legislature had agreed a resolution to remove the causes of Irish discontents and jealousies. This led to the repeal of both the English Declaratory Act, which had asserted the right of Westminster to legislate for Ireland and the Irish Act (Poynings' Law), which had meant that all bills passed in the Irish Parliament, with the exception of money bills, were subject to revision by the Privy Council of England.[57]

Delivering the 2005 Hugo Young Memorial Lecture, Brown cited the French political philosopher, Alexis de Tocqueville. Brown claimed that de Tocqueville had identified civic associations 'at the heart of America'.[58] In fact, in Democracy in America, de Tocqueville stated that 'the right of association was imported from England ... the liberty of association has become a necessary guarantee against the tyranny of the majority'.[59] Throughout, de Tocqueville's comparison was between America and England, rather than America and Britain; he saw a symbiotic relationship between political association and civic association, contending that 'civil associations, therefore, facilitate political association; but, on the other hand, political association singularly strengthens and improves associations for civil purposes'.[60] While Brown's British Way had permitted civic associations to sit alongside political associations in his native Scotland, strengthened and deepened through the restoration of the Scottish Parliament, Brown's vision of English democracy championed civic association but negated any suggestion of political association through English devolution: such a move would challenge the power and authority of constrained discretion. Paradoxically, de Tocqueville noted that England had never centralised its administration and believed that centralisation in nations could only exist 'by incessantly diminishing their local spirit'.[61]

Brown's use, and misquotation, of the work of George Orwell to substantiate the British Way is particularly important, because Orwell is the only significant figure from the Labour Party's history of ideas who Brown quotes regularly. Brown claimed that 'Orwell talked of a Britain known to the world for its "decency" ' and believed Britain in 1951 was 'still a country of fixed certainties – echoing Orwell's *Lion and the Unicorn*. In this book, Orwell asserted, 'in England such concepts as justice, liberty and objective truth are still believed in'.[62] Orwell subtitled that particular work, *Socialism and the English Genius* but Brown referred to, 'in Orwell's words, the British genius'.[63] Orwell had not been making a statement about British qualities; the work relentlessly focuses on England and Englishness. *The Lion and the Unicorn* ends with an essay on 'The English Revolution', which concludes that:

> ... the task of the bringing the real England to the surface, even the winning of the war, necessary though it is, is secondary ... I believe in England and I believe that we shall go forward.[64]

Gordon Brown's challenge as Prime Minister is that he believes in Britain and that it will go forward, at a time when a decreasing percentage of the population share his perspective. Brown looked for inspiration to the last Westminster major speech of a previous Prime Minister, Sir Winston Churchill. However, Churchill did not, as Brown claimed, state that Britain is defined by its sense of fair play.[65] Churchill made a speech on defence policy, in which he reaffirmed his government's commitment to the development of the hydrogen bomb and the maintenance of powerful conventional armed forces within the framework of the North Atlantic Treaty Organisation. He concluded it by hoping that 'the day may dawn when fair play, love for one's fellow men, respect for justice and freedom, will enable tormented generations to march forth serene and triumphant from the hideous epoch in which we have to dwell'.[66] Brown might also reflect on the fact that Churchill once said, 'there is a forgotten, nay almost forbidden word, which means more to me than any other. That word is England'.[67] The more he tries to forget or forbid it as the basis for an alternative national and political identity to Britain and Britishness, the more likely it will be that England will return to haunt Gordon Brown.

BROWN'S INGRATIATION OF THE SPORTING ENGLISH

One of Gordon Brown's principal tactics for diluting resurgent English nationalism and avoiding the possibility that it will develop into a political consciousness is to confine expressions of English identity to sport and culture. Since November 2005, he has sought to lead England's bid for the 2018 World Cup, just as Tony Blair successfully led the British bid for the 2012 Olympics. The Treasury has intruded on the Department for Culture, Media and Sport's responsibility for English football by conducting jointly with it a feasibility study on England's capacity to host the World Cup. When the study's report was published, in February 2007, it was carefully framed within a Unionist, United Kingdom-centric discourse. Instead of focusing on England's capacity, the study began by stating (in bold type), 'There is little doubt that the UK has the ability, capacity and reputation to host large sporting events'.[68]

The report's principal findings included the (not remotely Earth-shattering) revelations that:

> ... hosting the World Cup is likely to produce a positive economic impact as well as other associated intangible benefits ... there are at least eleven existing football stadia in England that could potentially host World Cup matches – with Wembley National Stadium providing a centrepiece ... there is a solid foundation of public support for England pursuing a bid for hosting a World Cup in 2018.[69]

There can be few better examples of an expensively commissioned report using taxpayers' money to state the patently obvious, for example, that fifty-six per cent of people were in favour of England making a World Cup bid.[70] Moreover, the study had no tangible output other than to provide 'a basis for further work by The FA to establish whether or not a bid to host the future World Cup should be made'.[71] The report merely served as a vehicle and platform for Brown to intrude on English sport.

Brown has also attempted to ingratiate himself with English football supporters and fans. Asked during a visit to Mumbai which team he would support should England's bid for the 2018 World Cup be successful, initially Brown answered 'I think the host'. When questioned, 'Not Scotland?', Brown responded, 'Well, of course, I want Scotland to do well but let's just see how it all works out'.[72] An embarrassed Brown later issued a statement that 'my ideal scenario is that Scotland play England in the final and Scotland win ... But if we don't qualify or we go out in an earlier round, then I would transfer my allegiance to the other home nation, England'. The absurdity of Brown's position had been exposed. To Alex Salmond, the leader of the Scottish National Party, Brown's comments had made him look 'ridiculous in Scotland and insincere in England'.[73]

During the 2006 World Cup, Scottish Cabinet ministers were surveyed to establish whether they would be supporting England (Scotland having failed to qualify for the tournament). Brown claimed that one of his favourite moments in football was Paul Gascoigne's goal in England's victory over Scotland at Wembley during the Euro '96 Championship. Brown also asserted that more than sixty per cent of Scots would be supporting England's attempt to win the World Cup. The Euro '96 match, together with England's 1997 draw against Italy in a World Cup qualifier in Rome, had been 'the most memorable' England games he had attended.[74]

Brown was the only Scottish Cabinet minister who did not refuse to answer the survey. His comments were met with incredulity by his own countrymen. Alex Salmond warned that 'real English football fans will begin to smell a rat'. Brown's comments were also described as 'a load of rubbish' and an electoral stunt by Turnbull Hutton, the Scottish businessman and former chairman of Raith Rovers, the Scottish League Division Two team based in Brown's constituency. Brown had helped Hutton to save Raith from bankruptcy in December 2005.[75]

Brown's claims appear even more incredible when his contribution to a 1994 collection of essays on football is taken into account. (One of the co-editors of the collection was Alistair Campbell, Tony Blair's future chief 'spin doctor'.) In their essays, MPs spelt out their devotion to football as 'The People's Game'. Brown's contribution was entitled 'Why Scotland Means The World To Me' and included the confession, 'you start young and you can't give up supporting Scotland', which makes a complete mockery of his 1997 claim about Gascoigne's goal in Euro '96.[76] Brown also celebrated the invasion and destruction of the Wembley pitch by Scottish supporters following Scotland's victory over England in the 1977 Home International Championship. Attributing 'the burden of national pride' carried by the Scottish football team on behalf of 'a country that was denied its own parliament', Brown also claimed 'English nationalism flowered on the playing fields of Eton', apparently referring to the reasons for the victory at the Battle of Waterloo wrongly attributed to Arthur Wellesley, the Duke of Wellington.[77] Subsequently, Brown denied that the political settlement that devolved power to the Scottish Parliament, the National Assembly for Wales and the Northern Ireland Assembly should extend to an English parliament. This has fuelled a resurgent English nationalism that extends far beyond the former officer class at Eton.

Brown has vocally supported the idea of a Great Britain football team, which Jack Straw, Brown's campaign manager for the Labour Party leadership, has proposed on a number of occasions. In November 2000, Straw stated, 'I personally look forward to the day when we have a British football team. I think we might start winning some games'.[78] Straw's suggestion was dismissed by Number 10 as a 'personal view' and rejected elsewhere with near universal and vehement condemnation, especially from Scotland.[79] This degree of hostility towards the idea of a Great Britain football team has not diminished. The Scottish Football Association and Football Association of Wales have ruled out their participation in a Great Britain team at the 2012 London Olympics.[80] In the politics of world football, the national associations of the United Kingdom have fought long and vigorously to retain their identity and the right to compete separately, rather than as a single Great Britain or United Kingdom team. The maintenance of four national teams also gives the associations the right to elect one of the vice-presidents of world football's governing body, FIFA. The idea is also loathed by representatives of supporters' organisations, who have no affinity with a politically contrived Great Britain team; it has never featured in the supporters' blueprint for the future of football.[81] In England and Wales, a poll conducted by the Football Supporters' Federation showed fifty-three per cent did not support a combined Home Nations' team.[82]

Beyond football, the 2012 London Olympics has assumed enormous importance to Brown's project to regenerate the United Kingdom and Britishness. In an attempt to avoid the possibility that the Olympics will be seen by the rest of the United Kingdom as a project solely for Londoners, the only consequence of which will be the diversion of £2.175 billion of National Lottery funding away from more worthy good causes, Brown announced two new initiatives in his 2006 Budget statement. First, before the 2012 Olympics, there would be a United Kingdom Schools' Olympics and second, there would be funding of thirty four million pounds for a new National Sports Federation (NSF).

The problem with these initiatives is that the governance of sport (together with arts and culture) within the United Kingdom is largely devolved, reflecting the fact that in most competitions other than the Olympic Games players tend to represent the constituent nations rather than the United Kingdom or Great Britain. For example, in Scotland, sportscotland, the national agency for sport, is accountable to the Scottish Executive and Scottish Parliament. The Scottish Institute of Sport, which provides support for Scotland's elite athletes, is separate from the English Institute of Sport and funded by the sportscotland Lottery Fund.[83] Although Brown's announcement of the new NSF implied that it was a United Kingdom institution, in practice its responsibility would be 'levering new and additional private investment into community sport in England' alone.[84]

CONCLUSION

Gordon Brown's British Way defined Britishness in terms of liberty for all, responsibility from all and fairness to all. Brown's political legacy, in terms of national identity and citizenship, is the delivery of liberty for some, responsibility from some and fairness to some. The citizens of England have not enjoyed the same liberty, defined in terms of Brown's defence of the individual against the arbitrary powers of the state, as citizens of the other constituent nations of the United Kingdom, where new, devolved, institutional checks and balances on state power have been created. The citizens of England have not been able to exercise the same degree of responsibility, defined in terms of Brown's willingness to embrace constitutional reform and break up centralised institutions. The absence of devolution has denied them the opportunity of extended democratic citizenship rights. The citizens of England have been treated unfairly, compared to citizens elsewhere in the United Kingdom.

Fifty-eight per cent of the White British population describe their national identity as English rather than British (thirty-six per cent);[85] the key challenge for England remains not to contrive a British Way but to define an inclusive and civic political identity or 'English Way'. This way must mirror the multicultural diversity of England's sporting and cultural institutions and the popular reclaiming of the Cross of St George. The task was given greater urgency by the May 2001 Oldham and July 2001 Bradford riots and renewed impetus by the increased electoral support for the British National Party in traditional working-class Labour constituencies in England (notably Burnley and Barking) and the London bombings of 7 July

2005 by three born-and-bred Yorkshiremen. Championing the introduction of British identity cards, Brown warned of 'the obvious vulnerability' to
identity theft.[86] However, in articulating the British Way, the real theft being
perpetrated by Brown has been that of English identity.

Public opinion turned markedly against Brown's British Way even
before he became Prime Minister. An April 2007 YouGov poll for the
Sunday Times found that seventy-six per cent of respondents thought it
unfair that Scottish MPs should be able to vote on matters affecting only
England when English MPs cannot vote on matters that affect only Scotland.
Only ten per cent thought the situation fair. Asked about the way England
should be governed in the light of devolution to Scotland and Wales, the
preferred solution (for fifty-one per cent) was to stop Scottish and Welsh
MPs voting on matters that affected only England, while twenty-one per
cent favoured an English Parliament with similar powers to the Scottish
Parliament. Only twelve per cent preferred to keep the current arrangements. In terms of government spending per head being about twenty per
cent higher in Scotland than in England, sixty-eight per cent thought this
unfair, compared with only sixteen per cent who thought it fair. To resolve
this situation, thirty-nine per cent thought Scottish taxes should be raised to
pay for the extra spending and thirty per cent that Scottish spending should
be cut to English levels. Only fifteen per cent thought the *status quo* the best
option. Fifty per cent thought the Scots ungrateful for their extra spending,
fifty-nine per cent thought English taxpayers were subsidising the other
constituent nations of the United Kingdom and seventy-eight per cent
thought it wrong for Scotland and Wales to have lower prescription charges
and lower university fees than England.[87]

During the Labour Party leadership campaign, Brown's campaign
manager, Jack Straw, sought to breathe new life into the British Way. He
asserted that:

> We need a British story [where] there is room for multiple and differ-
> ent identities but there has to be a contract that they will not take prece-
> dence over the core democratic values of freedom, fairness, tolerance
> and plurality that define what it means to be British. It is the bargain
> and it is non-negotiable.

Straw claimed that 'what we describe as Britishness in our story traces back
to our own Civil War, its resolution in 1688 – and the Treaty of Union in

1707' and that at the heart of this story lies 'the narrative of the Magna Carta, the Civil War, the Bill of Rights'.[88] As in Brown's analysis, herein lies a central flaw of the British Way. In using these examples, Straw was citing major events from the history of England and the constitutional development of English law. The 'our' in our own Civil War is England. What Straw described as Britishness was, in truth, his understanding of Englishness. Similarly, when Straw made the absurd claim, 'we are the only European nation', he was thinking of the United Kingdom and the British state but the historical lineage was of England and the English state.[89] One more conflation of England and the English with the United Kingdom and the British.

Straw thus highlighted the contradiction at the heart of the British Way. He noted that one in five neighbourhoods in England was racially mixed (that is, at least ten per cent of the population was from an ethnic minority) and that there was 'increasing integration for most people, in most areas, but increasing segregation for some in others'. He further noted how this divergence was highlighted in 2006 in *The State of the English Cities*.[90] Because of the historic and recent pattern of immigration into the United Kingdom, the challenge of integration and multiculturalism was – not exclusively but none the less predominantly – an English question. Moreover, Straw concluded that 'we can learn much from countries that have a more developed sense of citizenship and what goes with it'. In short, 'what goes with a more developed sense of citizenship' is a written constitution entrenching checks and balances on the power of the central executive, clearly defined civil and political rights and, above all, genuine political autonomy for cities, localities and other communities to raise taxes and allocate resources and design policies according to their own priorities, without their discretion being constrained by relentless centralised prescription and intervention.[91]

It would be possible to construct an alternative politics and inclusive concept of citizenship based on Brown's 'golden thread of liberty', Straw's 'core democratic values of freedom, fairness, tolerance and plurality' and the historical lineage and literary quotations that have been advanced to substantiate the British Way. However, that particular history and literature have given concrete expression to the possibility of an 'English Way'.

It would also be possible to construct a genuinely plural democratic political culture in England, to mirror its ethnic and multicultural diversity: Jack Straw himself once called on the Left to redefine its patriotism in the quest for a new England.[92] As Tony Benn once acknowledged, a radical English democratic tradition stretches from the English Civil War and the Levellers through to the Chartists of the mid-nineteenth century. These ideas, which informed Tom Paine's *Rights of Man* and both the French and American revolutions, might yet be brought home to England.[93] They could be combined with the radical liberalism of John Hobson and his proposals for proportional representation, the reform of the House of Lords and to the checking and balancing of the power of the Cabinet, to resolve the progressive dilemma of the relationship between liberalism and social democracy in the English path to modernity.[94]

The prerequisite for such an 'English Way' would be a written constitution, a Bill of Rights and, above all, an end to the centralised prescription inherent in constrained discretion and a reversal of more than thirty years' erosion of power of English local government.[95] As Prime Minister, Gordon Brown has demonstrated both in his draft legislative programme and White Paper on constitutional reform that he is not prepared to give away that political power.[96] Therefore, the legacy of the British Way for England remains parallel deficits in citizenship rights, democratic accountability and the denial of the expression of England's national identity as a distinct political community.

PART III

Gordon Brown's Foreign Policy Agenda

Chapter 6

New Atlanticism: The New Deal for Global Governance

INTRODUCTION: MAKING GLOBALISATION WORK FOR ALL

Gordon Brown has a very clear vision for global governance. He wants to make globalisation work for all, to assist the developing world through a Global New Deal that will tackle poverty in a modern Marshall Plan of multilateral co-operation.[1] During the second half of his decade as Chancellor of the Exchequer, Brown developed this agenda, to leave a very clear foreign policy legacy to the United Kingdom in relation to its policy on international development and the reform of the multilateral international organisations that were created at the end of the Second World War.

Brown's vision is of a project of restoration. He wants to re-establish the vision of 'a new public purpose based on high ideals' that inspired the interwar liberalism of the English economist John Maynard Keynes and the Democrat President Franklin D. Roosevelt.[2] This vision gave expression domestically to the New Deal in the United States during the 1930s and internationally to the Atlanticist multilateralism and co-operation of the mid- to late 1940s.

The earlier era witnessed the establishment of the Bretton Woods international economic order, characterised by the dominance of the dollar, fixed exchange rates and political controls on the movement of capital, the creation of the United Nations, the Marshall Plan for post-war reconstruction and the dawn of the 'Pax Americana'. Brown now wants to locate British foreign policy within a twenty-first century *Pax Americana*, where international peace and security is guaranteed by the active leadership and participation of the United States. This is an agenda for peace and security based on multilateral diplomatic and political co-operation, rather than aggressive unilateral military pre-emption. Brown intends to use this vision to distance himself and his government both from the failed neo-conservative 'war on terror', while retaining the primacy of Atlanticism and the 'special relationship' in British foreign policy and from any concerted attempt to trap the United Kingdom within the narrow confines of a European Union-led common foreign and security policy architecture (see Chapter Seven).[3]

Brown calibrates his vision by the same moral compass that oriented his 'British model' of political economy. He has called for 'a new paradigm which recognises our increased global interdependence and rejuvenates the earlier notion that an acceptable and sustainable international regime requires a moral underpinning'.[4] Like his domestic model, Brown's Global New Deal is based on learning some very important lessons from the errors of past governments, notably that 'neither isolationism nor the old *laissez-faire* will work. In the last fifty years no country has lifted itself out of poverty without participating in the global economy'.[5] As with the British model of political economy, there is no choice about the need to embrace globalisation: the choice is 'whether we manage globalisation well or badly, fairly or unfairly'.[6] Like his nationalisation of policy-making for public services in England, Brown's vision for global governance is top-down, technocratic and managerialist, shaped by his involvement in the work of a series of elite commissions and committees from the International Monetary Fund (IMF) to the United Nations.

Nationally, Brown's interest in foreign policy and issues of global governance is reflected in the triumvirate of White Papers, membership of elite committees and his involvement in commissioning reports on aspects of global governance. His desire to defeat global poverty and make globalisation and governance work for all was given concrete form in the three White Papers that mapped the Blair Government's policies on international development.[7] At Cabinet Committee level, Brown served as a member of the Ministerial Committee on Defence and Overseas Policy, whose remit was 'to set strategies for the Government's defence and overseas policy'. He also served on the Subcommittee on International Terrorism, which kept under review 'the Government's strategy for reducing the risk from international terrorism both in the United Kingdom and to its interests overseas'. (Significantly, Brown sought to distance himself from the consequences of the Blair Government's decision to participate in the invasion of Iraq. He sat neither on the Subcommittee on Iraq, whose remit was 'to set and monitor progress against the strategic objectives for British policy in relation to Iraq' nor the Subcommittee on Conflict Prevention and Reconstruction.[8]) Brown served as a member of the Commission for Africa and the Policy Review Working Groups chaired by Tony Blair on Britain and the World and Security, Crime and Justice.[9] As Chancellor of the Exchequer, Brown commissioned Sir Nicholas Stern to review the economics of climate change.[10]

Internationally, and as Chancellor of the Exchequer, Gordon Brown's longest-standing contribution to global governance was as Chairman of the IMF's most powerful committee, the International Monetary and Financial Committee (IMFC) from September 1999.[11] Under Brown's stewardship, the IMFC acted as the primary advisory committee to the IMF's Board of Governors, reporting on major issues, notably the management and adaptation of the international monetary and financial system, proposals for reform of the IMF's governance arrangements (through amendments to its *Articles of Agreement*) and dealing with 'sudden disturbances' that might threaten the international monetary and financial system.[12] Following the September 2005 World Summit, Brown served on the United Nations Secretary-General's High-level Panel on System-wide Coherence, which reported, in November 2006, on how the United Nations could overcome its fragmentation and help deliver the Millennium Development, and other internationally agreed, goals.[13]

The single most important legacy to global governance from Brown's desire to make globalisation work for all arose from the 2005 United Kingdom year-long leadership of the Group of Eight (G8) industrialised economies. During its leadership of the G8, which between 1 July and 31 December coincided with its Presidency of the Council of the European Union, the Blair Government sought to focus international attention on Africa and climate change. Gordon Brown was at the heart of this initiative, which was accompanied by the year-long 'Make Poverty History' campaign, led by an alliance of non-governmental organisations (NGOs). This followed the publication of the report of the Commission for Africa (Brown was one of its seventeen commissioners) and Brown's concerted attempts to attract international support for his International Finance Facility (IFF), a mechanism for accelerating the provision of Official Development Assistance (ODA) to Africa. The high point of this activity was the July 2005 G8 Gleneagles Summit, at which an agreement was reached to double annual world-wide ODA by fifty billion dollars, including an extra twenty-five billion pounds for Africa, and immediately to write off the debts of eighteen of the world's poorest countries.[14]

In this chapter, I shall explore the nature and legacy of Brown's desire to make globalisation work for all. I will evaluate the legacy of the Gleneagles Summit and how the G8 has failed (thus far) to furnish the resources required to deliver the Millennium Development Goals. The conclusion focuses on Brown's increasing emphasis, affirmed during the first month of his premiership, on the need for a new security architecture for the United Kingdom and a modified approach to global governance. This approach, which places increased emphasis on winning the battles of ideas and of hearts and minds in the fight against terrorism at home and abroad has remained implacably Atlanticist in its priorities and orientation, symbolised by Brown's commitment to renew the United Kingdom's independent nuclear deterrent.

My theme throughout this chapter is how Brown's desire has been compromised by his insistence on the market liberalism of the 'Washington Consensus', championing trade liberalisation and the neo-liberal orthodoxy of the IMF, World Bank and World Trade Organisation (WTO) at the expense of a more inclusive approach to global governance and a political economy of human development more attuned to the needs of the poorest countries.[15] (Throughout this chapter, neo-liberalism is used as a convenient shorthand to denote the ideology and policies, popularised during the 1980s by the governments of Margaret Thatcher and Ronald Reagan, which sought to roll back the frontiers of the state and roll forward the frontiers of the market through privatisation and the liberalisation and deregulation of markets.)

THE NEW ATLANTICISM

At first, Brown's focus as Chancellor was on the domestic monetary, fiscal and supply-side components of the British model of political economy, so it is perhaps not surprising that he did not make a major speech about global poverty until January 2000. In 1998, when the United Kingdom held both the Presidency of the Council of the European Union (EU) and the G8 in the immediate aftermath of the Asian financial crisis (which damaged global investor confidence and particularly the economies of South Korea and Thailand), the Blair Government chose to make achieving sustainable economic growth its central priority.[16] Brown focussed the attention of the May 1998 G8 Summit in Birmingham on strengthening the architecture of the international financial system and the identification of seven broad principles for growth and employment in the leading industrialised economies, rather than on the interests of developing countries.[17] When Brown was invited by Oxfam to deliver the Gilbert Murray Memorial Lecture, he identified two of the key facets of his perspective on global governance.

The first facet of Brown's vision for international development was its historical and intellectual debt to American liberalism, rather than the Labour Party's tradition of socialist internationalism or European social democracy. This debt was acknowledged by quotations from addresses by President Kennedy and Martin Luther King, the like of which had informed his father's sermons and helped orient Brown's moral compass. Brown cited Kennedy's invocation that 'If a free society cannot help the many who are poor, it cannot save the few who are rich' and King's belief that 'we are tied together in the single garment of destiny, caught in an inescapable network of mutuality'.[18] Brown also deployed a quote from an American academic, Professor James W. Stockinger, which later appeared in many of his speeches on poverty and development and became the signature statement of Brown's belief in the mutual dependence of humanity:

> It is the hands of others that grow the food we eat, sew the clothes we wear, build the homes we inhabit. It is the hands of others who tend us when we are sick and lift us when we fall. It is the hands of others who bring us into this world and lower us into the grave.[19]

The second facet was Brown's desire to define a new paradigm for international development. He contended that there was a need 'to move beyond the Washington Consensus of the 1980s, a creature of its times which narrowed our growth and employment objectives', which had 'proved inadequate for the insecurities and challenges of globalisation'.[20] As its successor, Brown proposed 'a new 2000 paradigm' which could not be 'a Washington

Consensus, but, as we have recognised in the poverty-reduction strategies, countries cannot claim ownership and make it part of their national consensus'. The four key elements of this new paradigm might be: recognition of 'the critical role of the public sector as well as the private', macroeconomic stability as 'an essential condition for growth' together with the pursuit of 'clear policy codes and principles' to ensure it, participation of the poorest countries in the global flow of capital, technology and ideas in a manner beneficial to their development and a recognition of the total interdependence of sustainable economic growth and social justice.[21]

Far from being a new paradigm, Brown's agenda was nothing more than a redefinition of development priorities within the neo-liberal orthodoxy of the Washington Consensus, with its emphasis on market liberalisation and deregulation. First, his emphasis on the critical role for the public sector appeared to be merely an endorsement of the World Bank's orthodoxy that the role of the state should be to build institutions for the market.[22] Second, his insistence on macroeconomic stability as a prerequisite of development and the pursuit of principles and codes to guarantee stability was little more than the sanction of the surveillance of its member states' economies conducted by the IMF. The highly prescriptive conditions of and structural adjustment required for multilateral loans threatened the sovereignty of the IMF and World Bank's client states by forcing them to undertake major reforms of their economies and societies which their populations had not chosen.

Third, the notion of the poorest economies engaging with globalisation in a manner beneficial to their development ignored the extent to which market liberalisation tended to reinforce the competitive advantage of the richest economies and accentuate global inequalities in income and wealth. Fourth, Brown's insistence on the interdependence of sustainable economic growth and social justice ignored the evidence from major international reports and summits of conflict both between growth and environmental sustainability and between market liberalisation and social justice for poorer economies. In 1987, the World Commission on Environment and Development (the Brundtland Report) concluded that a general acceleration of global economic growth would result in 'a mere perpetuation of existing economic patterns' and would not be sufficient to reduce dependence or inequalities.[23] A decade later, in a similar vein, the June 1997 United Nations General Assembly Special Session (Earth

Summit II) identified the 'real risk' that trade liberalisation could 'further marginalise' the least developed economies,[24] and that 'decisions on further liberalisation of trade should take into account effects on sustainable development'.[25]

A GLOBAL NEW DEAL THROUGH A MODERN MARSHALL PLAN

Brown's vision for global governance remains decidedly British and Atlanticist; not in any sense European. Brown sees no advantage whatsoever in contemplating further moves towards an ever-closer European political union with a common security and foreign policy agenda for the European Union. As in many other areas of politics, Brown has not sought inspiration from examples drawn from a European social democratic tradition, which would be a natural choice given the Labour Party's historic commitment to internationalism. Brown has looked instead to American liberalism and the example of the Democratic Secretary of State, George C. Marshall, and his programme for post-war reconstruction in Europe and the broader *Pax Americana*, created by the formation of multilateral institutions, notably the IMF and the World Bank.[26]

The vision for the Marshall Plan was set out in a speech at Harvard University made on the eve of the third anniversary of the D-Day landings. Marshall contended that although the American people were 'distant from the troubled areas of the Earth', nevertheless, the United States either had to provide Europe with 'substantial additional help or face economic, social and political deterioration of a very grave character'. Marshall asserted that the United States' Government's response should not be piecemeal but 'provide a cure rather than a mere palliative'.[27] Brown's preferred basis for global governance is a Labour Government working closely in partnership with a Democratic President of the United States to promote the global public good, prosperity and security.[28] Brown's vision is based on the historical precedent of multilateral co-operation but is a process of governance led by the rich industrialised economies rather than a truly global partnership.

The events of September 11th 2001 provided Brown with an international platform on which to confirm his commitment to establishment a new Marshall Plan and Global New Deal for tackling poverty. In the aftermath of the attack, Brown visited the United States to deliver two keynote addresses, in New York and Washington, setting out his vision for global governance. Brown's thesis was that 9/11 demonstrated that 'in the new global economy we are, all of us – the richest countries and the poorest countries – inextricably bound to one another by common interests, shared needs and linked destinies'. The choice facing the international community was 'whether we manage globalisation well or badly, fairly or unfairly [and] whether we are for social justice'. The opposing temptations of 'outdated protectionism and isolationism ... the old *laissez-faire* attitude of there is nothing that can be done' must be resisted. The alternative was to strengthen international cooperation by 'modernising our international rules and reforming the institutions of economic co-operation'.[29]

Brown claimed that his vision of a new global consensus was feasible. Even those campaigning for fair trade for developing countries must acknowledge:

> ... the importance of markets, the pivotal role of private capital and that while the unfettered power of any vested interest anywhere is unacceptable, private companies and private-not just public investments are crucial to making global economic development work in the interests of the excluded.[30]

This is both something of an over-exaggeration and an over-simplification of the degree of consensus at home and abroad. Fair trade campaigners, such as those who had protested at the WTO ministerial meetings in Seattle in 1999 and Doha in 2001, had acknowledged the importance of markets and the pivotal role of private capital but only to the extent that they believed globalisation to be a means to the extension of the power of transnational corporations.

Despite the weight of opposition, Brown maintained that his Global New Deal could be constructed on four building blocks: first, the creation of 'new rules of the game in codes and standards'. These would drive 'an improvement in the terms on which the poorest countries participate in the global economy and actively increase their capacity to do so'. Second, 'the adoption by business internationally of high corporate standards for engagement as reliable and consistent partners in the development process'. Third, building on the WTO ministerial meeting at Doha, 'the swift adoption of an improved trade regime essential for developing countries participation on fair terms in the world economy'. Fourth, 'a substantial transfer of additional resources from the richest to the poorest countries in the form of investment for development'.[31]

Underpinning each of these building blocks of Brown's modern Marshall Plan was the assumption that private capital, in the form of transnational corporations (TNCs) could be persuaded or manipulated to deliver the Global New Deal by investing in some of the poorest economies. However, the evidence from successive World Investment Reports produced by the United Nations is that the world's 60,000 or more TNCs and their 800,000 affiliates invest only where there is profit to be made. That means investment has overwhelmingly gone to the richest economies or to developing countries with major oil or mineral deposits. In 2000, when global Foreign Direct Investment (FDI) reached a record $1.3 trillion, the EU, United States and Japan accounted for seventy-one per cent of inward investment flow and eighty-two per cent of outward investment. Developing countries received only nineteen per cent of global FDI and the forty-nine least developed countries only 0.3 per cent. Africa's entire total was a paltry $9.1 billion.[32] By 2006, the distribution of private investment to the poorest economies had not altered significantly. During 2005 global FDI stood at $916 billion, of which the United Kingdom was the principal beneficiary, with $165 billion. Developing countries received $334 billion (thirty-six per cent of total FDI) but Africa's share (while a record) was only thirty-one billion dollars for the whole continent.[33]

Brown chose to overlook the growing evidence, manifest at the WTO's biennial ministerial meetings in Seattle and Doha, that the interests of the richest and poorer countries were diverging rapidly over the issue of trade liberalisation. Far from a global consensus, a fissure had developed between the richest economies (including the United Kingdom, who had pressed in Doha for broader and accelerated liberalisation of trade, especially in services) and the developing countries. The latter resisted the liberalisation of services until the richest countries had fully opened their markets for trade in agriculture, textiles and the other areas of trade where developing countries had a comparative advantage.[34] Moreover, the developing countries pointed out (correctly) that at a similar stage of their development, economies like that of the United States, Japan and the EU member states had all deployed tariff and non-tariff barriers to trade, to protect and nurture the infant industries on which their future prosperity depended. In the interest of fair trade, developing countries should be accorded the same opportunity and the 'one-size-fits-all' approach to trade liberalisation abandoned.

A PILLAR OF THE ESTABLISHMENT

The degree to which Brown's vision for global governance amounted to an adaptation of, rather than a genuine alternative to, the neo-liberal orthodoxy of market liberalisation and deregulation is best illustrated through Brown's most enduring practical contribution to global governance, as the Chairman (from September 1999) of the IMF's most powerful committee, the International Monetary and Financial Committee (IMFC).[35] Under Brown's stewardship, the IMFC acted as the primary advisory committee to the IMF Board of Governors. The IMFC reported on major issues, notably the management and adaptation of the international monetary and financial system, proposals for reform of the IMF's own governance arrangements (through amendments to its Articles of Agreement) and dealing with 'sudden disturbances' that might threaten the international monetary and financial system.[36] Over the fifteen meetings of the IMFC he chaired, Brown became a pillar of the IMF establishment.

From the very first meeting he chaired, in April 2000, at which the IMFC reaffirmed 'its strong support for the Fund's unique role as the cornerstone of the international monetary and financial community', Brown used the IMFC to endorse the neo-liberal orthodoxy of IMF policy and governance.[37] Any limited reforms proposed by the IMFC sought to strengthen and deepen the managerialist and technocratic role of the IMF in surveying the economies of its member states. These reforms were consistent with the desire of the United States' Department of the Treasury, under the Bush Administration, to put an end to the 'mission creep'[38] of the IMF and return it to its core mission of promoting international monetary co-operation and exchange rate stability.[39]In particular, under Brown's stewardship the IMFC adhered to the Bush Administration's objective of focusing the IMF on the prevention, rather than resolution, of financial crises and expanding the role of the private sector in crisis resolution, through the extension of Collective Action Clauses.[40] The IMFC also endorsed the IMF's role in poor countries, promoting policies such as the Contingent Credit Line (CCL), as 'indispensable' and lauding its interventions in financial crises such as that of Argentina in 2001, where the IMFC considered the IMF-supported programme to be 'an important and decisive step to boost confidence'.[41]

The IMFC's praise of the IMF flew in the face of the fact that not a single member state ever signed up to the CCL.[42] More damningly, in a series of highly critical reports, the IMF's Independent Evaluation Office (IEO) criticised the IMF's policies and prolonged use of its resources in poor countries.[43] The IEO recommended that:

> ... the IMF should strengthen the ability of its staff to analyse political economy issues in order to achieve a better understanding of the forces that are likely to block or enhance reforms and to take these into account in program design.

In particular, where the IMFC under Brown had praised the IMF's intervention in Argentina, the IEO criticised it for supporting Argentina 'despite repeated policy inadequacies'. It further claimed 'the IMF's surveillance and program conditionality were handicapped by analytical weaknesses and data limitations'.[44] Despite the repeated failings in IMF surveillance, the IMFC advocated that 'regional and global surveillance should play an increasingly important role and be better integrated with bilateral surveillance'.[45]

This advocacy of an expanded role for the IMFC was in spite of the fact every IMFC communiqué issued under Brown's chairmanship recommended the need for fiscal balance in the United States (lower public spending and/or higher taxation), structural reform in the European Union (greater liberalisation and deregulation of labour and product markets) and financial and corporate restructuring in Japan (fiscal consolidation and reduction of non-performing loans). The sheer repetition of this advice was indicative of the reluctance of the most powerful industrialised economies to give in to the IMFC's desire to micro-manage their domestic economic policies.[46]

THE INTERNATIONAL FINANCE FACILITY

Gordon Brown used the IMFC to power the spread of the British model of political economy and publicise the enduring success of the Brown Boom.

He also used it to promote his particular agenda for and innovations in international development, the most prominent of which was the creation of an International Finance Facility (IFF).

The fourth building block of Brown's modern Marshall Plan was 'a substantial transfer of additional resources from the richest to the poorest countries in the form of investment for development'.[47] In June 2001, a report prepared for the United Nations calculated that an extra fifty billion dollars a year in aid would be required if the international community were to finance the Millennium Development Goals (MDGs). Drawing on these findings and to make good the aid deficit, Brown initially advocated the creation of an International Development Trust Fund. This would have been overseen by a joint implementation committee of the IMF, the World Bank and possibly some member countries.[48]

By January 2003, the International Development Trust Fund had evolved into the IFF. To provide the additional aid required to meet the MDGs, the IFF proposed an extra fifty billion dollars in aid each year until 2015. As a temporary finance facility, rather than a development bank or aid agency, the IFF would organise the disbursement of aid in four- to five-year programmes, raising the money from international capital markets by issuing bonds, with legally binding commitments from the donors; bondholders would be repaid by the IFF. Aid would be disbursed over fifteen years, with the repayment phase lasting a further fifteen.[49] The additional aid would be disbursed through the existing multilateral and bilateral aid infrastructure. Introducing the IFF, Brown argued that, as the core of the modern Marshall Plan, it was based on 'the Marshall Plan's enduring values'. The IFF was urgently needed; it was known that in poor countries, some 115 million children were not able to go to school, 30,000 infants were dying every day and more than two billion people were living on an income of less than two dollars a day. The IFF could fund development that would mean 'the difference between life and death'.[50] The Treasury argued that the IFF would be a practical and cost-effective measure. Having the financial backing of the governments of leading industrialised economies, the IFF bonds would attract high credit ratings. There was also 'a strong moral case for bringing forward these additional resources'.[51]

The IFF for Immunisation was launched in 2006, to provide funding for health and immunisation programmes in seventy of the world's poorest countries. Its rate of return was estimated at 'well over twenty-five per cent'.[52]

The IFF was publicly welcomed by Kofi Annan, Nelson Mandela, Pope John Paul II and Bob Geldof. Mandela, for example, described the IFF as 'an absolutely necessary and timely initiative and deserves an active response from all members of the international community'.[53] However, the United States' Treasury steadfastly refused to stand shoulder-to-shoulder with Brown in the moral crusade against global poverty, because the IFF was not consistent with George W. Bush's Administration's agenda for fighting the economic dimension of its 'war on terror'.[54]

The IFF was also heavily criticised by influential voices within the NGO community. The influential London-based campaigning NGO, the World Development Movement (WDM), pointed out that, according to the Treasury's own calculations, the IFF was likely to raise, on average, an extra nineteen billion dollars per year (at 2006 prices), rather than the fifty billion dollar target. While WDM estimated that the IFF would provide an additional $209 billion in aid (at 2006 prices) between 2006 and 2017, this sum would be more than offset by the repayments that would have to be made from aid budgets, to IFF bondholders between 2018 and 2032. WDM asserted that there would be (at 2006 prices) $316.6 billion less available for aid during this period, meaning that 'the IFF will result in an overall net loss of some US $108 billion less than would otherwise have been available in total aid between 2006 and 2032'. Moreover, WDM calculated that while the IFF would disburse $500 billion over its lifetime, because of the interest payments to bondholders it would cost $720 billion to finance: a net loss of $220 billion.[55]

Similar criticisms came from the Washington-based think tank, the Centre for Global Development (CGD), which is dedicated to reducing global poverty and inequality. It identified ten myths pertaining to the IFF, including the assertion that the IFF would create additional resources for development and that its additional financing costs were defensible. CGD observed that these costs were probably not justified, because the donors 'will pay *at least twenty-four billion dollars in extra interest costs, over and above the regular interest charges*'.[56] Furthermore, CGD disputed whether, because of the likely backlash against aid in the US Congress, American participation in the IFF was either essential or possible and it questioned the capacity both of the IFF to disburse an extra fifty billion dollars a year and to help achieve the Millennium Development Goals. While the myth of 'doubling aid to halve poverty' might sound attractive, CGD described this as 'utterly implausible'. Consequently, CGD concluded that other options for increasing aid to developing countries merited consideration, 'including a more vigorous appeal for more aid through the normal budgetary processes and long-term constituency building'. While such options might be less exciting than Brown's IFF, they might 'nonetheless [be] more transparent, accountable and democratic'.[57]

THE COMMISSION FOR AFRICA

Scepticism also surrounded another of the Blair Government's major innovations in international development, in which Gordon Brown played a major role. As one of seventeen commissioners, Brown contributed to the production of the report of the Commission for Africa. Chaired by Tony Blair, the Commission was launched in February 2004. Its five formal objectives included a commitment 'to generate new ideas and action for a strong and prosperous Africa'.[58]

Unfortunately, the Commission failed to generate the progressive global consensus Brown envisaged. Before the publication of its final report, the Commission was warned by a parliamentary select committee that it should first do no harm and should focus on policy coherence for development and press 'for action on global governance, to ensure that Africa had a louder voice in international organisations such as the United Nations, the World Bank and the International Monetary Fund'.[59] This call was echoed by the United Kingdom NGO, ActionAid, which asserted that 'the first step in supporting African development must be to do no harm'.[60] Indeed, ActionAid created its own 'African Commission for Britain', an all-African panel whose membership, including Michael Camdessus, the former Managing Director of the IMF and Ralph Goodale, Canada's Minister of Finance, contrasted vividly with the Commission for Africa's majority of white commissioners.[61]

When the Commission for Africa published its final report on 11 March 2005, its recommendations did not receive universal approval. The Commission recommended 'significant transfers of money' from richer countries to fund: improved governance and capacity building (an additional up to £3.5 billion), Education for All (an additional seven to eight billion dollars per year), improved public health services (an additional seven to eight billion dollars), investment in infrastructure (an extra ten billion dollars a year to 2010, rising to twenty billion dollars a year to 2015), increased trade through a completion of the Doha Round of world trade talks by the end of 2006, the elimination of export subsidies and trade-distorting support for agriculture by 2010, 'untied, predictable, harmonised' aid, total debt cancellation 'as soon as possible' and a greater voice for African countries in multilateral institutions.[62] Far from generating a new global consensus, both the Blair Government and the Commission came under sustained criticism.

John Hilary, Director of Campaigns and Policy at the campaigning NGO, War on Want, described the report as a 'damning indictment' of the Blair Government's policies of trade liberalisation and privatisation.[63] Hilary highlighted the discrepancy between the Commission's assertion that 'forcing poor countries to liberalise through agreements is the wrong approach to achieving growth and poverty reduction',[64] and the Blair Government's commitment to trade liberalisation as an instrument, as described in the DTI publication, *Making globalisation a force for good.*[65]

Furthermore, despite running to no fewer than 461 pages, the report made no recommendations about climate change and side-stepped a detailed analysis of the impact of transnational corporations on African development.[66] As WDO concluded, in overall terms the report amounted to a backward step from the much clearer and more extensive commitments arising from the twin reports of the Brandt Commission, which had helped initiate the debate on global governance.[67]

THE LEGACY OF THE GLENEAGLES G8 SUMMIT

The failure of major international agents (notably the Bush Administration) to provide substantial backing for the Commission for Africa's recommendations and the hostile reception of the Commission's report by major United Kingdom-based NGOs were particularly damaging for Brown's ambition to foster a New Deal for global poverty. The Blair Government had made Africa and climate change two key themes of the United Kingdom's Presidency of the G8 in 2005. They also featured prominently in the priorities of the United Kingdom's simultaneous presidency of the European Union.[68] The Blair Government had actively courted the global 'Make Poverty History' campaign, in which United Kingdom NGOs were the prime movers, to mobilise popular support for concerted international action on Africa and climate change. For those very same NGOs to criticise the Commission for Africa's report, one of the focal points of the dual G8/EU Presidencies was, at best, an acute political embarrassment.

At the conclusion of the summit of the G8 leaders in Gleneagles in July 2005, a communiqué was issued that included a commitment to double worldwide official development aid by 2010, providing an extra fifty billion dollars per annum, including an annual increase of twenty-five billion dollars for Africa. In addition, there were commitments both to write off the debts of eighteen of the world's poorest countries, at a cost of forty billion dollars, and to end export subsidies.[69] For both Brown and Blair, these commitments amounted to one of their most important legacies to global governance and the attempt to reduce global poverty.

However, the record since the Gleneagles summit has demonstrated Brown's difficulties in generating a new global consensus. The Development Assistance Committee (DAC) of the Organisation for Economic Cooperation and Development (OECD) reported that its twenty-two members provided $103.9 billion in aid during 2006 – but this amounted to 5.1 per cent less than in 2005, measured in constant dollar terms. In real terms, this constituted the first decrease in Official Development Assistance (ODA) since 1997. Most significantly, it meant that the Gleneagles G8 Summit commitment to double aid to Africa by 2010 had become much harder to accomplish. While in 2006 the United Kingdom's $12.2 billion ODA represented an annual increase of 13.1 per cent, reflecting larger contributions to international organisations, the United States' fell by twenty per cent, Japan's by 9.6 per cent, Canada's by 9.2 per cent and Italy's by thirty per cent.[70] Other members of the G8 had not rallied to Brown's quest for a Global New Deal nor been prepared to stand shoulder-to-shoulder to deliver the financial commitment that would make a new Marshall Plan feasible.

One of the institutional legacies of the Commission for Africa was the creation of an African Progress Panel (APP) of six eminent figures, including the former United Nations Secretary-General Kofi Annan, the former IMF Managing Director, Michel Camdessus and Bob Geldof, the founder and Chair of Band Aid, Live Aid and Live8. In its first communiqué, the Panel noted that 'in a globalised world, the stability and prosperity of the world is at risk when an entire continent is lagging behind'. At the midpoint of the Millennium Development Goals (MDGs), 'sub-Saharan Africa is the only region which, at current rates, will meet none of the MDG targets by 2015'. During 2006, the continent of Africa achieved a growth rate of 5.4 per cent, well below the seven per cent annual growth needed to reduce African poverty substantially. Moreover, Africa's share of world trade fell, during 2005, by two per cent, pointing to the failure of the trade liberalisation championed by Brown to yield a significant developmental divided for the poorest economies. The APP further identified the shortfall in international aid, despite the G8 commitments made at Gleneagles: the 'G8 governments need to make urgent budget provisions of more than five billion dollars every year, to find the twenty-five billion dollars which they have pledged by 2010'. At the same time, the Education for All Fast Track Initiative, championed by Brown,[71] confronted 'a funding gap of at least US$2.5 billion'.[72]

The most damning criticism of the failure of the international community to deliver on its pledges for aid and debt cancellation has come from the coalition of NGOs who formed the 'Make Poverty History' campaign. That coalition, and its campaign that accompanied the United Kingdom's Presidency of the G8 and EU (which Tony Blair and Gordon Brown actively courted to rally support for their agenda for international development) was reborn as 'The World Can't Wait'. It has sought to address the issues, surrounding debt cancellation, trade justice, vital public services and climate change, on which the G8 and EU failed to deliver during 2005.[73] In a series of highly critical reports and in damning evidence given to a series of parliamentary select committees, United Kingdom-based NGOs identified the flaws in Brown's agenda. In particular, they criticised his – and the Blair Government's – insistence on trade liberalisation by developing countries. For example, Christian Aid identified how 'trade liberalisation has cost sub-Saharan Africa US$272 billion over the past twenty years', a sum which far exceeds the forty billion dollars of aid agreed at the Gleneagles summit.[74] For its part, the World Development Movement identified the United Kingdom's unjust contribution to global climate change (one of the two priorities for the Presidency of the G8). And ActionAid not only repeatedly highlighted the failure of the G8 to meet its targets on debt, trade and aid but also identified a gap of $8.1 billion in funding in 2007 for achieving universal access to HIV infection prevention, treatment and care by 2010.[75]

Even multilateral international organisations have had to acknowledge the shortcomings in global governance and the lack of progress towards the Millennium Development Goals (MDGs). In their annual Global

Monitoring Report, the World Bank and IMF recognise that, five years after 189 states signed the Millennium Declaration pledge to deliver the MDGs by 2015, 'many countries – particularly in Africa and South Asia – are off track [with] over ten million children dying annually of readily preventable diseases'. Despite this, the G8 commitments on aid 'risk remaining unfulfilled'.[76] In a similar vein, the World Economic Forum's Global Governance Initiative (GGI), which monitors annual progress on a range of internationally agreed human development objectives, vividly demonstrated the failure of the international community to deliver anything like Brown's global New Deal or Marshall Plan. A GGI score of ten out of ten would signify adequate human developmental progress; in its first three annual reports, the GGI failed to register a single mark higher than a paltry five (for progress in addressing health and poverty during 2005). Indeed, during 2005, peace and security could score only three, while progress on human rights and the environment was a lamentable two out of ten.[77] In the face of such sustained failure, the World Bank conceded that, while it still believed Brown's priorities (institutionalised in the British model of political economy) of 'macro-economic stability, domestic liberalisation and openness [to] lie at the heart of any sustained growth process', it had to concede that 'the options for achieving these goals vary widely'.[78]

Despite the legion of evidence that the existing pattern of global governance has failed to deliver the MDGs, Gordon Brown has remained steadfastly committed to strengthening and deepening existing multilateral institutions, because of their Atlanticist provenance and the manner in which their governance and policies have permitted the export of the British model of political economy. While Chairman of the IMFC, Brown remained convinced that 2005 had witnessed: 'the first steps to make poverty history and now we must ensure 2005 is remembered not as a one-off but as the beginning of step change in international development'.[79]

Furthermore, in spite of increasing incidences of major financial crises both in developed economies (South Korea, 1997) and developing countries (Mexico, 1994, Russia, 1998, Argentina, 2001), Brown remained adamant that 'stronger IMF surveillance will be critical to resolving the current imbalances and maintaining global economic stability in the medium term'. In short, the IMF could be reformed to deliver prosperity for all by making it 'fit for purpose', by giving it greater power to survey its member states' economies and financial systems through 'a new approach to multilateral surveillance, taking into account the linkages and spillover effects of one country's policies on others in the global economy'.[80] In a classic conflation of his own agenda with that of other interested parties, Brown claimed to be able to identify 'a new consensus developing that an emerging market country and a developing country responding to globalisation will need to have stability, will need to have private as well as public investment'.[81] However, as the sheer weight of evidence submitted to parliamentary select committees by academics, NGOs and critics of the IMF demonstrated, Brown, in believing that such a new consensus exists, might find himself in a small minority.[82]

RENEWING THE 'SPECIAL RELATIONSHIP' IN THE AGE OF INTERDEPENDENCE

As the likelihood of his succeeding Tony Blair became a strong probability rather than a possibility, Gordon Brown returned to the American liberalism of the 1960s Democratic Party for the inspiration to define the agenda for global governance and international development that would shape the foreign policies of his Government.

Brown asserted that because of the rapid and extensive transformation of the global economy, we are witnessing an 'emerging new world order [which] cannot work unless we recognise that we are in age of interdependence'.[83] The concept of an age of interdependence was deployed by President John F. Kennedy during a speech in July 1963, at the height of the Cold War and in the aftermath of the Cuban Missile Crisis. Just months before his assassination, Kennedy claimed that 'the age of interdependence is here'.[84]

President Kennedy's thesis was that the United States' West European allies in the North Atlantic Treaty Organisation (NATO) were 'committed to the path of progressive democracy – to social justice and economic reform attained through the process of debate and reform'. Kennedy sought to champion progressive democracy as a path, superior to communist dictatorship, to modernisation, growth and prosperity. The age of interdependence had arisen because it was 'increasingly clear that the United States and Western Europe are tightly bound by shared goals and mutual respect', wherein 'the central moving force of our great adventure is enduring mutual trust'.[85] Brown wants to develop this same enduring mutual trust in contemporary global governance. It might appear perplexing that a Labour Prime Minister has chosen to build his vision for the future of global governance on a concept developed by a Cold War warrior, given the Labour Party's strong historic commitments to internationalism and pacificism. If, however, Brown's legacy to global and domestic security is taken fully into account, then it becomes apparent that in his premiership, he is seeking to strengthen and deepen, rather than dilute or abandon the trans-Atlantic 'special relationship'.

While he may have refused to embrace the rhetoric of George W. Bush's 'Axis of evil' or Tony Blair's 'Arc of extremism', Brown, nevertheless, steadfastly remained shoulder-to-shoulder with Number Ten and the White House in their post 9/11 war on terror. Brown was one of the 412 MPs who, on 18 March 2003, voted in favour of the United Kingdom using 'all means necessary to ensure the disarmament of Iraq's weapons of mass destruction'.[86] In November 2006, Brown visited British troops in Basra, describing the Prince of Wales' Royal Regiment (known as 'the Tigers') as 'proud and courageous tigers and everyone in Britain is very proud of you'.[87] In March 2007, Brown flew unexpectedly to Helmand Province, Afghanistan, where he stated that, 'achieving security must be our first priority'.[88] Most importantly and almost unnoticed, given the periodic public furore over alleged equipment shortages and deficiencies, as Chancellor of the Exchequer, Brown financed a significant real increase in the United Kingdom's defence spending.

When the Blair Government first took office, the July 1998 Comprehensive Spending Review noted that the United Kingdom's defence spending had 'fallen by some twenty-three per cent in real terms and the Armed Forces have been reduced by almost a third since 1990'. The Government's Strategic Defence Review envisaged 'a radical modernisation of the United Kingdom's defence forces', to be achieved while delivering 'real savings to the taxpayer' from 'within a defence budget that will continue to fall as a share of GDP'.[89] By July 2000, Brown's second Spending Review reflected a changing security agenda. The involvement of British armed forces in Kosovo, East Timor and Sierra Leone meant that defence spending would increase in real terms for the first time in more than a decade, albeit at only 0.3 per cent in real terms per year.[90]

The events of 9/11 marked a sea change in the security agenda: Brown contended that 'Britain's international engagement ... has assumed new importance'.[91] In the July 2002 Spending Review, Brown announced a 1.2 per cent real terms increase, the largest sustained increase in defence spending for twenty years. This was accompanied by parallel increases in the budgets of the Foreign Office, the British Council and the BBC World Service, together with a huge increasing in spending on international development, yielding 'A thirty-five per cent real terms increase since 2001, a ninety-three per cent real terms increase since 1997'.[92] Reflecting this change in the commitment to security at home and abroad, the 2002 Pre-Budget Report redefined the Blair Government's central objective to include 'security for all' for the very first time (a commitment that has remained).[93]

The fiscal prudence of the British model of political economy during the Blair Government's first term left a significant legacy to the United Kingdom's expenditure on both cultural and indirect influences (soft power) and military action (hard power) during New Labour's second term.[94] The greatest dividend of Brown's prudence came after the March 2003 invasion of Iraq. While he maintained a conspicuous public silence on the conduct of the war and its aftermath, in subsequent Budget statements and in the Pre-Budget Report, Brown highlighted the commitment of additional resources to the wars in Iraq and Afghanistan. Not once did he question the efficacy or legitimacy of this expenditure. Having allocated three billion pounds for the war in Iraq in his April 2003 Budget, together with an extra £330 million for additional domestic counter-terrorism measures, in December 2003 Brown announced the 'money set aside for the war against terror including in Afghanistan and for our action in Iraq is £5.5 billion'.[95] In his July 2004 Spending Review statement, Brown announced a further annual average increase of 1.4 per cent, equivalent to an additional £3.7 billion a year by 2007–08 but supplemented by £2.8 billion of efficiency savings over the 2004 Spending Review period.[96] Whenever resources have been needed, Brown's fiscal legacy for global governance has been to make fighting the war against terror overseas a core priority.

THE BATTLE FOR HEARTS AND MINDS

9/11 brought about a sea change in the priority Brown gave to security issues overseas; the terrorist attacks on the London transport system on 7 July 2005 brought about a similar change to his perspective on the implications of global terrorism for domestic security. Brown asserted that since 9/11, the Treasury had, in effect, become a department of security. Indeed, he claimed that 'it is not just the Treasury that is a department of security. So too is almost every other department'. This was because 'addressing the reality, causes and roots of international terrorism is one of the greatest new challenges of our times'.[97] For this reason, the second 2007 Comprehensive Spending Review, the framework for the expenditure priorities not only for the three years until 2009–2010 but also for the policy priorities of the Brown Government for the next decade, identified global uncertainty as one of the principal long-term challenges facing the United Kingdom.[98]

As in other areas of global governance, Brown asserted that the 'British way' to act together, both globally and nationally, is through the construction of 'a unified national consensus'. Because globalisation afforded new opportunities to terrorist networks, Brown advocated steps 'to isolate extremists from the moderate majority'. The model for the fight against international terrorism must be the 'cultural Cold War – a Cold War of ideas and values – and one in which the best ideas and values eventually triumphed'.[99] The Internet has allowed terrorist networks to exchange ideas; Brown has urged that these ideas be openly discussed, so that the moderate majority can 'win the global battle for hearts and minds'.[100]

Although the full forces of the mass media, the arts, literature, foundations, trusts, civil society and civic organisations must be engaged in this battle for hearts and minds, Brown looks to the resources of the state to lead the war against terrorism, noting the investment of two billion pounds a year on counter-terrorism and resilience, a doubling of expenditure since 9/11. Brown has strongly affirmed the introduction of biometric passports, the United Kingdom's movement towards 'an integrated electronic border security system', the extension of pre-charge detention powers from fourteen to twenty-eight days (and beyond, if warranted) and, above all, the introduction of national identity cards. Brown has, opportunistically, linked the war against terrorism with his desire to strengthen the celebration of British national identity by advocating 'the ideals of Britishness' as another bulwark against extremism. In short, 'global terrorism must be fought globally – with all the means at our disposal: military, security, intelligence, economics and culture'.[101]

Drawing on the insights of another eminent American Democratic politician from the Cold War era, Dean Acheson, the former Secretary of

State in the Truman Administration, Brown concluded that if the battle for hearts and minds is to be won, peace and prosperity must be seen as indivisible.[102] Ironically, it was Acheson who famously observed that 'Great Britain has lost an empire and has not yet found a role'.[103] For Brown, the quest for a new global role for the United Kingdom in the twenty-first century means, above all, that the 'special relationship' with the United States will endure. Brown's determination to maintain this primacy in the United Kingdom's Atlanticist foreign policy has been demonstrated by his stance on the UK's independent nuclear deterrent. When the issue was debated in the House of Commons, Brown voted in favour of renewing the United Kingdom's Trident nuclear submarine system. The Government secured the support of 409 MPs and a majority of 248. No fewer than ninety-five Labour MPs voted for an amendment which stated that the case for renewal had not yet been proven and therefore a decision should be delayed and eighty-eight voted against the Government's motion. The dissenters included sixteen former ministers; four were former Cabinet ministers.[104] Intriguingly, sixty of the ninety-five unconvinced of the case for renewal later nominated Brown as Blair's successor, as did forty-eight of the eighty-eight rebels who voted against the Government.[105] There may be trouble ahead in future Parliamentary votes on Trident's renewal.

CONCLUSION

From his tenure as Chancellor of the Exchequer, Gordon Brown's legacy to global governance is a vision rooted in the ideology and institutions of the American liberalism of the 1930s' New Deal and the post-war multilateralism of the Marshall Plan and the *Pax Americana*. Brown looks to that particular ideological and institutional legacy as a model for global governance in the twenty-first century. He is as determinedly, if not more, committed as Tony Blair to writing new chapters in the 'special relationship' with the White House. The only significant difference so far has been the greater emphasis that Brown has placed on issues of international development and economic governance, compared to Blair's more vigorous espousal of the legitimacy of the 'war on terror'.[106] While some of Brown's proposals, notably the International Finance Facility, have been imaginative, they have been cast firmly within the tenets of the neo-liberal Washington Consensus, with its unassailable faith in the merits of liberalisation, deregulation and privatisation as the basis for development. During his tenure as Chairman of the IMFC, Brown steadfastly toed the establishment line in relation to the governance of the IMF and other multilateral institutions.

Through international co-operation and the reform of international institutions, notably the United Nations, the North Atlantic Treaty Organisation, the IMF and the World Bank, Brown continues to believe that globalisation can be made to work 'to ensure prosperity and opportunity for not just some people but all people'.[107] His thesis is that the global public good, notably in energy and natural resources, the environment and the fight against terrorism, will only be secured through co-operation. For international co-operation to be feasible, there must be both 'reformed international institutions and more effective multilateral networks'. While the post-1945 Bretton Woods system of international institutions, crafted for 'a world of sheltered economies and just fifty states, is not yet broken', it is nevertheless 'urgently in need of modernisation and reform [for] a world of two hundred states and an open globalisation'.[108]

Brown does not envisage that the United Kingdom will stand down from its permanent seat on the United Nations' Security Council to make way for new twenty-first century powers, such as India and China. Speaking during an official visit overseas while 'Prime Minister-in-waiting', Brown acknowledged India's 'right to an increased voice, side by side with the responsibilities of an economic openness and enhanced international co-operation that come with it'.[109] His balancing of India's rights with its responsibilities sent a clear message about twenty-first century global governance and the contribution that British foreign policy will make to it. India must open up its protected markets to foreign (not least British) investment, in the same way that the United Kingdom has liberalised its markets. India and other developing economies must join the international club on his terms. Just like the European Union, they must converge towards the British model and embrace the Brown Government's agenda for global governance.

Chapter 7

Global Europe: Convergence Towards the British Model

INTRODUCTION

If control over the agenda for the reform of public services in England was the greatest source of friction in domestic policy between Tony Blair and Gordon Brown, the United Kingdom's attitude towards the European Union (EU) was the greatest source of tension in foreign policy. While committed wholeheartedly to the United Kingdom's membership of the EU, Brown is, nevertheless, a confirmed Euro-sceptic and in his pro-European realism, wants the EU to converge towards the British model of political economy. The necessity of that convergence has been institutionalised in the 'Five Tests' that must be passed before the people of the United Kingdom are invited to vote in a referendum on participation in the single European currency. Brown, in his vision of a Global Europe based on pro-European realism, has explicitly rejected the idea of ever closer political union as the future for the EU. Indeed, he has designated that earlier model as merely the first, past and completed phase in the history of European integration.

Brown's political legacy as Chancellor of the Exchequer was the obstruction – repeatedly and successfully – of Tony Blair's stated ambition to place the United Kingdom at the heart of Europe. The United Kingdom did not participate in the first wave of European Monetary Union (EMU). During New Labour's first term, Brown quickly, and decisively, ruled out the United Kingdom's participation in the Single European currency for the lifetime of that Parliament. During the Blair Government's second term, Brown devised a complex array of detailed studies and tests to evaluate progress towards convergence between the United Kingdom economy and the euro-zone. Those studies concluded that it was not then in the United Kingdom's national interest to replace the pound with the euro. Nor is there any prospect, in the immediate or foreseeable future, that the Brown Government will do so. Brown's British model of political economy and unprecedented political power as a peace-time Chancellor was built on the foundation of the national rather than the supra-national control of monetary, fiscal and enterprise policy. The Treasury, under Gordon Brown and outside the euro-zone, not the European Central Bank within it, shaped the United Kingdom's engagement with the European single market. For Brown and his political allies, the vindication of that strategy has been the sustained growth of the national economy outside the euro-zone.

Gordon Brown became Prime Minister at a particularly sensitive time for the EU. Having marked the fiftieth anniversary of the creation of the European Economic Community on 25 March 1957, the European Council held a summit meeting in Germany on 21 and 22 June 2007, to debate the future of the *Treaty Establishing a Constitution for Europe*. The summit was held just after the second anniversary of referendums in which the French and Dutch people had voted 'no' to the Treaty and the European Council's call, in the aftermath of the Constitution's rejection, for a 'period of reflection'.[1]

Brown's reflection on the first fifty years of European integration is that its first phase is over. That phase, of regional economic integration, reconstruction of trade and investment links, development of 'new policies and institutions as the foundation of a common market' and the strengthening and then enlargement of the Single Market, has been supplanted by a second phase. For Brown, the EU must 'move on from the older, inward-looking model to become a more flexible, reforming, open and globally-oriented Europe'.[2] As with so many other aspects of his domestic and international political agenda, Brown has identified globalisation, and the competitive challenge posed by the United States, Japan, China and India, as the justification for major institutional and policy changes at the supra-national level.

The challenge which confronted the Brown Government was that both the European Commission and the political elites of many of the other EU member states remain convinced that the European Constitution can – and should – be revived. For many in France, the principal reason for voting '*non*' in the May 2005 referendum was that the document before them amounted to what Andrew Rawnsley called '*une constitution Blairiste*'.[3] Despite the fact that the EU Constitutional Convention was led by the former French President, Valéry Giscard d'Estaing, there was a widespread belief on both the French Left and Right that the Blair Government had subverted the Constitution. Rather than a further step towards an ever-closer political union, the '*non*' camp was convinced that the Constitution represented a drift towards the Anglo-American model of capitalism and a dismantling of the European social model of comprehensive welfare benefit entitlements. At the same time, high-profile representatives of foreign manufacturers in the United Kingdom criticised the Blair Government's failure to adopt the single European currency and identified how the resulting uncertainty about the pound's future value against the euro had threatened future investment.[4]

For its part, and in the debates held during the period of official reflection under its 'Plan D for Democracy, Dialogue and Debate', the European Commission concluded that there is 'a strong wish by Europe's citizens for more EU action in many areas: on creating jobs, managing globalisation, fighting terrorism and organised crime, promoting sustainable development and solidarity'.[5] The Commission conceded that only forty-seven per cent of its citizens had a positive image of the EU and only forty-four per cent trusted the EU but nevertheless asserted that 'the European Union has never been more needed but rarely more questioned'.[6] It has therefore sought to identify 'A Citizens' Agenda' for Europe, to 'deliver peace, prosperity and solidarity in a new context, globalisation'. Brown's problem is that although the political rhetoric might appear to be converging towards his vision of a 'Global Europe', in practice large parts of the European Commission still believe that globalisation is best addressed by sustaining 'publicly funded health care, social protection and pensions'; somewhat distant from the proposals for wholesale structural reform advanced by the Treasury during Brown's tenure as Chancellor.

As in other areas of domestic and foreign policy, Gordon Brown has sought vigorously to engage in and win the battle of ideas about the future of the EU. There is little sign of any progressive consensus about the future pattern of European integration. In this chapter, I shall set out Gordon Brown's particular vision for the European Union and the United Kingdom's position within it and document how Brown's development of the British model of political economy and broader advocacy of the Anglo-American model of capitalism led to the development of a vision for Europe that is, largely, in accordance with the tenets of Margaret Thatcher's Bruges speech to the College of Europe. I shall then explore the 'Five Tests' for sterling's entry to the single European currency and how Brown, and Ed Balls, developed a very precise agenda for reform of the economic policies of the EU and European Central Bank and in particular the Growth and Stability Pact. The Treasury used the March 2000 Lisbon Summit of the EU as a platform to legitimise Brown's agenda for wholesale structural reform of the Single Market towards a more liberalised and deregulated model. This culminated in Brown's vision of a 'Global Europe' for the twenty-first century and the desire for the other member states of the EU to converge towards the British model of political economy.

THE LESSONS OF 'BLACK WEDNESDAY'

For many eminent social democratic commentators, whether the United Kingdom should align its strategic political and economic interests more closely with those of the United States or the EU is far more than a simple foreign policy choice. The inability of successive post-war British Prime Ministers (including Clement Attlee, Harold Wilson and James Callaghan), to cast off the cloak of the British Empire and move the United Kingdom closer to Europe, was described by Young, in *This Blessed Plot*, as Britain's failure 'to reconcile the past she could not forget with the future she could not avoid'.[7] According to Professor Andrew Gamble, for the British state, 'it is not a matter simply of economics or of politics or of international relations: it goes to the heart of the political identity and political economy of this state formed over a very long period of development';[8] the Labour Party should embrace Europe 'as a model both for capitalism and for welfare and for democracy, to join the euro and to participate fully in developing Britain's European identity and deepening the integration of Europe'.[9] For the *Observer* columnist Will Hutton, 'the quest for European Union is one of the great rousing and crucial political projects of our time' and therefore the United Kingdom should join the euro.[10] For these commentators, the United Kingdom's stance towards European integration is much more than simply a question of whether or not to join the euro. It should be seen as 'a question about what values should underpin the building of Britain's economic and social model'.

This is not a view currently shared by Gordon Brown but it was not ever thus. Speaking at the Trades Union Congress on 8 September 1988, Jacques Delors, the President of the European Commission, appeared to provide the Labour movement with a means to roll back the frontiers of a decade of Thatcherism by embracing the European Community's economic and social model of 'co-operation as well as competition'.[11] During the 1992 General Election campaign, the Labour Party promised to 'promote Britain out of the European second division into which our country has been relegated by the Tories'. Having cast off its overt Euro-scepticism of a decade earlier, the Party would keep the pound within the European Exchange Rate Mechanism (ERM) but play an active role in negotiations on the EMU.[12] However, on 16 September 1992, the United Kingdom suffered the national humiliation of 'Black Wednesday' when currency speculators operating on the City of London's foreign exchange markets drove the pound out of the ERM's fixed exchange rate regime. This happened despite the Major Government's having, within less than four hours, raised interest rates from ten per cent to twelve per cent and then to fifteen per cent, and spent billions of pounds of foreign exchange buying sterling in a vain attempt to maintain the pound within the permitted variation from its central parity of DM2.95.[13] The Major Government's counter-inflationary strategy was destroyed at a stroke, together with its reputation for economic competence. The Chancellor of the Exchequer, Norman Lamont, paid for the crisis with his job.

Gordon Brown and Ed Balls learnt important lessons about the future conduct of British economic policy and its relationship to EMU from the events of 'Black Wednesday'; lessons that provided the foundations of the British model of political economy (as I outlined in Chapter Three). Brown's initial reaction was to suggest that 'Black Wednesday' had demonstrated that Europe was still the answer.[14] More, rather than less, European co-operation was needed 'to diminish the power and role of speculators'. Brown explicitly rejected the idea that a freely-floating pound, outside the

ERM, could provide the 'managed and stable exchange rate essential for sustainable growth'. Brown argued that 'The credibility of Europe depends on the ability of Governments to act together to deal with the problems of the economy'.[15] Above all, Brown wanted to avoid the Labour Party being once more depicted as 'the party of devaluation'.

At this time, Ed Balls did not share Brown's analysis. His lessons from the debacle were much clearer: the ERM had ensnared the pound in a Euro-monetarist trap. The key challenge for the Labour Party was to provide the United Kingdom with an 'alternative but credible policy framework and promote growth and full employment at the same time'.[16] The United Kingdom could not rejoin EMU until there was convergence between a British 'new economic deal for the 1990s' and a non-monetarist 'European policy which puts growth, employment and political integration before over-rigid attachments to fixed monetary rules.[17] This would rule out the United Kingdom's participation in EMU indefinitely, because of the irreconcilable nature of the projects of Labour's domestic modernisation and EMU, unless the latter was prepared to converge towards the former.

Brown was duly persuaded by Balls, and by the policies pursued by the Clinton Administration in the United States, that priority should be given to the construction of a non-monetarist economic policy based on national economic choices rather than supra-national co-operation through EMU. He began to cast off his previous attachment to supply-side socialism, with its roots in continental European national political economy and embrace supply-side liberalism, with its roots in North American capitalism. For Brown, the key point of the victory of the New Democrats in Congress was that:

> Clinton found an echo throughout America for his central idea that government had responsibilities to the whole community to deal with the huge problems of unemployment, the weakness of the American manufacturing sector and training in skills and, of course, for the argument that there were entrenched elites in American society, that were denying people opportunity.[18]

Drawing on the lessons from the New Democrats and the nascent 'Clintonomics', Labour's new economic policy could more effectively secure macro-economic stability and fiscal discipline and confront the challenges posed by globalisation and the impact of new information and communication technologies from outside the ERM and EMU. In New Labour's economic policy, EMU would be subordinate to national monetary and fiscal policy choices.[19] Labour would continue to support EMU but with the strong qualification that 'convergence of the real economic performance of member states is a vital pre-condition of any moves towards economic and monetary union'.[20]

THE 'FIVE TESTS' (PLUS TWO)

In its 1997 General Election manifesto, the Labour Party promised 'a fresh start in Europe, with the credibility to achieve reform'. British leadership in Europe would be based on the vision of Europe as 'an alliance of independent nations choosing to co-operate to achieve the goals they cannot achieve alone'. (This particular section of the manifesto was headed by a picture of Tony Blair taking the lead in talks with an attentive Jacques Chirac.) However, there was also an equivocal statement of opposition to a European federal super-state and a commitment to basing participation in the single currency on 'a hard-headed assessment of Britain's economic interests'.[21] Moreover, the manifesto recognised 'formidable obstacles' in the way of British participation in the first wave of EMU. The economic prerequisite would be 'genuine convergence' among participating economies. The political prerequisites would be Cabinet and Parliamentary approval before a 'Yes' vote in a future referendum.[22]

The United Kingdom's presidency of the European Council (for six months from 1st January 1998) was an opportunity for Brown and the Treasury to ensure the priority of national economic policy over EMU. Any ambitions for sterling to make a belated bid for participation in the first wave of EMU that Tony Blair might have harboured were quickly dashed in a series of decisive moves Brown made.[23] First, he announced the decision to give the Bank of England operational independence over the implementation of monetary policy. Second, his statement of the Blair Government's central economic objectives did not include sterling's participation in his first wave of EMU. Third, in his first major statement of New Labour's European agenda, Brown made it plain that Britain wished to exercise leadership in Europe on New Labour's terms, rather than those of its EU partners.

This speech appears to have been the only occasion during his Chancellorship when Brown actually used the term the 'third way', referring to New Labour's 'third way of economic reform' as an alternative to 'the old choices between a federal versus non-federal Europe and between a social market and a free-market Europe or old style regulation versus crude deregulation ... We reject both the federal way forward and the regulatory way ahead'.[24] Brown based Britain's claim to leadership in Europe on what he termed 'British genius': uniquely British values and qualities such as a commitment to openness to trade, outward-looking and internationalist instincts, connections which stretched across the world, creativity and adaptability as a nation, insistence on the importance of public services and openness in the running of institutions. Brown conceded that Britain shared certain qualities with other European states, such as the importance attached to hard work, self-improvement through education, fair play and opportunity for all but the others, he claimed, were 'uniquely British'.[25] Asserting that Britain had a unique claim to such qualities was flying in the face of centuries of European history, and not least of developments since the end of the Second World War. Many EU states could stake at least an equal claim to such qualities in their national character and political cultures. For example, the much higher share of national income devoted to public spending in general and key public services such as health care in particular, and the resistance to privatisation and deregulation might have suggested that France and Germany had a stronger claim to reverence for the importance of public services.

The most important aspect of Brown's speech was the specification of five tests that would provide 'a hard-headed assessment of Britain's economic interests' and a basis on which to decide whether it was appropriate for the United Kingdom to join EMU. These tests were: first, whether joining EMU would create better conditions for firms contemplating long-term investment in Britain, second, whether joining EMU would benefit the United Kingdom's financial services, third (and notwithstanding long-term benefits from EMU), whether there was sufficient compatibility between business cycles and economic structures in Britain and Europe to enable euro interest rates to be permanently lived with, fourth, whether there was sufficient flexibility within EMU to deal with emergent problems and fifth ('the bottom line'), whether joining EMU would promote Brown's central economic objectives of 'higher growth, stability and a lasting increase in jobs'.[26]

Brown's claims, as the basis for Britain's agenda in Europe, were likely to offend some EU states, because of their rather arrogant and imprudent nature. However, Brown's speech was designed to appeal to a domestic audience, not a continental European one. He had spelt out five economic tests for determining whether it was in the United Kingdom's interest to participate in EMU but Brown's strategy was really dictated by a sixth and seventh pair of hidden (and political) tests that were the true 'bottom line'. The sixth was whether a United Kingdom referendum on EMU could be won. This was far from a foregone conclusion. In November 1997, an opinion poll revealed that fifty per cent of those questioned opposed United Kingdom participation in the euro. Furthermore, sixty-five per cent of respondents thought such participation would mean the United Kingdom having to stay in the EU forever. No fewer than thirty-five per cent favoured outright withdrawal from the EU.[27] The seventh – and most important – test was whether EMU would fatally undermine the Treasury's control over domestic economic and social policy choices by taking away discretion over the design of monetary and fiscal policy. Since it would, there could be no question of the United Kingdom participating in EMU.

Brown's speech was, in effect, a justification for not taking advantage of Labour's landslide General Election victory to set an early referendum on the principle of entry to the euro. The radicalism of Brown's immediate reforms to monetary and fiscal policy, through the new role for the Monetary Policy Committee of the Bank of England and the Government's 'golden rules' and spending review, was not matched by similar radicalism in his attitude to Europe. For the Treasury to have agreed to an early referendum would have meant threatening Brown's unprecedented control over domestic policy. Becoming a party to the European Central Bank's Stability and Growth Pact would have meant constraints on his freedom to use fiscal policy to drive New Labour's domestic modernisation agenda. By making the United Kingdom's participation in the euro-zone dependent on major structural reforms to its EU partners' economies, so that they converged towards the British model, Brown knew full well that the United Kingdom was effectively ruling itself out of joining the euro for at least a decade.

Brown claimed that 'the Government is throwing open the EMU debate' but in effect he was closing it down.[28] This was confirmed in his first major Westminster statement on EMU, in which he asserted that Britain had faced 'no question more important and more contentious than that of our relationship with Europe ... The decision on a single currency is probably the most important this country is likely to face in our generation'. While there were obvious benefits from EMU, 'in terms of trade, transparency of costs and currency stability', there were three 'issues of principle' that had to be surmounted before Britain could join the euro: whether EMU would work economically, whether a common monetary policy would represent an unconstitutional loss of economic sovereignty and whether the consent of the British people could be secured in a referendum.[29]

Brown confirmed that the Blair Government's conclusion on EMU, based on an application of the five economic tests, was that 'there is no proper convergence between the British and the other European economies now'. The Treasury study revealed important structural differences between the United Kingdom economy and those of other European countries: trade patterns, North Sea oil, company finance, the housing market and notable weaknesses 'in the level of skills, the high numbers of workless households and high levels of long-term unemployment'.[30] Therefore, the United Kingdom did not seek membership of the single currency on 1st January 1999. While there was 'no need, legally, formally or politically, to renounce our option for the period between 1st January 1999 and the end of the Parliament, nor would it be sensible to do so', Brown effectively ruled out United Kingdom entry to EMU for the lifetime of the Parliament, because there was 'no realistic prospect' of the demonstration of 'convergence which is sustainable and settled rather than transitory'. The policy would not change 'barring some fundamental and unforeseen change in economic circumstances'. Brown claimed: 'the essential decision is economic'.[31]

On the contrary, for Brown the essential decision was and always would be, political. Brown had guaranteed Treasury control over monetary and fiscal policy for the duration of New Labour's first term. More importantly, he had, at Tony Blair's expense, entrenched his political control over resource allocation and domestic policy design in England.

THE POLITICS OF 'PRO-EUROPEAN REALISM'

Although Gordon Brown claimed that the Blair Government was 'the first British government to declare for the principle of monetary union. The first to state that there is no over-riding constitutional bar to membership', he had, simultaneously, ruled out the practice of monetary union and constructed an effective Treasury bar to membership.[32]

Brown undermined Blair's oft-stated ambition to place Britain at the heart of Europe. On 5th April 1995, Blair had made a speech on 'Britain in Europe' to the Royal Institute of International Affairs (RIIA) at Chatham House, in which he stated that 'Europe is the only route through which Britain can exercise power and influence. If it is to maintain its historic role as a global player, Britain has to be a central part of the politics of Europe'.[33] Brown's speech to the RIIA at Chatham House two years later crushed that Prime Ministerial vision and weakened Blair's authority. There had been no mention of the 'five tests' during the 1997 General Election campaign or in the Labour Party manifesto. The tests were contrived by Balls and Brown without Blair's involvement. Blair's economic advisor, Derek Scott, later confirmed that Number Ten found it extremely difficult to secure information on key economic decisions from the Treasury. Scott claimed 'the Chancellor's office had instructed all officials within the department that any contact they had with me to be reported, together with the subject discussed'.[34]

The source of the greatest friction between Blair and Brown came on 18th October 1997. The *Times* newspaper carried the headline, 'Brown Rules Out Single Currency for Lifetime of this Parliament'; the *Sun* 'Brown Says No to the Euro'.[35] This information had been leaked to the media by Charlie Whelan, Brown's 'spin doctor'. A vital decision on British government policy had been made without the express knowledge or authorisation of the Prime Minister or the Foreign Secretary or any discussion by the Cabinet. As one influential commentator on New Labour suggested:

> Manoeuvring between its two leading men, exacerbated by the mutual loathing and paranoia of their entourages and further aggravated by the government's haphazard forms of decision-making, was creating mayhem in the most fundamental area of foreign and economic affairs.[36]

The political legacy of this confusion further poisoned the working relationship between Brown and Blair. Personally, the EMU debacle led to weeks of political backbiting between the Blair and Brown camps carried out through their media proxies, culminating in the reported allegation that

Blair believed Brown to possess 'psychological flaws'.[37] On policy, Brown was happy to announce to Parliament both the United Kingdom's Action Plan to create lasting employment and the Treasury's Guide to the Single Currency.[38] However, when it came to the announcement of the United Kingdom's National Changeover Plan for the introduction of the euro (which would come after a referendum vote in favour of EMU), Brown was insistent that Blair make the statement at Westminster.[39]

Brown wanted to distance himself from EMU and for Blair to make a statement to Parliament that would vindicate the Treasury's strategy towards the United Kingdom's participation. Blair's statement, on 23 February 1999, on the National Changeover Plan served precisely those purposes. By affirming that the five tests would have to be passed before a referendum could be held, Blair effectively confirmed that the Treasury, not Number Ten, would decide on the United Kingdom's entry into the euro.[40] In its 2001 General Election manifesto, the Labour Party reiterated its commitment in principle to join a successful single currency but promised an assessment of the UK's standing in the five tests early in the next Parliament.[41] Blair stated, in answer to a parliamentary question, that 'early in the next parliament would of course be within two years'.[42] When the General Election was held on 7th June 2001, it appeared Blair had for once entrapped Brown into a definitive timetable for an assessment that could lead to eventual United Kingdom entry to the euro-zone. However, Blair had not anticipated the lengths to which Brown and the Treasury would go to demonstrate that there was not a clear and unambiguous case for joining EMU.

When the Treasury published its assessment of the five tests for United Kingdom membership of the single currency on 9th June 2003, it produced not one report but eighteen studies that analysed the economic implications of joining the euro-zone in the minutest detail.[43] Their excessive length was an elaborate smoke-screen for the fact that the United Kingdom's participation in EMU was quintessentially a political decision that would be made by Brown and the Treasury, not by Tony Blair or the Cabinet collectively. In the two years before the studies' publication, Brown and Balls delivered a series of keynote speeches and lectures in which they set out, with increasing confidence, the principles and policies of their 'British model' of political economy, reiterated the importance of the five economic tests and identified a series of major structural reforms that would have to be undertaken before the United Kingdom could participate in EMU. Most importantly, they made it increasingly apparent that, with the British economy out-performing its major continental European rivals in employment growth, the convergence would have to predominantly be of the euro-zone economies towards the British model, rather than vice versa.

Immediately after the June 2001 General Election, in a major speech to a City of London audience, Brown defined his approach to EMU as 'one of pro-euro realism'. He claimed that 'a Europe reformed is a Europe that serves Britain and Europe best'. There would have to be urgent reform of the EU budget and the Common Agricultural Policy. The future of the EU must be 'not a federalist one but one in which independent nation states work together to shape the decisions', with increasing 'mutual recognition of national standards and solutions based on exchange of information, peer review and benchmarking rather than the central imposition of "one size fits all." ' While the EU single market must 'rightly, have a social dimension', at the same time, it must make 'subsidiarity or national decision-making the way forward'. There must be 'tax competition not tax harmonisation', with the new Europe being 'outward-looking rather than inward-looking' on trade policy.[44] The message of Brown's speech was clear. Major reforms to the EU would be needed before the United Kingdom could contemplate its involvement in EMU, including structural convergence towards the British model of market liberalisation and deregulation.

Speaking in Oxford in 2002, on the tenth anniversary of the publication of his path-breaking analysis of Euro-monetarism, Ed Balls sought to give the Treasury's five tests greater historical gravitas by locating them within a broader analysis of Britain's relative economic decline. He claimed that the five tests were based on four vital lessons the Treasury had learned from the United Kingdom's return to the Gold Standard in April 1925. First, in 1925 the British Government had not ensured that 'economics, not politics, was the deciding factor on the timing and manner of decision'. Second, this particular decision had been made 'not from a position of strength but from weakness'. Third, the decision had not been based on 'a proper assessment of the long-run economic consequences'. Fourth, at the time, the government had not undertaken 'a full economic analysis of the economic consequences, including any short-term transitional issues so that the economic consequences were fully understood'. For Balls, the lessons of history for the Treasury's assessment of the five tests were clear.[45] The assessment would be based on economics, not politics, made from a position of strength (delivered by the British model) and follow a proper assessment of the long-term consequences of EMU. Pro-European realism would rule the Blair Government's policy.

When the Treasury published a major assessment of the five economic tests, it concluded, in overall terms, the United Kingdom had indeed:

> ... made real economic progress towards meeting the five economic tests. But, on balance, though the potential benefits of increased investment, trade, a boost to financial services, growth and jobs are clear, we cannot at this point in time conclude that there is sustainable and durable convergence or sufficient flexibility to cope with any potential difficulties within the euro area. So, despite the risks and costs from delaying the benefits of joining, a clear and unambiguous case for UK membership of EMU has not at the present time been made and a decision to join now would not be in the national economic interest.[46]

Brown's statement to Parliament confirmed that only the third and fourth of the five tests, on investment and financial services respectively, had been passed. The first test on convergence, the second test on flexibility and the critical fifth test on employment, stability and growth had not. Price inflation in the British housing market (a source of economic volatility during the past fifty years) was a particular structural difference between the United Kingdom and the euro-zone remained and dictated 'a cautious approach'.[47] Therefore, the United Kingdom would not be joining the euro-zone for the foreseeable future, especially since the housing market was one of the principal engines of the consumption-led growth which characterised the British model of political economy.

CONVERGENCE TOWARDS THE BRITISH MODEL

Gordon Brown used his statement on 9th June 2003 on the Treasury's assessment of the five tests to announce the implementation of further major reforms of the United Kingdom economy, to promote the process of 'sustainable and durable convergence'.[48] With increasing confidence in the British model of political economy, arising from the Treasury's rejection of a clear and unambiguous case for EMU, Brown and Balls developed a major critique of the European Central Bank (ECB) and the European Stability and Growth Pact, as supra-national instruments of macro-economic stability. Balls developed the thesis, which underpinned the Treasury's June 2003 assessment, that operating outside the euro-zone, the British model enjoyed a much greater range of macro-economic policy options and was able to respond to any shock which might threaten domestic growth and stability. Outside the euro-zone, the Treasury had recourse to monetary policy, exchange rate adjustment, fiscal policy and flexibility in wages and prices if it wished to respond to an economic shock. Balls asserted that the British model of monetary and fiscal policy had institutionalised the 'principles of modern macro-economic policy' and that the European Growth and Stability Pact should be modernised to embrace them.[49] The British model's range of policy instruments would narrow significantly if the United Kingdom were to join the euro-zone.

Balls asserted that the monetary policy, as a country-specific stabiliser, would be diluted in the euro-zone because the ECB, unlike the Treasury, would respond to an overall euro-inflation objective, rather than one for the British economy alone. In the euro-zone, the Treasury would no longer have the pound's nominal exchange rate as a tool of exchange rate adjustment. The only remaining macro-economic policy options would be flexibility in prices, quantities and capital movements or a greater use of fiscal policy as an instrument for domestic stabilisation. Balls was convinced that, because an over-reliance on flexibility in wages and prices could be potentially damaging for both stability and growth, the ECB and European Growth and Stability Pact must place a greater emphasis on fiscal policy as a source of stability.[50] Therefore, the United Kingdom – and all the other existing euro-zone member states – must consider how a flexible and legitimate national régime for fiscal policy might be designed to operate in the euro-zone. The clear implication was that the existing European Growth and Stability Pact was insufficiently flexible and illegitimate.

Despite the Treasury's reticence, the United Kingdom might be able to join the euro, through the modernisation of the European Growth and Stability Pact so that it converged towards the Treasury's model of constrained discretion. To extend the first principle of constrained discretion, the specification of long-term objectives, to fiscal policy within the euro-zone, Balls proposed that, subject to the ECB's inflation target, the objective should be to minimise deviations of national output and employment from the national economy's trend growth rate. To avoid the possibility of confusion and conflict between national fiscal policy and that operating in the wider euro-zone, Balls proposed that there should be a mechanism to trigger adjustments in national fiscal policy, if there were a prospect of significant deviation of the national economy from a stable path.[51] In its assessment paper, *Fiscal Stabilisation and EMU*, the Treasury proposed a rule for fiscal policy based on an output gap of 1–1.5 per cent.[52] In other words, if the national economy were to deviate from its sustainable path of growth by more than 1–1.5 per cent, a fiscal policy response would be triggered. This trigger would operate subject to the two elements of the Treasury's existing rules-based approach to fiscal policy: the 'golden rule' and the sustainable investment rule.

Balls contented that there were four reasons why this trigger would work effectively for the United Kingdom and other member states within a modernised European Growth and Stability Pact. First, it would avoid excessive instability in national output. Second, because the fiscal trigger would be symmetrical, it could equally be triggered to induce fiscal tightening, should a national economy be growing in an inflationary manner. Third, the trigger, while predictable, would not be automatically implemented: the sole obligation of national governments would be to justify to their Parliament and financial markets why they had chosen to act on fiscal policy or not. Fourth, the trigger would create an explicit link between flexibility and sustainability across the economic cycle and the level of net debt, because it would only operate subject to the existing net debt and sustainable public finances rules in British model of fiscal policy.[53]

The British model provided the European Growth and Stability Pact with a blueprint for its modernisation. The Pact must ensure that within EMU, fiscal activism by individual countries was 'predictable, exceptional and confined to low debt countries'. Members must be committed to 'fiscal discipline, symmetrical over the cycle for all countries', allowing low debt countries only to use fiscal stabilisation measures to ensure stability and growth, consonant with low debt and sustainable public finances and 'effectively enforced fiscal co-ordination between national governments'.[54] To achieve this, the mechanistic and asymmetrically applied annual rules of the European Growth and Stability Pact, with their target of annual reduction of budget deficits by 0.5 per cent of gross domestic product (GDP), should be replaced by guiding principles allowing for constrained discretion, that is, the British model's 'clear pre-commitment to flexible operating rules'.

Balls called for a more prudent interpretation of the European Growth and Stability Pact; an evolution in its institutional design that would give greater flexibility by allowing low debt economies to use discretionary fiscal policy to support stability and growth. This would mean agreement by the Council of the ECB that low debt economies, like the United Kingdom, should be able to breach the three per cent of GDP deficit rule for 'exceptional and temporary reasons'. There would need to be greater fiscal co-ordination within the Council of the ECB and a strengthening of independent monitoring, surveillance and transparency, possibly by creating an inter-governmental 'fiscal surveillance committee ... staffed by Member State and European Commission representatives, with delegated authority to conduct analysis and surveillance of national fiscal policies and advise the Council'.[55]

Balls and Brown wanted the euro-zone to converge towards the British model of monetary and fiscal policy. That was their prerequisite for sterling's. Just as, under their stewardship, British economic policy had evolved from the flawed policies of Lawson, Major and Lamont into the British model, so now EMU must cast off European monetarism. Their conceit was that, having worked nationally, the British model 'can be made to work in monetary unions too'.[56] Balls first advocated this expansion of the British model at a time when he could confidently predict that the Government would meet its 'golden rule' of fiscal policy, with an annual average surplus over the economic cycle of 0.2 per cent of GDP (fourteen billion pounds) and meet the net debt rule with a margin of 4.5 per cent of GDP (sixty-four billion pounds). This was before Brown had three times had to redefine his definition of the United Kingdom's economic cycle to meet his own fiscal rules (see Chapter Three).

GLOBAL BRITAIN, GLOBAL EUROPE

Gordon Brown and Ed Balls's ambition to export the British model of political economy to the euro-zone was not confined to monetary and fiscal policy. Brown attempted to press other EU economies to transform their prospects for more rapid growth and employment by converging towards the supply-side liberalism of the Anglo-American model of capitalism. Much of the political momentum for this initiative arose from the

European Council's Lisbon Summit of 23–24 March 2000. This Summit marked a turning point in supra-national policy, in that it committed the EU 'to strengthen employment, economic reform and social cohesion as part of a knowledge-based economy'.[57] This agenda sought to draw the EU into a process of political, economic and social renewal whose rhetoric, language and content bore, in many respects, a marked similarity to New Labour's domestic modernisation agenda. The Summit's agenda was based on the conviction that the EU was faced by 'a quantum shift resulting from globalisation and the challenges of a new knowledge-driven economy' which was 'affecting every aspect of people's lives' and which would require 'a radical transformation of the European economy'[58].

Confronted with this challenge, the European Council set the EU the new strategic goal of becoming 'the most competitive and dynamic knowledge-based economy in the world, capable of sustainable economic growth and better jobs and greater social cohesion'.[59] This meant three things for supra-national policy. First, preparation for the transition to a knowledge-based economy and society through better policies for the information society and for research and development and an acceleration of the process of structural reform for competitiveness and innovation and the completion of the internal market. Second, the modernisation of the European social model through investment in people and the combating of social exclusion. Third, the application of 'an appropriate macro-economic policy mix' to sustain the healthy economic outlook and favourable growth prospects for the EU.[60]

From the perspective of Brown's agenda of supply-side liberalism for enhancing competitiveness, the key insight was the recognition granted to the role of the entrepreneur, enterprise, innovation and productivity growth in this new strategic agenda for the EU. The Lisbon Summit acknowledged the direct dependence both of the competitiveness and dynamism of businesses on 'a regulatory climate conducive to investment, innovation and entrepreneurship'. It also recognised the need to redirect public spending 'towards increasing the relative importance of capital accumulation – both physical and human' and the need to adapt the European model of developed systems of social protection to create an 'active welfare state' which would ensure that work was worth it. The Summit agreed that this agenda should be pursued through 'A fully decentralised approach', which would accord priority to the states and regions of the EU and through the development of 'variable forms of partnership'.[61] In short, the supra-national agenda of social and economic renewal was moving much closer, at least in rhetoric, towards New Labour's modernisation agenda.[62]

The confirmation that the EU agenda on competitiveness could converge with that of Brown and the Treasury came with the publication of the EU's programme for enterprise and entrepreneurship for the period which would cover the Blair Government's second term. The European Commission proposed 'a systematic approach to foster entrepreneurship in the new economy', by encouraging 'risk-taking and the spirit of enterprise', because 'Entrepreneurship is the key to the new economy'.[63] The EU must become 'Enterprise Europe', where 'anyone with a commercially feasible idea should be able to realise it, with access to the best technology, and then deliver it, by the best possible means, to the appropriate market'.[64]

This approach to creating a more dynamic European enterprise culture brought supra-national policy closer to the British model. Since the mid-1990s, it had sought to benchmark national economy performance against a range of indicators of enterprise, productivity and innovation; a trend which was widened and deepened by New Labour's fixation on performance and output indicators. Throughout, the United States was identified as the model to follow. It was to the Treasury's advantage that the EU's Action Plan for Entrepreneurship also identified a widening productivity gap between the EU and the US. It lamented the fact that (in October 2003) only four per cent of Europeans stated that they had been engaged in creating a business or being an entrepreneur, compared with eleven per cent of Americans. While forty-four per cent of Americans thought that a business should still be started if there were a risk of failure, only twenty-nine per cent of Europeans concurred.[65]

Gordon Brown sought to exploit this favourable environment for policy by developing an analysis of EU economic performance and competitiveness policy based on his vision of 'Global Europe'. Repeating the pattern of the British model, globalisation became a political weapon in a series of Treasury reports justifying major structural changes and supply-side reforms of continental European economies.[66] In a speech at a Confederation of British Industry conference on 'Competitiveness in Europe-Post Enlargement', rather than setting out how the United Kingdom would seek to converge with the euro-zone, Brown provided his audience with an agenda on how the newly expanded EU should converge with the 'British model' of stability and enterprise.

Brown claimed that globalisation had placed Europe's competitive advantage under a severe, triple, threat that came first from the developing economies, which he claimed could account for half of all global manufacturing exports in twenty years; second, from Asia, to which five million European and American jobs might be out-sourced and third, from China, which was already a larger market for Volkswagen than Germany.[67] Brown portrayed the history of supra-national integration as a process which had created the world's first modern trade block but which had now entered a second phase of 'Global Europe': a Europe facing global competition. Brown did not acknowledge that European integration might fundamentally have been about the vision of an ever-closer political union rather than simply a matter of economics. Instead, he claimed that globalisation demanded 'a programme of liberalisation, tax reform, new employment policies, the opening up of trade and commerce and a modern monetary and fiscal regime'[68].

Brown set out a five-point framework to enable the EU to converge with the supply-side liberalism of the Anglo-American model of capitalism. First, the EU must follow the British example of delegating responsibility for liberalisation to competition authorities, rather than politicians, to accelerate the creation of more open and flexible markets. Second, accelerated liberalisation would require openness, flexibility and competition in taxation. Notions of tax harmonisation, underpinning the idea of an ever-closer political union must be abandoned, not only because they would reduce competitiveness but also because they would be 'unacceptable to the peoples of Europe because decisions on what to tax, and how, reflect national choices and cultures'.[69] Despite this emphasis on the importance of national cultural factors, Brown contended that harmonisation of corporation tax and Value Added Tax must also be abandoned because of the constraints imposed by open global markets.

Brown's third prerequisite for the more competitive enlarged Europe was for it to copy the British example of the New Deal. Passive labour markets, with their implicit inflexibility and welfare dependency, must be abandoned in favour of an active labour market policy. In this way, certain EU states might cut their levels of forty to sixty per cent of unemployment lasting for more than a year and converge on the American figure of only twelve per cent. Fourth, the enlarged EU should meet the competitive challenge posed by globalised trade by abandoning what Brown portrayed as its 'Fortress Europe' approach in favour of leadership of the World Trade Organization, in part-nership with the US. Brown claimed that a 'properly sequenced' programme of reforms might create a million jobs in the US and EU, boosting Europe's growth rate by two per cent and the US's by one per cent.[70]

The fifth and final prerequisite was a 'proactive and forward looking' monetary and fiscal policy to address the challenge posed by globalised markets, which the United Kingdom had achieved this through the rules-based approach of the 'British model' for stability. The existing terms of the European Central Bank's Stability and Growth Pact were inappropriate. It was wrong for the European Commission to penalise countries for using fiscal policy to support monetary policy, by making 'sensible investments to improve infrastructure and public services' and thereby combat low growth, especially where countries had 'a position of low debt and of con-sumption covered by revenues'.[71] In an enlarged EU of 25 member states, Brown's conclusion was that reform was 'not just desirable [but] an urgent necessity'. Liberalisation, flexibility and economic reform should be accomplished through 'inter-governmental co-operation' and not, he clearly implied, through closer political union or endorsement of the draft EU Constitution.[72]

GLOBAL EUROPE AND THE 2005 UNITED KINGDOM EU PRESIDENCY

Gordon Brown's commitment to pro-European realism and his vision of a Global Europe was demonstrated during the United Kingdom's presidency of the European Council which ran from 1st July–31st December 2005, forming the twin themes of his contribution to it.

Brown developed the thesis that the EU was entering a second phase of its history. Flows of capital, companies and brands, which had, during an earlier era of European integration, moved from the national to the European level were becoming increasingly global. The inward-looking 'old trade bloc Europe', with its outmoded vision of 'a single currency and per-haps even a federal fiscal policy with tax harmonisation and then ... a supra-national state', must urgently make the transition to an outward-looking Global Europe.[73] This change was made necessary by a circumstance unforeseen by the founders of European integration: the rise of China and

India and other Asian economies from which goods can be obtained and to which investment may flow.

Brown's contention was that Europe was still less competitive in the five key areas of growth, labour market performance, skills, innovation and enterprise. His remedy was the extension of the supply-side liberalism of the British model to the whole EU. Globalisation must be managed well and equitably, through economic and social policies designed to provide the requisite flexibility and fairness to deliver full employment for the twenty million unemployed in Europe.[74] With China and Asia engaged in 'a race to the top', Europe 'must continuously upgrade skills and technology and raise our game'. For Brown, full participation in the new global economy offered the double dividend of efficiency and productivity gains for companies and lower prices for consumers.[75]

In Brown's vision of Global Europe, the United States remained the benchmark for unfavourable comparisons of European economic performance. In terms of growth, Brown asserted that American living standards were more than 30 per cent higher than in the EU. Annual average growth in per capita GDP since 1996 was 0.5 per cent lower in the euro area than in the United States and poor labour market performance was estimated to account for two-thirds of this gap in living standards. Brown highlighted the paltry level of 40.2 per cent employment for Europeans aged 55–64 in 2003, compared with sixty per cent in the United States and sixty-two per cent in Japan. The EU needed to create 22 million jobs by 2010 to meet the targets established at the Lisbon Summit. There was a huge disparity between the EU's 41.8 per cent rate of long-term unemployment (those out of work for more than twelve months) and the 12.7 per cent rate in the United States.[76] Brown did not mention that this might be due to the more generous pension entitlements in the EU member states but the clear implication was that in Global Europe, people would have to work longer.

Brown noted that the EU states had created more than seven million new jobs between 1997 and 2002 in knowledge-intense services but that skill levels were higher in the United States, Canada and Japan and were rising more quickly in emerging markets. In terms of innovation, the EU states had less than half the number of patent applications (per capita) in 2002 than the United States and Japan, while business research and development was almost fifty per cent higher in the United States. (Brown did not supply sources for these statistics.) In terms of enterprise, Brown claimed that total entrepreneurial activity in the United States, Canada and China was 'double or treble that in the large EU member states'.[77]

The message was clear. Europe faced an actual or potential gap in its economic performance and international competitiveness in growth, labour market skills, innovation and enterprise. To create prosperity, full employment and security for all European citizens, the older, inward-looking model of European integration must be supplanted by 'a more flexible, reforming, open and globally-oriented Europe', embracing 'flexibility, dynamism and entrepreneurship supported by an active and responsive labour market policy'.[78] This was something to which Margaret Thatcher or the late Lord Keith Joseph could have objected little.

To deliver Brown's 'full-employment Global Europe', the EU must embrace the economic and social reforms characteristic of the British model of political economy developed by Brown and Balls at the Treasury. Brown emphasised the importance of learning from international practice: for both macro-economic and micro-economic policy, the EU must draw the same lessons from the political economy of the United States as the British model. He insisted that 'there can be no security without change'.[79] However, this strategy must be carried out by the co-operation of national governments rather than through the deepening of supra-national political integration. Brown was equally adamant that policies 'must reflect national traditions and electoral preferences'.[80] Global Europe could be achieved only through 'a new commitment to reform – to complete the Single Market, promote better regulation, encourage innovation and refocus the EU budget'.[81]

In terms of the policy priorities of the United Kingdom's presidency, the first step for the achievement of Global Europe was a political commitment to the completion of the Single Market. For Brown, this entailed liberalisation of EU markets for telecommunications, electricity, gas and commercial services, the elimination of inefficient state subsidies and the implementation of 'an independent and pro-active competition policy'. Furthermore, the EU should deliver 'open, flexible and competitive tax systems across the EU', because 'neither the demands of the modern global economy, nor the principles of subsidiarity and political legitimacy can justify harmonisation of tax rates or bases at an EU level'. Brown held that fair tax competition, rather than harmonisation reflected 'the realities of the global economy' and respected 'the fundamentally national nature of public services needs and economic management challenges that govern-ments face'.[82] The EU must adopt 'a risk-based approach to regulation' and reduce the burden of regulation, including the Union's 'enormous and unwieldy rulebook'. Brown's demand for greater investment in research and development and policies to stimulate private investment and innova-tion led him to the thorny issue of reform of the EU budget which, for him, was 'also key' and must become 'fit for purpose' to meet 'the science, skills and infrastructure challenges of global change'.[83]

To ensure that Global Europe was outward-looking, Brown was adamant that the EU must not retreat behind protectionist policies but must see America, Asia and the rest of the world as partners in a discussion about 'common approaches to regulation, competition and transatlantic commerce'. Global Europe would only be possible through a long-term programme of economic reform in five key areas: structural, budgetary, social, regulatory and trade reform.[84] Brown consigned political integration to history but, as with many other areas of his politics, his analysis was built on weak arguments. For example, he claimed it was 'an implicit assumption of European development that what happened within the European Union mattered far more than what was happening outside it'[85] but, by definition, integration could hardly be anything other than inward-looking.

Conspicuously absent from Brown's vision for the EU was any notion that the way forward might be to develop a common European citizenship and identity based on shared values. Brown's preoccupation in his 'British Way' was the reinvention of British citizenship and identity based on shared British values: a task which had no supra-national dimension. For the EU, the challenge of globalisation demanded rethinking of 'the most basic of political assumptions that have underlain 50 years of development'. Specifically, two assumptions that must be rethought were 'that we would move from being economically integrated at a national level to being eco-nomically integrated at a European level [and] that cultural and political integration would follow economic integration'.[86] Brown specifically rejected the assumption that 'a European identity could supersede national identities' because of the dominance of globalisation over Europe and the assumption about the old European model both because of the EU Constitution referendum results in France and the Netherlands and the reaction across the EU to a period of low growth. For Brown, the referen-dums demonstrated how identities had 'remained rooted in the nation state

– and that familiar national, cultural and political attachments are important', not least in relation to 'issues of what is taxed and by whom'. Brown's 'pro-European realism' remained based on 'the founding case for the European Union, the benefits of co-operation among nation states for peace and prosperity but strengthened by the insistence that Europe looks outwards as a Global Europe'.[87]

THE SUPRA-NATIONAL PRIORITIES FOR A BROWN GOVERNMENT

To consolidate his influence over the Blair Government's policy on Europe, Brown sat on two Cabinet Committees: the Cabinet Ministerial Committee on European Policy, whose remit was to determine the United Kingdom's policies on European Union issues and to oversee the United Kingdom's relations with other member states and principal partners of the European Union and the Ministerial Committee on European Union Strategy, whose remit was to oversee the Government's European strategy and the presentation of the Government's European policy.[88] Long before he acceded to the role of Prime Minister, the priorities of a future Brown Government's EU reform agenda were identified.

The central objective of Brown's strategy is maintaining the pressure on the EU to converge towards the British model of political economy.[89] In a joint paper with the Department of Trade and Industry, the Treasury spelled out its vision for the EU Single Market in the twenty-first century. The Treasury contended that progress towards greater employment, growth, choice and prosperity for Europe's citizens and businesses had been slowing and so wanted the EU to embrace Brown's vision of a Global Europe by adopting 'a much more outward-looking, global perspective'. This would require a rethinking of 'the traditional model for the Single Market – one that seeks to achieve integration through legislation and the harmonisation of rules'. The Treasury wanted 'a new strategy for the Single Market that calls for a renewed focus on its core purpose – to provide jobs, growth and prosperity for Europe's citizens'. This would mean an emphasis on action 'in those areas where the economic benefits are greatest'. Policy must become 'more tailored, proportionate and flexible'.[90]

The Treasury approach to the Single Market was based on four principles. First, the EU must 'be clear about the purpose – focusing policy on outcomes of promoting jobs, growth and prosperity, by creating a dynamic and competitive Single Market'. The EU must copy Brown's output-centric approach to policy-making and delivery of services. Second, the EU must 'be focused on priorities – adopting a more systematic approach with policy priorities set according to sound analysis of where the economic benefits are greatest'.[91] In other words, the EU must both converge towards the British model (with its emphasis on constrained discretion and evidence-based reforms) and simultaneously abandon the political project of an ever-closer union through, for example, harmonisation of fiscal policy.

Third, the EU must 'take action at the right level – emphasising co-operation and applying the principle of subsidiarity'. Responsibility for policy design and resource allocation must be taken by national government and, where necessary, taken back from supra-national bodies. Fourth, the EU must 'deliver a modern and flexible framework – policy makers should embrace a wider range of policy tools, including more pro-active use of competition policy'.[92] The EU must continue with the Anglo-American model of capitalism, through accelerated market liberalisation, deregulation and privatisation. Taxes on businesses, both large and small, must be cut and the costs of social welfare, in the context of an ageing population, must be transferred from the general taxpayer to the individual consumer.

The Treasury contended that the benefits of convergence towards the British model would be significant. For example, insufficient liberalisation of EU gas markets was estimated to have cost Europe's energy consumers forty billion pounds during 2007, while the European Central Bank calculated that further competition reform could yield energy price cuts of up to thirty-six per cent.[93] The maintenance of costly subsidies and barriers to external trade and investment arising from protectionist 'tariffs, quotas and unjustifiably restrictive standards' may have cost Europe's consumers 600–700 billion euros (seven per cent of EU GDP) during 2007.[94] Opening up the EU's network industries, for example airlines, electricity, gas, post, rail-freight and passenger services and telecommunications could increase EU welfare by 1.3–1.7 per cent. This would mean an extra seventy-five to ninety-five billion euros of income for the EU economy and the creation of 140,000 to 360,000 jobs.[95] In telecommunications alone, the Treasury noted that liberalisation across the EU might cut prices by about eleven per cent, expand the market by four per cent and increase cross-border trade by twenty-nine per cent.[96]

Having helped, some fifteen years earlier, to initiate Gordon Brown's intellectual reflection on British economic policy and its relationship to European integration, in the weeks before Brown became Prime Minister, Ed Balls published a new essay about the future direction of policy towards the EU. Although he modestly subtitled his essay, *A City minister's perspective*, given the timing of its publication there was little doubt that it fully reflected Brown's agenda for the future of the EU, especially since Balls underlined the case for Brown's 'hard-headed pro-Europeanism'.[97]

Balls's position as City minister was doubly significant; for both Brown and Balls, the City of London's innovative and liberal markets were their blueprint for the future liberalisation of the EU single market. Particularly conspicuous in Balls's agenda was the open dismissal of further consideration of deeper integration and closer European political union. He depicted the advocacy of 'a continental identity both economically and politically' as an outdated product of the Cold War.[98] There was no attempt to engage with, for example, the ambitions of the German Chancellor, Angela Merkel, to revive a slimmed-down version of the European Constitution. Balls looked to a Europe based on 'an inclusive globalisation', where EU-level action is taken, only if it is appropriate, proportionate and flexible and in the national interests of its member states.[99]

The Brown Government's commitment to the pro-European realism of Global Europe was illustrated during his first month in office. David Miliband, the Foreign Secretary, affirmed the United Kingdom's commitment to the EU as an asset in economic terms, an asset in tackling crime and 'a greater asset in foreign policy – not substituting for nation states but giving better expression to the common commitments of nation states'.[100] In the foreword to his Government's White Paper on the British approach to the July 2007 Intergovernmental Conference, Gordon Brown stated that the Blair Government had set out its 'red lines' at the June 2007 European Council, which had ensured that 'there would not be a transfer of power away from the UK on issues of fundamental importance to our sovereignty'.[101] The mandate Brown specified for the Intergovernmental Conference would ensure the intact maintenance of the United Kingdom's labour and social legislation, the protection of its common law system, police and judicial processes, the protection of its tax and social security systems and the preservation of its independent foreign and defence policy. Furthermore, the proposed EU Reform Treaty would, for the first time, make it clear that national security would remain a matter for member states. This agenda would enable the EU 'to move on from debates about institutions to creating the outward-facing, flexible Europe that we need to meet the fundamental challenges of globalisation'.[102] The EU would be aligned with the Brown Government's pro-European realism.

CONCLUSION

One of Gordon Brown's most important political and economy policy legacies is the fact that the pound is not part of EMU. By keeping it out, Brown retained control over the United Kingdom's monetary and fiscal policy and thereby consolidated the British model of political economy. In the process, he frustrated Tony Blair's desire to place the United Kingdom at the heart of Europe and ensured that Europe continued to be subordinate to Atlanticism in British foreign policy. In his pro-European, realist vision of Global Europe, Brown staked out the terms of future engagement with European integration during his premiership.

The United Kingdom will not be joining the euro; neither will it be seeking to revive the European constitution nor move towards closer political union. Brown's 'British Way' is focussed on shoring up the British Union, not deepening the European Union. The path to modernity lies with the market liberalism of the United States rather than the social democratic traditions of continental Europe, even though the latter's philosophical roots are much closer to the Labour Party's historical development. Atlanticism will continue to take precedence over European integration in British foreign policy. The Anglo-American model of capitalism will continue to enjoy supremacy, both moral and political, over its inflexible continental European rival.

Brown's stance means that the Labour Party will find it more difficult to portray the Conservative Party as being more Euro-sceptic. Brown's perspective on the challenges of globalisation and European integration is very similar to David Cameron's, in his vision of 'The 3G Europe', with the priorities of 'Globalisation, Global Warming, Global Poverty'[103] This is a prime example of British politics having become stranded on an ideological common ground. Brown remains wedded to a vision of Europe that encompasses willing and active co-operation between sovereign EU member states, the tackling of present problems in a practical manner, however difficult that might prove, the encouragement of enterprise, the avoidance of protectionism and the maintenance of British and European security through Atlanticist structures like NATO.

The irony is that these are the guiding principles of a vision of Europe set out by a previous British Prime Minister in 1988, speaking to the College of Europe.[104] The author of that infamous Bruges speech was none other than Margaret Thatcher.

Chapter 8

Conclusion

INTRODUCTION

The purpose of this concluding chapter is twofold: first, to complete the evaluation of Gordon Brown's politics and legacy by exploring the nature of his economic legacy and political inheritance and second, to identify the priorities and policy agenda established during the early weeks of the Brown Government, which have reflected many of the policies analysed in earlier chapters of the book. In this chapter, I shall consider whether the 'heavy-weight' force of Brown's 'big clunking fist' has succeeded in delivering a major departure from the legacy of New Labour, in terms of domestic and foreign policy and a new politics and style of government and assess whether Gordon Brown is best for England and ultimately best for Britain.[1]

Gordon Brown's central role in the Blair Governments ensured that when he became Labour Party leader on 24th June 2007, and Prime Minister on the 27th, he carried a major political legacy. Gordon Brown has travelled a personal political odyssey, from parliamentary and supply-side socialism to the more recent sympathetic and supply-side liberalism of the New British Enlightenment that will shape the agenda of his Government. That journey has come full circle: Brown has returned to the American liberalism of the 1930s New Deal and 1960s Great Society eras first taught to him by his father. His personal moral compass is calibrated against the liberalism of Adam Smith, fellow Scot and son of Kirkcaldy, ideas which are a significant departure from and alien to, the mainstream history and traditions of the Labour Party. Gordon Brown is the third British Prime Minister, following Margaret Thatcher and Tony Blair, to base his modernisation programme on an ideology rooted in liberalism, implemented through a statecraft that entails further centralised state control.

The major components of Gordon Brown's domestic policy agenda are first, that he has delivered the supply-side liberalism of the British model of political economy, together with its abandonment of the Labour Party's long-standing commitment to state-led industrial modernisation. In its place, the British model favours an alternative economic strategy, centred on the City of London's liberalised financial markets, the domestic property market and consumer-led growth. Second, Brown has nationalised the processes of policy design and resource allocation for the public services in England. Third, he has constructed a 'British Way' for national identity and citizenship, in an attempt to answer the 'Kirkcaldy and Cowdenbeath Question' of why he, as an MP for a Scottish constituency in a devolved United Kingdom, should be able to exercise such unchecked and unbalanced political power in England. However, the British Way conflates and confuses examples of actually of England and Englishness with Britain and Britishness.

In Gordon Brown's foreign policy agenda, the roots of his vision of a New Atlanticism and quest for a global New Deal on poverty lie in the agenda of multilateral institutions and co-operation fashioned by American liberalism at the end of the Second World War. This passionate Atlanticism contrasts with the Euro-scepticism of Brown's 'pro-European realism' and in his vision of a Global Europe he has abandoned the quest for an ever-closer political union, in favour of convergence towards the British model of political economy.

Even before he became Prime Minister, Gordon Brown was locked in a battle of ideas with David Cameron, for liberalism and the common ground in British politics. After a decade of almost relentless policy initiatives and an unprecedented volume of peacetime legislation, in his leadership acceptance speech, Brown told the Labour Party that 'as people's aspirations and priorities change, we the Labour Party must renew ourselves as the party of change'.[2] Outside 10 Downing Street, in his first speech as Prime Minister, Brown told the electorate that he had listened and learnt and that his arrival as Prime Minister would mark the start of a period of change in British politics. His government would deliver 'change in our NHS, change in our schools, change with affordable housing, change to build trust in government, change to protect and extend the British way of life'. Brown promised to build 'a government that uses all the talents'.[3] Opinion polls in July 2007 suggested a 'Brown Bounce' to a recovery in the Labour Party's popularity to a six percentage point lead.[4]

GORDON BROWN'S ECONOMIC LEGACY

The economic legacy of Gordon Brown's decade as Chancellor of the Exchequer is mixed. The British model of political economy and its underlying supply-side liberalism delivered a decade of uninterrupted economic growth, not an inconsiderable achievement given the travails of previous Labour governments during the United Kingdom's post-war relative economic decline. When Brown left the Treasury, the economy was still growing. In the first three months of 2007, the United Kingdom GDP grew by 0.7 per cent and its level was 2.9 per cent higher than in the same quarter of 2006.[5] In 2005, the United Kingdom had total assets of £7,600 billion, including £3,356 billion in residential housing and £1,842 billion of pension fund and life assurance investments.[6] However, it must be remembered that the Brown Boom's record and legacy of sustained growth, low inflation and high levels of employment actually began in the three months following 'Black Wednesday' (16 September 1992) and was sustained for nearly five years before Brown became Chancellor.[7]

In becoming a more affluent society, the United Kingdom also saw increases in the inequalities in the distribution of income and wealth. The IFS noted that 'income growth since 2004–05 has tended to be faster the higher are incomes', with incomes among the richest fifth of the United Kingdom rising by 1.5 per cent but incomes among the poorest fifth falling by 0.4 per cent.[8] In that respect, the Brown Boom continued the trend experienced under the Thatcher and Major Governments. During the latter half of the 1980s, the wealthiest one per cent of the population owned between seventeen and eighteen per cent of United Kingdom wealth; during Brown's tenure as Chancellor, that proportion increased to between twenty and twenty-four per cent of total wealth.[9]

The very rich prospered the most under Gordon Brown. This conclusion was confirmed by a major study from the Joseph Rowntree Foundation which found that between 2003 and 2005 'areas with the highest average incomes experienced the greatest increases, in both absolute and relative terms, while some areas with the lowest average incomes experienced declining incomes, increasing polarisation'.[10] Between 1999 and 2003, wealth rose most in areas in a band between 50–100 miles from London but fell most in the cities of northern England and across Scotland.[11] The Brown Boom accentuated both the income gap between the very rich and very poor and the inequalities in wealth between the North and the South East.

Brown's immediate legacy to Alistair Darling, his successor as Chancellor, was the first rise in the rate of relative poverty in the United Kingdom either since 1996–1997 (before housing costs (BHC) were taken into account) or 1997–1998 (after housing costs, AHC). Between 2004–2005 and 2005–2006, the number of people living in relative poverty (in households with less than sixty per cent of the median income) had risen from 12.1 million to 12.7 million AHC and from 10 million to 10.4 million BHC. Despite this, Brown's overall legacy was a fall in relative poverty from 25.3 per cent to 21.6 per cent AHC and from 19.4 per cent to 17.6 per cent BHC. The future difficulty this has created for the Brown Government is that the target for cutting child poverty (by a quarter from its 1998–1999 level) is now further away. In 2005–2006, child poverty had only been cut by fourteen per cent AHC or eighteen per cent BHC from its 1998–1999 level. For the Brown Government to meet the stated objective of halving of child poverty (from its 1998–1999 level) by 2010–2011, an annual average of more than 200,000 children will have to be lifted out of poverty each year until 2012. This follows annual falls of fewer than 100,000 since 2000. The IFS has estimated that to have 'a 50:50 chance of meeting its target' the Brown Government will have to spend an additional four billion pounds a year (on the per-child component of the child tax credit) by 2010–2011.[12]

Brown's prudential legacy is equally mixed. The initial prudence in the public finances delivered by the British model of political economy has long since disappeared, replaced by growing public and private imprudence. By the end of April 2007, the United Kingdom's public sector net debt amounted to £497.7 billion (thirty-seven per cent of GDP). This is a marked deterioration from the end of 2001–2002, when the debt stood at £317.6 billion (30.7 per cent of GDP).[13] Brown borrowed to spend but the fiscal consequences have come home to roost for Alistair Darling. And the degree to which private imprudence has become a characteristic of British society is reflected in the record levels of personal debt and insolvency. Britain's personal debt grows by £1 million every four minutes. At the end of April 2007, total personal debt in the United Kingdom was £1,325 billion, with an annual growth rate of 10.4 per cent (£114 billion). In England and Wales, during the first quarter of 2007, there were 30,075 individual insolvencies (an annual increase of 23.9 per cent) and 33,715 mortgage repossessions, a ten per cent increase on the previous quarter.[14]

The political consequences of imprudence may rebound on Brown at the next General Election. In December 2006, the British Social Attitudes survey revealed rapidly declining public support for the imposition of higher taxation to finance better public services. When the Blair Government first took office, sixty-three per cent of those questioned supported increasing taxation and services on health, education and social benefits, compared to thirty-four per cent who wanted them to remain the same or be cut. By 2002, after Gordon Brown had increased National Insurance to finance additional spending on the National Health Service, those figures remained virtually unchanged. However, following the Blair Government's third consecutive General Election victory, public support for higher taxation and spending on the public services declined to forty-six per cent, with forty-nine per cent wanting taxation and spending to remain the same or be reduced. These statistics were almost identical to the statistics recorded during the second Thatcher Government in 1986. In particular, the survey identified stronger opposition to higher taxation among younger people. Only thirty-eight per cent of eighteen to thirty-four year-olds favoured increased taxation and spending, compared with fifty per cent of those aged fifty-five and over.[15]

Alistair Darling has also to deal with the consequences of rising inflation. In the year to March 2007, inflation (as measured by the Consumer Prices' Index, (CPI) rose by 3.1 per cent. This was its highest level since CPI was adopted as the Government's preferred measurement of inflation, the worst since August 1992 and up from the 1.1 per cent figure recorded for the year to March 2004. Inflation, as measured by the Retail Prices Index for all items (including mortgage payments, indirect taxation and utility bills), rose in the year to March 2007 by 4.8 per cent, compared to 2.6 per cent in the year to March 2004.[16] Since the CPI inflation rate had risen more than one per cent above the Government's two per cent target, under the 'Open Letter' system the Governor of the Bank of England had to write to the Chancellor explaining what action would be taken to counter these inflationary pressures, the first occasion on which this had been necessary. A period of higher interest rates became inevitable.[17] This coincided not only with the pound rising to a twenty-six-year high against the dollar but also with the United Kingdom's monthly trade deficit averaging more than four billion pounds (around four per cent of GDP) and the monthly deficit on trade in goods averaging more than £6.5 billion (around six per cent of GDP).[18] The United Kingdom's £7.8 billion surplus on trade in services during the first quarter of 2007 was nowhere near sufficient to compensate for the £20.7 billion deficit on trade in goods.[19]

The Brown Government also faces pressures on housing, public services and the wider infrastructure, that arise from the continuing high levels of net migration to the United Kingdom (or rather, to the overcrowded south-east of England, where the problems are writ largest in Greater London). During 2005, an estimated 565,000 immigrants entered the United Kingdom intending to live for at least one year, a lower figure than the record of 582,000 in 2004 but sufficient to produce net migration of 185,000 or the addition of around 500 people to the population each day. Of these, almost ninety-two per cent migrated to England and nearly half to London and the south-east.[20] This compounds the most intractable legacy of Brown's tenure at the Treasury; the strengthening and deepening of the trend towards a lack of affordable housing.

Between 1995 and 2005, the average house price in the United Kingdom almost trebled, from £66,786 to £183,966, and the average price of a first house rose by 204 per cent from £46,489 to £141,229.[21] With the number of households in England and Wales set to grow by an annual average of 223,000 up to 2030, one report forecast that by 2026, the cheapest twenty-five per cent of houses will cost ten times the average earnings of the poorest twenty-five per cent of people. At the end of 2006, the ratio was seven times and at the Millennium under four times. In 2007, a survey found that more than eighty per cent of people thought the government should be doing more to make housing more affordable, that nearly half of people aged under thirty-five thought their standard of living would be lower than their parents because of rising house prices and around one third of non-home owners thought they would never be able to buy a house.[22] There is a danger that Brown's most lasting economic legacy as Chancellor would be to have helped raise unrealistic popular expectations of constantly rising incomes and living standards, only for those dashed expectations to present him with new and possibly insurmountable problems as Prime Minister.

To meet these challenges, the Brown Government has made housing one of its priorities. In so doing, it has exposed many of the paradoxes and tensions that surround Gordon Brown's attempts to convince the electorate that he has listened and learnt from them and that the Labour Party, in its third term of office, is still 'the party of change'.[23] The Brown Government's draft legislative programme included a Housing and Regeneration Bill, for England and Wales.[24] Yvette Cooper, the Minister for Housing (to whom Brown extended the right to attend Cabinet meetings), published a Green Paper on housing policy in England, which committed the Government to an annual house-building target for England of 240,000 new houses by 2016 (compared to the former target of 200,000), the delivery of two million new homes in England by 2016, three million by 2020 and the creation of five new English eco-towns, designed to zero carbon standards.[25]

Gordon Brown had sat in Cabinet meetings and committees for a decade; he had orchestrated two Comprehensive Spending Reviews and three biennial Spending Reviews and delivered eleven Budget statements and ten Pre-Budget Reports, all incorporating major decisions on housing policy and expenditure. If, in July 2007, 'putting affordable within the reach not just of the few but the many' had become 'vital both to meeting individual aspirations and a better future for our country' (meaning England), why had he not done more to build affordable social housing during the previous decade?[26] It could not have been for the lack of advice. In an avalanche of reports, select committees, housing charities and other interested parties had demanded urgent action. For example, in December 1997, a report from the Joseph Rowntree Foundation pointed out that a substantial proportion of new households in the twenty years to 2017 would need to be accommodated in the social rented sector. The report noted an annual shortfall of 50–60,000 homes in the house-building programme to 2016, very close to the Brown Government's proposed annual increase of 40,000 homes announced in July 2007.[27]

In effect, a decade had been wasted. Government statistics revealed that local authorities had built a paltry 1011 new council houses in 1997–1998; just 185 houses had been built in 2002–2003; the highest figure was 439, built in 2000–2001.[28] The crisis in affordable housing that the Brown Government has inherited is a direct economic, social and political legacy of the policies pursued during Gordon Brown's tenure as Chancellor. For a decade, Brown failed to reverse the trend of the sale of council housing. Moreover, the number of new houses built each year and registered to social landlords declined, from 25,414 in 1997–1998 to only 16,342 in 2002–2003.[29] At the same time, Brown did nothing to curtail the demand for new housing.

The Brown Government will not be able to indefinitely ignore the additional strains on housing and the infrastructure of public services (especially in London and the South-East of England), arising from new immigrants, who account for the 713,000 National Insurance numbers allocated to overseas (non-United Kingdom) nationals during 2006–2007; 2.54 million since 2002–2003.[30]

GORDON BROWN'S POLITICAL INHERITANCE

Gordon Brown's immediate political inheritance from Tony Blair was not promising. Following the Labour Party's electoral losses in the May 2007 local government and devolved institution elections, there was an urgent need to reverse negative electoral and opinion poll trends. However, all was far from lost. In Scotland, the Labour Party lost four seats but lost power to the Scottish National Party (SNP) by only one seat (forty-six Labour seats to the SNP's forty-seven). In Wales, the decline in Labour's support from 38.3 per cent of the vote in 2003 to 30.9 per cent in 2007 left it with only twenty-six members of the National Assembly (compared to 30 before the election) but despite this reversal, Labour remained the largest single party and still a full nine percentage points ahead of the Conservatives. Divisions and prevarication between the Welsh Liberal Democrats and Plaid Cymru allowed Labour's Rhodri Morgan to return as First Minister, at the head of a minority administration.

Paradoxically, the political situation in Wales and Scotland might be to Brown's advantage in the longer term. In the fullness of time, the electoral reverses of May 2007 can be presented as the electorate's final verdict on Tony Blair as Prime Minister; that, in short, the electorate was using its last opportunity to remind Blair of the depth of public disquiet and anger about the war in Iraq and the arguments that were used originally to justify the March 2003 invasion. In Scotland, the election of Alex Salmond as First Minister of a minority administration dependent on the support of other parties has enabled Brown to contrast his own experience and decisive actions on major issues of domestic and foreign policy with Salmond's prevarication. The need to negotiate a coalition of support on all major issues confronting the Scottish Parliament will provide Brown with ample opportunities to expose the fault-lines and weaknesses in the Nationalist's agenda. The SNP has no prospect whatsoever of gaining majority support for a referendum on Scottish independence. Consequently, it will not be able to deliver on its principal electoral promise and the greatest threat to the British Union.

Gordon Brown's principal electoral challenges lie in England, a fact reflected in the launch of his Labour Party leadership campaign 'Gordon Brown for Britain', in a series of visits to marginal constituencies across London and the Home Counties. Following its loss of 319 seats and seventeen councils in the May 2006 English local government elections, the Labour Party lost a further 911 seats and eight councils in the May 2007 elections. However, its estimated share of the national vote rose from twenty-six per cent in 2006 to twenty-seven per cent in 2007, while the Conservative Party's estimated share remained at forty per cent. Brown's challenge will be to close this gap further. As the 'Brown Bounce' of renewed popularity during the Brown Government's first few weeks in office demonstrated, this is by no means impossible.

All the top jobs in the Cabinet changed hands when Brown formed his first Cabinet, which will considerably help the task of rebuilding electoral popularity and refreshing the Government's agenda and image. Brown's appointments of David Miliband as Foreign Secretary, Douglas Alexander as International Development Secretary, Jacqui Smith as Home Secretary, Ed Balls as Children, Schools and Families Secretary and Ed Miliband as Minister for the Cabinet Office has enabled him to contrast his 'Cabinet of all the (younger) talents' with David Cameron's combination of no fewer than fourteen Old Etonian front bench spokesmen (plus three in his private office). Moreover, Cameron's Shadow Cabinet is based on politicians associated with the failed Major Government (William Hague, David Davis, Liam Fox and David Willetts) and the ineffective Hague and Howard Conservative Party leaderships (Liam Fox, Andrew Lansley, Oliver Letwin and Theresa May).

STRANDED ON THE COMMON GROUND: THE FIGHT FOR LIBERALISM

In the run-up to the next General Election, the key ideological contest between Gordon Brown and David Cameron (assuming Cameron survives as Conservative Party leader) will be over who is the truest advocate of liberalism in twenty-first century British politics. Their degree of agreement is striking both in their political philosophy and in their respective agendas for domestic and foreign policy. The danger of Brown's sympathetic liberalism is that it strands him on the political and philosophical territory occupied by the Conservative Party from the mid-1970s onwards. Brown has occupied Keith Joseph's 'common ground', a political agenda embracing the moral and material benefits of the market order and a politics based on a descending hierarchy of 'values, aspiration, understanding, policies'. For Joseph, the common ground was the territory occupied by those politicians whose aim is to transform the expectations of government in pursuit of prosperity, low inflation, private profit and investment, 'housing choice, decent education, less dependency, less crime' and 'freedom within the law to run our own lives'.[31]

David Cameron has described the political philosophy that underpins his domestic and foreign policy agendas as liberal conservatism.[32] Cameron's belief is that 'we need a new liberal Conservative consensus on our country'.[33] This philosophy purports to believe in individual freedom and social responsibility, rather than state control. It is a vision whose aims and values are based on the need for 'a responsibility revolution', embracing personal responsibility, professional responsibility, civic responsibility and corporate responsibility.[34]

The forthcoming battle of ideas for the common ground in British politics will be between Gordon Brown's sympathetic liberalism and David Cameron's liberal conservatism. It will be fought across an ideological and political territory defined by Margaret Thatcher and Sir Keith Joseph in the late 1970s. The ultimate victor in the battle of ideas might prove to be Thatcherism itself.[35]

The key electoral fight for the common ground at the next General Election will be in England, in particular the marginal constituencies in London, the Home Counties and the Midlands that were instrumental in the General Election victories of the Blair-led Labour Party and the Margaret Thatcher-led Conservative Party. David Cameron's strategy to win Middle England is clear: he has attempted to put the Conservative Party in a position to be the natural inheritor of Tony Blair's legacy. In defining modern conservatism, Cameron asserted that the Conservative Party has long since been victorious in the battle of ideas. Indeed, its principal problem 'arose from the triumph of our ideas' and not knowing how to deal with that victory.[36] Cameron's analysis is simple: Margaret Thatcher defeated both Old Labour and the British Disease of economic decline and trades union unrest by identifying 'a means of transforming both the British economy and British society' and transformed Britain into 'a more middle-class country with a functioning market economy', based on 'monetary and fiscal control matched by supply-side reform'. For Cameron, 'the Thatcher revolution' changed the Labour Party and brought about Tony Blair's New Labour project of social justice and economic efficiency. Blair failed to deliver 'neither economic efficiency, nor social justice', because of his pre-occupation with spin and the short-term and with 'the quest for a legacy becoming an all-consuming mission'.[37] For Cameron, 'Social justice and economic efficiency' are on the common ground of British politics'.[38]

The challenge for the Conservative Party has been to come to terms with its victory in the battle of ideas. Before Brown became Prime Minister, Cameron's strategy was to place the Conservative Party as the natural successor to Tony Blair's reforms, because of their alleged philosophical and policy debt to and inheritance from Thatcherism. On the critical issue of public services, Cameron argued that Blair was right to seek investment in and reform of those services; his failure and legacy was that 'his reforms were faltering, half-hearted and ultimately thwarted'.[39] In his speeches, Cameron has sought to portray those failures as a result of Gordon Brown's shortcomings. Brown imposed reform of the public services 'through centralised command and control, with targets and inspections' and the investment delivered a poor return because of the waste of 'billions of pounds on the bureaucratic apparatus needed to operate a command and control system' and the 111 new quangos established since 1997. Moreover, as the pre-election Warwick Agreement, between the Labour Party and the unions demonstrated, 'the trades unions act as a powerful brake on reform'. Consequently, Cameron concluded, 'the task for a modern Conservative Party is to deliver the radical reform that Labour are temperamentally and politically incapable of'.[40]

The Conservative Party has portrayed Gordon Brown as 'a "road block" to further reform' of the public services. It has portrayed itself as the natural inheritors of Blair's legacy of choice and competition and as drivers of higher standards in delivery of services, given what has been being depicted as a 'growing consensus between the current Prime Minister [Blair at the time the speech was made] and the Conservative Party', which Brown is deemed not to share.[41] In practice, there is evidence of a growing convergence in ideas between Gordon Brown and David Cameron. For example, Gordon Brown has described Robert Kennedy as 'my moral beacon' and written an effusive essay praising Kennedy's moral courage and vision in identifying a 'genuinely original vision of empowerment', embracing 'not just freedom from but freedom to'.[42] For his part, and in articulating his perspective on civil society and the need for 'a revolution in responsibility', David Cameron cited Robert Kennedy's critique of Gross National Product for failing to 'allow for the health of our education, the quality of their education or the joy of their play'.[43]

There is also growing evidence of convergence between Brown and Cameron in economic policy. For example, Brown's 2007 Budget confirmed that that the Spending Review covering 2008–09 until 2010–11 would see a growth in current public spending at an average of 1.9 per cent a year in real terms. This would be a slower rate of increase than Brown's forecast rates of GDP growth of 2.75 to 3.25 per cent in 2007 and a trend of between 2.5 and 3 per cent in the following years.[44] In this, Brown had moved towards the second of the Cameron-led Conservative Party's three Sound Money Tests: 'Sharing the Proceeds'. This test is that 'Over time, and only when the country can afford it, we will move in the direction of lower taxes. We will do this by sharing the proceeds of economic growth between lower taxes and well-funded public services'.[45] Both Cameron and Brown have also committed themselves to rebuilding trust in politics and expressed their commitment to maintaining the British Union.[46]

In terms of foreign policy, both Gordon Brown and David Cameron have indicated that theirs will be based on what they determine to be the British national interest. Cameron, in a lecture given on 11th September 2006, said his policy would be founded on the principles of a strategy arising from more than the simple exercise of military force, an understanding that democracy cannot be imposed from the outside, a commitment to a new multilateralism and be a policy based on moral authority.[47] The greatest convergence has been in relation to the European Union. The pro-European realism of Gordon Brown's vision of a 'Global Europe' is matched by Cameron's vision of 'The 3G Europe'.[48] Neither wants further European integration through closer political union and neither wants a revival of the European Constitution.

The fight for the common ground in British politics between Brown and Cameron is centred on the publication of the Treasury's second Comprehensive Spending Review and the final reports of the Conservative Party's six Policy Review Groups, which Cameron established. In the years before the next General Election, Brown's political strategy will be to contrast his experience and record as Chancellor of the Exchequer and Prime Minister with David Cameron's inexperience. Cameron's vulnerability on this and the fragile nature of the Conservative Party's opinion poll lead have been exposed by the divisions among the Shadow Cabinet and parliamentary party over Cameron's announcement that it would not establish any more grammar schools. In the immediate aftermath of a week of divisive infighting over Conservative education policy, an ICM opinion poll revealed that eighty-five per cent of respondents saw Brown as more experienced than Cameron, compared to only seven per cent support for Cameron. No fewer than fifty-four per cent thought Brown to be more competent (compared to twenty-nine per cent support for Cameron), while fifty-three per cent thought Brown to be the stronger leader (compared to thirty-three per cent support for Cameron).[49]

Brown will also be able to expose the degree to which Cameron's Policy Reviews are led by yesterday's failed politicians. For example, the Economic Competitiveness Policy Group is co-chaired by John Redwood, quintessentially Thatcherite and formerly Head of the Prime Minister's Policy Unit under Margaret Thatcher. Redwood, an Englishman, was also formerly Secretary of State for Wales, who infamously (and hilariously) attempted to mouth, in Welsh, the words of Hen Wlad Fy Nhadau (Land of My Fathers), the Welsh national anthem, which he manifestly did not know. The Social Justice Policy Group is led by Iain Duncan Smith, former Conservative Party leader and self-styled 'Quiet Man', who singularly failed to revive his party's electoral fortunes. The Globalisation and Global Poverty Group is led by Peter Lilley, former Deputy Leader of the Conservative Party, who held responsibility for policy formation during William Hague's unsuccessful tenure as party leader. It will be simple for a Brown Government to portray Cameron's Conservative Party as privileged, class-ridden and burdened with the figures of a failed Conservative past.

The evidence of the first month of the Brown Government was that he had successfully surmounted any short-term problems arising from the political legacy left by Tony Blair. By the end of July 2007, the Labour Party had risen to thirty-eight per cent in an ICM poll, well ahead of the Conservative Party on thirty-two per cent and a reversal of the trend since Cameron's election as Conservative leader. Equally important, no fewer than forty-nine per cent of respondents thought Brown's leadership style represented a real change (compared to thirty-five per cent who did not), while forty-three per cent thought Brown had brought a real change in policy direction (compared to thirty-six per cent who did not). Twenty-one per cent of people stated that their opinion of Brown had gone up since he had become Prime Minister; twenty-one per cent of respondents stated that their opinion of David Cameron had declined during the same period.[50] On this evidence, Gordon Brown had won the first round in the battle for the common ground in British politics.

THE AGENDA FOR CHANGE OF THE BROWN GOVERNMENT

The principal challenge that Brown confronted as Prime Minister was to reinvigorate a government in its third term. Brown's strategy, from the start, was to use the language of change. In words reminiscent of Blair a decade earlier, Brown promised to form 'a new government with new priorities to meet the new challenges ahead'.[51] Setting out his government's agenda for reform, Brown identified 'A Britain changing because of global economic competition, climate change, security and terrorism and of course rising aspirations'.[52] He sought to distance himself from the unpopular elements of the Blair legacy while identifying his distinct domestic and foreign policy changes.

Brown was helped by the fact that he had orchestrated detailed preparations for a Brown Government for at least two years before he became Prime Minister. The process had effectively begun on 19 July 2005, with the announcement of the launch of the second Comprehensive Spending Review. This would report in 2007, having identified the further investments and reforms required to equip the United Kingdom for 'the global challenges of the decade ahead'.[53] By setting the priorities for ten years to come, Brown ensured that his control over domestic policy, foreign policy and global governance would endure, whether or not he became Prime Minister.

In November 2006, the Treasury published its study of the long-term opportunities and challenges confronting the United Kingdom. Although the study was prefaced by an introduction jointly signed by both Blair and Brown, in practice the five challenges and opportunities identified by the document reflected themes familiar from Brown's speeches, Pre-Budget Reports and Budget statements. More importantly, they set the framework for the policies and priorities of the future Brown Government. The first challenge was demographic and socio-economic change and the need to address 'rapid increases in the old-age dependency ratio on the horizon and rising consumer expectations of public services'.[54] This signalled that in the Brown premiership there will be no let-up in the pace of welfare reform or the transfer of the responsibilities for funding welfare from the general tax-payer to the individual citizen.

The second challenge was globalisation, a core element of Brown's 'British model' of political economy. The study focused on 'the intensification of cross-border economic competition, with new opportunities for growth, as the balance of international economic activity shifts towards emerging markets such as China and India'.[55] This was the central theme of Brown's vision of Global Europe writ large. In a Brown Government, there would be no reduction in the liberalisation and deregulation demanded by supply-side liberalism. The third challenge confronting the United Kingdom in the decade ahead was technological change and 'the rapid pace of innovation and diffusion, which will continue to transform the way people live and open up new ways of delivering public services'.[56] This theme had been repeatedly underlined during a decade of Brown's Pre-Budget Reports but if it were to become a priority for the public services, the Brown Government would clearly have to get to grips, very quickly, with the delayed and hugely over-budget (£12.4 billion) implementation of information technology to National Health Service data in England.[57]

The fourth challenge was 'continued global uncertainty with on-going threats of international terrorism and global conflict and the continued imperative to tackle global poverty'. During 2006, Brown announced his intention to give a greater priority to security and claimed that, in the aftermath of the 7 July 2005 London bombings, 'in effect the Treasury itself had to become a department for security'.[58] Preparations for the 2007 CSR included the conduct of a review of counter-terrorism and security.[59] The likelihood that a Brown government would introduce a single security budget, accompanied by a reorganisation of Whitehall to a give greater institutional profile to homeland security, was confirmed by Brown in a House of

Commons statement on 25 July 2007.[60] The innovation of the International Finance Facility (IFF) and in particular the IFF For Immunisation, allied to the commitments on global poverty made at the Gleneagles' G8 Summit, gave Brown a policy framework within which to continue to work for the 2015 Millennium Development Goals.

The fifth and final challenge was the 'increasing pressures on our natural resources and global climate, requiring action by governments, businesses and individuals to maintain prosperity and improve environmental care'.[61] This appeared to be one area where Brown had been less vocal than David Cameron, however, the preparation for the publication of the results of the 2007 CSR included the commissioning of the Stern Review on the economics of climate change.[62] Before its publication, Brown finally spelt out his priorities for climate change, locating his agenda for the environment within the liberalism of the political economy of John Maynard Keynes. Brown noted that, in 1944, Keynes defined what he believed to be 'the foundations of economic policy: that is for government to ensure the twin objectives of high and stable levels of growth and employment'.[63] Brown's thesis for the decade ahead was that 'there is a third objective on which our economies must be built and that is environmental care. Environmental sustainability is not an option: it is necessity'.[64] Brown's 'new synthesis' of 'economic growth, social justice and environmental care' advancing together would be based on the liberalism of an earlier member of the Liberal Party, rather than on a figure from the history of Labour Party doctrine, such as the tradition of ethical socialism. For Brown, economic growth and social justice could be reconciled with environmental care; something that was widely challenged by environmentalists. For the Brown government, policies for growth that incorporate the requisite technology and resources would yet be capable of surmounting poverty, underdevelopment and environmental degradation.

Brown's thesis is that 'it is through the new economics of climate change that a new global consensus for tackling environmental change can be built'.[65] For Brown, climate change is not only an environmental issue but also 'most definitely an economic issue ... one of justice as much as of economic development'.[66] Once more, Brown has placed his faith in the capacity of economics and the technical expertise of unelected economists to provide the solution to major public policies, demonstrated in his role in commissioning the Stern Review. Brown's conviction is that there are two reasons why it is both more urgent and more possible to construct a global consensus for tackling environment change, based on economic growth and technological innovation: first, the rising cost of energy has driven the quest for greater efficiency and diversity of supply and second, there is both a convergence between and an unprecedented mutual reinforcement of the economic agenda and the environmental agenda. This has created economic opportunities for companies, universities and social enterprises in Britain in 'new markets; new jobs; new technologies; new exports'.[67]

Brown has pointed to the ability of Britain to cut its greenhouse gas emissions during a period of high growth but this glosses over the fact that the United Kingdom has lost a large part of its manufacturing industry. He also wants to 'strongly support the innovation of carbon trading', not least because this could benefit the City of London as its global centre[68] and has identified the environment as a means to promote his agenda for a Global Europe. Brown has defined his ultimate environmental goal as a global carbon market, with the global environmental market having a potential value of $700 billion by 2010.[69] As in other fields, and following the publication of the Stern Review, Brown's favoured policy innovations are the creation of a new commission to identify detailed proposals to enable Britain to lead the development and maximise the opportunities of the new low-carbon economy in the coming decade. This followed the announcement, in the March 2006 Budget, of the creation of a National Institute of Energy Technologies, a public-private partnership of engineers, scientists and companies set the objective of raising one billion pounds to co-ordinate investment in science and technology in accordance with the new market incentives. Brown also wants to establish a further independent body 'to work with the government on how efforts to reduce emissions should be spread over time and across the economy'.[70]

In relation to climate change and sustainable development, Brown's conclusion is that 'great challenges require great acts of statesmanship', as exemplified by the 'path-breaking statesmanship and leadership' that brought about the Marshall Plan of the 1940s and the creation of the United Nations, the International Monetary Fund and the World Bank. He believes that 'international co-operation built on bold, innovative stewardship' could realise 'the ideal of an international community acting for the public good; for the present generation and for generations to come'.[71] It is apparent that the same preference for multilateral co-operation, based on the

Atlanticist model established during the late 1940s, will continue to be the support of the Brown Government's approach to certain major issues of global governance. However, in other areas of foreign policy, notably the 'war on terror' in Iraq, there may be greater political advantage in a clear and early break with not only the rhetoric but also the substance of the Blair Government's foreign policies.

THE BATTLE FOR HEARTS AND MINDS: BRITAIN AS A GLOBAL HUB

If Gordon Brown is decisively to defeat David Cameron in the fight for the common ground in British politics, his greatest immediate challenge in foreign policy as Prime Minister will be to extricate his government from the damaging legacy of the war on terror in Iraq.

Interviewed on BBC television in January 2007, Brown said there were two clear lessons to be learnt from the war in Iraq. The first lesson, related to Iraq itself, is that there should have been a much earlier 'passage of authority to the local population'.[72] In May 2007, Brown reminded the Labour Party that in Iraq 'there is only one province left to hand back. There were 44,000 troops in Iraq, there are now 7,000 going down to 6,000' and that therefore there was no need to be hurried into an early announcement on a definitive timetable for a final British withdrawal from Iraq because it had already largely taken place.[73] The fact that Brown has chosen not to criticise the American decision to dismantle the former Bathist regime or the slow pace of reconstruction – and thereby to forget the lessons learnt in Japan and Germany at the end of the Second World War – is indicative of the underlying strength of Brown's faith in Atlanticism.

Brown claimed the second lesson, related to the more general war on terror, would be both 'of huge significance in the years to come' and 'almost a big change in the way we've got to look at these issues'. The lesson was that while military action, policing, intelligence and security work 'can achieve a great deal', they will not be sufficient by themselves. The core of British foreign policy under the Brown Government is the doctrine that 'you will not win against extremist terrorist activities and particular the propaganda activities, unless you have this battle of hearts and minds that is won'. In his major speeches on security, Brown has repeated the mantra that this battle is like the Cold War: the 'cultural war that had to be fought against communism from the 1940s and 50s onwards'. For Brown, that is 'in a sense the model for what we've got to do here'.[74] This view is shared by David Cameron, who in a further point of foreign policy convergence, has built the liberal conservatism of his foreign policy on the recognition that communism was defeated 'in the battle of ideas', rather than by the military.[75]

Continuity in British foreign policy under a Brown government comes from the priority afforded to Atlanticism and the continuation of the 'special relationship' over European integration and stout opposition to a revival of the European Union constitution to facilitate closer political union. Brown has claimed that 'The British national interest is what I and my colleagues are about' and the tacit assumption is that the pursuit of that interest overseas is synonymous with Atlanticism. Brown has stated how he looks forward to working with President George W. Bush and has reminded interviewers that he has already worked with 'major figures in previous United States' administrations, notably Alan Greenspan, Robert Rubin and Larry Summers.[76]

The Brown Government wasted little time in setting out its commitment to a New Atlanticism in British foreign policy. David Miliband, the Foreign Secretary, confirmed that the United Kingdom would bring together 'a unique set of alliances' in Europe, alliances with the United States and 'some vital developing countries like India'. At its heart, Britain and its cities would serve as a global economic hub, through the City of London, a global cultural hub, not least through the work of the British Council, and have the potential to be a global hub for political and scientific collaboration.[77] The interdependence of domestic and foreign policy would be reflected in a foreign policy that sought to win the battle of ideas by using British strength in international engagement to be 'a force for good in the world'.[78] To become that force, the Brown Government would acknowledge the growing power of India and China and the 'growing mismatch between national power and global problems', combining in its foreign policy 'the soft power of ideas and influence and the hard power of economic and military incentives and interventions'.[79]

In effect, the Brown Government had returned to the multilateralist principles identified in Robin Cook's vision of an ethical dimension to British foreign policy and more fully elaborated in Tony Blair's doctrine of an international community.[80] British power in foreign policy would be derived from winning the battle of ideas, exercising influence within multilateral institutions and the European Union to give them a strong sense of purpose, providing incentives and sanctions through the use of harder power and engaging in direct intervention when appropriate, as in Kosovo in 1999.[81] However, in advancing this vision of a New Atlanticism, the Brown Government offered no guarantee that it would not be prepared to back military sanctions against Iran, should it continue to defy diplomatic pressure from the United Nations to close its uranium enrichment programme.

A key appointment that demonstrated the Brown Government's commitment to a New Atlanticism based on multilateral co-operation was that of Lord Malloch Brown to the new ministership for Africa, Asia and the United States. During his tenure as the United Nations' Deputy Secretary-General and Chief of Staff to the former United Nations' Secretary-General Kofi Annan, Malloch Brown had angered the Bush Administration by his repeated criticism of the United States' policy towards the United Nations. For example, in June 2006, Malloch Brown contended that 'even as the world's challenges are growing, the UN's ability to respond is being weakened without US leadership'. He further asserted that no President since Harry Truman in the late 1940s had thought 'managing global security and development issues through the network of a United Nations was worth the effort' and the Bush Administration had adopted counter-productive 'maximalist positions when it could be finding middle ground'.[82] John Bolton, the United States' Ambassador to the United Nations retorted that such remarks by a senior United Nations' official were 'a very, very grave mistake' whose 'condescending and patronising tone' had delivered 'a very serious affront' to the American people.[83]

Shortly after his appointment at the Foreign Office, Malloch Brown stated his belief that British foreign policy should not be so reliant on the United States.[84] This followed a major speech given in Washington DC by Douglas Alexander, the Secretary of State for International Development, in which he set out the Brown Government's vision of 'an alliance of opportunity'. According to this vision, the whole international community must rally to the Brown Government's cause of advancing change through common values and new alliances must be formed based on those values. Words and actions alike must demonstrate that 'we are: internationalist not isolationist, multilateralist not unilateralist, active not passive and driven by core values consistently applied, not special interests'. Because isolationism did not work in an interdependent world, global civilisation must be guaranteed by a multilateralist, not unilateralist, approach to 'a rules-based international system'. Global challenges must involve the active engagement of the United States and a global community capable of acting together 'through modern effective institutions, including a reformed United Nations, International Monetary Fund, World Bank, World Trade Organization and European Union'.[85]

Douglas Alexander claimed that the Brown Government's foreign policy would be driven by core values, such as opportunity, responsibility and justice, rather than special interests. However, the Brown Government's vision of the United Kingdom as a global hub is largely built on a desire to defend the special interests in global commerce of the City of London's financial markets. Furthermore, the Government's announcement of its commitment to increase defence spending from thirty-four billion pounds in 2008–2009 to £36.9 billion in 2010–2011 and to order two 65,000 tonne aircraft carriers at an estimated cost of £3.9 billion, each equipped with thirty-six Joint Strike Fighter aircraft at a further estimated cost of more than five billion pounds, reflects the continuing influence of the special interests of the United Kingdom's warfare state in British foreign and security policy.[86]

Some interpreted Alexander's speech as a veiled critique of the Bush Administration and a signal that the Brown Government would distance itself from the 'special relationship'. However, the announcement to Parliament on 25 July 2007, two days before the Summer Recess and with no debate, that the Government had agreed to a request from the Bush Administration to upgrade the Ballistic Early Missile Warning System radar at RAF Fylingdales in North Yorkshire, to enable it to contribute to the controversial United States' ballistic missile defence system, confirmed that the 'special relationship' would be strengthened and deepened, rather than weakened, in Brown's New Atlanticism.[87]

One strategic advantage in the timing of Brown's succession to Tony Blair was that the campaign for the November 2008 United States' Presidential election had already begun and the hawkish neo-conservatism of the Bush Administration had little more than a year to run. There was mounting evidence, not least from the Bush Administration itself, of the failure of its strategy for security and reconstruction in Iraq. For example, in its July 2007 *Initial Benchmark Assessment Report*, the Administration conceded that there had been satisfactory progress in only eight out of the eighteen benchmarks set by the US Congress for evaluating progress in Iraq.

The Iraqi Government had failed to make satisfactory progress on a wide range of vital issues, including the establishment of an independent Electoral Commission, electoral law, provincial council authorities and a date for provincial elections. It had also failed to put in place the conditions for a general amnesty, a successful militia disarmament programme, the even-handed enforcement of the law and an expansion in the number of Iraqi Security Forces' units capable of operating independently. The Iraqi Government had also managed to disburse only twenty-two per cent of its capital budget for reconstruction.[88]

Against this backdrop of strategic failure in United States' security policy, the likely successors to George W. Bush, at least those from the Democratic Party, have already indicated their strong commitment to an agenda of multilateralist co-operation, fully in accordance with Gordon Brown's New Atlanticism. Hillary Clinton, a leading contender for the Democratic Party nomination for President, has argued that the United States 'must, by word and deed, renew internationalism for a new century [and] blend both idealism and realism in the service of American interests'.[89] Clinton's chief rival for the Democratic nomination, Barack Obama, has also committed himself to multilateral co-operation, stating that 'no country has a bigger stake than we do in strengthening international institutions – which is why we pushed for their creation in the first place and why we need to take the lead in improving them'.[90]

For Gordon Brown, there is every prospect of a new chapter of Atlanticist co-operation opening up in the 'special relationship'; a relationship reminiscent of the agenda pursued by Tony Blair and Bill Clinton during the last years of the old Millennium.

A NEW KIND OF POLITICS, A NEW STYLE OF GOVERNMENT

Five months before he became Prime Minister, Gordon Brown identified the principal challenges that would confront Britain during the next decade, which he claimed were quite different from those of the past ten years. First, there would be 'a security challenge that is quite unprecedented'. Second, there would be 'an environmental challenge that nobody really thought about in the same way as they do now in 1997'. Third, there would be 'an economic challenge'.

From Brown's perspective, the common denominator of this triumvirate was that it required 'a new kind of politics in this country. And it needs a new style of government in the future'.[91] Brown made a number of claims about the nature of government he will lead: first, the past propensity for the state to intervene, through 'a top-down approach' with a 'government that simply pulled the levers' would not work in the future. Second, asked whether his government would be based less on spin and more on collective Cabinet government, Brown did not address either but asserted that his government would be 'a government of all the talents. And that doesn't mean just the talents of one political party. I think you've got to use the talents of the wider community'.[92] This was an indication of Brown's preparedness to draw on Cabinet ministerial talent from beyond the ranks of the Labour Party and also signalled his willingness to follow Tony Blair's example when facing certain contentious decisions, such as voting on the decision to renew the United Kingdom's nuclear deterrent or to extend the right to detain terrorist suspects for more than 28 days, to mobilise the support of MPs from other parties to overcome the opposition of backbench Labour MPs. Third, Brown had asserted that his was 'a patriotic vision', based on a rejection of 'the idea of the state as being an over-bearing state', for 'that cannot be the government of the future'. Fourth, Brown defined the role of the state as 'the servant state', one in which the government serves the people by talking, consulting and debating, with the 'responsible citizen, the active citizen empowered to be more involved in their community life' as 'a great theme of the future'. This new style of government, Brown claimed, would not constitute a change of style for him.[93]

The new politics that Brown identified would require 'a new settlement over these next few years between, if you like, the executive, the legislature and that is the power of Parliament and the House of Commons and the people themselves'. Brown claimed that this would entail 'a more accountable government, a stronger parliamentary democracy and a more active population'.[94] Pressed by his interviewer, the journalist Andrew Marr, Brown went on to give the clearest indication of what he has ruled out during his premiership. Greater accountability would not mean that the people of England's elected representatives will be the sole determinants of the passage of legislation affecting England. Brown has insisted on 'British votes for English laws', as the accompaniment to 'Scots votes for Scots laws' in the Scottish Parliament. A stronger parliamentary democracy will not mean

'English votes for English laws' nor will the population of England be empowered to become more active citizens by voting in a referendum on the establishment of an English Parliament. This agenda was confirmed by the Brown Government's draft legislative programme and in particular the Green Paper on constitutional reform. Intriguingly, both documents were given the title *The Governance of Britain*, even though both referred to the constitutional future of the United Kingdom.

In their foreword to the Green Paper, Gordon Brown and Jack Straw (Secretary of State for Justice and Lord Chancellor) stated their commitment 'to forge a new relationship between government and citizen and begin the journey towards a new constitutional settlement – a settlement that entrusts Parliament and the people with more power'.[95] However, the details revealed that the Brown Government would not entrust the people of England with the same extension of democratic power and citizenship rights which had been provided to the people of the other constituent territories of the United Kingdom. The Government stated that it would:

> ... better enable local people to hold service providers to account; place a duty on public bodies to involve local people in major decisions; [and] assess the merits of giving local communities the ability to apply for devolved or delegated budgets.[96]

Devolution in Brown's native Scotland meant that Scottish citizens, through their directly elected representatives, had the freedom to hold service providers to account and to decide when to devolve or delegate budgets. In England, by contrast, the Brown Government proposed to maintain its capacity to determine these decisions in Whitehall, despite the Green Paper's admission that 'power remains too centralised and too concentrated in government'.[97]

Rather than introducing a new style of politics and a new style of government, the Brown Government has maintained central control over political power, policy design and resource allocation in England. As a substitute for devolution to directly-elected representatives of the people of England, the Brown Government created nine regional ministers for England (based on administrative boundaries rather than actual English identities) and suggested the creation of nine regional select committees to hold those ministers to account.[98] This proposal owed more to the desire to manage territory than to any notion of devolution or enhanced citizenship.

On becoming Prime Minister, Brown indicated that he had listened and learnt from the people. However, there had never been any calls for either regional ministers or regional select committees. The November 2004 referendum that overwhelmingly rejected the Blair Government's proposal for a regional assembly for the North East demonstrated the popular English reaction to expensive 'talking shops' that would not involve genuine devolution of political power or the opportunity for local people to have greater control over the decisions affecting important aspects of their lives, such as schools and hospitals. The Brown Government's proposals for constitutional reform in England have simply reiterated his vision of a Britain of nations and regions (discussed in Chapter Five), which identified the nations as Scotland, Wales and Britain, dividing England into administrative regions with which its people have no popular identification.

The prospects for greater accountability through a new style of politics and government have not been enhanced by the attitude of Brown and his closest political allies to freedom of information. On 18th May 2007, Ed Balls, Gordon Brown's closest political ally and Jacqui Smith, then Chief Whip, were among 78 Labour MPs who voted to exempt MPs' correspondence from freedom of information legislation.[99] Balls's and Smith's votes, and Brown's refusal to oppose the legislation, did not augur well for greater transparency under a Brown Government. Neither did the fact that the Treasury, under Brown, had conducted an eighteen-month rearguard action to prevent the *Sunday Times* obtaining documents relating to the advice received in 1999 by Brown and the Treasury from the Bank of England and gold traders about the sale of four hundred tons of gold, more than half the United Kingdom's reserves. The sale was controversial, because the gold was sold when world gold markets were at a twenty-year low, at prices between $256 and $296 an ounce (an average of $275). Among gold traders, the sale became known as the 'Brown Bottom'. The price of gold has since risen to $685 an ounce; a potential loss to the British taxpayer of more than two billion pounds.[100] The *Sunday Times* discovered that both the Bank's officials and the private gold traders had warned Brown, who was not at the crucial meeting, that there could not have been a more inopportune moment to sell. However, their advice was ignored by Brown and his inner circle of advisers.

In its first month, the Brown Government demonstrated considerable continuity, in its style of politics and government, with Blair's. This was particularly marked in its approach to the government of England: old habits died hard. Despite the promises of Cabinet government and a more collegiate style of decision-making, Gordon Brown's first major U-turn on policy, breaking with the legacy of the Blair Government, was a telling indictment of his statecraft. Rather than consulting with his Cabinet colleagues, the Parliamentary Labour Party or local councillors about the abandonment of plans for a super-casino in Manchester, Brown chose to use the coded language of a reply during Prime Minister's Question Time to announce a change in policy. He noted the absence of a consensus within the two Houses of Parliament about super-casinos, even though he had personally voted for the Gambling Act 2005 at every single stage of the legislation (whereas Tony Blair had frequently abstained) and stated that it was 'an issue that is now subject to reflection over the next few months'.[101] That statement was later confirmed, by anonymous Whitehall sources, to mean that the plans for the super-casino were (as quoted in the *Guardian* on 26th June 2007) 'dead in the water'.[102] This style of unilateral decision-making did not bode well for transparency and collegiality under the Brown Government.

IS GORDON BROWN BEST FOR ENGLAND?

In his January 2007 interview with Andrew Marr, Gordon Brown conceded that 'I know that England is eighty-five per cent of the Union' but then added 'and England at any point can out-vote the rest of the Union'.[103] This is entirely disingenuous: politics at Westminster is divided not by nationality but by party political affiliation. As long as MPs from other parts of the United Kingdom are able to vote on laws that affect only England, the elected representatives of the people of England will be denied the autonomous politics that devolution has extended to the other parts of the United Kingdom.

In effect, Brown's 'new politics' and 'new style of government' have entrenched the same political asymmetries and democratic deficit as the old. The 'British Way' has left the ultimate postcode lottery of citizenship entirely untouched. The electorate of Brown's Kirkcaldy and Cowdenbeath constituency has the power directly to elect representatives to make laws in the Scottish Parliament that affect Scots alone, while also electing a politician who has continued to make policy for and determine the allocation of resources in England. The citizens of Cowdenbeath and Kirkcaldy do not, and will not have to, experience those policies in their schools and hospitals. The people of England have not been, and will not be, able to hold Gordon Brown (or any other MP representing a Scottish, Welsh or Northern Irish constituency), directly to account either for their policy decisions in Cabinet and Whitehall or their votes at Westminster which have affected England alone.

Brown has not provided an answer to the question of why devolution should empower the citizens of Scotland, Wales and Northern Ireland but not those of England. He has justified devolution in terms of the need 'to recognise the different views and the decision making processes in some other parts of the country. But at the end of the day this is a union that is built around an England that is eighty-five per cent of the Union'.[104] That is in no sense an explanation as to why devolution should be confined to 'some other parts of the country' and not allowed to England. If England is eighty-five per cent of the United Kingdom, that would appear to be the strongest-possible reason for recognising the distinctiveness of England as a political community.

Brown, and Douglas Alexander, have defended the *status quo* of the British Union on the grounds that:

> A million Scots live south of the border – more than three-quarters of a million people who live in Scotland were born in England. Half of us have relatives in England and people throughout all parts of the UK move freely to set up home.[105]

This is another spurious argument: devolution has extended democratic citizenship to the constituent nations of the United Kingdom, each of which has a citizenry and electorate drawn from many nations. Brown has asserted that it 'is not the institutions alone' (the monarchy, House of Commons, National Health Service, BBC and Army) but 'in the end, the shared values that bind' the British Union together. Given that Brown has indicated those shared values include the people's commitment to parliamentary democracy, it is paradoxical that eighty-five per cent of the population should be excluded from the entrenchment of those shared values through devolution. They are denied Robert Kennedy's politics of empowerment, with its 'more modern conception of freedom – not just freedom from but freedom to'.[106]

Conceding that there are 'various ways that Englishness can be recognised', Brown has remained adamant that England will never be recognised as a political community in its own right. He wants to confine the debate about English identity to questions of the English national character and its distinct qualities (hence the reference to 'Englishness') and thereby avoid any debate about England as a democratic nation and distinct, plural and multicultural political community in its own right. Purportedly, this is because 'a policy of English votes for English laws would in the end break up the United Kingdom because the executive would have to owe its authority to simply the English members'.[107] This is logically inconsistent: the Scottish Parliament owes its authority to its Scots members, the National Assembly for Wales to its Welsh members and the Northern Ireland Assembly to its Irish members. There is no logical reason to prevent the exercise of political power in England having to owe its authority to members for English constituencies. Brown knows this.

It is hard to escape the conclusion that Gordon Brown cannot contemplate the fact that his Prime Ministership would see him enjoying a much weaker capacity to control England, after a decade in which the nationalisation of policy-making gave him, as Chancellor of the Exchequer, unprecedented power to allocate resources and determine policy choices there. It is simply a case of the triumph of personal political ambition over equity and the 'politics of empowerment'. The ultimate paradox is that by denying the people of England the same democratic power to determine their future as that enjoyed elsewhere in the Union, Brown may have accelerated the demise of the United Kingdom. There is consistent opinion poll evidence of diminishing support for the British Union and growing support for the recognition of England as a separate democratic political community.

An ICM opinion poll, commissioned for *The Sunday Telegraph* in November 2006, found that, of respondents in England, no fewer than sixty-eight per cent wanted an English Parliament with similar powers to the Scottish Parliament and forty-eight per cent wanted independence for England. In Scotland, fifty-eight per cent supported the idea of an English Parliament, while forty-five per cent approved of independence for England. No fewer than sixty-two per cent of English respondents and forty-six per cent of Scottish respondents thought Scottish MPs should not be able to vote on English laws, when English MPs cannot vote on Scottish laws. Sixty per cent of English respondents thought higher government spending per head in Scotland than in England was unjustified. As many as twenty-six per cent of Brown's fellow countrymen and women described themselves as 'Scottish, not British', compared to only sixteen per cent of English respondents but even this figure, extrapolated to the whole English population, would mean around eight million people in England no longer described themselves as British – equivalent to the entire population of Scotland and Wales.[108]

Gordon Brown's sensitivity to these trends in public opinion in both England and Scotland has become more noticeable. He has appeared acutely conscious of the threat such trends potentially pose to his ambition to remain Prime Minister of the United Kingdom and to deliver a fourth consecutive General Election victory for the Labour Party, which he counters by reiterating his familiar mantra that 'We need a United Kingdom' because its constituent nations are 'stronger together but weaker apart'. Brown has also asserted that the time has come for the supporters of the Union 'to speak up, to resist any drift towards a Balkanisation of Britain' and returned to his familiar theme of the importance of the forging of shared national objectives and the same sense of national mission in peacetime that was prevalent in wartime.[109]

The political asymmetries of devolution, promoted by the government in which (as a prominent supporter of devolution) he served for a decade, do not add up. The restoration of the Scottish Parliament has given Scots the opportunity politically to forge their shared national objectives in vital areas such as education and health. The National Assembly for Wales has given the Welsh a similar chance and the Northern Irish Assembly theirs. The missing link is the same freedom for English.

The growing demands and popular support, both North and South of the border, for 'English votes for English laws' are not, as Brown has portrayed them, 'a Trojan horse for separation'.[110] They are simply a desire to restore equilibrium to an unbalanced and asymmetrical constitutional settlement and a popular expression of the sense of 'fair play' that Brown attributed to Winston Churchill.[111] (Ironically, Churchill once identified 'England' as his favourite word.) Brown has asserted that there is a:

> ... dangerous drift in anti-Union sentiment today. For while it is healthy to recognise the distinctiveness of each nation, we will all lose if politicians play fast and loose with the Union and abandon national purpose to a focus on what divides.

What Brown has never explained is why the distinctiveness of the other constituent nations of the United Kingdom may legitimately be recognised politically, through devolution, but England must be denied this recognition. All that Brown has to offer the English is for St George's Day to 'be given greater pride of place as a celebration'.[112] Ultimately, this a question of power: for a decade, as Chancellor of the Exchequer, Gordon Brown exercised unprecedented political power over the allocation of resources and the design of policy in England. He simply refuses to contemplate giving away that power. In so doing, he has risked the United Kingdom he claims to wish to save.

The political sensitivity of the three-hundredth anniversary of the political union of England and Wales with Scotland, especially in advance of the May 2007 Scottish Parliament elections, was illustrated by the very low-key official government celebrations that marked the occasion. Gordon Brown was particularly conspicuous by his absence. The urgency of Brown's attempts to revive Britishness, especially among the English, were given renewed impetus by the publication of the twenty-third British Social Attitudes Survey. This revealed a dramatic decline in the proportion of the British population who state 'British' to be the best or the only way to describe themselves. This figure fell from fifty-two per cent in 1996 to forty-four per cent in 2005. In England, in 1992 as many as sixty-three per cent of people had identified 'British' as the best or the only way to define their national identity. That figure had now declined to only forty-eight per cent. During the same period, the number of people identifying 'English' as their best or only identification had risen from thirty-one to forty per cent. In Brown's native Scotland, only fourteen per cent of people identified themselves as 'British', compared to seventy-nine per cent who defined their best or sole identity as 'Scottish'.[113]

To counter such trends, two ministers in the Blair Government had proposed that British identity be bolstered by a range of new measures. Ruth Kelly, then Secretary of State for Communities and Local Government and Liam Byrne, then Minister of State for Immigration and Asylum, proposed the designation of a 'British National Day' and the possibility of 'a new "State of the Nation" address for the Prime Minister', to accompany the State Opening of Parliament.[114] However, Kelly and Byrne failed to acknowledge that the written constitutions of states such as Australia and the United States have incorporated many more institutional checks and balances on the power enjoyed by their Prime Minister and President. To define 'a sharper identity for England', Kelly and Byrne accepted the need to debate 'the English question' but asserted 'the seductive-sounding call for

English votes on English laws or some kind of English parliament would simply be unworkable. It would lead to constitutional chaos or worse could ultimately jeopardise the future of the union itself'.[115] On the contrary, an English Parliament would be workable, as are legislatures in the United States, Canada, Australia, Germany, India and all the great democracies of the world, and as the English Parliament once was itself, before the creation of the United Kingdom in 1707.

The only possibility is of constitutional chaos if the Brown Government 'British Way' continues to ignore the English question. There is a very real possibility that, after the next General Election, the Labour Party will be the largest party at Westminster, possibly holding an overall United Kingdom-wide majority but that the Conservative Party could have a majority of parliamentary seats in England (it won more English votes than the Labour Party at the 2005 General Election). If a Brown Government, either on its own or in coalition with other political parties, seeks to pass legislation affecting England alone using the votes of MPs representing constituencies from the other nations of the United Kingdom, there is likely to be constitutional chaos and the future of the British Union will be jeopardised.

Brown's political fate will depend on whether he can persuade Rupert Murdoch to continue to align his media empire with New Labour (in recent years, he accompanied Tony Blair on his trips to visit Murdoch). Brown has great sensitivity on the issue of the question of the nationality of his constituency in a devolved settlement. Given the huge political asymmetries and fiscal imbalances of the Blair decade, especially in relation to spending on health care and other front-line public services, it is precisely the populist sort of question on which Murdoch tabloid editors love to campaign.

IS GORDON BROWN BEST FOR BRITAIN?

Brown's vision for his Prime Ministership is rooted in American liberalism, rather than the traditions of the British Labour Party. As Prime Minister, Gordon Brown wants to build 'a strong economy and a good society' for Britain.[116] 'Good society' is a concept drawn directly from the 1930s New Deal reconstruction of American liberalism (Walter Lipmann), the Great Society liberalism of the 1960s (Robert Kennedy) and its proposed revival during the 1990s (John Kenneth Galbraith).[117] Brown has identified his personal policy priorities as Prime Minister as lying in the 'good society', stating that 'education will be the priority, it will have pride of place and indeed it's my passion'.[118] This vision is identical to that of Tony Blair who, almost exactly a dozen years earlier in 1995, stated that 'education will be the passion of my government'.[119]

In his book *Courage: Eight portraits*, Brown identified his admiration for those who have been 'driven and sustained by higher ideals' and stated his belief that such courage 'can continue to transform our world today'.[120] More specifically, Brown identified Robert Kennedy 'as the first modern political leader – prepared to break with old conventions and offer a wholly distinct message that transcended both the old right and the old left'.[121] Ironically, given his general disdain for the term, Brown has claimed that Kennedy was seeking the path of 'a third way'.[122] Not content to remain 'in the control zone of his party's establishment', Kennedy 'took risks, was prepared to change course, tried to move the whole of the American democratic establishment into new territory and genuinely broke new ground'.[123]

If Gordon Brown is to recapture the four million voters and 200,000 members who have deserted the Labour Party since the 1997 General Election and to persuade Middle England not to abandon New Labour for David Cameron's liberal conservatism, the sympathetic liberalism of his 'British Way' will need to show similar moral courage and political leadership. Brown may also reflect on the fact that the gradual political collapse of American liberalism and the Great Society programmes during the late 1960s, allied to the collapse of the Bretton Woods international economic order in the early 1970s, ushered in the era of 'Reaganomics' and Thatcherism. As Prime Minister, Gordon Brown will not be best for Britain nor for the Labour Party if the 'British Way' bequeaths a similar political legacy.

The greatest irony of Brown's attachment to the vision of the good society is that the philosophy of his moral beacon, Robert Kennedy, requires him to undertake the political actions he is least minded to implement. If Brown is to be best for Britain, follow Kennedy's example, genuinely break new political ground and move the British democratic establishment into genuinely new territory, he must first abandon the central prescription for his nationalisation of policy making and resource allocation in England, restore genuine Cabinet government and not (as in the U-turn over super-casinos) discard it when it suits his purpose. He must institute collective discussion of major policy decisions, rather than use the Cabinet as a rubber stamp, presenting it with policies, already leaked to the media, as a political *fait accompli.*

Second, he must ensure that Westminster is not exempt from freedom of information legislation and apply to it the standards of transparency and accountability required of other public institutions. Third, on economic policy, Brown must incorporate greater transparency into his 'British model' of political economy and subject the conduct of fiscal policy to the same degree of independent scrutiny as the conduct of monetary policy. He must incorporate mortgage interest payments into the official calculation of inflation and the Bank of England's monetary policy deliberations, so that they reflect the real cost of living people experience.

Fourth, on reform of the public services, he must resist the temptation to continue the permanent revolution of top-down reforms which the nationalisation of policy design and resource allocation in England has made possible. Finally – and more so than at any time since the Suez Crisis of 1956 – Brown has the opportunity to recast British foreign policy. To make foreign policy fit for its purpose in the twenty-first century, he must renew his commitment to international development and a global war on poverty but set these within a more inclusive approach to global governance, rather than a narrower Atlanticist-based multilateralism. In casting Britain as a global hub, foreign policy must recognise the interests of people and communities beyond London and its financial markets.

Above all, in terms of identity and citizenship, Brown must correct the asymmetries and imbalances in the democratic voice and accountability that the Blair Government's devolution agenda bequeathed to England. People must no longer be treated as passive consumers, whose only concern is for the further extension of market-led services. The public realm must be reinvigorated and people re-engaged as active citizens, with real power over the decisions that affect the communities, policies and services that shape their lives. The *sine qua non* is that England must be granted the self-determination to vote on policies and issues that affect it alone that devolution has extended to the other constituent nations of the United Kingdom.

If Brown believes that the essence of Britishness and the British Way is liberty for all, responsibility from all and fairness to all, he must extend the same liberties to the people of England as are enjoyed elsewhere in the United Kingdom. If he believes in Robert Kennedy's politics of empowerment, he must enable English citizens to rediscover the responsibility of civic duty so England is no longer treated in an unfair manner. That redress of inequity must extend to a full assessment of the territorial allocation of public expenditure within and between the constituent nations of the United Kingdom, to replace the archaic, pre-Thatcher, Barnett Formula.

Failure to institute any of these measures will mean, irrespective of whether they are best for Britain, Gordon Brown and his British Way will not be best for England.

Endnotes

PREFACE

1. H. M. Treasury, *Public Expenditure Statistical Analyses 2007*, Cm. 7091 (London: The Stationery Office, 2007), Table 9.2, p. 115.
2. Ministry of Justice, *The Governance of Britain – The Government's Draft Legislative Programme*, Cm. 7175 (London: The Stationery Office, 2007); Ministry of Justice, *The Governance of Britain*, Cm. 7170 (London: The Stationery Office, 2007).

INTRODUCTION

1. H. M. Treasury, *Budget 2007, Building Britain's Long-Term Future: Prosperity and fairness for families. Economic and fiscal strategy report and financial statement and budget report.* HC. 342 (London: The Stationery Office, 2007), p. 3.
2. H. M. Treasury, *Pre-Budget Report, Investing in Britain's Potential: Building our long-term future*, Cm. 6984 (London: The Stationery Office, 2006), p. 14.
3. Ibid.
4. YouGov, *YouGov/Daily Telegraph Survey, March 21–22 2007* (London: YouGov, 2007).
5. Electoral Calculus, *Recent opinion polls* (London: Electoral Calculus, 2007), available online at http://www.electoralcalculus.co.uk (accessed 26 March 2007).
6. YouGov, *Budget Polls for Daily Telegraph-Trends* (London: YouGov, 2007).
7. Ipsos MORI, *Satisfaction With The Chancellor Trends, Agreement With Government's Policies* (London: Ipsos MORI, 2006). The Economic Optimism Index (EOI) records the percentage difference between those who think the

general economic condition of the country will improve over the next twelve months and those who think it will not.

8. MORI, *Political Monitor: State of the economy – last 12 months* (London: MORI, 2007).
9. YouGov, *YouGov/Daily Telegraph Survey Results, 19–21 February 2007* (London: YouGov, 2007).
10. Populus, *Political Attitudes, 2–4 March* (London: Populus, 2007).
11. ICM Research, *The Guardian Poll, 16–18 February* (London: ICM Research, 2007).
12. G. Hurst and F. Yeoman, 'Prospect of Brown as Leader Fails to Lift MPs on the Margins,' *The Times*, 26 February 2007.
13. A. Thomson and R. Sylvester, 'Clarke on Brown: He lacks courage and vision, he's delusional and a control freak,' *The Daily Telegraph*, 10 September 2006.
14. N. Timmins, ''Stalinist' Brown, by Ex-Cabinet Secretary,' *Financial Times*, 20 March 2007.
15. Ibid.
16. A. Rawnsley, *Servants of The People: The inside story of New Labour* (London: Penguin, 2000), p. 150.
17. Press Association, 'Blair Denies Calling Brown 'Psychologically Flawed',' *The Guardian*, 17 January 2007.
18. J. Smith, 'Row Reignites as Clarke Vents Anger at 'Stupid' Brown,' *Press Association*, 8 September 2006.
19. The 2020 Vision, *The 2020 Vision: Towards a progressive century. Mission statement for the 2020 Vision*, available online at http://www.the2020vision.org/uk/index.php/pages/have-your-say/the-2020-vision (accessed 25 March 2007).
20. P. Routledge, *Gordon Brown: The biography* (London: Simon and Schuster, 1988); W. Keegan, *The Prudence of Mr Gordon Brown* (Chichester: John Wiley & Sons, 2003); and T. Bower, *Gordon Brown* (London: HarperCollins, 2004).
21. See for example, D. Scott, *Off Whitehall: A view from Downing Street by Tony Blair's adviser* (London: I. B. Tauris, 2004); and J. Naughtie, *The Rivals: The intimate story of a political marriage* (London: Fourth Estate, 2002).
22. Supply-side economics focuses on improving economic growth and performance not only by enhancing the efficiency with which resources are allocated in the production of existing goods and services but also by expanding the total volume of production through investment in new technologies, businesses and human and physical infrastructure. It stands in contrast to Keynesian economics, with its emphasis on the short-term manipulation of demand to maintain full employment.

CHAPTER 1

1. M. Thatcher, *Let Our Children Grow Tall: Selected speeches 1975–77* (London: Centre for Policy Studies, 1977), p. 51.
2. For Joseph, the middle ground was nothing more than 'a compromise between politicians, unrelated to the aspirations of the people,' 'a slippery slope to socialism and state control' and a guarantor of 'the left-wing ratchet.' Sir K. Joseph, *Stranded on the Middle Ground? Reflections on Circumstances and Policies* (London: Centre for Policy Studies, 1976), pp. 19, 21.
3. Ibid., pp. 21, 25.
4. Sir K. Joseph, *Hansard*, 21 May 1979, c. 706.
5. T. Blair, *Change and National Renewal* (London: The Labour Party, 1994).
6. T. Blair, *New Britain: My vision of a young country* (London: Fourth Estate, 1996), p. 56.
7. Ibid., p. 13.
8. Ibid., p. 20.
9. The Labour Party, *New Labour: Because Britain deserves better* (London: The Labour Party, 1997), pp. 3–4.
10. The Conservative Party, *The Conservative Party 1979 General Election Manifesto* (London: Conservative Central Office, 1979). The manifesto referred only to a commitment 'to sell back to private ownership the recently nationalised aerospace and shipbuilding concerns' and the aim 'to sell shares in the National Freight Corporation to the general public,' p. 15.
11. The term 'Thatcherism' was popularised first in a series of articles in *Marxism Today*. These articles are reproduced in S. Hall and M. Jacques (ed.), *The Politics of Thatcherism* (London: Lawrence and Wishart, 1983).
12. T. Blair, *The Third Way: New politics for the new century* (London: The Fabian Society, 1998); A. Giddens, *The Third Way: The renewal of social democracy* (Cambridge: Polity Press, 1988).
13. W. Clinton, *State of the Union*, The White House, Washington DC, 27 January 1998. The peripheral importance of the Third Way to Clinton's politics was demonstrated by the devotion of only one per cent of the 957 pages of his biography to this subject. See W. Clinton, *My Life* (London: Hutchinson, 2004), pp. 381–382, 813, 854, 878–879, 907–908 and 934.
14. These speeches can be viewed on the website of the Margaret Thatcher Foundation, www.margaretthatcher.org.
15. G. Brown, *Moving Britain Forward: Selected speeches 1997–2006* (edited by W. Stevenson) (London: Bloomsbury, 2006). A more comprehensive collection of Brown's speeches was published simultaneously in G. Brown, *Speeches, 1997–2006* (London: Bloomsbury, 2006).

16. G. Brown, 'Securing Our Future,' speech at the Royal United Services Institute, London, 13 February 2006.

17. G. Brown, 'We Will Always Strive to be on Your Side,' speech to the Labour Party Conference, Manchester, 25 September 2006.

18. G. Brown, 'Meeting the Terrorist Challenge,' speech given to Chatham House, London, 10 October 2006.

19. G. Brown, 'We Will Always Strive to be on Your Side,' speech to the Labour Party Conference, Manchester, 25 September 2006.

20. For an insider's perspective on Blair's commitment, see P. Ashdown, *The Ashdown Diaries: Volume two 1997–1999* (London: Penguin, 2002).

21. D. Marquand, *The Progressive Dilemma: From Lloyd George to Kinnock* (London: Heinemann, 1991).

22. T. Blair, *The Third Way: New politics for the new century* (London: The Fabian Society, 1998), p. 1. For a detailed analysis of the Third Way, see S. Lee, *Blair's Third Way* (London: Palgrave Macmillan, 2008).

23. Home Office, *The Report of the Independent Commission on the Voting System*, Cm. 4090-I (London: The Stationery Office, 1998).

24. The Labour Party, *New Labour Because Britain Deserves Better: The 1997 general election manifesto* (London: The Labour Party).

25. Among its principal recommendations, the Jenkins Commission advocated 'a two-vote mixed system, which can be described as either limited AMS or AV Top-up', be introduced throughout the United Kingdom, as 'the best alternative to First Past the Post.' Under the AMS (Additional Member System) or AV (Alternative Vote) Top-up system, 'voters cast two distinct votes – the first for a constituency MP and the second a party vote,' Home Office, *The Report of the Independent Commission on the Voting System*, Cm. 4090-I (London: The Stationery Office, 1998), Chapter 9, Glossary.

26. B. Crick, 'Still Missing: A public philosophy,' *Political Quarterly*, 68, 4, 1997, pp. 344–351; B. Pimlott, 'New Labour, New Era,' *Political Quarterly*, 68, 4, 1997, pp. 325–334; and C. Crouch, 'The Terms of the Neo-Liberal Consensus,' *Political Quarterly*, 68, 4, 1997, pp. 352–371.

27. B. Gould, 'The Long Retreat from Principle,' *New Statesman*, 29 January 1999.

28. D. Marquand, 'After Euphoria: The dilemma of New Labour,' *Political Quarterly*, 68, 4, 1997, pp. 335–343.

29. G. Brown, speech to the Labour Party Conference, Brighton, 27 September 2004.

30. W. H. Greenleaf, *The British Political Tradition. Volume Two: The ideological heritage* (London: Methuen, 1983), p. 359.

31. S. Webb, *The Basis & Policy of Socialism* (London: Fabian Socialist Series No.4, 1908), p. 71.

32. Recent examples of technocratic reports commissioned by Brown have included H. M. Treasury, *Prosperity for All in the Global Economy: World class skills* (The Leitch Review of Skills) (London: H. M. Treasury, 2006); H. M. Treasury, *Barker Review of Land Use Planning: Final Report – Recommendations* (London: H. M. Treasury, 2006); H. M. Treasury, *Stern Review: The Economics of Climate Change* (London: H. M. Treasury, 2006).
33. N. Dennis and A. H. Halsey, *English Ethical Socialism: Thomas More to R. H. Tawney* (Oxford: Clarendon Press, 1988), p. 1.
34. Ibid., pp. 4–5.
35. M. Carter, *T. H. Green and the Development of Ethical Socialism* (Exeter: Imprint Academic, 2003), p. 172.
36. N. Dennis and A. H. Halsey, *English Ethical Socialism: Thomas More to R. H. Tawney* (Oxford: Clarendon Press, 1988), p. 150.
37. G. Brown, 'Interview with Lynn Barber,' *The Daily Telegraph*, 10 July 1995, cited in P. Routledge, *Gordon Brown: The biography* (London: Pocket Books, 1998), p. 25.
38. Ibid., p. 25.
39. G. Brown, 'We Will Always Strive to be on Your Side,' speech to the Labour Party Conference, Manchester, 25 September 2006.
40. Ibid.
41. This thesis was most clearly developed in G. Brown, British Council Annual Lecture, 7 July 2004.
42. A prime example is provided by G. Brown, The Hugo Young Memorial Lecture, 13 December 2005.
43. G. Brown, 'We Will Always Strive to be on Your Side,' speech to the Labour Party Conference, Manchester, 25 September 2006.
44. G. Brown, 'Interview with Paul Routledge,' 20 April 1997, cited in P. Routledge, *Gordon Brown: The biography* (London: Pocket Books, 1998), p. 27.
45. *Student*, 9 November 1972, cited in P. Routledge, *Gordon Brown: The biography* (London: Pocket Books, 1998), p. 56.
46. J. Allison, *Guilty by Suspicion* (Glendaruel: Argyll Publishing, 1995), p. 119, cited in P. Routledge, *Gordon Brown: The biography* (London: Pocket Books, 1998), p. 96.
47. The first Red Paper, B. Cuddihy (ed.), *The Red Paper on Education* (Edinburgh: Edinburgh University Student Press, 1970), had been published in 1970 as a forum for the Left to express an alternative to C. B. Cox and A. E. Dyson (ed.), *The Black Papers on Education* (London: Davis-Poynter, 1971).
48. G. Brown, 'Introduction: The socialist challenge,' to G. Brown (ed.), *The Red Paper on Scotland* (Edinburgh: Edinburgh University Student Press, 1975), p. 7.

49. Ibid., pp. 7–8

50. Ibid., p. 8.

51. Ibid., p. 8.

52. Ibid., p. 8.

53. Ibid., p. 9.

54. Ibid., p. 10.

55. Ibid., p. 11.

56. Ibid., p. 13.

57. Ibid., p. 14.

58. Ibid., p. 17.

59. Ibid., p. 18.

60. Despite his scepticism about the benefits of devolution, Brown was later chosen to chair the Scottish Labour Party's Devolution Committee, at the tender age of twenty-seven. However, other prominent figures within the Scottish Labour Party retained Brown's scepticism. For example, devolution was dismissed by Robin Cook, a fellow graduate of Edinburgh University, as 'irrelevant to the real problems we face. Given the present economic situation, to go ahead with devolution seems to be like fiddling while Rome Burns.' R. Cook, cited in P. Routledge, *Gordon Brown: The biography* (London: Pocket Books, 1998), p. 81.

61. Ibid., p. 19.

62. G. Brown, *The Labour Party and Political Change in Scotland, 1918–1929* (Edinburgh University: Edinburgh University PhD thesis, 1981).

63. F. W. Jowett, *Socialism in Our Time* (London: Independent Labour Party, 1926), p. 4.

64. J. Maxton, *New Leader*, 9 January 1928, cited in G. Brown, *Maxton* (Edinburgh: Mainstream Publishing, 1986), p. 182.

65. G. Brown, *Maxton* (Edinburgh: Mainstream Publishing, 1986), p. 294.

66. G. Brown, 'Social Security,' *Hansard*, 27 July 1983, cc. 1239–1244.

67. Ibid., c. 1240.

68. Ibid., c. 1243.

69. Ibid., c. 1244.

70. G. Brown, 'Introduction' to G. Brown and R. Cook (ed.), *Scotland: The Real Divide. Poverty and Deprivation in Scotland* (Edinburgh: Mainstream, 1983), p. 9.

71. Ibid., pp. 16, 19.

72. Ibid., pp. 21–22.

73. The Labour Party, *Report of the Annual Conference of the Labour Party 1985* (London: The Labour Party, 1986), p. 114.

74. N. Kinnock, *Making Our Way: Investing in Britain's future* (Oxford: Basil Blackwell, 1986), p. vi.

252   Endnotes

75. Labour Party, *Social Justice & Economic Efficiency: First report of Labour's policy review for the 1990s* (London: The Labour Party, 1988), pp. 3, 4.
76. Labour Party, *Meet the Challenge, Make the Change: A new agenda for Britain* (London: The Labour Party, 1989), p. 6.
77. Labour Party, *Looking to the Future* (London: The Labour Party, 1990), pp. 5, 7.
78. Labour Party, *Opportunity Britain: Labour's better way for the 1990s* (London: The Labour Party, 1991), pp. ii, 5.
79. Labour Party, *It's Time to Get Britain Working Again: Labour's election manifesto* (London: The Labour Party, 1992), pp. 12–13.
80. For a concise analysis of the British tradition of state-led industrial modernisation programmes, see S. Lee, 'Manufacturing,' in D. Coates (ed.), *Industrial Policy in Britain* (London: Macmillan, 1996).
81. G. Brown, *Where There is Greed: Margaret Thatcher and the betrayal of Britain* (Edinburgh: Mainstream Publishing, 1989), pp. 3, 6.
82. Ibid., p. 10.
83. Ibid., p. 23.
84. Ibid., p. 61.
85. The developmental state has been defined by academics as one 'whose politics have concentrated sufficient power, autonomy and capacity at the centre to shape, pursue and encourage the achievements of explicit developmental objectives, whether by establishing and promoting the conditions and direction of economic growth or by organising it directly or a varying combination of both,' A. Leftwich, 'Bringing Politics Back in: Towards a model of the developmental state,' *Journal of Development Studies*, 31, 3, 1995, pp. 400–427. For an explanation of the concept of the developmental state, see S. Lee 'Developmental State,' in R. Barry Jones (ed.), *The Routledge Encyclopaedia of International Political Economy*, Volume 1 (London: Routledge, 2001), pp. 343–346.
86. F. List, *The National System of Political Economy* (London: Longmans, Green and Company, 1928). List's agenda for industrialising economies is summarised in M. Shafaeddin, *What Did Frederick List Actually Say? Some Clarifications on the Infant Industry Argument* (Geneva: United Nations Conference on Trade and Development, Discussion Paper No.149, 2000).
87. F. List, *The National System of Political Economy* (London: Longmans, Green and Company, 1928), pp. 116, 150.
88. Labour Party, *Made in Britain* (London: The Labour Party, 1992).
89. P. Anderson, 'Stable Climate for Business Planned,' *Tribune*, 10 January 1992.
90. C. Hughes and P. Wintour, *Labour Rebuilt: The New Model Party* (London: Fourth Estate, 1990), p. 135.
91. T. Blair, *Change and National Renewal* (London: The Labour Party, 1994).

92. P. Anderson, 'The Tribune Interview: Gordon Brown,' *Tribune*, 1 January 1993.

93. Ibid.

94. Ibid.

95. Ibid.

96. N. Kinnock, 'Introduction' to Labour Party, *Opportunity Britain: Labour's better way for the 1990s* (London: The Labour Party, 1991), p. iii.

97. G. Brown, *Fair Is Efficient: A socialist agenda for fairness* (London: The Fabian Society, 1994), p. 1.

98. Ibid., p. 2.

99. Ibid., p. 3.

100. Ibid., p. 3.

101. Ibid., p. 3.

102. R. H. Tawney, *Equality* (London: Unwin Books, 1931), p. 268, cited in G. Brown, *Fair Is Efficient: A socialist agenda for fairness* (London: The Fabian Society, 1994), p. 3.

103. A. Bevan, *In Place of Fear* (London: William Heinemann, 1952), p. 170, cited in G. Brown, *Fair Is Efficient: A socialist agenda for fairness* (London: The Fabian Society, 1994), p. 3.

104. G. Brown, *Fair Is Efficient: A socialist agenda for fairness* (London: The Fabian Society, 1994), p. 3.

105. D. Miliband, 'Introduction' to D. Miliband (ed.), *Reinventing the Left* (Cambridge: Polity Press, 1994), pp. 5–8.

106. G. Brown, 'The Politics of Potential: A new agenda for Labour,' in D. Miliband (ed.), *Reinventing the Left* (Cambridge: Polity, 1994), p. 114.

107. Ibid., p. 115.

108. Ibid., p. 115.

109. Ibid., p. 119.

110. Ibid., p. 119.

111. A. Phillips, 'Comment: Whose community? Which individuals?' in D. Miliband (ed.), *Reinventing the Left* (Cambridge: Polity, Press), p. 124.

112. J. Smith, 'Reclaiming the Ground,' The R. H. Tawney Memorial Lecture, 20 March 1993, cited in G. Brown, 'John Smith's Socialism: His writings and speeches,' in G. Brown and J. Naughtie (ed.), *John Smith: Life and soul of the party* (Edinburgh: Mainstream Publishing, 1994), p. 67.

113. G. Brown and T. Wright, 'Introduction' to G. Brown and T. Wright (ed.), *Values, Visions and Voices: An anthology of socialism* (Edinburgh: Mainstream, 1995), p. 14.

114. Ibid., p. 16.

115. Ibid., pp. 16–17.

116. Ibid., p. 17.
117. Ibid., pp. 18–19.
118. Ibid., p. 19.
119. G. Brown and T. Wright, 'Introduction' to G. Brown and T. Wright (ed.), *Values, Visions and Voices: An anthology of socialism* (Edinburgh: Mainstream, 1995), pp. 25–26.
120. T. Blair, speech to business leaders, Singapore, 7 January 1996.
121. W. Hutton, 'Fool's Gold in a Fool's Paradise,' *The Observer*, 2 June 1996.
122. Ibid.
123. Labour Party, *New Labour, New Life for Britain* (London: The Labour Party, 1996).
124. For a detailed analysis of the evolution of Labour Party policy on economy and society during this period, see S. Lee, 'Finance for Industry,' in J. Michie and J. Grieve Smith (ed.), *Creating Industrial Capacity: Towards full employment* (Oxford: Oxford University Press, 1996); and S. Lee, 'Competitiveness and the Welfare State in Britain,' in M. Mullard and S. Lee (ed.), *Social Policy in Europe* (Cheltenham: Edward Elgar 1997).
125. T. Blair, speech at a Fabian Society Commemoration of the Fiftieth Anniversary of the 1945 General Election, 5 July 1995, in T. Blair, *New Britain: My vision of a young country* (London: Fourth Estate, 1996), p. 13.
126. Ibid., p. 20.
127. Ibid., p. 16.
128. T. Blair, 'Why I am a Christian,' *The Sunday Telegraph*, 7 April 1996, in T. Blair, *New Britain: My vision of a young country* (London: Fourth Estate, 1996), pp. 59–60.
129. T. Blair, 'The Young Country,' speech to the Labour Party Conference, Brighton, 3 October 1995, in T. Blair, *New Britain: My vision of a young country* (London: Fourth Estate, 1996), p. 62.
130. T. Happold and K. Maguire, 'Revealed: Brown and Blair's pact,' *The Guardian*, 6 June 2003.
131. M. Kettle, 'The Granita Guarantee Decoded,' *The Guardian*, 6 June 2003.
132. Labour Party, *A New Economic Future for Britain: Economic and employment opportunities for all* (London: The Labour Party, 1995), p. 4.
133. Labour Party, *New Labour: Because Britain deserves better* (London: The Labour Party, 1997), pp. 3–4.
134. Labour Party, *A New Economic Future for Britain: Economic and employment opportunities for all* (London: The Labour Party, 1995), p. 28.
135. Department of Trade and Industry, *DTI – Department for Enterprise* (London: Her Majesty's Stationery Office, 1988), p. ii.

CHAPTER 2

1. G. Brown, The 1997 Allied Dunbar/Spectator Lecture, reprinted as G. Brown, 'Outward Bound,' *The Spectator*, 8 November 1997, pp. 15–16.
2. G. Brown, 'Modernising the British Economy: The new mission for the Treasury,' 30th Anniversary Lecture to the Institute of Fiscal Studies, London, 27 May 1999.
3. G. Brown, speech at the Smith Institute, London, 15 April 1999.
4. Ibid.
5. G. Brown, 'Civic Society in Modern Britain,' The 17th Arnold Goodman Lecture, Merchant Taylor's Hall, London, 20 July 2000.
6. A. Seldon and S. Ball (ed.), *The Conservative Century* (London, Macmillan, 1994).
7. I. McLean and G. Lodge, *The Progressive Consensus in Perspective* (London: Institute for Public Policy Research, 2007), p. 3.
8. J. M. Keynes, *The Economic Consequences of the Peace* (London: Macmillan, 1920); J. M. Keynes, *The End of* Laissez-Faire (London: L and V. Woolf at the Hogarth Press, 1926); J. M. Keynes, *The General Theory of Employment, Interest and Money* (London: Macmillan and Co., 1936); J. M. Keynes, *How to Pay for the War: A radical plan for the Chancellor of the Exchequer* (London: Macmillan, 1940). For an analysis of Keynes' liberalism on the development of economic policy in the interwar period, see A. Booth, *British Economic Policy 1931–49: Was there a Keynesian revolution?* (London: Harvester Wheatsheaf, 1989).
9. The ideas and policies for full employment were identified by the wartime Minister of Reconstruction in the White Paper, *Employment Policy*, Cmnd. 6527 (London: His Majesty's Stationery Office, 1944).
10. Lord W. Beveridge, *Social Insurance and Allied Services* (London: Her Majesty's Stationery Office, 1942); Lord W. Beveridge, *Full Employment in a Free Society* (London: George Allen & Unwin, 1944).
11. In her speeches, Thatcher paid tribute frequently to the work of Adam Smith and Friedrich Hayek. For example, in a single speech Thatcher once paid tribute to the importance of moral philosophy for both the American Declaration of Independence and contemporary political economy and the contribution played by Hayek in demonstrating that Keynes would have opposed the inflationary post-war policies of Keynesians (M. Thatcher, Walter Heller International Finance Lecture, Roosevelt University, Chicago, 22 September 1975, reproduced in The Thatcher Archive, CCOPR 789/75, available online from the Thatcher Foundation at www.margaretthatcher.org/speeches/displaydocument.asp?docid=102465 (accessed 30 March 2007).

12. For an analysis of Sir Keith Joseph's political philosophy, including his debt to liberalism, see K. Bosanquet, 'Sir Keith's Reading List,' *Political Quarterly*, 52, 3, 1981, pp. 324–341.

13. N. Lawson, 'The New Conservatism,' Lecture to the Bow Group, 4 August 1980, reproduced as Annexe I of N. Lawson, *The View from No.11: Memoirs of a tory radical* (London: Bantam Press, 1992), p. 1041.

14. T. Blair, speech to the Annual Conference of the Confederation of British Industry, 13 November 1995, in T. Blair, *New Britain: My vision of a young country* (London: Fourth Estate, 1996), p. 110.

15. G. Brown, CAFOD Pope Paul VI Memorial Lecture, London, 8 December 2004.

16. Ibid.

17. See for example, G. Brown, 'Foreword' to I. McLean, *Adam Smith, Radical and Egalitarian: An interpretation for the twenty-first century* (Edinburgh: Edinburgh University Press, 2006), pp. viii-ix.

18. G. Brown, CAFOD Pope Paul VI Memorial Lecture, London, 8 December 2004.

19. A. Smith, *The Theory of Moral Sentiments* (London: A Millar, 1759; Indianapolis: LibertyClassics edition, 1982), p. 1.

20. 'This can only happen if we build from solid foundations of prudent economic management,' G. Brown, 'Statement from the Chancellor of the Exchequer: Central economic objectives of the new Government,' *H. M. Treasury Press Release*, 6 May 1997 (London: H. M. Treasury, 1997).

21. A. Smith, *The Theory of Moral Sentiments* (London: A Millar, 1759; Indianapolis: LibertyClassics edition, 1982), p. 216.

22. Ibid., p. 215.

23. Ibid., p. 217.

24. I. McLean, *Adam Smith, Radical and Egalitarian: An interpretation for the twenty-first century* (Edinburgh: Edinburgh University Press, 2007), p. xix

25. Ibid., pp. 142–143.

26. Ibid., p. 145.

27. Ibid., p. 120.

28. Ibid., p. 138.

29. A. Smith, *An Inquiry into the Nature and Causes of the Wealth of Nations, Book II* (Glasgow, 1759), V.ii.b., cited in I. McLean, *Radical and Egalitarian: An interpretation for the twenty-first century* (Edinburgh: Edinburgh University Press, 2006), p. 76.

30. A. Smith, *The Theory of Moral Sentiments* (London: A Millar, 1759; Indianapolis: LibertyClassics edition, 1982), p. 55.

31. G. Brown, 'Introduction' to the 'Can Both the Left and Right Claim Adam Smith?' Enlightenment Lecture, Playfair Library Hall, Old College, Edinburgh University, 25 April 2002.

32. G. Brown, First Donald Dewar Memorial Lecture, Glasgow University, 12 October 2006.
33. Ibid.
34. J. Sacks, *The Politics of Hope* (London: Vintage, 2000), pp. 1–4, 112–120.
35. A. Smith, *The Wealth of Nations: Books I – III* (Harmondsworth: Penguin, 1983), p. 512, partially cited in G. Brown, First Donald Dewar Memorial Lecture, Glasgow University, 12 October 2006.
36. G. Brown, First Donald Dewar Memorial Lecture, Glasgow University, 12 October 2006.
37. A. Greenspan, The Adam Smith Memorial Lecture, Kirkcaldy, 6 February 2005.
38. M. King, 'Trusting in Money: From Kirkcaldy to the MPC,' The Adam Smith Memorial Lecture, Kirkcaldy, 29 October 2006.
39. J. Sacks, *The Politics of Hope* (London: Vintage, 2000); J. Sacks, *The Dignity of Difference: How to avoid the clash of civilisations* (London: Continuum, 2006).
40. J. Sacks, *The Politics of Hope* (London: Vintage, 2000), p. 2.
41. Ibid., pp. 3–4, 47.
42. Ibid., p. 64.
43. J. Sacks, *The Dignity of Difference: How to avoid the clash of civilisations* (London: Continuum, 2006), p. 3.
44. Sacks has argued that a covenant occurs 'when two individuals or groups, differing perhaps in power but each acknowledging the integrity and sovereignty of the other, pledge themselves in mutual loyalty to achieve together what neither can achieve alone.' Ibid., p. 202.
45. Ibid., pp. 14, 35.
46. Ibid., p. 17.
47. Ibid., p. 78.
48. Ibid., p. 87.
49. Ibid., pp. 88–89.
50. Ibid., p. 98.
51. Advocates of comparative advantage, such as Adam Smith and David Ricardo, argued that 'by specialising in producing and trading those goods for which they have greater cost advantage, nations and their populations maximise their access to wealth and welfare.' R. Korzeniewicz, 'Comparative Advantage and Unequal Exchange,' in P. O'Hara (ed.), *Encyclopedia of Political Economy, Volume I* (London: Routledge, 1999), p. 127.
52. Sacks, *The Dignity of Difference*, p. 101.
53. Ibid., p. 103.
54. Ibid., p. 202.
55. Ibid., p. 205.
56. G. Brown, CAFOD Pope Paul VI Memorial Lecture, 8 December 2004.

57. G. Brown, The Hugo Young Memorial Lecture, Chatham House, London, 13 December 2005.
58. Ibid.
59. G. Brown, speech to the National Council of Voluntary Organisations' Annual Conference, London, 9 February 2000.
60. Ibid.
61. G. Brown, 'Civic Society in Modern Britain,' 17th Arnold Goodman Lecture, Merchant Taylor's Hall, London, 20 July 2000.
62. G. Brown, speech to the National Council of Voluntary Organisations' Annual Conference, London, 9 February 2000.
63. G. Brown, 'Civic Society in Modern Britain,' 17th Arnold Goodman Lecture, Merchant Taylor's Hall, London, 20 July 2000.
64. Ibid.
65. Ibid.
66. G. Brown, speech to the Volunteering Conference, London, 31 January 2005.
67. M. Sandel, 'What Money Can't Buy: The moral limits of markets.' The Tanner Lectures on Human Values, delivered at Brasenose College, Oxford, 11 and 12 May 1998, cited in G. Brown, 'A Modern Agenda for Prosperity and Social Reform,' speech to the Social Market Foundation, Cass Business School, London, 3 February 2003.
68. M. Sandel, 'What Money Can't Buy: The moral limits of markets.' The Tanner Lectures on Human Values, delivered at Brasenose College, Oxford, 11 and 12 May 1998.
69. Ibid.
70. G. Brown, speech at the Smith Institute, London, 15 April 1999.
71. M. Walzer, *Spheres of Justice: A defense of pluralism and equality* (New York: Basic Books, 1983), p. 100, cited in G. Brown, 'State and Market: Towards a public interest test,' *Political Quarterly*, 73, 2003, pp. 268–284, cf p. 269.
72. A. Okun, *Equality and Efficiency: The big tradeoff* (Washington DC: The Brookings Institution, 1975), p. 119, cited in G. Brown, 'State and Market: Towards a public interest test,' *Political Quarterly*, 73, 2003, pp. 268–284, cf p. 269.
73. J. Pechman (ed.), *Economics for Policymaking: Selected essays of Arthur M. Okun* (Cambridge, Massachusetts: The MIT Press, 1983), pp. 634–635.
74. G. Brown, Keynote speech at the 2004 National Council for Voluntary Organisations' Annual Conference, London, 18 February 2004.
75. G. Brown, speech to the Volunteering Conference, London, 31 January 2005.
76. Ibid.
77. D. Brooks, 'Questions of Culture,' *New York Times*, 19 February 2006, cited in G. Brown, First Donald Dewar Memorial Lecture, Glasgow University, 12 October 2006.

78. M. Yoe, 'Everybody's a critic,' *The University of Chicago Magazine*, February 2004.
79. J. Q. Wilson, *The Moral Sense* (New York: The Free Press, 1993), p. xiv.
80. Ibid., p. xiii.
81. G. Brown, 'Politics as a moral duty,' speech to the Labour Party Annual Conference, Brighton, 26 September 2005.
82. J. Q. Wilson, *The Moral Sense* (New York: The Free Press, 1993), p. xiii.
83. N. Temko, 'Brown: my mother's pain shaped my life,' *The Observer*, 8 October 2006.
84. J. Q. Wilson, *The Moral Sense* (New York: The Free Press, 1993), p. 251, cited in G. Brown, CAFOD Pope Paul VI Memorial Lecture, 8 December 2004.
85. J. Q. Wilson, *The Moral Sense* (New York: The Free Press, 1993), p. 244.
86. The White House, 'President Honours 2003 Presidential Medal of Freedom Recipients,' *White House Press Release*, 23 July 2003.
87. J. Q. Wilson, *The Moral Sense* (New York: The Free Press, 1993), p. vii.
88. Elsewhere, Wilson has defined moral sense as 'a directly felt impression of some standards by which we ought to judge voluntary action. The standards are usually general and imprecise.' J. Q. Wilson, *On Character* (Washington DC: The AEI Press, 1995), p. 192.
89. J. Q. Wilson, *The Moral Sense* (New York: The Free Press, 1993) pp. xi-xii.
90. Ibid., p. 250.
91. Ibid., p. 231.
92. Ibid., p. 234.
93. J. Q. Wilson, *On Character* (Washington DC: The AEI Press, 1995), pp. 198, 202.
94. Ibid., p. 205.
95. Wilson, *The Moral Sense* p. 240
96. J. Campbell, *The Power of Myth* (New York: Broadway Books, 1988), p. 123. This quotation was cited by Gordon Brown in his CAFOD Pope Paul VI Memorial Lecture, London, 8 December 2004, and in his speech at the Muslim News Awards for Excellence, 23 March 2005.
97. J. Campbell, *The Power of Myth* (New York: Broadway Books, 1988), p. 5.
98. Ibid., p. 13.
99. Ibid., pp. 9, 24.
100. Ibid., p. 28.
101. Ibid., p. 31.
102. G. Brown, *Courage: Eight portraits* (London: Bloomsbury, 2007), p. 1.
103. G. Himmelfarb, *The Roads to Modernity: The British, French and American Enlightenments* (New York: Alfred A. Knopf, 2004).
104. See for example, G. Himmerlfarb, *The De-Moralisation of Society: from*

Victorian virtues to modern values (London: Institute for Economic Affairs Health and Welfare Unit, 1995).

105. See for example, I. Kristol, *Neoconservatism: The autobiography of an idea* (New York: The Free Press, 1995). Kristol has impeccable right-wing credentials, being a longstanding Senior Fellow at the free market American Enterprise Institute and the founder of the journals *The Public Interest* and *The National Interest*. In recent years the latter journal has seen an embittered debate between the neo-conservatives Francis Fukuyama and Charles Krauthammer about the efficacy of the Bush Administration's 'War on Terror.' In July 2002, Kristol was awarded the Presidential Medal of Freedom by George W. Bush.

106. G. Himmelfarb, *The Roads to Modernity: The British, French and American Enlightenments* (New York: Alfred A. Knopf, 2004), p. 5.

107. Ibid., p. 150.

108. Ibid., pp. 19–20.

109. Ibid., p. 13.

110. Himmelfarb later describes Adam Smith as 'one of England's most eminent philosophers,' Ibid., p. 69.

111. Ibid., pp. 66–67.

112. Ibid., p. 233.

113. Ibid., p. 231.

CHAPTER 3

1. Indeed, Cowley has noted that 'in December 1993 the Gallup 9000 poll – an aggregate of all the polls Gallup conducted that month – showed that just under nineteen per cent of the public thought the Conservatives could better handle the economy compared with fifty-one per cent who chose Labour, a gap of thirty-two percentage points. Throughout 1994 and 1995 the gap averaged at least twenty-five percentage points,' P. Cowley, 'The Conservative Party: Decline and fall,' in A. Geddes and J. Tonge (ed.), *Labour's Landslide* (Manchester: Manchester University Press, 1997), p. 40.

2. E. Balls, 'Delivering Economic Stability,' Oxford Business Alumni Annual Lecture, Merchant Taylors' Hall, London, 12 June 2001.

3. International Monetary Fund, 'IMF Executive Board Concludes 2005 Article IV Consultation with the United Kingdom,' *Public Information Notice No.06/24*, 3 March 2006 (Washington, DC: International Monetary Fund). Available online: http://www.imf.org/external/np/sec/pn/2006/pn0624.htm (accessed 1 March 2007), p. 1; International Monetary Fund, *United Kingdom:*

2006 article IV consultation – staff report, March 2007 (Washington DC: International Monetary Fund, 2007), p. 3.

4. H. M. Treasury, *Pre-Budget Report. Investing in Britain's Potential: Building our long-term future*, Cm. 6984 (London: H. M. Treasury, 2006), p. 14.

5. G. Brown, Budget Statement, 17 March 2004; G. Brown, Budget Statement, 16 March 2005.

6. G. Brown, 'Modernising the British Economy: The new mission for the Treasury,' *Treasury Press Release 86/99*, 27 May 1999.

7. International Monetary Fund, *United Kingdom: 2006 article IV consultation – staff report, March 2007* (Washington DC: International Monetary Fund, 2007), p. 22.

8. For the thesis of the Treasury's 'contempt for production,' see S. Pollard, *The Wasting of the British Economy: British economic policy 1945 to the present* (London: Croom Helm, 1982), p. 73. For the thesis of the 'core institutional nexus,' composed of the Bank of England, City of London and Treasury, see G. Ingham, *Capitalism Divided? The City and Industry in British Social Development* (London: Macmillan, 1984). For the thesis of the frustration of successive state-led modernisation programmes, see S. Newton and D. Porter, *Modernisation Frustrated: The politics of industrial decline in Britain since 1900* (London: Unwin Hyman, 1988).

9. G. Brown, 'Modernising the British Economy: The new mission for the Treasury,' *Treasury Press Release 86/99*, 27 May 1999.

10. G. Brown, *In My Way* (Harmondsworth: Penguin, 1971), pp. 104–105.

11. C. Johnson, *MITI and the Japanese Miracle: The growth of industrial policy, 1925–1975* (Stanford University Press, 1982), p. 323.

12. E. Balls, J. Grice and G. O'Donnell (ed.), *Microeconomic Reform in Britain: Delivering opportunities for all* (London: Palgrave Macmillan, 2004), pp. 6, 8.

13. It is this continuity of ideology and policy that has led one influential commentator on British politics to see the transition from Thatcher to Major, Major to Blair, and from Blair to Brown, as a political and economic revolution in three acts, S. Jenkins, *Thatcher & Sons: A revolution in three acts* (London: Allen Lane, 2006).

14. W. Keegan, *The Prudence of Mr Gordon Brown* (Chichester: John Wiley, 2003), p. 130.

15. E. Balls, *Euro-Monetarism: Why Britain was ensnared and how it should escape* (London: Fabian Society, 1992), p. 3.

16. Ibid., pp. 10–11, 14.

17. Ibid., p. 15.

18. Ibid., pp. 18, 23.

19. Ibid., p. 16.

20. Ibid., pp. 17–18.
21. E. Balls, 'Delivering Economic Stability,' Inaugural Oxford Business Alumni Lecture, Merchant Taylors' Hall, London, 12 June 2001.
22. E. Balls, 'Stability, Growth and UK Fiscal Policy,' Inaugural Ken Dixon Lecture, Department of Economics, University of York, 23 January 2004. Monetarism is the belief among certain economists that the money supply is the most important factor affecting economic performance in general and the rate of inflation in particular. The belief that economic stability and low inflation could be best achieved by governmental control of the money supply was popularised by the American economist Milton Friedman during the late 1960s and given effect by the policies of the Thatcher Governments and Reagan Administration during the 1980s. The Brown/Balls model was 'post-monetarist' because it had moved on from this economic policy agenda.
23. M. Friedman, 'The Role of Monetary Policy,' *The American Economic Review*, 58, 1, 1968, pp. 1–17. Friedman's work was cited in G. Brown, 'The Conditions For Full Employment: The Mais Lecture,' City University, London, 19 October 1999 and E. Balls, 'Open Macroeconomics in an Open Economy,' *Scottish Journal of Political Economy*, 45, 2, 1998, pp. 113–132, cf. 118.
24. E. Balls, 'Stability, Growth and UK Fiscal Policy,' Inaugural Ken Dixon Lecture, Department of Economics, University of York, 23 January 2004.
25. Ibid.
26. G. Brown, 'Statement from the Chancellor on the Central Economic Objectives of the New Government,' *H. M. Treasury Press Release*, 6 May 1997 (London: H. M. Treasury, 1997).
27. Minister of Reconstruction, *Employment Policy*, Cmnd. 6527 (London: His Majesty's Stationery Office, 1944), p. 3.
28. In economic policy-making, monetary policy refers to the policies adopted by monetary authorities, in this case the Treasury and the Bank of England, in pursuit of stable prices, low inflation and confidence in the currency. Fiscal policy refers to government policy towards government income (i.e. through taxation and revenue collection) and expenditure.
29. G. Brown, 'Statement from the Chancellor on the Central Economic Objectives of the New Government,' *H. M. Treasury Press Release*, 6 May 1997 (London: H. M. Treasury, 1997).
30. G. Brown, speech to the Royal Institute for International Affairs, Chatham House, London, 17 July 1997.
31. E. Balls, J. Grice and G. O'Donnell (ed.), *Microeconomic Reform in Britain: Delivering opportunities for all* (London: Palgrave Macmillan, 2004), p. 381.
32. E. Balls, 'Stability, Growth and UK Fiscal Policy,' Inaugural Ken Dixon Lecture, Department of Economics, University of York, 23 January 2004.

33. E. Balls, 'Open Macroeconomics in an Open Economy,' *Scottish Journal of Political Economy*, 45, 2, 1998, p. 121.
34. E. Balls, J. Grice and G. O'Donnell (ed.), *Microeconomic Reform in Britain: Delivering opportunities for all* (London: Palgrave Macmillan, 2004), p. 381.
35. E. Balls, 'Open Macroeconomics in an Open Economy,' *Scottish Journal of Political Economy*, 45, 2, 1998, pp. 113–132, cf. p. 120.
36. M. King, 'Credibility and Monetary Policy: Theory and evidence,' *Scottish Journal of Political Economy*, 42, 1, 1995, pp. 1–19, cf.17–18.
37. E. Balls, 'Open Macroeconomics in an Open Economy,' *Scottish Journal of Political Economy*, 45, 2, 1998, p. 122.
38. G. Brown, 'Foreword' to E. Balls, J. Grice and G. O'Donnell (ed.), *Microeconomic Reform in Britain: Delivering opportunities for all* (London: Palgrave Macmillan, 2004), p. xiii.
39. E. Balls and G. O'Donnell (ed.), *Reforming Britain's Economic and Financial Policy: Towards greater economic stability* (Houndmills: Palgrave Macmillan, 2002), pp. 5–8.
40. Ibid., pp. 17–18.
41. Labour Party, *New Labour: Because Britain deserves better* (London: The Labour Party, 1997), p. 13.
42. H. M. Treasury, 'Remit for the Monetary Policy Committee,' *H. M. Treasury Press Release 64/97*, 12 June 1997
43. E. Balls, 'Stability, Growth and UK Fiscal Policy,' Inaugural Ken Dixon Lecture, Department of Economics, University of York, 23 January 2004.
44. H. M. Treasury, *The Strength to Take the Long-Term Decisions for Britain: Seizing the opportunities of the global recovery. Pre-budget report 2003*, Cm. 6042 (London: The Stationery Office, 2003), p. 3.
45. H. M. Treasury, *Budget 2007. Building Britain's Long-Term Future: Prosperity and fairness for families. Economic and fiscal strategy report and financial statement and budget report*, HC. 342 (London: The Stationery Office, 2007), pp. 20–21.
46. Office for National Statistics, *Consumer Price Indices: June 2007* (London: Office for National Statistics, 2007), p. 1.
47. Ibid., p. 20.
48. A. Dilnot and P. Johnson (ed.), *Election Briefing 1997* (London: Institute for Fiscal Studies, 1997), p. i.
49. E. Balls and G. O'Donnell (ed.), *Reforming Britain's Economic and Financial Policy: Towards greater economic stability* (Houndmills: Palgrave Macmillan, 2002), p. 19.
50. A. Dilnot and P. Johnson (ed.), *Election Briefing 1997* (London: Institute for Fiscal Studies, 1997), p. i.

51. Ibid., pp. 14–16.
52. H. M. Treasury, *Fiscal Policy: Lessons from the last economic cycle* (London: H. M. Treasury, 1997), p. 1.
53. G. Brown, speech at the Lord Mayor's Dinner, Mansion House, London, 12 June 1997.
54. E. Balls, 'Stability, Growth and UK Fiscal Policy,' Inaugural Ken Dixon Lecture, Department of Economics, University of York, 23 January 2004.
55. Institute for Fiscal Studies, *The IFS Green Budget: January 2006* (London: Institute for Fiscal Studies, 2006), p. 45.
56. Ibid., p. 37.
57. Ibid., pp. 26, 32.
58. Ibid., pp. 38–40.
59. E. Balls, 'Stability, Growth and UK Fiscal Policy,' Inaugural Ken Dixon Lecture, Department of Economics, University of York, 23 January 2004.
60. Ibid.
61. G. Brown, *G8 and other International Issues.* Evidence given to the House of Commons Treasury Select Committee, 19 July 2005, Session 2005–2006, HC. 399-I (London: The Stationery Office, 2005), Q7.
62. H. M. Treasury, *Britain Meeting the Global Challenge: Enterprise, fairness and responsibility. Pre-budget report December 2005*, Cm. 6701 (London: H. M. Treasury), p. 208.
63. H. M. Treasury, *Investing in Britain's Potential: Building our long-term future. Pre-budget report 2006*, Cm. 6984 (London: The Stationery Office, 2006), p. 218.
64. Institute for Fiscal Studies, *Public Finance Bulletin*, 20 March 2007 (London: Institute for Fiscal Studies, 2007), p. 2.
65. H. M. Treasury, *Budget 2007. Building Britain's Long-Term Future: Prosperity and fairness for families. Economic and fiscal strategy report and financial statement and budget report*, HC. 342 (London: The Stationery Office, 2007).
66. R. Chote and C. Emmerson, *The Public Finances: Election briefing 2005* (London: Institute for Fiscal Studies, 2005), p. 4.
67. Office for National Statistics, *Public Sector Finances June 2007* (London: Office for National Statistics, 2007), p. 1
68. C. Frayne, 'Public Finances,' presentation at the Institute for Fiscal Studies' Post-Budget Briefing, 23 March 2007.
69. House of Commons Treasury Committee, *The 2006 Pre-Budget Report, Second Report of Session 2006–07*, HC. 115 (London: The Stationery Office, 2007), p. 20.
70. G. Brown, 'Foreword' to E. Balls, J. Grice and G. O'Donnell, *Microeconomic Reform in Britain: Delivering opportunities for all* (London: Palgrave Macmillan, 2004), p. xii.

71. E. Balls, *Euro-Monetarism: Why Britain was ensnared and how it should escape* (London: Fabian Society, 1992), p. 18.
72. Ibid., p. 21.
73. Ibid., pp. 22–23.
74. Ibid., p. 23.
75. Ibid., p. 23.
76. Ibid., p. 23.
77. G. Brown, speech at the Lord Mayor's Banquet, Mansion House, London, 21 June 2006.
78. Ibid.
79. Business Guardian, 'Banking Bonanza – How the Profits Stack Up,' *Guardian Unlimited*, 15 April 2007.
80. Ibid.
81. E. Balls, 'The City as the Global Finance Centre: Risks and opportunities,' speech at Bloomberg, City of London, 14 June 2006.
82. H. M. Treasury, 'Economic Secretary Leads Discussion on City Competitiveness,' *H. M. Treasury Press Release 102/06* (London: H. M. Treasury, 2006).
83. House of Lords, *Overseas Trade. Report of the House of Lords Select Committee, 1984–85 Session*, HL.41-I (London: Her Majesty's Stationery Office, 1985), p. 6.
84. E. Balls, 'Britain's Next Decade,' The Fabian Lecture, 1 November 2006.
85. Institute for Fiscal Studies, *The IFS Green Budget: January 2006*, p. 61.
86. Office for National Statistics, *Business Investment: Revised results – 4th quarter 2006* (London: The Stationery Office, 2007), p. 1.
87. House of Commons Treasury Committee, *The 2006 Pre-Budget Report. Second Report of Session 2006–07*, HC. 115 (London: The Stationery Office, 2007), pp. 7–8.
88. Office for National Statistics, *International Comparisons of Productivity, 21 February 2007* (London: The Stationery Office, 2007), p. 10.
89. G. Brown, 'Exploiting the British Genius – The Key to Long-Term Economic Success,' speech to the Confederation of British Industry, 20 May 1997.
90. G. Brown, speech at the Confederation of British Industry President's Dinner, London, 22 April 1998.
91. P. Aldrick and E. Conway, 'Brown's Pension Grab Secret is Revealed,' *The Daily Telegraph*, 31 March 2007.
92. Office for National Statistics, *Balance of Payments 4th Quarter and Annual 2006* (London: The Stationery Office, 2007), pp. 1–3; Office for National Statistics, *Balance of Payments 1st Quarter 2007* (London: Office for National Statistics, 2007), p. 1.

93. Ibid., p. 10.
94. Institute for Fiscal Studies, *The IFS Green Budget: January 2006* (London: Institute for Fiscal Studies, 2006) p. 58.
95. Office for National Statistics, *The Pink Book: 2006 edition* (London: The Stationery Office, 2006), p. 96.
96. Ibid., p. 78.
97. Office for National Statistics, *Balance of Payments 4th Quarter and Annual 2006* (London: The Stationery Office, 2007), p. 8.
98. Stephen Nickell, *The UK Current Account Deficit and All That* (London: Bank of England, 2006), p. 2.
99. Association of Payment Clearing Systems (APACS), 'Record number of transactions on plastic cards over festive season,' *APACS Press Release*, 2 January (London: Association of Payment Clearing Systems, 2007).
100. Credit Action, *Debt Facts and Figures: Compiled 1 February 2007* (Lincoln: Credit Action, 2007). Available online: http://www.creditaction.org.uk/debtstats.htm (accessed 1 March 2007).
101. Citizens Advice, '2007 starts with fifteen per cent more debt problems than 2006,' *Citizens Advice Press Release*, 16 February (London: Citizens Advice, 2007). Available online: http://www.citizensadvice.org.uk/press_041006 (accessed 1 March 2007).
102. Credit Action, *Debt Facts and Figures: Compiled 1 February 2007* (Lincoln: Credit Action, 2007). Available online: http://www.creditaction.org.uk/debtstats.htm (accessed 1 March 2007).
103. N. Lawson, *The View from No.11: Memoirs of a tory radical* (London, Bantam Press, 1992), pp. 366–367, 631.
104. Halifax, *Halifax House Price Index: January 2007* (Halifax: Halifax plc, 2007).
105. Ibid.
106. Credit Action, *Debt Facts and Figures: Compiled 1 February 2007* (Lincoln: Credit Action, 2007). Available online: http://www.creditaction.org.uk/debtstats.htm (accessed 1 March 2007).
107. The Guardian/Reward Technology Forum (RTF) Directors' Pay Survey, *The Guardian*, 2 October 2006.
108. N. Isles, *The Risk Myth: CEOS and labour market risk* (London: The Work Foundation, 2006).
109. G. Brown, 'Exploiting the British Genius – The Key to Long-Term Economic Success,' speech to the Confederation of British Industry, 20 May 1997.
110. Commission on Public Policy and British Business, *Promoting Prosperity: A business agenda for Britain* (London: Vintage, 1997).

111. Gordon Brown, *Pre-Budget Report statement to the House of Commons, 6 December 2006* (London: H. M. Treasury, 2006). Available online: http://www.hm_treasury.gov.uk/pre_budget_report/prebud_pbr06/prebud _pbr06_speech.cfm (accessed 27 February 2007).

CHAPTER 4

1. Labour Party, *New Labour: Because Britain deserves better* (London: The Labour Party, 1997), p. 5.
2. Ibid., p. 20.
3. Ibid., p. 13.
4. Ibid., p. 21.
5. A. Goodman and L. Sibieta, *Public Spending on Education in the UK*. Prepared for the Education and Skills Select Committee (London: Institute for Fiscal Studies, 2006), pp. 9–10.
6. Department of Health, *Department of Health Departmental Report 2007* (London: Department of Health, 2007), pp. 128–129.
7. Ipsos MORI, *Ipsos MORI Delivery Index*, 16 May 2007 (London: Ipsos MORI, 2007).
8. V. Garrow and E. Sterling, *The Management Agenda 2007: Overview of findings* (Horsham: Roffey Park Institute, 2007), p. 2.
9. British Medical Association, speech by Dr Jonathan Fielden, Chairman of the Central Consultants and Specialists' Committee, Westminster Conference Centre, London, 6 June 2007.
10. Cabinet Office, *Ministerial Committees of the Cabinet and Policy Review Working Groups: Composition and terms of reference* (London: Cabinet Office, 2006), p. 35.
11. Department of Health, *The NHS Plan: A plan for investment, a plan for reform*, Cm. 4818 (London: The Stationery Office, 2000), p. 11.
12. E. Balls, J. Grice and G. O'Donnell (ed.), *Microeconomic Reform in Britain: Delivering opportunities for all* (Houndmills: Palgrave Macmillan, 2004), p. 18.
13. Office of Public Services Reform, *Reforming Our Public Services: Principles into practice* (London: The Prime Minister's Office of Public Services Reform, 2002), p. 17.
14. Ibid., pp. 2–3, 28.
15. E. Balls, J. Grice and G. O'Donnell (ed.), *Microeconomic Reform in Britain: Delivering opportunities for all* (Houndmills: Palgrave Macmillan, 2004), p. 9.
16. T. Blair, interview with *Breakfast With Frost*, BBC 1, 16 January 2000, cited in A. Rawnsley, *Servants of the People: The inside story of New Labour* (London: Penguin, 2001), p. 337.

17. Brown was reported to have told Blair, 'you have stolen my fucking Budget,' cited in A. Rawnsley, *Servants of the People: The inside story of New Labour* (London: Penguin, 2001), p. 338.
18. D. Wanless, *Securing our Future Health: Taking a long-term view* (London: H. M. Treasury, 2002).
19. This was published as Prime Minister's Strategy Unit, *Health Strategy Review: Analytical report* (London: Prime Minister's Strategy Unit, 2002).
20. H. M. Treasury, *Opportunity and Security For All: Investing in an enterprising, fairer Britain. New Public Spending Plans 2003–2006*, Cm. 5570 (London: The Stationery Office, 2002), p. 2; D. Wanless, *Securing our Future Health: Taking a long-term view* (London: H. M. Treasury, 2002), p. 75.
21. D. Osborne and T. Gabeler, *Reinventing Government: How the entrepreneurial spirit is transforming the public sector* (Reading, Massachusetts: Addison-Wesley, 1992), p. xix.
22. Ibid., pp. 19–20.
23. Ibid., p. xxi.
24. Ibid., pp. 23–24.
25. Ibid., p. 35.
26. Ibid., p. 40.
27. Ibid., p. 45.
28. C. Thain and M. Wright, *The Treasury and Whitehall: The planning and control of public expenditure, 1976–1993* (Oxford: Clarendon Press, 1995), p. 537.
29. For a concise analysis of this approach, see S. Lee and R. Woodward, 'Implementing the Third Way: The delivery of public services under the Blair Government,' *Public Money and Management,* October-December 2002, pp. 1–8.
30. H. M. Treasury, *Modern Public Services: Investing in reform. Comprehensive Spending Review: New public spending plans 1999–2000*, Cm. 4011 (London: The Stationery Office, 1998), p. 6.
31. R. Chote, C. Emmerson and C. Frayne, *The Public Finances: Election briefing 2005* (London: Institute for Fiscal Studies, 2005), p. 7; C. Emmerson and C. Frayne, *Public Spending: Election briefing 2005* (London: Institute for Fiscal Studies, 2005), p. 2.
32. R. Chote, C. Emmerson and C. Frayne, 'Public Spending Pressures,' in R. Chote, C. Emmerson, R. Harrison and D. Miles (ed.), *The IFS Green Budget: January 2006* (London: Institute for Fiscal Studies, 2006), pp. 74, 76.
33. H. M. Treasury, *Building Opportunity and Security for All: 2000 spending review. New public spending plans 2001–2004* (London: H. M. Treasury, 2000), pp. 1–2.
34. H. M. Treasury, *Opportunity and security for all: Investing in an enterprising, fairer Britain. 2002 Spending Review: New Public Spending Plans 2003–2006*, Cm. 5570 (London: The Stationery Office, 2002), pp. 2–3.

35. H. M. Treasury, *Stability, Security and Opportunity for All: Investing for Britain's long-term future. 2004 Spending Review: New Public Spending Plans 2005–2008*, Cm. 6237 (London: The Stationery Office, 2004), pp. 85, 93.

36. E. Balls, J. Grice and G. O'Donnell (ed.), *Microeconomic Reform in Britain: Delivering opportunities for all* (Houndmills: Palgrave Macmillan, 2004), p. 346.

37. H. M. Treasury, *Modern Public Services for Britain: Investing in reform. Comprehensive Spending Review: new public spending plans 1999–2002*, Cm. 4011 (London: The Stationery Office, 1998), p. 13.

38. H. M. Treasury, *Service Delivery Agreements and Technical Notes*, Available online: http://www.hm-treasury.gov.uk./Spending_Review/Spending_Review_2000/Service_Delivery_Agreements/spend_sr00_sda_index.cfm (accessed 10 June 2007).

39. Treasury Select Committee, *H. M. Treasury. Third Report from the House of Commons' Treasury Select Committee, Session 2000–2001*, HC. 73-I (London: The Stationery Office, 2001), paras 19–21.

40. Ibid., paras 31–32.

41. Ibid., para 48.

42. H. M. Treasury/Cabinet Office, *Delivering Decision Making: 1-Delivering better public services: refining targets and performance management* (London: H. M. Treasury, 2004); H. M. Treasury/Office of the Deputy Prime Minister/ Department of Trade and Industry, *Devolving Decision Making: 2-Meeting the regional economic challenge: Increasing regional and local flexibility* (London: H. M. Treasury, 2004).

43. H. M. Treasury, *Budget 2007: Building Britain's long-term future: prosperity and fairness for families. Economic and Financial Statement and Budget Report*, HC. 342 (London: The Stationery Office, 2006), p. 153.

44. Department for Communities and Local Government, *Strong and Prosperous Communities: The Local Government White Paper*, Cm. 6939-II (London: The Stationery Office, 2006), pp. 4–5, 122. For a more detailed analysis of the impact of constrained discretion on the English regions, see S. Lee, 'Constrained Discretion and English Regional Governance: The case of Yorkshire and the Humber,' in J. Bradbury (ed.), *Devolution, Regionalism and Regional Development in the UK* (London: Taylor & Francis, 2007).

45. E. Balls, G. O'Donnell and J. Grice (ed.), *Microeconomic Reform in Britain: Delivering opportunities for all* (London: Palgrave Macmillan, 2004), pp. 6, 8.

46. Ibid., p. 380.

47. Ibid., p. 17.

48. Ibid., p. 17.

49. G. Brown, 'State and Market: Towards a public interest test,' *The Political Quarterly*, 74, 3, 2003, p. 267.
50. Ibid., p. 267.
51. Ibid., p. 268.
52. M. Sandel, *What Money Can't Buy: The moral limits of markets*. The Tanner Lectures on Human Values, delivered at Brasenose College, Oxford, 11 and 12 May 1998, cited in G. Brown, 'A Modern Agenda for Prosperity and Social Reform,' speech to the Social Market Foundation, Cass Business School, London, 3 January 2003.
53. Ibid., p. 270.
54. Ibid., pp. 271–272.
55. Ibid., pp. 277–278.
56. Ibid., pp. 279–280.
57. H. M. Treasury, *Investing in Britain's Potential: Building our long-term future. Pre-budget report*, Cm. 6984 (London: The Stationery Office, 2006), p. 246.
58. Ibid., p. 246.
59. See for example, A. Pollock, *NHS plc: The privatisation of our health care* (London: Verso, 2005).
60. The role of consultants in inflating PFI projects has been documented extensively in D. Craig and R. Brooks, *Plundering the Public Sector* (London: Constable, 2006).
61. P. Gosling, *PFI: Against the public interest* (London: UNISON, 2005).
62. UNISON, *Private Finance Initiative (PFI): The case against PFI* (London: UNISON, 2007). Available online: http://www.unison.org.uk/pfi/caseagainst.asp (accessed 10 June 2007).
63. A. Pollock and D. Price, *Public Risk for Private Gain? The public audit implications of risk transfer and private finance* (London: UNISON, 2004), p. 3.
64. A. Pollock, D. Price and S. Player, *The Private Finance Initiative: A policy built on sand* (London: UNISON, 2005).
65. Ibid., p. 3.
66. H. M. Treasury, *PFI: Meeting the investment challenge* (London: H. M. Treasury, 2003).
67. A. Pollock, D. Price and S. Player, *The Private Finance Initiative: A policy built on sand* (London: UNISON, 2005), p. 3.
68. House of Commons Committee of Public Accounts, *Update on PFI Debt Refinancing and the PFI Equity Market. Twenty-fifth Report on Session 2006–07*, HC. 158 (London: The Stationery Office, 2007), p. 7.
69. G. Brown, 'State and Market: Towards a public interest test,' *The Political Quarterly*, 74, 3, 2003, pp. 281–282.

70. Ibid., p. 282.
71. Ibid., p. 283.
72. Ibid., p. 277.
73. H. M. Treasury, *Public Expenditure Statistical Analyses 2007*, Cm. 7091 (London: The Stationery Office, 2007), pp. 131–132.
74. D. Wilkes, 'Postcode Lottery for Cancer Wonder Drug,' *The Daily Mail*, 10 April 2006.
75. House of Commons Committee of Public Accounts, *The NHS Cancer Plan: A progress report, HC. 791* (London: The Stationery Office, 2005).
76. The Northern Way was established in 2004 by bringing together the RDAs in the North East, North West and Yorkshire and the Humber. It was intended to create 'a new system of regional government for the North' that would permit 'the regions to plan more strategically, establish priorities and take key decisions on a region-wide basis,' Office of the Deputy Prime Minister, *Draft Regional Assemblies Bill: Policy statement* (London: Office of the Deputy Prime Minister, 2004), pp. 3–4.
77. E. Balls, G. O'Donnell and J. Grice (ed.), *Microeconomic Reform in Britain: Delivering opportunities for all* (London: Palgrave Macmillan, 2004), pp. 17, 346.
78. G. Brown, 'Introduction' to E. Balls, G. O'Donnell and J. Grice (ed.), *Microeconomic Reform in Britain: Delivering opportunities for all* (London: Palgrave Macmillan, 2004), p. xiii.
79. G. Brown, speech to the Labour Party Conference, 26 September 2005.
80. Ibid.
81. H. M. Treasury, *Budget 2007: Building Britain's long-term future: Prosperity and fairness for families. Economic and financial statement and budget report*, HC. 342 (London: The Stationery Office, 2006), p. 148.
82. ICM Research, *March 2007 Poll* (London: ICM Research, 2007), p. 4.
83. Ipsos MORI, *Public Expectations About The NHS-Government Delivery Index* (London: Ipsos MORI, 2007), pp. 1–2.
84. Ipsos MORI, *10 Years of Blair: How did he do?* Poll, 10 May 2007 (London: Ipsos MORI, 2007).
85. ICM Research, *Political Trust*. A poll prepared on behalf of the *Sunday Telegraph*, 30–31 May 2007 (London: ICM Research).
86. A. Johnson, 'NHS Next State Review,' *Hansard*, 4 July 2007, cc. 961–962.
87. Department of Health, 'Shaping Health Care for the Next Decade,' 4 July 2007, p. 1.
88. Department for Children, Schools and Families, 'Ed Balls Appointed Secretary of State for Children, Schools and Families,' 28 June 2007, p. 2.
89. G. Brown, presentation at the Public Service Reform Conference: Twenty-first century public services – learning from the front line,' London, 27 March 2007.

90. G. Brown, remarks at the Twenty-first Century Public Services: Putting People First Conference, Queen Elizabeth II Conference Hall, London, 6 June 2006.
91. G. Brown, presentation at the Public Service Reform Conference: Twenty-first century public services – learning from the front line,' London, 27 March 2007.
92. Ibid.
93. Ibid.
94. G. Brown, remarks at the Twenty-first Century Public Services: Putting People First Conference, Queen Elizabeth II Conference Hall, London, 6 June 2006.
95. H. M. Treasury, *Budget 2007: Building Britain's long-term future: Prosperity and fairness for families. Economic and financial statement and budget report*, HC. 342 (London: The Stationery Office, 2007), p. 139.
96. H. M. Treasury, *Stability, Security and Opportunity for All: Investing for Britain's long-term future. 2004 spending review: New public spending plans 2005–2008*, Cm. 6237 (London: The Stationery Office, 2004), p. 85; H. M. Treasury, *Opportunity and Security For All: Investing in an enterprising, fairer Britain. New public spending plans 2003–2006*, Cm. 5570 (London: The Stationery Office, 2002), p. 59; H. M. Treasury, *Prudent for a Purpose: Building opportunity and security for all. New public spending plans for 2001–2004* (London: The Stationery Office, 2000), section 7.19.
97. H. M. Treasury, *Releasing resources to the front line: Independent Review of Public Sector Efficiency by Sir Peter Gershon* (London: H. M. Treasury, 2004), p. 35.
98. H. M. Treasury, *Long-term Opportunities and Challenges for the UK: Analysis for the 2007 Comprehensive Spending Review* (London: H. M. Treasury, 2006), p. 24.
99. D. Coats, *Efficiency, efficiency, efficiency. The Gershon Review: Public service efficiency and the management of change* (London: The Work Foundation, 2004), p. 4.
100. Healthcare Commission, *Briefing note: NHS trust declarations on standards for 2006/2007* (London: Healthcare Commission, 2007), p. 8.
101. Ibid., p. 4.
102. H. M. Treasury, *Budget 2007: Building Britain's long-term future: Prosperity and fairness for families. Economic and financial statement and budget report*, HC. 342 (London: The Stationery Office, 2006), p. 148.
103. Department of Health, *NHS Financial Performance Quarter Four 2006–7* (London: Department of Health, 2007), p. 1.
104. UNISON/Compass, *Voices for Real Reform: A public service discussion paper*

based on a joint Compass and UNISON Summit January 2007 (London: Compass and UNISON, 2007), pp. 2–3.

105. Ibid., p. 4.
106. T. Blair, speech to the Venture Capitalists' Association Conference, London, 6 July 1999.
107. T. Blair, speech to the Labour Party Conference, Bournemouth, 28 September 1999; BBC, 'Blair's Stern Lesson for Teachers,' BBC News, 21 October 1999.
108. A. Goodman and L. Sibieta, *Public spending on education in the UK*. Prepared for the Education and Skills Select Committee (London: Institute for Fiscal Studies, 2006), pp. 1, 7.
109. G. Brown, transcript of interview with Andrew Marr for the Sunday AM programme, 7 January 2007. Available online: http://www.bbc.co.uk/1/hi/uk_politics/6241819.stm (accessed 8 January 2007).
110. Ibid.
111. Ibid.
112. P. Wintour, 'Brown Backs City Academies with Words and Cash,' *The Guardian*, 20 March 2007.
113. G. Brown, 'Financial Statement,' 22 March 2006, c. 287–302.
114. '£34 Billion Schools Bonanza,' *The Daily Mirror*, 23 March 2006, cited in A. Goodman and L. Sibieta, *Public Spending on Education in the UK*. Prepared for the Education and Skills Select Committee (London: Institute for Fiscal Studies, 2006), p. 2.
115. A. Goodman and L. Sibieta, *Public Spending on Education in the UK*. Prepared for the Education and Skills Select Committee (London: Institute for Fiscal Studies, 2006), p. 2.
116. H. M. Treasury, 'Modern Public Services: Investing in Reform,' *Her Majesty's Treasury Press Release HMT 1*, 14 July 1998. Brown was criticised for a lack of transparency by a parliamentary select committee, which recommended that this confusing practice should be ended. House of Commons Treasury Committee, *The New Fiscal Framework and the Comprehensive Spending Review. Eighth Report of Session 1997–98*, HC. 960-I (London: The Stationery Office, 1998), para 33.
117. Ibid., p. 7.
118. G. Brown, transcript of interview with Andrew Marr for the Sunday AM programme, 7 January 2007. Available online: http://www.bbc.co.uk/1/hi/uk_politics/6241819.stm (accessed 8 January 2007).
119. H. M. Treasury, *Budget 2007: Building Britain's long-term future: Prosperity and fairness for families. Economic and financial statement and budget report*, HC. 342 (London: The Stationery Office, 2006), p. 140.
120. House of Commons Committee of Public Accounts, *Financial Management in*

the NHS. *Seventeenth Report of Session 2006–07*, HC. 361 (London: The Stationery Office, 2007), p. 5.

121. P. Hewitt, speech at the London School of Economics, 14 June 2007.

122. House of Commons Office of the Deputy Prime Minister: Housing, Planning, Local Government and the Regions Committee, *The Draft Assemblies Bill. First Report of Session 2004–05*, H. C. 61-I (London: The Stationery Office, 2004), p. 6.

123. The Cabinet Office, *Building on Progress: Public services* (London: Prime Minister's Strategy Unit, The Cabinet Office, 2007), p. 7.

124. Ibid., p. 15.

125. Ibid., p. 39.

126. H. M. Treasury/Cabinet Office, *The Future Role of the Third Sector in Social and Economic Regeneration: Interim report* (London: H. M. Treasury, 2006).

127. This thesis has been developed brilliantly in D. Marquand, *Decline of the Public* (Cambridge: Polity, 2004).

128. Ipsos MORI, *Ipsos MORI Delivery Index*, 16 May 2007 (London: Ipsos MORI, 2007).

129. YouGov, *YouGov/Daily Telegraph Survey Results*, 21–23 May 2007 (London: YouGov, 2007), pp. 4–5.

CHAPTER 5

1. G. Brown, Annual British Council Lecture, London, 7 July 2004; G. Brown, 'The Future of Britishness,' speech to the Fabian Society 'Future of Britishness' conference, London, 14 January 2006; G. Brown, 'Securing Our Future,' lecture at the Royal Institute of International Affairs, Chatham House, London, 13 February 2006; 'Brown's Language Call to Migrants,' *BBC News*, 6 June 2006.

2. G. Brown, 'Britain Leading in Europe,' speech by the Chancellor of the Exchequer to the Royal Institute of International Affairs, London, 7 July 1997.

3. House of Commons, Higher Education Bill in Standing Committee H, 4 March 2004, c. 504.

4. G. Himmelfarb, *The Roads to Modernity: The British, French and American Enlightenment* (New York: Alfred A. Knight, 2004).

5. J. Q. Wilson, *The Moral Sense* (New York: The Free Press, 1993), cited in G. Brown, CAFOD Pope Paul VI Memorial Lecture, 8 December 2004.

6. N. Dennis and A. H. Halsey, *English Ethical Socialism: Thomas More to R. H. Tawney* (Oxford: Clarendon Press, 1988), p. 4.

7. A rare example was when Brown noted 'Crosland's study of the values of British

democratic socialism is a compelling case to focus on what a great influence on him, R. H. Tawney, called the extraordinary potential of ordinary people,' G. Brown, 'Foreword' to A. Crosland, *The Future of Socialism* (London: Constable, 2006 edition), p. x.

8. G. Brown, 'Outward Bound,' *The Spectator*, 8 November 1997, pp. 15–16.
9. G. Brown, speech at the Smith Institute, London, 15 April 1999.
10. G. Brown, British Council Annual Lecture, London, 7 July 2004.
11. Ibid.
12. For example, '...only English and Welsh MPs will be entitled to vote on Government Bills relating to England and Wales. And English MPs alone will vote on the remaining laws which apply exclusively to England,' Conservative Party, *Time For Common Sense: 2001 Conservative Party General Election Manifesto* (London: The Conservative Party, 2001), p. 11 ; 'We will act to ensure that English laws are decided by English votes,' Conservative Party, *Are You Thinking What We're Thinking. It's Time For Action* (London: Conservative Party, 2005), p. 22.
13. D. Cameron, 'Modernisation with a purpose,' 6 February 2006.
14. Conservative Party, 'Ken Clarke's Democracy Taskforce Restoring Trust in Politics,' *Conservatives.com*. Available online: http://www.conservatives.com/tile.do?def=democracy.taskforce.page (accessed 25 May 2007).
15. 'English voters "oppose Scots PM",' *BBC News*, 14 May 2006.
16. 'England' in the Encyclopaedia Britannica, *The New Encyclopaedia Britannica*, (Chicago: Encyclopaedia Britannica, 2002), pp. 496–497.
17. Royal Commission on the Constitution 1969–1973, *Volume I: Report*, Cmnd. 5460 (London: Her Majesty's Stationery Office, 1973), p. 159.
18. Royal Commission on the Constitution 1969–1973, *Volume II: Memorandum of Dissent*, Cmnd. 5460-I (London: Her Majesty's Stationery Office, 1973), p. viii.
19. G. Brown, 'We Have Renewed Britain; Now We Must Champion It,' *The Guardian*, 27 February 2006.
20. Ibid.
21. G. Brown, speech at the University of Manchester Institute of Science and Technology, 26 January 2001.
22. G. Brown, speech to the Sustainable Communities Summit, Manchester, 2 February 2005.
23. G. Brown, 'Prosperity and Justice for All,' speech to the Labour Party Annual Conference, Brighton, 27 September 2004.
24. T. Dalyell, *Devolution: The End of Britain?* (London: Jonathan Cape, 1977), p. 247.
25. Prime Minister's Office of Public Services Reform, *Reforming Our Public*

Services: Principles into practice (London: Prime Minister's Office of Public Services Reform, 2002), pp. 12, 28.

26. E. Balls, J. Grice and G. O'Donnell, *Microeconomic Reform in Britain: Delivering opportunities for all* (London: Palgrave Macmillan, 2004).

27. T. Shifrin, 'Scotland Launches Youth Volunteering Programme,' *The Guardian*, 11 May 2004.

28. Scottish Executive, 'Programme for Young Volunteers,' *Scottish Executive News Release*, 11 May 2004. Available online: http://www.scotland.gov.uk/News/Releases/2004/05/5496 (accessed 15 May 2007).

29. Russell Commission, *A National Framework for Youth Action and Engagement: The Report of the Russell Commission* (London, The Stationery Office, 2005), pp. 169–170.

30. Russell Commission, *The Russell Commission-Frequently Asked Questions.* Available online: http://www.russellcommission.org/faq/index.html (accessed 11 May 2006).

31. G. Brown, speech at the Smith Institute, London, 15 April 1999

32. Ibid.

33. Cited in D. Blair, 'Mbeki Lambasts Brown for "Imperial Nostalgia",' *Daily Telegraph*, 30 May 2005.

34. Cited in M. Kearney, 'Brown Seeks Out "British Values",' *BBC News*, 14 March 2005.

35. Cited in ' "No UK Apology" for Colonial Past,' *BBC News*, 15 Jan 2005.

36. S. Milne, 'Britain: Imperial Nostalgia,' *Le Monde Diplomatique*, May 2005, cited in T. Mbeki, 'Lies Have Short Legs!' *ANC Today*, Vol.5, No.21, 27 May 2005.

37. J. A. Hobson, *Imperialism: A Study* (London: George Allen and Unwin, 1902).

38. G. Brown, 'The Future of Britishness,' speech to the Fabian Society 'Future of Britishness' conference, London, 14 January 2006.

39. Cited in M. Mendle, 'Putney's Pronouns: Identity and Indemnity in the Great Debate' in M. Mendle (ed.), *The Putney Debates of 1647: The Army, the Levellers and the English State* (Cambridge: Cambridge University Press, 2001), pp. 136–137.

40. G. Brown, 'The Future of Britishness,' speech to the Fabian Society 'Future of Britishness' conference, London, 14 January 2006.

41. F. de Voltaire, *Letters Concerning the English Nation* (London: C. Davis and A. Lyon, 1733), p. 34.

42. G. Brown, The Hugo Young Memorial Lecture, Chatham House, London, 13 December 2005.

43. C.-L. de Montesquieu, '*Notes on England*, with commentary, translation and annotations by Iain Stewart,' *Oxford University Comparative Law Forum*, 6. Available online: http://www.ouclf.iuscomp.org (accessed 23 December 2006).

44. N. Cronk, 'Introduction' to N. Cronk (ed.), *Letters Concerning the English Nation* (Oxford: Oxford University Press, 1994), p. xvii.

45. T. Pangle, *Montesquieu's Philosophy of Liberalism: A commentary on 'The Spirit of the Laws'* (Chicago:University of Chicago Press, 1973), p. 228.

46. E. Burke, *Reflections on the Revolution in France*, (first published in 1790; Buffalo, New York: Prometheus Books, 1987), p. 51.

47. Ibid., pp. 93, 133.

48. T. Furniss, 'Cementing the Nation: Burke's *Reflections* on nationalism and national identity,' in J. Whale (ed.), *Edmund Burke's 'Reflections on the Revolution in France: New interdisciplinary essays* (Manchester, Manchester University Press, 2000), pp. 123, 125.

49. C. Connolly, '*Reflections* on the Act of Union,' in J. Whale (ed.), *Edmund Burke's Reflections on the Revolution in France: New interdisciplinary essays* (Manchester: Manchester University Press, 2000), pp. 185–186.

50. T. Gray, 'Elegy Written in a Country Churchyard,' in A. Quiller-Couch (ed.), *The Oxford Book of English Verse: 1250–1900* (Oxford: Oxford University Press, 1919), p. 533, cited in G. Brown, The Hugo Young Memorial Lecture, Chatham House, London, 13 December 2005.

51. W. Wordsworth, 'England, 1802,' in A. Quiller-Couch (ed.), *The Oxford Book of English Verse: 1250–1900* (Oxford: Oxford University Press, 1919), p. 618.

52. W. Hazlitt, *Political Essays with Sketches of Public Characters* (London: William Hone, 1819), p. viii, cited in G. Brown, 'The Future of Britishness,' speech to the Fabian Society 'Future of Britishness' conference, London, 14 January 2006.

53. W. Hazlitt, *Political Essays with Sketches of Public Characters* (London: William Hone, 1819), p. viii

54. G. Brown, 'The Future of Britishness,' speech to the Fabian Society 'Future of Britishness' conference, London, 14 January 2006.

55. S. Gwynn, *Henry Grattan and His Times* (Dublin: Browne and Nolan, 1939), p. 129.

56. Ibid., pp. 236–238.

57. R. McDowell, *Ireland in the Age of Imperialism and Revolution 1760–1801* (Oxford: Clarendon Press, 1979), p. 249.

58. G. Brown, The Hugo Young Memorial Lecture, Chatham House, London, 13 December 2005.

59. A. de Tocqueville, *Democracy in America* (originally published in 1835; specially edited and abridged by Richard Heffner: New York: Mentor, 1956), p. 97.

60. Ibid., p. 205.

61. Ibid., p. 64.

62. G. Orwell, *The Lion and the Unicorn: Socialism and the English genius* (first published in 1941; London: Secker and Warburg, 1962), pp. 19–20, cited in

G. Brown, The Hugo Young Memorial Lecture, Chatham House, London, 13 December 2005.

63. G. Brown, speech at the Smith Institute, London, 15 April 1999.

64. G. Orwell, *The Lion and the Unicorn: Socialism and the English genius* (London: Secker and Warburg, 1962), p. 96.

65. G. Brown, The Hugo Young Memorial Lecture, Chatham House, London, 13 December 2005.

66. W. Churchill, 'Motion on the Statement on Defence, 1955, Command Paper No.9391,' *Official Record*, 1 March 1955, c. 1906.

67. Churchill was cited by a Scot, James Gray MP, representing an English constituency (North Wiltshire), during a parliamentary debate Gray had introduced on the topic of 'Constitutional Reform (England).' Having introduced himself as 'an honorary Englishman' and after citing Churchill, Gray concluded his speech, 'Now is the time for the House to speak for England,' *Hansard*, 9 June 1999, cc. 581, 586.

68. H. M. Treasury, *Hosting the World Cup: A feasibility study* (London: H. M. Treasury, 2007), p. 5.

69. Ibid., p. 3.

70. Ibid., p. 35.

71. Ibid., p. 4.

72. BBC, 'World Cup Own Goal for Chancellor,' *BBC News*, 19 January 2007. Available online: http://news.bbc.co.uk/1/hi/scotland/6280663.stm (accessed 21 May 2007).

73. Ibid.

74. E. Harrell, 'Brown's Fond Memories of Gazza's Goal Against Scots,' *The Scotsman*, 22 May 2006. Available online: http://www.news.scotsman.com/politics.cfm?id=757742006 (accessed 21 May 2007).

75. Ibid.

76. G. Brown, 'Why Scotland Means the World to Me,' in D. Bull and A. Campbell (ed.), *Football and the Commons People* (Sheffield: Juma, 1994), p. 142.

77. Ibid., p. 145.

78. BBC, 'Government Rejects "Britain FC" Plans,' *BBC News*, 29 November 2000.

79. J. Naughtie, 'A British Football Team? No Chance,' *The Guardian*, 30 November 2000.

80. BBC, 'No Scots for GB Olympic Football,' *BBC News*, 11 November 2005.

81. Football Supporters' Federation, *Football – Our Game! The fans' blueprint for the future of the beautiful game* (Kingston On Thames: Football Supporters' Federation, 2006).

82. Football Supporters' Federation, 'FSF Poll Results: "Do you support a combined Home Nations team for the 2012 London Olympics?"' (Kingston On

Thames, Football Supporters' Federation 2007). Available online: http://www.fsf.org.uk/site-pages/poll_olympic.html (accessed 25 May 2007).

83. Reflecting the devolved nature of sport, the arts and culture in Scotland, the Scottish Executive had published its first National Cultural Strategy as early as August 2000, *Creating Our Future, Minding Our Past* (Edinburgh: Scottish Executive, 2000).

84. National Sports Foundation, 'About the Foundation' (London: National Sports Foundation, 2007). Available online: http://www.nationalsports foundation.org/about_foundation.html (accessed 25 May 2007).

85. Office for National Statistics, *Social Trends 36* (London: Palgrave Macmillan, 2006), p. 3.

86. G. Brown, 'Securing our Future,' speech at the Royal United Services Institute, London, 13 February 2006.

87. YouGov, *YouGov/Sunday Times Survey Results* (London: YouGov, 2007), pp. 4–5.

88. J. Straw, 'We Need a British Story: Nationality should not require individuals to give up distinctive cultural attributes,' *The Sunday Times*, 29 April 2007.

89. Ibid.

90. Office of the Deputy Prime Minister, *State of the English Cities* (London: Office of the Deputy Prime Minister, 2006).

91. These arguments are developed further in S. Lee, *Blair's Third Way* (London: Palgrave Macmillan, 2008); S. Lee, 'Constrained Discretion and English Regional Governance: The case of Yorkshire and the Humber' in J. Bradbury (ed.), *Devolution, Regionalism and Regional Development in the UK* (London: Taylor Francis, 2007), pp. 240–272; and S. Lee, 'The Competitive Disadvantage of England,' in K. Cowling (ed.), *Industrial Policy in Europe: Theoretical perspectives and practical proposals* (London: Routledge, 1999), pp. 88–117.

92. J. Straw, 'Reclaiming the Flag: It's time the left redefined its patriotism,' *New Statesman and Society*, 24 February 1995, p. 24.

93. Jonathan Freedland has conflated English ideas into British ideas about liberty and democracy to make the case for a British republic, which might equally and more appropriately (given their particular intellectual and political lineage) be applied to the constitutional future of England. J. Freedland, *Bring Home the Revolution: The case for a British Republic* (London: Fourth Estate, 1998).

94. J. A. Hobson, *The Crisis of Liberalism: New issues of democracy* (London: P. S. King and Son, 1909).

95. The possibility of an English Way, in accordance with these principles, is outlined in S. Lee, *Blair's Third Way* (London: Palgrave Macmillan, 2008).

96. Ministry of Justice, *The Governance of Britain – The Government's Draft Legislative Programme*, Cm. 7175 (London: The Stationery Office, 2007);

Ministry of Justice, *The Governance of Britain*, Cm. 7170 (London: The Stationery Office, 2007).

CHAPTER 6

1. H. M. Treasury, *Tackling Poverty: A global new deal. A modern Marshall Plan for the developing world* (London: H. M. Treasury, 2002). Although this document was published as a Treasury strategy, it was actually based on two speeches given by Gordon Brown in the immediate wake of 9/11, namely G. Brown, speech to the Federal Reserve, New York, 16 November 2001; and G. Brown, speech at the Press Club, Washington DC, 17 December 2001. These speeches were also adapted into G. Brown, 'Governments and Supranational Agencies: A new consensus?' in J. Dunning (ed.), *Making Globalisation Good: The moral challenges of global capitalism* (Oxford: Oxford University Press, 2004), pp. 320–332.

2. G. Brown, 'Governments and Supranational Agencies: A new consensus?' in J. Dunning (ed.), *Making Globalisation Good: The moral challenges of global capitalism* (Oxford: Oxford University Press, 2004), p. 320.

3. For an analysis of Blair's foreign policy and its close alignment with the neo-conservatism of George W. Bush, see S. Lee 'The Politics of Globalisation and the War on Terror,' in M. Mullard and B. Cole (ed.), *Globalisation, Citizenship and the War on Terror* (Cheltenham: Edward Elgar, 2007).

4. G. Brown, 'Governments and Supranational Agencies: A new consensus?' in J. Dunning (ed.), *Making Globalisation Good: The moral challenges of global capitalism* (Oxford: Oxford University Press, 2004), p. 320.

5. H. M. Treasury, *Tackling Poverty: A global new deal. A modern Marshall Plan for the developing world* (London: H. M. Treasury, 2002), p. 2.

6. G. Brown, 'Governments and Supranational Agencies: A new consensus?' in J. Dunning (ed.), *Making Globalisation Good: The moral challenges of global capitalism* (Oxford: Oxford University Press, 2004), p. 322.

7. Department for International Development, *Eliminating World Poverty: A challenge for the 21st century*, Cm. 3789 (London: The Stationery Office, 1997); Department for International Development, *Eliminating World Poverty: Making globalisation work for the poor*, Cm. 5006 (London: The Stationery Office, 2000); and Department for International Development, *Eliminating World Poverty: Making governance work for the poor*, Cm. 6876 (London: The Stationery Office, 2006).

8. Cabinet Office, *Ministerial Committees of the Cabinet and Policy Review Working Groups: Composition and terms of reference* (London: Cabinet Office, 2006), p. 35.

9. Ibid., pp. 54–55; and Commission for Africa, *Our Common Interest: Report of the Commission for Africa* (London: Commission for Africa, 2005).

10. N. Stern, *The Economics of Climate Change: The Stern Review* (London: H. M. Treasury and Cabinet Office, 2006). Stern had served as the Chief Economist at the World Bank between 2000 and 2003 before becoming Second Permanent Secretary at the Treasury and Director of Policy and Research for the Commission for Africa.

11. International Monetary Fund, 'Interim Committee Selects UK's Brown as New Chairman,' *International Monetary Fund Press Release No.99/41*, 10 September 1999 (Washington DC: International Monetary Fund, 1999), p. 1.

12. International Monetary Fund, 'IMF Board of Governors Approves Transformation of Interim Committee,' *International Monetary Fund Press Release No.99/47*, 30 September 1999 (Washington DC: International Monetary Fund, 1999), p. 1.

13. United Nations, *Delivering as One: Report of the Secretary-General's high-level panel on UN system-wide coherence in the areas of development, humanitarian assistance and the environment* (New York: United Nations, 2006), p. 1.

14. Group of Eight (G8), *The Gleneagles Communiqué* (London: Group of Eight, 2005), pp. 15–28.

15. For a detailed analysis, critique and alternative to the 'Washington Consensus,' see S. Lee and S. McBride, 'Introduction: Neo-liberalism, state power and global governance in the twenty-first century,' and S. Lee and S. McBride, 'Conclusion: The need to rebuild the public domain,' in S. Lee and S. McBride (ed.), *Neo-Liberalism, State Power and Global Governance* (London: Springer-Verlag, 2007).

16. Group of Eight (G8), *The Birmingham Summit 15–17 May 1998 Communiqué* (Toronto: G8 Information Centre, 1998), p. 1.

17. H. M. Treasury, 'G7 Report on Strengthening the Architecture of the Global Financial System,' *H. M. Treasury Press Release 79/98*, 15 May 1998; H. M. Treasury, 'Seven Principles for Jobs: G8 agrees new agenda,' *H. M. Treasury Press Release 25/98*, 22 February 1998.

18. President John F. Kennedy, Inaugural Address to the American people, Capitol Building, Washington DC, 20 January 1961; M. Luther King, Jr., 'Remaining Awake Through a Great Revolution,' sermon delivered at the National Cathedral, Washington DC, 31 March 1968.

19. The poem appears in J. Stockinger, 'Locke and Rousseau: Human nature, human citizenship and human work,' unpublished PhD dissertation, Department of Sociology, University of California, Berkeley, 1990, cited in R. Bellah, R. Marsden, W. Sullivan, A. Swidler and S. Tipton, *The Good Society* (New York: Vintage Books, 1992), p. 104.

20. Ibid.
21. Ibid.
22. This commitment had been embodied in World Bank, *The State in a Changing World: The 1997 World Development Report* (New York: Oxford University Press, 1997).
23. World Commission on Environment and Development, *Our Common Future* (Oxford: Oxford University Press, 1987), p. 89.
24. United Nations, *Programme for the Further Implementation of Agenda 21: Adopted by the Special Session of the General Assembly*, 23–27 June 1997, published as Annex 4 of D. Osborn and T. Bigg, *Earth Summit II: Outcomes and analysis* (London: Earthscan, 1998), p. 144.
25. United Nations, *Report of the UN Secretary-General: Overall progress achieved since the United Nations Conference on Environment and Development*, E/CN.17/1997/Z, 31 January 1997, published as Annex 3 of D. Osborn and T. Bigg, *Earth Summit II: Outcomes and analysis* (London: Earthscan, 1998), p. 95.
26. For a critical perspective on the role of the Marshall Plan in fostering the Pax Americana, see C. Mee, *The Marshall Plan* (New York: Simon and Schuster, 1984). For an analysis of New Deal liberalism and its role in fostering both the inter-war New Deal and post-war international reconstruction, see A. Brinkley, *The End of Reform: New deal liberalism in recession and war* (New York: Vintage Books, 1996).
27. George C. Marshall, speech at Harvard University, Cambridge, Massachusetts, 5 June 1947.
28. For an analysis of the impact of the Marshall Plan on Britain during the Attlee Government, see H. Pelling, *Britain and the Marshall Plan* (London: Macmillan, 1988).
29. H. M. Treasury, *Tackling Poverty: A global new deal. A modern Marshall Plan for the developing world* (London: H. M. Treasury, 2002), pp. 1–2. This pamphlet was based on G. Brown, speech at the Federal Reserve, New York, 16 November 2001; and G. Brown, speech at the Press Club, Washington DC, 17 December 2001.
30. Ibid., p. 3.
31. Ibid., pp. 7–8.
32. United Nations Conference on Trade and Development, *World Investment Report 2001: Promoting linkages* (New York: United Nations, 2001), p. xiii.
33. United Nations Conference on Trade and Development, *World Investment Report 2006: FDI from developing and transition economies; implications for development* (New York: United Nations, 2006), p. xvii.
34. A detailed analysis of the demise of the Doha 'Development' Round of trade negotiations has been provided by The World Development Movement, *The*

Death of the Doha "Development" Round (London: World Development Movement, 2006) and W. Bello, 'Why Today's Collapse of the Doha Round Negotiations is the Best Outcome for Developing Countries,' *Focus on the Global South*, 25 July 2006, p. 1. The absence of a global consensus between Gordon Brown's advocacy of market liberalisation and Trade Justice campaigners' demands for an alternative approach to WTO negotiations can be gauged from the World Development Movement's Trade campaign briefings (available at http://www.wdm.org.uk/resources/briefings/trade/index.htm).

35. International Monetary Fund, 'Interim Committee Selects UK's Brown as New Chairman,' *International Monetary Fund Press Release No.99/41*, 10 September 1999 (Washington DC: International Monetary Fund, 1999), p. 1.

36. International Monetary Fund, 'IMF Board of Governors Approves Transformation of Interim Committee,' *International Monetary Fund Press Release No.99/47*, 30 September 1999 (Washington DC: International Monetary Fund, 1999), p. 1.

37. International Monetary Fund, *Communiqué of the International Monetary and Financial Committee of the Board of Governors of the International Monetary Fund*, 16 April 2000 (Washington DC: International Monetary Fund, 2000), pp. 1, 6.

38. US Treasury, *Report on Implementation of Recommendations made by the International Financial Institutions Advisory Commission* (Washington DC: Office of Public Affairs, 2001), p. 2.

39. International Monetary Fund, *Articles of Agreement of the International Monetary Fund: Article I-purposes* (Washington DC: International Monetary Fund, 2007), p. 1.

40. For a detailed analysis of the economic dimension of the 'war on terror' and the Bush Administration's agenda for the World Bank and IMF, see S. Lee, 'Building Institutions for Freedom: The economic dimension of the "war on terror",' in M. Mullard and B. Cole (ed.), *Globalisation, Citizenship and the War on Terror* (Cheltenham: Edward Elgar, 2007).

41. International Monetary Fund, *Communiqué of the International Monetary and Financial Committee of the Board of Governors of the International Monetary Fund*, 29 April 2001 (Washington DC: International Monetary Fund, 2001), p. 2.

42. For a critical overview of the role of the IMF, see S. Lee, 'The International Monetary Fund,' *New Political Economy*, 7, 2, 2002, pp. 283–298.

43. Independent Evaluation Office, *Evaluation of Prolonged Use of IMF Resources* (Washington DC: International Monetary Fund, 2002).

44. Independent Evaluation Office, *Report on the Evaluation of the Role of the IMF in Argentina, 1991–2001* (Washington DC: International Monetary Fund, 2004), p. 6.

45. International Monetary Fund, *Communiqué of the International Monetary and Financial Committee of the Board of Governors of the International Monetary Fund*, 16 April 2005 (Washington DC: International Monetary Fund, 2005), p. 3.
46. For a detailed and critical analysis of the role of the IMF in the governance of global financial markets, see S. Lee, 'Global Governance and the International Monetary Fund,' in G. Hook and H. Dobson (ed.), *Global Governance and Japan: The institutional architecture* (London: Routledge, 2007), pp. 126–142.
47. H. M. Treasury, *Tackling Poverty: A global new deal. A modern Marshall Plan for the developing world* (London: H. M. Treasury, 2002), p. 8.
48. Ibid., p. 34.
49. H. M. Treasury/Department for International Development, *International Finance Facility* (London: H. M. Treasury/Department for International Development, 2003), pp. 4–5.
50. G. Brown, speech to the Royal Institute for International Affairs/Chatham House Conference on 'Financing Sustainable Development, Poverty Reduction and the Private Sector: Financing common ground on the ground,' Chatham House, London, 22 January 2003.
51. H. M. Treasury/Department for International Development, *The International Finance Facility* (London H. M. Treasury/Department for International Development, 2005), p. 1.
52. Ibid., p. 14.
53. Ibid., p. 17.
54. For an explanation of why the Bush Administration has refused to back the IFF, see S. Lee, 'Building Institutions for Freedom: The economic dimension of the "war on terror",' in M. Mullard and B. Cole (ed.), *Globalisation, Citizenship and the War on Terror* (Cheltenham: Edward Elgar, 2007).
55. World Development Movement, *The International Finance Facility: Boon or burden for the poor?* (London: World Development Movement, 2005), pp. 5–6.
56. T. Moss, *Ten Myths of the International Finance Facility* (Washington DC: Centre for Global Development, 2005), p. 6.
57. Ibid., pp. 9–10.
58. The five formal objectives of the Commission are listed at Commission for Africa, 'Objectives of the Commission' (London: Commission for Africa, 2004). Available online: http://www.commissionforafrica.org/english/about/objectives.html (accessed 1 May 2007).
59. House of Commons International Development Committee, *The Commission for Africa and Policy Coherence for Development: First do no harm.* First

Report of Session 2004–05, HC. 123 (London: The Stationery Office, 2005), p. 30.

60. ActionAid, 'ActionAid Turns Tables with an African Commission for Britain,' 23 February 2005. Available online: http://www.actionaid.org/pages.aspx? PageID=35&ItemID=53 (accessed 1 May 2007).

61. The Africa Commission for Britain identified ten actions that Britain must take to support Africa's development, including the cessation of export dumping and African countries being forced to open their markets; the cancellation of un-payable debts; the reduction of carbon emissions; the untying of economic policy conditions to aid; and ensuring access to free and comprehensive treatment for all people living with HIV and AIDS. The African Commission for Britain, *Ten Actions Britain Must Take to Support Africa's Development* (London: ActionAid International, 2005), p. 3.

62. Commission for Africa, *Our Common Interest: Report of the Commission for Africa* (London: Commission for Africa, 2005), pp. 60–79.

63. War on Want, 'Africa Commission Issues "Damning Indictment" of UK Policy,' 11 March 2005 (London: War on Want, 2005), p. 1.

64. Ibid., p. 285.

65. Department of Trade and Industry, *Making Globalisation a Force for Good*, Cm. 6278 (London: The Stationery Office, 2004).

66. World Development Movement, *Commission for Africa: WDM analysis of the final report* (London: World Development Movement, 2005), pp. 1–2.

67. Ibid., pp. 5–7. See Brandt Commission, *North-South: A programme for survival. Report of the Independent Commission on International Development Issues* (London: Pan Books, 1980); Brandt Commission, *Common Crisis. North-South: Co-operation for world recovery* (London: Pan Books, 1983).

68. Full details of the United Kingdom's priorities for its Presidency of the G8 and European Union are available from http://www.g8.co.uk and http://www. eu2005.gov.uk.

69. The Foreign Office, *The Gleneagles Communiqué* (London: The Foreign Office, 2005).

70. Organisation for Economic Co-operation and Development, 'Development Aid from OECD Countries Fell 5.1 per cent in 2006,' *OECD News Release*, 3 April 2007 (Paris: Organisation for Economic Co-operation and Development, 2007), pp. 1–2.

71. G. Brown, 'Our 2p Pledge to All Children,' *The Guardian*, 4 January 2007.

72. Africa Progress Panel, *Africa Progress Panel Communiqué* (London: Africa Progress Panel, 2007), pp. 1–6.

73. The World Can't Wait, *The World Can't Wait– For What?* (London: The World

Can't Wait, 2007). Available online: http://www.yourvoiceagainstpoverty.
org.uk/about-us/ (accessed 15 May 2007).

74. Christian Aid, *The Economics of Failure: The real cost of "free" trade for poor countries* (London: Christian Aid, 2005), p. 1.

75. World Development Movement, *Climate Calendar: The UK's unjust contribution to global climate change* (London: World Development Movement, 2007); P. Watt and T. Sharman, *The G8 summit in 2006* (London: ActionAid, 2006); ActionAid, *Delivering the 2010 Target: Financing universal access to HIV and AIDS treatment* (London: ActionAid, 2007), p. 1.

76. The World Bank, *Global Monitoring Report 2006* (Washington DC: The World Bank, 2006), p. xvii-xviii.

77. World Economic Forum, *Global Governance Initiative: Annual Report 2006* (Geneva: World Economic Forum, in partnership with The Centre for International Governance Innovation, 2006), pp. 5–6.

78. The World Bank, *Economic Growth in the 1990s: Learning from a decade of reform* (Washington DC: The World Bank, 2006), p. xii.

79. G. Brown, 'Foreword' to H. M. Treasury, *Meeting the Challenges of Globalisation for All: The UK and the IMF 2005* (London: H. M. Treasury, 2006), p. 3.

80. G. Brown, 'Foreword' to H. M. Treasury, *The UK and the IMF Report 2006: Reform to deliver prosperity for all* (London: H. M. Treasury, 2007), p. 1.

81. G. Brown, oral evidence, 11 May 2006, to the House of Commons Treasury Committee, *Globalisation: The role of the IMF. Ninth Report of Session 2005–06*, HC. 875 (London: The Stationery Office, 2006) Ev.37, answer to Q.164.

82. See, for example, the written and oral evidence given to the House of Commons Treasury Committee, *Globalisation: The role of the IMF. Ninth Report of Session 2005–06*, HC. 875 (London: The Stationery Office, 2006). For an analysis of the critique of the IMF's role, see S. Lee, 'Global Governance and the International Monetary Fund,' in G. Hook and H. Dobson (ed.), *Global Governance and Japan: The institutional architecture* (London: Routledge, 2007), pp. 126–142.

83. G. Brown, 'Foreword' to H. M. Treasury, *The UK and the IMF Report 2006: Reform to deliver prosperity for all* (London: H. M. Treasury, 2007), p. 1.

84. J. F. Kennedy, remarks in Naples at NATO Headquarters, 2 July 1963, in *John F. Kennedy: Public papers of the Presidents of the United States* (Washington DC: United States Government Printing Office, 1963), p. 552.

85. Ibid., pp. 550–551.

86. Debate on Iraq, *Hansard*, 18 March 2003, c. 911.

87. BBC, 'Brown Makes First Visit to Iraq,' *BBC News*, 18 November 2006.

88. Mark Oliver, 'Brown Surprises Troops in Afghanistan,' *The Guardian*, 30 March 2007.

89. H. M. Treasury, *Modern Public Services for Britain: Investing in reform. Comprehensive spending review: New public spending plans 1999–2002*, Cm. 4011 (London: The Stationery Office, 1998), paras 14.3–14.5.

90. H. M. Treasury, *Prudent for a Purpose: Building opportunity and security for all. New public spending plans for 2001–2004* (London: The Stationery Office, 2000), p. 1.

91. G. Brown, 'Statement by the Chancellor of the Exchequer on the 2002 Spending Review,' *Hansard*, 15 July 2002, cc. 21–30.

92. Ibid.

93. H. M. Treasury, *Steering a Steady Course: Delivering stability, enterprise and fairness in an uncertain world. Pre-budget report 2002* (London: The Stationery Office, 2002), p. 1.

94. 'Soft power' is the term coined by the American political scientist, Joseph Nye, to denote 'the ability to get what you want through attraction rather than coercion or payments.' Nye has argued that the soft power of a country rests primarily on its culture, its political values and its foreign policies. Hard power, by contrast, refers to military and economic might. See J. Nye, *Soft Power: The means to success in world politics* (New York: Public Affairs, 2004), pp. x, 11.

95. G. Brown, 'Budget Statement,' *Hansard*, 9 April 2003; G. Brown, 'Pre-Budget Report Statement,' *Hansard*, 10 December 2003, cc. 1061–1086.

96. H. M. Treasury, 'Further boost for Britain's armed forces,' *H. M. Treasury Press Notice A7*, 12 July 2004.

97. G. Brown, 'Securing Our Future,' speech at the Royal United Services Institute, London, 13 February 2006.

98. H. M. Treasury, *Long-Term Opportunities and Challenges for the UK: Analysis for the 2007 Comprehensive Spending Review* (London: The Stationery Office, 2006), pp. 105–107.

99. G. Brown, 'Securing Our Future,' speech at the Royal United Services Institute, London, 13 February 2006.

100. G. Brown, 'Meeting the Terrorist Challenge,' speech at Chatham House, London, 10 October 2006.

101. Ibid.

102. G. Brown, 'Meeting the Terrorist Challenge,' speech at Chatham House, London, 10 October 2006.

103. D. Acheson, speech at the Military Academy, West Point, 5 December 1962.

104. BBC, 'Trident Plan Wins Commons Support,' *BBC News*, 18 May 2005.

105. Labour Party, 'Gordon Brown is the Candidate for Leader of the Labour Party,' 18 May 2007. Available online: http://www.labour.org.uk/leadership/Gordon_brown123 (accessed 18 May 2007).

106. For an analysis of Blair's foreign policy and why he has so closely aligned himself with the neo-conservatism of George W. Bush, see S. Lee 'The Politics of Globalisation and the War on Terror,' in M. Mullard and B. Cole (ed.), *Globalisation, Citizenship and the War on Terror* (Cheltenham: Edward Elgar, 2007).
107. G. Brown, speech at the Confederation of Indian Industry, Bangalore, 17 January 2007.
108. Ibid.
109. Ibid.

CHAPTER 7

1. European Commission, *Communication from the Commission to the Council, the European Parliament, the European Economic and Social Committee and the Committee of the Regions: The Commission's contribution to the period of reflection and beyond: Plan-D for Democracy, Dialogue and Debate*, COM (2005) 494 final (Brussels: Commission of the European Communities, 2005), p. 2.
2. G. Brown, 'Global Britain, Global Europe: A Presidency founded on pro-European realism,' speech at the Mansion House, London, 22 June 2005.
3. A. Rawnsley, 'In France it's Under Constitution Blairiste,' *The Observer*, 31 October 2004.
4. 'Whether Paid in Sterling or Euro, Honda is Here to Stay,' *Financial Times*, 23 May 2007.
5. European Commission, *Communication from the Commission to the European Council: A citizens' agenda. Delivering results for Europe*, COM (2006) 211 final (Brussels: Commission of the European Communities, 2006), p. 2.
6. European Commission, *Communication from the Commission to the Council, the European Parliament, the European Economic and Social Committee and the Committee of The Regions: The Commission's contribution to the period of reflection and beyond: Plan-D for Democracy, Dialogue and Debate*, COM (2005) 494 final (Brussels: Commission of the European Communities, 2005), p. 3; European Commission, *Communication from the Commission to the European Council: A citizens' agenda. Delivering results for Europe*, COM (2006) 211 final (Brussels: Commission of the European Communities, 2006), p. 2.
7. H. Young, *This Blessed Plot: Britain and Europe from Churchill to Blair* (London: Macmillan, 1998), p. 1.
8. A. Gamble, *Between Europe and America: The future of British politics* (Houndmills: Palgrave Macmillan, 2003), p. 1.

9. Ibid., p. 230.

10. W. Hutton, *The World We're in* (London: Little Brown, 2002), p. 2.

11. J. Delors, speech to the Trades Union Congress, Brighton, 8 September 1988.

12. Labour Party, *It's Time to Get Britain Working Again: Labour's election manifesto* (London: The Labour Party, 1992, p. 27.

13. For a more detailed analysis of the events of 'Black Wednesday,' see P. Stephens, *Politics and the Pound: The Conservatives' struggle with Sterling* (London: Macmillan, 1996).

14. G. Brown, 'Europe Still the Answer,' *Tribune*, 25 September 1992, p. 8.

15. P. Anderson, 'New Economics. The Tribune Interview: Gordon Brown,' *Tribune*, 1 January 1993, p. 5.

16. E. Balls, *Euro-Monetarism: Why Britain was ensnared and how it should escape* (London: The Fabian Society, 1992), p. 10.

17. Ibid., p. 23.

18. P. Anderson, 'New Economics. The Tribune Interview: Gordon Brown,' *Tribune*, 1 January 1993, p. 5.

19. Labour Party, *A New Economic Future for Britain: Economic and employment opportunities for all* (London: The Labour Party, 1995), pp. 4–5.

20. Labour Party, *Economic Renewal in the European Union: The UK Labour party and the Delors white paper on growth, competitiveness and employment* (London: The Labour Party, 1994), p. 1.

21. Labour Party, *New Labour: Because Britain deserves better* (London: The Labour Party, 1997), p. 37.

22. Ibid., pp. 37–38.

23. The Labour Party's agenda for the UK Presidency of the EU during the first half of 1998 were: rapid completion of the single market; EU enlargement with the requisite institutional reforms; urgent reform of the Common Agricultural Policy; greater openness and democracy in EU institutions; retention of the national veto over key matters of national interest such as taxation and bud-getary matters, immigration, defence and security; and a British signature on the Social Chapter, Ibid., p. 37.

24. G. Brown, 'Britain Leading in Europe,' speech to the Royal Institute for International Affairs, Chatham House, London, 17 July 1997.

25. Ibid.

26. Ibid.

27. MORI, *Attitudes to Europe in Great Britain, 13–14 November* (London: Market Opinion Research International, 1997).

28. Ibid.

29. G. Brown, 'Statement on European Monetary Union,' 27 October 1997, cc. 583–588.

30. H. M. Treasury, *UK Membership of the Single Currency: An assessment of the Five Economic Tests* (London: H. M. Treasury, 1997), pp. 5–6.
31. G. Brown, 'Statement on European Monetary Union,' 27 October 1997, cc. 583–588.
32. Ibid.
33. T. Blair, *New Britain: My vision of a young country* (London: Fourth Estate, 1996), p. 283.
34. D. Scott, *Off Whitehall: A view from Downing Street by Tony Blair's adviser* (London: I. B. Taurus, 2004), p. 23.
35. *The Times*, 17 October 1997; *The Sun*, 17 October 1997.
36. A. Rawnsley, *Servants of the People: The inside story of New Labour* (London: Penguin Books, 2001), p. 83.
37. A. Rawnsley, 'What Blair Really Thinks of Brown,' *The Observer*, 18 January 1998.
38. H. M. Treasury, 'Getting Europe to Work: Building a strong European economy. Chancellor launches UK Action Plan to create lasting jobs in Europe,' 4 June 1997; H. M. Treasury, 'Chancellor Publishes Business Guide to Single Currency,' 24 July 1997.
39. A. Rawnsley, *Servants of the People: The inside story of New Labour* (London: Penguin Books, 2001), pp. 235–236.
40. For a more detailed account of the political machinations between Brown and Blair over EMU, see R. Peston, *Brown's Britain* (London: Short Books, 2005), pp. 178–245, and T. Bower, *Gordon Brown* (London: HarperCollins, 2004), pp. 247–252, 313–317.
41. Labour Party, *Ambitions for Britain: Labour's manifesto 2001* (London: The Labour Party, 2001), p. 13.
42. T. Blair, *Hansard*, 7 February 2001, c. 918.
43. The eighteen EMU studies that comprise the Treasury's assessment of United Kingdom membership of the single currency are available online: http://www.hm-treasury.gov.uk/documents/international_issues/the_euro/assessment/report/euro_assess03_repindex.cfm (accessed 21 May 2007).
44. G. Brown, speech at the Mansion House, City of London, 20 June 2001.
45. E. Balls, 'Why The Five Economic Tests?,' The 2002 Alec Cairncross Lecture, Oxford, 4 December 2002.
46. H. M. Treasury, *UK Membership of the Single Currency: An assessment of the Five Economic Tests*, Cm. 5776 (London: The Stationery Office, 2003), p. 6.
47. G. Brown, 'Statement on Economic and Monetary Union,' 9 June 2003, cc. 407–415.
48. Ibid.

49. E. Balls, 'Stability, Growth and UK Fiscal Policy,' The Inaugural Ken Dixon Lecture, Department of Economics, University of York, 23 January 2004.
50. Ibid.
51. Ibid.
52. H. M. Treasury, *Fiscal Stabilisation and EMU: A discussion paper* (London: H. M. Treasury, 2003).
53. E. Balls, 'Stability, Growth and UK Fiscal Policy,' The Inaugural Ken Dixon Lecture, Department of Economics, University of York, 23 January 2004.
54. Ibid.
55. Ibid.
56. Ibid.
57. European Council, 'Presidency Conclusions, Lisbon European Council, 23–24 March,' *Press Release* (Brussels: Commission of the European Communities, 2000), p. 1.
58. Ibid., p. 1.
59. Ibid., p. 2.
60. Ibid., p. 2.
61. Ibid., pp. 5, 7, 9, 11.
62. This trend was deepened by the publication of the updated version of the EU's post-Lisbon agenda for innovation policy which noted the importance for long-term growth of increasing investment in R&D towards three per cent of GDP, *European Commission, Fostering Structural Change: An industrial policy for an enlarged Europe*, COM (2004) 274 final (Brussels: Commission of the European Communities, 2004), p. 4. This closely paralleled the trajectory of Treasury policy under Gordon Brown who had identified similar targets for the United Kingdom.
63. European Commission, *Towards Enterprise Europe: Work programme for enterprise policy 2000–2005*, SEC (2000) 771 (Brussels: Commission of European Communities, 2000), pp. 2–3.
64. European Commission, *Challenges for Enterprise Policy in the Knowledge-Driven Economy: Proposal for a Council decision on a multinational programme for enterprise and entrepreneurship (2001–2005)*, COM (2000) 256 final/2 (Brussels: Commission of the European Communities, 2000), p. 4.
65. European Commission, *Action Plan: The European agenda for entrepreneurship*, COM (2004) 70 final (Brussels: Commission of the European Communities, 2004), p. 4.
66. H. M. Treasury, *European Economic Reform: Meeting the challenge* (London: H. M. Treasury, 2001); H. M. Treasury, *Realising Europe's Potential: Economic reform in Europe* (London: H. M. Treasury, 2002); H. M. Treasury, *Meeting the Challenge: Economic reform in Europe* (London: H. M. Treasury, 2003); H. M.

Treasury, *Advancing Long-Term Prosperity: Economic reform in an enlarged Europe* (London: H. M. Treasury, 2004); H. M. Treasury, *Growth and Opportunity: Prioritising economic reform in Europe* (London: H. M. Treasury, 2005).
67. G. Brown, speech at the Confederation of British Industry Conference on 'Competitiveness in Europe-Post Enlargement,' 12 May 2004.
68. Ibid.
69. Ibid.
70. Ibid.
71. Ibid.
72. Ibid.
73. G. Brown, *Global Europe: Full-employment Europe* (London: H. M. Treasury, 2005), p. 1.
74. Ibid., pp. 1–2.
75. Ibid., pp. 7–8.
76. Ibid., pp. 8–9.
77. Ibid., p. 10.
78. Ibid., p. 10.
79. Ibid., p. 11.
80. Ibid., p. 12.
81. Ibid., p. 12.
82. Ibid., p. 13.
83. Ibid., pp. 13–14.
84. Ibid., p. 15.
85. Ibid., p. 3.
86. G. Brown, 'Global Britain, Global Europe: A Presidency founded on pro-European realism,' speech at the Mansion House, London, 22 June 2005.
87. Ibid.
88. Cabinet Office, *Ministerial Committees of the Cabinet and Policy Review Working Groups: Composition and terms of reference* (London: Cabinet Office, 2006), pp. 27–28.
89. See for example, H. M. Treasury, *The Case for Open Markets: How increased competition can equip Europe for global change* (London: H. M. Treasury, 2006).
90. H. M. Treasury/Department of Trade and Industry, *The Single Market: A vision for the 21st century* (London: The Stationery Office, 2007), p. 3.
91. Ibid., p. 3.
92. Ibid., p. 4.
93. Ibid., p. 12.
94. Ibid., p. 19.
95. Ibid., p. 23.

96. Ibid., p. 39.
97. E. Balls, *Britain and Europe: A City minister's perspective* (London: Centre for European Reform, 2007), p. 3.
98. Ibid., p. 4.
99. Ibid., pp. 21, 39.
100. D. Miliband, 'New Diplomacy: Challenges for Foreign Policy,' speech at the Royal Institute of International Affairs, Chatham House, London, 19 July 2007.
101. G. Brown, 'Foreword' to Foreign and Commonwealth Office, *The Reform Treaty: The British approach to the European Union Intergovernmental Conference*, July 2007, Cm. 7174 (London: The Stationery Office, 2007), p. 1.
102. Ibid., p. 1.
103. D. Cameron, 'The EU – A New Agenda for the 21st Century,' speech at the Movement for European Reform conference, Brussels, 6 March 2007.
104. M. Thatcher, speech to the College of Europe, Bruges, 20 September 1988.

CHAPTER 8

1. This was the term used by Tony Blair to hail his successor as Prime Minister following the 2006 Queen's Speech, BBC, 'Blair Hails Heavyweight Successor,' *BBC News*, 15 November 2006.
2. G. Brown, speech to the Labour Party, Manchester, 25 June 2007.
3. G. Brown, inaugural speech as Prime Minister, Downing Street, 27 June 2007.
4. J. Glover, 'Tory Voters Turn Against Cameron,' *The Guardian*, 25 July 2007.
5. Office for National Statistics, *UK Output, Income and Expenditure: 1st quarter 2007* (London: Office for National Statistics, 2007), p. 1.
6. Office for National Statistics, *Social Trends No.37: 2007 edition* (London: Palgrave Macmillan, 2007), pp. 69–70.
7. This was pointed out in the 1997 Conservative Party manifesto, which alluded to the likelihood of a sixth successive year of economic growth, itself 'a postwar record'; inflation below four per cent, itself 'the longest period of low inflation for almost half a century'; unemployment at its lowest level for six years; and mortgage rates 'at their lowest levels for thirty years.' Conservative Party, *You Can Only be Sure with the Conservatives: The Conservative manifesto* (London: Conservative Party, 1997), p. 6.
8. M. Brewer, A. Goodman, A. Muriel and L. Sibieta, *Poverty and Inequality in the UK: 2007* (London: Institute for Fiscal Studies, 2007), p. 1.
9. Office for National Statistics, *Social Trends No.37: 2007 edition* (London: Office for National Statistics, 2007), p. 70.

10. D. Dorling, J. Rigby, B. Wheeler, D. Ballas, B. Thomas, E. Fahmy, D. Gordon and R. Lupton, *Poverty, Wealth and Place in Britain, 1968 to 2005* (York: Joseph Rowntree Foundation, 2007), p. xiii.
11. Ibid., p. xiii.
12. Ibid., p. 2.
13. Office for National Statistics, *Public Sector Finances: April 2007* (London: Office for National Statistics, 2007), pp. 1–2.
14. Credit Action, *Debt Facts and Figures: Compiled 1 June 2007* (Lincoln: Credit Action, 2007), pp. 1–2.
15. National Centre for Social Research, 'Brown Faces Growing Tax Resistance,' *Press Release*, 6 December 2006 (London: National Centre for Social Research), pp. 1–2.
16. Office for National Statistics, *Consumer Price Indices: March 2007* (London: Office for National Statistics, 2007), p. 1.
17. Bank of England, *Open Letter from Mervyn King, The Governor of the Bank of England to The Chancellor of the Exchequer, 16 April 2007* (London: Bank of England, 2007).
18. Office for National Statistics, *UK Trade: February 2007* (London: Office for National Statistics, 2007); Office for National Statistics, *Press Briefing on UK, Trade World– February 2007* (London: Office for National Statistics, 2007), p. 1.
19. Office for National Statistics, *UK Trade: March 2007* (London: Office for National Statistics, 2007), pp. 2, 6.
20. Office for National Statistics, *International Migration: Migrants entering or leaving the United Kingdom and England and Wales, 2005* (London: Office for National Statistics, 2007), p. 4.
21. Office for National Statistics, *Social Trends No.37: 2007 edition* (London: Office for National Statistics, 2007), pp. 140–141.
22. National Housing and Planning Advice Unit, *Affordability Matters* (London: National Housing and Planning Advice Unit, 2007), pp. 4, 22.
23. G. Brown, speech to the Labour Party, Manchester, 25 June 2007.
24. Ministry of Justice, *The Governance of Britain: The Government's draft legislative programme*, Cm. 7175 (London: The Stationery Office, 2007), p. 46.
25. Department for Communities and Local Government, *Homes for the Future: More affordable, more sustainable*, Cm. 7191 (London: The Stationery Office, 2007), p. 7.
26. G. Brown, 'Statement on Draft Legislative Programme,' *Hansard*, 11 July 2007, c. 1149.
27. D. Maclennan, G. Meen, K. Gibb and M. Stephens, *Fixed Commitments, Uncertain Incomes: Sustainable owner-occupation and the economy* (York: Joseph Rowntree Foundation, 1997).

28. Department for Communities and Local Government, *Table 208, Housebuilding: Permanent dwellings started, by tenure and country* (London: Department for Communities and Local Government, 2007).

29. Ibid.

30. Office for National Statistics, *National Insurance Number Allocations to Overseas Nationals Entering the UK 2006/07* (London: Office for National Statistics, 2007), p. 1.

31. Sir K. Joseph, *Stranded on the Middle Ground: Reflections on circumstances and policies* (London: Centre for Policy Studies, 1976), pp. 27–33.

32. D. Cameron, 'A Liberal Conservative Consensus to Restore Trust in Politics,' speech, Bath, 22 March 2007; D. Cameron, 'A New Approach to Foreign Affairs: Liberal conservatism,' Annual J. P. Morgan Lecture at the British American Project, 11 September 2006.

33. D. Cameron, 'A Liberal Conservative Consensus to Restore Trust in Politics,' speech, Bath, 22 March 2007.

34. D. Cameron, 'Foreword' to Conservative Party, *Built to Last: The aims and values of the Conservative Party* (London: Conservative Party, 2006), p. 3.

35. This thesis has been developed by S. Jenkins, *Thatcher and Sons: A revolution in three acts* (London: Allen Lane, 2006).

36. D. Cameron, 'Modern Conservatism,' speech at Demos, London, 30 January 2006.

37. Ibid.

38. Ibid.

39. D. Cameron, 'The Need for Public Service Reform,' speech at Portsmouth, 9 September 2005.

40. Ibid.

41. G. Osborne, 'Only Conservatives Can Maintain Public Service Reform,' speech to Policy Exchange, London, 30 May 2007.

42. G. Brown, 'My Moral Beacon,' *New Statesman and Society*, 30 April 2007; G. Brown, 'Robert Kennedy,' in G. Brown, *Courage: Eight portraits* (London: Bloomsbury, 2007), p. 115.

43. R. F. Kennedy, 'What do we Stand for? The Liberation of the Human Spirit,' speech to the Commonwealth Club of California, San Francisco, 4 January 1968, cited in D. Cameron, 'Civility and Civil Progress,' speech at the Royal Society, London, 23 April 2007.

44. H. M. Treasury, *Budget 2007. Building Britain's Long-Term Future: Prosperity and fairness for families. Economic and fiscal strategy report and financial statement and budget report*, HC. 342 (London: The Stationery Office, 2007), pp. 3, 5.

45. G. Osborne, speech to the Confederation of British Industry, London, 7 March 2007. The Conservative Party's other two Sound Money Tests are the 'Stability

Test,' which dictates that 'economic stability will always be our priority. We will not cut taxes if that puts at risk the low interest rates and low inflation that families and businesses depend on. We will not be making up front promises of overall tax cuts at the election – promises we couldn't be sure I could keep;' and the 'Manifesto Test,' which states that 'no policy proposals with implications for public spending are Conservative Party policy until they have been approved by me and David Cameron, passed by the Shadow Cabinet and appear in our draft manifesto.' Ibid.

46. The convergence between Brown and Cameron on the future of the British Union is shown by G. Brown, 'Stronger Together Weaker Apart,' speech, Edinburgh, 8 September 2006; D. Cameron, 'I Support the Union for What it can Achieve in the Future,' speech, Gretna Green, 19 April 2007

47. D. Cameron, 'A New Approach to Foreign Affairs: Liberal conservatism,' Annual J. P. Morgan Lecture at the British American Project, 11 September 2006.

48. D. Cameron, 'The EU – A New Agenda for the 21st Century,' speech to the Movement for European Reform Conference, Brussels, 6 March 2007.

49. M. Kite, T. Harper and M. Goslett, 'Cameron Much Weaker than Brown, say voters,' *The Sunday Telegraph*, 3 June 2007.

50. J. Glover, 'Tory Voters Turn Against Cameron,' *The Guardian*, 25 July 2007.

51. G. Brown, speech to the Labour Party, Manchester, 25 June 2007.

52. G. Brown, speech at the Queen Elizabeth II Conference Centre, London, 9 July 2007.

53. H. M. Treasury, '2007 Comprehensive Spending Review,' *CSR microsite*. Available online: http://www.hm-treasury.gov.uk/spending_review/spend_csr07/spend_csr07_index.cfm (accessed 5 June 2007).

54. H. M. Treasury, *Long-Term Opportunities and Challenges for the UK: Analysis for the 2007 Comprehensive Spending Review* (London: The Stationery Office, 2006), p. 6.

55. Ibid., p. 6.

56. Ibid., p. 6.

57. The National Audit Office has estimated the total cost of the ten-year National Programme for Information Technology in the NHS in England at £12.4 billion, although it has acknowledged that Lord Warner, the Minister of State for Reform, has stated 'the full cost of the Programme was likely to be nearer twenty billion pounds.' National Audit Office, *Department of Health: The national programme for IT in the NHS*, HC. 1173 (London: The Stationery Office, 2006), pp. 5–6.

58. G. Brown, 'Securing Our Future,' speech at the Royal United Services Institute,

London, 13 February 2006. See also G. Brown, 'Meeting the Terrorist Challenge,' speech at Chatham House, London, 10 October 2006.

59. Among its objectives, the Review will 'map existing counter-terrorism and security strategy across Government' and 'consider the systems of governance and accountability for counter-terrorism spending and delivery, including the case for a single security budget.' H. M. Treasury, *Review of Counter-Terrorism and Security: Terms of reference* (London: H. M. Treasury, 2006), p. 1.

60. G. Brown, 'Statement on National Security,' *Hansard*, 25 July 2007, cc. 841–845.

61. H. M. Treasury, *Long-Term Opportunities and Challenges for the UK: Analysis for the 2007 Comprehensive Spending Review* (London: The Stationery Office, 2006), p. 6.

62. H. M. Treasury, *Stern Review on the Economics of Climate Change* (London: The Stationery Office, 2007).

63. G. Brown, 'Protecting and Improving our Environment,' in P. Bill (ed.), *The Green Shift: Environmental policies to match a changing public climate* (London: The Smith Institute, 2006), p. 8

64. Ibid., p. 8.

65. Ibid., p. 8.

66. Ibid., p. 9.

67. Ibid., p. 10.

68. Ibid., p. 11.

69. Ibid., p. 12.

70. Ibid., pp. 12, 14.

71. G. Brown, 'Protecting and Improving our Environment' in P. Bill (ed.), *The Green Shift: Environmental policies to match a changing public climate* (London: The Smith Institute, 2006).

72. G. Brown, transcript of interview with Andrew Marr for the Sunday AM programme, 7 January 2007. Available online: http://www.bbc.co.uk/1/hi/uk_politics/6241819.stm (accessed 8 January 2007).

73. G. Brown, answer given at the Fabian Society Leadership Hustings, Institute of Education, London, 13 May 2007.

74. G. Brown, transcript of interview with Andrew Marr for the Sunday AM programme, 7 January 2007. Available online: http://www.bbc.co.uk/1/hi/uk_politics/6241819.stm (accessed 8 January 2007).

75. D. Cameron, 'A New Approach to Foreign Affairs: Liberal conservatism,' Annual J. P. Morgan Lecture at the British American Project, 11 September 2006.

76. Greenspan had served as Chairman of the Federal Reserve Board and was invited by Brown to Kirkcaldy in 2006 to deliver the annual Adam Smith

Lecture. Robert Rubin and Larry Summers had served the Clinton Administration; Rubin between January 1993 and July 1999 as Director of the National Economic Council and Treasury Secretary (from January 1995), and Summers as Rubin's successor as Treasury Secretary until 2001.

77. D. Miliband, 'Interview,' *The Financial Times*, 9 July 2007.
78. D. Miliband, 'New Diplomacy: Challenges for foreign policy,' speech at the Royal Institute of International Affairs, Chatham House, London, 19 July 2007.
79. Ibid.
80. For an analysis of Robin Cook's 'ethical dimension' and Tony Blair's 'doctrine of international community, see S. Lee, 'The Politics of Globalisation and the War on Terrror,' in M. Mullard and B. Cole (ed.), *Globalisation, Citizenship and The War on Terror* (Cheltenham: Edward Elgar, 2007).
81. D. Miliband, 'New Diplomacy: Challenges for foreign policy,' speech at the Royal Institute of International Affairs, Chatham House, London, 19 July 2007.
82. M. Malloch Brown, United Nations Deputy Secretary-General, 'Power and Super-Power: Global leadership in the twenty-first century,' address to the Century Foundation and Centre for American Progress, New York, 7 June 2006.
83. United States' Department of State, 'UN Official's Remarks a "Grave Mistake", US's Bolton Says,' 7 June 2006 (Washington DC: United States' Department of State, 2006).
84. R. Sylvester and A. Thomson, 'Mark Malloch Brown: "Let's not just rely on US,' *The Daily Telegraph*, 14 July 2007.
85. D. Alexander, speech delivered at the Council on Foreign Relations, Washington DC, 12 July 2007.
86. D. Browne, 'Statement on CSR and Aircraft Carriers,' *Hansard*, 25 July 2007, cc. 865–867. The 'warfare state' is frequently deployed as a convenient shorthand for that part of the institutional architecture of the British state that is devoted to the management of the armed forces, military strategy and procurement and defence industrial policy. For a detailed analysis of the role of the warfare state in British grand strategy during the twentieth century, see D. Edgerton, *Warfare State Britain, 1920–1970* (Cambridge: Cambridge University Press, 2006).
87. D. Browne, 'Statement on Ballistic Missile Defence,' *Hansard*, 25 July 2007, cc. 72–73.
88. National Security Council, *Initial Benchmark Assessment Report* (Washington, DC: National Security Council, 2007), pp. 12–23.
89. H. Clinton, 'Challenges Facing the United States in the Global Security Environment,' speech to the Council on Foreign Relations, New York, 31 October 2006.

90. B. Obama, *The Audacity of Hope: Thoughts on reclaiming the American Dream* (New York: Crown Publishers, 2006), p. 320.
91. G. Brown, transcript of interview with Andrew Marr for the Sunday AM programme, 7 January 2007. Available online: http://www.bbc.co.uk/1/hi/uk_ politics/6241819.stm (accessed 8 January 2007).
92. Ibid.
93. Ibid.
94. Ibid.
95. G. Brown and J. Straw, 'Foreword' to Ministry of Justice, *The Governance of Britain*, Cm. 7170 (London: The Stationery Office, 2007), p. 5.
96. Ministry of Justice, *The Governance of Britain*, Cm. 7170 (London: The Stationery Office, 2007), p. 8.
97. Ibid., p. 10.
98. Ibid., pp. 38–39.
99. House of Commons, 'Division No.119,' *Hansard*, 18 May 2007, c. 890.
100. H. Watt and R. Winnett, 'Goldfinger Brown's £2 Billion Blunder in the Bullion Market,' *The Sunday Times*, 15 April 2007.
101. G. Brown, 'Reply to Question 2, Prime Minister's Questions,' *Hansard*, 11 July 2007, c. 1438.
102. T. Branigan and P. Wintour, 'Brown U-Turn over Plan for Supercasino,' *The Guardian*, 26 June 2007.
103. G. Brown, transcript of interview with Andrew Marr for the Sunday AM programme, 7 January 2007. Available online: http://www.bbc.co.uk/1/hi/uk_ politics/6241819.stm (accessed 8 January 2007).
104. Ibid.
105. G. Brown and D. Alexander, *Stronger Together: The 21st century case for Scotland and Britain* (London: The Fabian Society, 2007), p. 25.
106. G. Brown, 'Robert Kennedy,' in G. Brown, *Courage: Eight portraits* (London: Bloomsbury, 2007), p. 115.
107. G. Brown, transcript of interview with Andrew Marr for the Sunday AM programme, 7 January 2007. Available online: http://www.bbc.co.uk/1/hi/uk_ politics/6241819.stm (accessed 8 January 2007).
108. P. Hennessy and M. Kite, 'End of the Union? England Wants its Independence,' *The Sunday Telegraph*, 26 November 2006.
109. Gordon Brown, 'We Need a United Kingdom,' *The Daily Telegraph*, 13 January 2007.
110. Ibid.
111. Ibid.
112. Ibid.
113. National Centre for Social Research, 'New British Social Attitudes Report

Published Today,' *Press Release*, 24 January (London: National Centre for Social Research, 2007), pp. 1–2.

114. R. Kelly and L. Byrne, *A Common Place* (London: Fabian Society, 2007), pp. 4, 22.

115. Ibid., p. 24.

116. Labour Party, 'Today Gordon Brown Accepted the Nomination as Leader of the Labour Party,' 17 May 2007. Available online: http://www.labour.org.uk/ leadership/Gordon_brown (accessed 22 May 2007).

117. The vision of the 'good society' is set out in W. Lippmann, *The Good Society* (London: George Allen & Unwin, 1937); R. Kennedy, *To Seek a Newer World* (New York: M Joseph, 1968); and J. K. Galbraith, *The Good Society: The humane agenda* (Boston: Houghton Mifflin, 1996).

118. G. Brown, transcript of interview with Andrew Marr for BBC One's *Sunday AM* programme, 7 January 2007. Available online: http://news.bbc.co.uk/1/ hi/programmes/sunday_am/6238645.stm (accessed 18 May 2007).

119. T. Blair, 'Realising our True Potential,' speech at the Institute of London, University of London, 23 June 1995, reproduced in T. Blair, *New Britain: My vision of a young country* (London: Fourth Estate, 1996), p. 159.

120. G. Brown, *Courage: Eight portraits* (London: Bloomsbury, 2007), pp. 3–7.

121. Ibid., p. 6.

122. Ibid., p. 116.

123. Ibid., p. 135.

Index